Television and Culture in Putin's Russia

This book examines television culture in Russia under the government of Vladimir Putin. In recent years, the growing influx into Russian television of globally mediated genres and formats has coincided with a decline in media freedom and an increase in government control over the content and style of television programmes. All three national channels (First, Russia and NTV) have fallen victim to Putin's power-obsessed regime. Journalists critical of his Chechnya policy have been subject to harassment and arrest; programmes courting political controversy, such as Savik Shuster's *Freedom of Speech* (*Svoboda slova*) have been taken off the air; coverage of national holidays like Victory Day has witnessed a return of Soviet-style bombast; and reporting on crises, such as the Beslan tragedy, is severely curtailed.

The book demonstrates how broadcasters have been enlisted in support of a transparent effort to install a latter-day version of imperial pride in Russian military achievements at the centre of a national identity project over which, from the depths of the Kremlin, Putin's government exerts a form of remote control. However, central to the book's argument is the notion that because of the changes wrought upon Russian society after 1985, a blanket return to the totalitarianism of the Soviet media has, notwithstanding the tenor of much western reporting on the issue, not occurred. Despite the fact that television is nominally under state control, that control remains remote and less than wholly effective, as amply demonstrated in the audience research conducted for the book, and in analysis of contradictions at the textual level. Overall, this book provides a fascinating account of the role of television under President Putin, and will be of interest to all those wishing to understand contemporary Russian society.

Stephen Hutchings is Chair in Russian Studies at the Department of Russian Studies, University of Manchester, UK. He is the author of *Russian Literary Culture in the Camera Age: The World as Image* (2004), and co-editor of *Soviet and Post-Soviet Screen Adaptations of Literature: Screening the World* (co-edited with Anat Vernistki, 2004), both published by Routledge.

Natalia Rulyova is Lecturer in Russian at the Centre for Russian and East European Studies, University of Birmingham, UK.

BASEES/Routledge Series on Russian and East European Studies

Series editor: Richard Sakwa
Department of Politics and International Relations, University of Kent

Editorial Committee:
Julian Cooper, *Centre for Russian and East European Studies, University of Birmingham*
Terry Cox, *Department of Central and East European Studies, University of Glasgow*
Rosalind Marsh, *Department of European Studies and Modern Languages, University of Bath*
David Moon, *Department of History, University of Durham*
Hilary Pilkington, *Department of Sociology, University of Warwick*
Stephen White, *Department of Politics, University of Glasgow*

Founding Editorial Committee Member:
George Blazyca, *Centre for Contemporary European Studies, University of Paisley*

This series is published on behalf of BASEES (the British Association for Slavonic and East European Studies). The series comprises original, high-quality, research-level work by both new and established scholars on all aspects of Russian, Soviet, post-Soviet and East European Studies in humanities and social science subjects.

Television and Culture in Putin's Russia

Remote control

Stephen Hutchings and Natalia Rulyova

Routledge
Taylor & Francis Group

LONDON AND NEW YORK

Transferred to digital printing 2010

First published 2009
by Routledge
2 Park Square, Milton Park, Abingdon, Oxon OX14 4RN

Simultaneously published in the USA and Canada
by Routledge
270 Madison Ave, New York, NY 10016

Routledge is an imprint of the Taylor & Francis Group, an informa business

© 2009 Stephen Hutchings and Natalia Rulyova

Typeset in Times New Roman Times by
Taylor & Francis Books

British Library Cataloguing in Publication Data
A catalogue record for this book is available from the British Library

Library of Congress Cataloging in Publication Data
Hutchings, Stephen C.
Television and culture in Putin's Russia : remote control / Stephen
Hutchings, Natalia Rulyova.
    p. cm.
  Includes bibliographical references and index.
  1. Television and politics–Russia (Federation) 2. Television broadcasting
  of news–Russia (Federation) I. Rulyova, Natalia. II. Title.
  PN1992.3.R8H88 2009
302.23'450947–dc22   2008042323

ISBN 978-0-415-41907-9 (hbk)
ISBN 978-0-415-59050-1(pbk)
ISBN 978-0-203-09163-0 (ebk)

For Our Families

Contents

Illustrations

Figures

Tables

Acknowledgements

As always, thanks are due to a number of people and institutions without whose support this book could not have been written. We should first pay tribute to Peter Sowden, the commissioning editor at Routledge, whose enthusiasm and support were a real inspiration to us to see the project through to the end. We were lucky enough to benefit from the wisdom of a number of scholars whilst researching and writing the book. They are too numerous to name in full, but we should perhaps single out David MacFadyen, Birgit Beumers, Tony Anemone, Elena Prokhorova, Nancy Condee and Rosina Marquez-Reiter. Two anonymous readers at Routledge also provided excellent guidance in the initial stages. The patience and understanding shown by the entire Routledge team at all stages has, indeed, been exemplary. We cannot fail to mention the highly professional expertise and support provided by Donal O'Brien, our Senior Technician at the University of Surrey. Our gratitude extends to the Arts and Humanities Research Council under whose funding scheme research for the book was conducted, to the Universities of Manchester, Birmingham and Surrey for providing the ideal working environment, and to staff at the Universities of St Petersburg, Perm, and Voronezh, and to Internews Moscow, for their help with organising our focus groups. Finally, we must pay tribute to the forbearance of our families throughout the project's duration and it is to them that we dedicate this book.

Stephen Hutchings and Natalia Rulyova

Introduction

All in the name

All that the reader needs to know about this book is contained in its title. So, as a preliminary to the more detailed exposition of its background, aims and methods which follows, let us take each component of the title in turn, beginning with 'Television and Culture'.

First and foremost, the phrase confirms that we are interested in television's location in contemporary post-Soviet Russian culture, signalling that our allegiances are primarily with the Cultural Studies rather than the Political Science wing of Media Studies. We are concerned less with the political and socio-economic determinants of Russian television discourse than with the cultural meanings that the medium generates, both at the level of text, and at that of audience.

But also significant is the fact that we have opted for the copulative 'and', rather than the comparative 'as' ('Television as Culture'); the latter would imply, misleadingly for our purposes, that the medium is usually studied outside of its cultural dimension, but that we have chosen, unusually, to treat it in this aspect in order to gain new insight. Nor, however would the adjectival '*Television* Culture' correctly convey our intentions. Here, the medium is subordinated to the more inclusive category of 'Culture', creating the impression that we are leaving aside the essence of television in order to study one of its peripheral features ('television culture' rather than 'television' itself).

The title 'Television and Culture' recognises television's ambiguous societal status, an ambiguity replicated in academic discourse about the medium: it clearly operates within culture but it is sufficiently ubiquitous to be capable of driving cultural development at large and is even partly constitutive of culture in its modern form. Paradoxically, television's very importance means that it must be considered apart from culture, yet it also seeps into its every nook and cranny. This, in turn, signals that television provides the perfect object of analysis for standard cultural studies paradigms, but that it exceeds the scope of those paradigms. It is at this point that we must qualify our assertion that the book is located primarily within Cultural Studies. For we will argue that, given television's elusive status, no existing academic field of study is entirely adequate to the issues that it raises. As Colin McCabe puts it:

> to treat television as a unified cultural form ... is to confuse electronic hardware with cultural form ... all that it is possible to do is to examine the diverse and incomparable ways in which the developing technology interacts with the reality or fiction that it frames.
>
> (McCabe 1999: 98)

This ambiguity, born of television's very ubiquity, makes the opening of a dialogue between Cultural Studies and adjacent disciplines such as Political Science imperative. Finally, we will demonstrate that the dilemmas we have highlighted are expressed with a particular acuity in post-Soviet television.

The latter discussion brings us neatly to the second component of our title: 'in Putin's Russia', about which, other than the particular national focus that it gives to our analysis, there are two things worth highlighting. For by linking phrases containing, respectively, the words 'culture' and 'Putin', we are foregrounding our interdisciplinary pitch: the intention to bring those 'soft-edged' humanities angles on television which eschew anything as crudely empirical as consideration of a particular political leader's impact on a national media system into open dialogue with the 'hard-edged' social science approaches for which such considerations are standard fare. But the phrase 'in Putin's Russia' has temporal as well as disciplinary ramifications. It betrays an attachment to a discrete, relatively short segment of the recent past. The very temporal uncertainty (Putin's post-presidential clout renders moot the question of whether this is a study of the present or the past) self-reflexively encapsulates one of the central questions under consideration in the book: that of the extent to which Vladimir Putin has been able to impose his agenda on a television system which, notwithstanding the considerable political muscle at the President's disposal, must also respond to trends in global communications and audience cultures.

There is another, related aspect to the temporal issue. The phrase 'in Putin's Russia' clearly connotes a preference for a cross-sectional, synchronic analysis over a diachronic account of developments in Russian television of the post-Soviet period. We make no apologies for nailing our colours to the synchronic mask. However, we would also wish to cite Jakobson's and Tynianov's insistence that any synchronic system develops through time and therefore has a diachronic dimension, just as any diachronic series can only be properly analysed in its systemic manifestation: 'Pure synchronism ... proves to be an illusion: every synchronic system has its past and its future as inseparable structural elements of the system' (Jakobson and Tynianov 1978: 79).

Diachrony does matter to our project since one of the tasks we set ourselves is to try to unpick the two components of the much (ab)used, hyphenated 'post-Soviet'. We need to determine just what the Soviet residue in contemporary Russian television is, and in what ways it has been transformed into the 'post-Soviet'. Following the logic of Jakobson and Tynianov, our argument will be that the 'post' and the 'Soviet' can best be understood in their mutual relationship, rather than in the sequence from one ('Soviet') to the other ('post-Soviet'), and, more particularly that the conception of the 'Soviet' in Russian television is a construct of the post-Soviet present rather than a passive reflection of the communist past.

The meaning of the third element of our title – 'Remote control' – is overdetermined. First, it recognises the decline in media freedom and the increase of government control over the content and style of television programmes which has occurred under Putin, whose efforts to install a latter-day version of imperial pride in Russian military achievements at the centre of a national identity project amount to a form of remote *control*. Yet, precisely because of the recent changes wrought upon Russian society, a blanket return to the totalitarianism of the Soviet media has not occurred. The fact that Russian television now operates in a global 'infosphere'; the inherently porous boundaries between television texts and their contexts; the growing 'conversationalisation' of media discourse (Fairclough 1995: 5, 10–11); the influence of the market imperative; television's twin, and contradictory, national-centripetal and local-centrifugal emphases; the lack in post-Soviet Russia of an established mechanism for mediating between public and private spheres; and the persistently low cultural status that the medium enjoys in Russia all conspire to ensure that the control that Putin nominally exercises remains *remote* and less than wholly effective.

Our subtitle acquires its definitive motivation from the multiplicity of viewing modes, identifications and ways of incorporating television into the discourses of everyday life revealed by the fieldwork which represents one of the book's principal innovations. The autonomy in the way that post-Soviet viewers exercise their viewing choices is symbolised in the image of the *remote control* device.

By way of expanding on the context for our study, let us provide some preliminary background on the book's two key terms: control and meaning.

Control

Since its emergence, television has proved something of a dilemma to governments wishing to exploit its potential as a propaganda tool. For television is driven by competing centripetal and centrifugal tendencies. The easy accessibility of television technology makes for maximum penetration potential (hence the term 'broadcast'). Almost every home in any country will have at least one television set; it requires little obvious intellectual effort and governments therefore have the power to insinuate themselves into the intimacy of every living room. Moreover, the huge resources required to run a television station and the need to have untrammelled access to broadcasting frequencies mean that it comes with a built-in control mechanism which authoritarian governments have not been slow to exploit. The centripetal tendencies are further enhanced by television's associations with the objectivity of the camera. It is easier for a government to validate the veracity of the message it is disseminating if it is grounded in the authenticity of the photographic image rather than the suspect rhetoric of the printed word. In all these senses, then, television offers the supreme propaganda tool.

But for the same reasons, it is also a totalitarian's nightmare. Precisely because of its associations with the concrete and the authentic, and because of its easy accessibility, television has the tendency to increase the desire for broadcasting geared to the specific and the local; if we are given access to how people live at the centre, then why should we not be accorded the same insights into our own lives? The other side to this point is that an insight into the intimate details of life at the centre may create the desire that those details be replicated at the peripheries ('if them, why not us?'). Furthermore, 'the camera doesn't lie' is a double-edged maxim; one small slip in applying it is sufficient for a half-truth to be downgraded to a lie.[1]

The unique advantage that television offers over other camera technologies is its inherent associations with live, face-to-face, second-person address modes. Whilst this principle, too, if deployed with care, can enhance the veracity of a political message (a leader communicating in 'real time' is more compelling than a taped interview), the unpredictability that it brings leads to potentially catastrophic losses of control. Thus, television's centrifugal tendencies are as powerful as the centripetal forces of which they are merely the obverse.

It is hardly surprising, then, that the Soviet Communist Party deliberated at some length before deciding in 1965 to proceed with the development of a national television system. One of the conditions was that television be tied closely to the Party's control structures and to this end Gostelradio (State Television and Radio) was established with a rigid pyramidal structure headed by the Politburo, with party input into key personnel appointments and with a Department of Information and Propaganda dominating broadcasting schedules at every level. Soviet television programming was from its inception controlled from the centre. The agenda for news broadcasting was driven by the press and throughout its period of operation, the visual image was strictly subordinate to the written word of party directives and *Pravda* editorials; the official metrics for television news bulletins was that of 'pages' of script read. Entertainment programming, though not ignored, was given a limited quota of airtime and considered to be of secondary importance, whilst national schedules were structured around the propaganda needs of the Communist Party.[2]

Despite this, television ownership grew rapidly during the 1960s and by the end of the decade virtually every home had access to the four main national channels. Viewing figures for the main evening news bulletin, *Vremia*, remained at well over 50 million throughout the late Soviet period – a statistic of which commercial channels in the west would have been deeply envious. During the late 1960s and 1970s, the Union republics (except Russia) were given their own television channels on which they were permitted to broadcast in languages other than Russian, and on local issues. As early as the 1970s, the Communist Party was issuing directives against 'localism', fearful of a rise in national sentiment causes by television's promotion of ethnic and regional loyalties. Two developments which did much to precipitate the end of the Soviet Union were the battle between Soviet troops and local activists around the Vilnius television tower in January 1991, and Eltsyn's insistence in 1990 that Russia be given its own broadcasting time on Union frequencies.

The spread of TV to the outer reaches of the Soviet Union also meant that rural dwellers in Siberia or Kazakhstan were treated to intimate views of the insides of Moscow apartments, only to be struck by the superior quality of living enjoyed by their metropolitan compatriots. A still more dangerous product of television's involuntary attention to extraneous detail was the tendency of Soviet viewers to watch reports on demonstrations in western cities less for the voiced-over clichés about worker oppression than for the well-stocked shops and fashionably dressed shoppers glimpsed in the camera footage.

The camera also has an inconvenient familiarising function. Stalin's mystique is largely attributable to the fact that the Soviet people very rarely saw live images of him. In the television era, such selective visibility was not an option. One of the most surprising images for Soviet viewers in the mid-1960s was that of Brezhnev (General Secretary of the Communist Party) and Kosygin (Prime Minister) sharing an intimate joke caught on camera in an unguarded moment during an otherwise highly ritualised press conference. Such details simultaneously humanised and familiarised the Communist leaders, diminishing their aura and symbolic power.

As Brezhnev became ever more addicted to the symbolism of power (his lapels famously drooping with multiple self-awarded medals), he also cut an increasingly decrepit figure impossible to hide from the unforgiving television eye. The extensive series of unofficial Brezhnev jokes which circulated throughout the Soviet Union owed much to television images of the leader.

Also impossible for the Soviet leadership to conceal indefinitely was the growing penetration of western popular culture. This became a frequent topic of agonising debate in the Politburo during the 1970s. With the Baltic republics able to receive Finnish television, the increasing influence of Voice of America and Radio Free Europe, and the advent of the VCR machine, Soviet television had no option but to respond by developing a home-grown popular culture suited to the needs of a Communist Party ever paranoid about losing its grip on power. As a result, a unique brand of Soviet television detectives and spy thrillers emerged, along with variety, comedy and game shows reflecting native traditions such as the still vibrant oral culture, and concerts of insipid, officially manufactured popular music.

These efforts met with some success, particularly in the realm of television drama, where series such as the detective thriller *The Place of Rendezvous cannot be Changed* (*Mesto vstrechi izmenit' nel'zia*) starring Vysotskii, and the spy series *Seventeen Moments of Spring* (*Semnadsat' mgnovenii vesni*; 1973), acquired a popularity which still resonates today. But this popularity was in part due to the ambiguity which both series embraced. Thus, *Seventeen Moments* featured the legendary Shtirlitz, played by Viacheslav Tikhonov. His exploits as a Soviet agent (Maksim Isaev) working behind German lines in the Second World War under a false German persona, encouraged viewers to imagine the Russian Self as Other in a potentially subversive way. Significantly, the hero entered unofficial folklore as Shtirlitz rather than Isaev. And *The Place* offered a provocative portrayal of a detective willing to bend the law in order to uphold it

Soviet television emphasised high literary values as a means of demarcating native television culture from decadent western consumerist 'trash'. For this reason a spate of well-produced, if stodgy, adaptations of literary classics occupied a prominent place in the schedules. The selection of texts for adaptation often reflected current government policy. For example, the 1970s, the period of détente, saw several respectful television adaptations of western literary classics, including a production of Jerome K. Jerome's *Three Men in A Boat* in which the narrator's playful request at the beginning of each episode for parents to send their children to bed demonstrated the maturing of a self-conscious television culture capable of accommodating foreign texts to domestic viewing habits; and a version of the Sherlock Holmes stories so popular that Russian tourists would regularly make pilgrimages to Holmes's fictitious flat in Baker Street, London.

Such adaptations, however, soon succumbed to the late Soviet tendency to read (and write) 'between the lines' (*mezhdu strokami*). The success of Mark Zakharov's 1980 television adaptation of Eric von Raspe's *Adventures of Baron von Munchausen* rested on the film's ideologically subversive play with the notion of 'image as truth and word as lie' (the story centres on a character who tells tall tales about fantastical adventures he claims to have endured) in a subtle critique of Soviet anti-western propaganda.[3]

Foreign classics featured alongside resurrected native classics as part of a policy of bolstering pride in the Russian contribution to world culture. However, there were good ideological reasons why Dostoevskii's works had lain dormant during the Stalin period, and why, with some exceptions, even Turgenev, with his enlightened liberalism, had not featured prominently in the Soviet literary canon. Far from confirming the validity of this canon, the spate of Chekhov and Turgenev serialisations raised questions about the exclusion of texts whose luxuriant television production, intentionally or otherwise, encouraged nostalgia for pre-revolutionary values and lifestyles.

Another awkward irony arose from the juxtaposition of these weighty literary adaptations with earlier Bolshevik antagonism high culture. Dziga Vertov's call for a cinema freed from the shackles of enslavement to bourgeois literary culture became a rallying cry for the post-revolutionary cinematic avant-garde (Vertov 1984). In an inversion of this axiom, the traditional, high-budget adaptation of the literary classic reinforced an ideological commitment to protecting precious Russian literary culture from the tide of western visual trash flooding people's homes. The success of government-financed television adaptations of Dostoevskii's *The Idiot* in 2004; Pasternak's *Doctor Zhivago* (*Doktor Zhivago*) and Solzhenitsyn's *First Circle* (*V kruge pervom*) in 2005; and Bulgakov's *The Master and Margarita* (*Master i Margarita*) in 2006, offer recent illustrations of the durability of this trend.

Even during the Soviet period, though, government control over the full semiotic context in which television operated (as opposed to its structure and scheduling policies, and the content of its broadcasts) was far from complete. The themes we will pursue are all traceable to this long-gestating breakdown in semiotic hegemony.

Post-Soviet television began in earnest with the arrival of glasnost. But, contrary to romanticised western notions of glasnost as the arrival of democratic decentralisation, the policy was originally driven by a centralising mission to exploit local antagonisms to government orthodoxies as a weapon with which to defeat the conservative enemies of perestroika at the heart of the regime. Glasnost was a Leninist principle rather than a gesture towards western-style democracy. Soviet television in the late 1980s was characterised by uncompromising exposés of corruption and inefficiency and hand wringing about the excesses of the Stalinist past. It was then that the culture of investigative journalism first established itself in the Soviet Union – an important development not entirely undermined by the retrenchments of the Putin era.

Television was more than the tool of glasnost. It was in fact synonymous with the policy. Early glasnost rhetoric focused on a 'making universally visible' – or televising – of the previously hidden. The titles of the flagship glasnost programmes are revealing: *The Glance* (*Vzgliad*) and *The Spotlight of Perestroika* (*Prozhektor perestroika*) both emphasise the role of light and vision (McNair 1991). Television was also crucial to the accompanying principle of 'timeliness' (*operativnost'*) – the notion that a modern, technology-led economy requires the rapid dissemination of information. For this reason, live broadcasting became one of the major innovations of the Gorbachev period, beginning with broadcasts from the chambers of central and local government. Live talk shows, press conferences and interviews, and, most famously, live television link ups (or *telemosty*) followed suit, with the debate between Soviet and American youth co-hosted by Vladimir Pozner and Phil Donahue marking a milestone in world television history.

The emphasis on investigative exposé and live broadcasting had unintended consequences, generating a flood of nationalist extremism and other voices opposed, from a variety of stances, altogether to the Soviet regime, and so strengthening rather than weakening the conservative forces of opposition to Gorbachev. As a result, there ensued a reining back of glasnost, a virtual end to live broadcasting and calls from Leonid Kravchenko, the head of State Television, for a return to 'positive' Soviet news values.

But things had progressed too far and the worst fears of those who had, from the outset, warned about the dangerous ambiguities of television were about to be realised. Ironically, in one last-ditch effort to draw upon the vast resources available to a state with complete oversight of television, in March 1991 Gorbachev mounted a successful publicity campaign in support of his plea for a 'yes' vote in a referendum on maintaining the Soviet Union intact. But the success was short lived, cut short by the August 1991 coup in which, once again, television played the key role. The conflict at the heart of the *Vremia* news team and the eventual decision to broadcast the full picture of the drama unfolding on the streets of Moscow, the infamous 'trembling fingers' of the coup leaders as they nervously faced the international press, included in rather than edited out of the conference footage after the intervention of the *Vremia* editor, have all become part of the mythology of the coup.[4] Here, television's capacity for capturing extraneous detail is transformed into an overt weapon of rebellion wielded by the very guardians of central control. The abiding symbolism of the events of August 1991 also owe their currency to television as images of Eltsyn standing on a Red Army tank fomenting democratic revolt made their way into living rooms across an astonished world. The way in which Russian television has converged with the very dramas which it represents is a recurrent theme in this book.

The events of 1991 did not mark the advent of a powerful 'fourth estate'. Eltsyn's hold on power remained precarious and whilst the principles of freedom of speech first enshrined under Gorbachev in the 1990 Press Act were basically adhered to, Eltsyn reasserted government control over television broadcasting through economic means. Retaining ownership of the main national channels, he reduced their share of government subsidies as part of the economic liberalisation pursued in the early post-Soviet years, making television dependent on advertising income and government favour. Arguably, his policy was vindicated by the events of 1993 when a counter-revolution led by an alliance of old communists and proto-fascists launched, through the Duma in which they held democratic sway, a bid to establish power over broadcasting and wrest power from Eltsyn.

During the constitutional crisis of October 1993 which ended with troops storming the seat of parliament, an assault was launched by a baying crowd of extremists on Moscow's main television tower. Programmes were suspended on all stations but one (TV2) which continued to broadcast dramatic interviews with government troops about to do battle with the mob, accompanied by the sound of studio windows shattering.[5] Once again, television was thrust to the forefront of its own news agenda. This time, paradoxically, television defended democracy and free speech by deploying its resources *against* forces sympathetic to a democratically elected parliament.

Despite a short-lived clampdown on the media, the period between 1993 and 1996 was marked by the emergence of the oligarchs as a force in media ownership, with Boris Berezovskii, at that time close to the Kremlin, obtaining a controlling share in Channel 1 (renamed ORT); and the mayor of Moscow, Iurii Luzhkov, linked to the energy industry, gaining a significant stake in TVS. It also saw the arrival of Russia's first politically independent television channel – NTV – with the backing of Berezovzkii's rival, Vladimir Gusinskii. With its critical stance towards the government's first Chechen campaign in 1995, NTV produced the first Russian example of television forcing the government to change course (Eltsyn negotiated a hasty peace settlement in 1996 in advance of his re-election campaign). It swiftly established a reputation as the channel for the oppositional intelligentsia, hosting programmes such as *Puppets* (*Kukly*) – the bitingly satirical Russian version of the British *Spitting Image* – whose makers Eltsyn attempted unsuccessfully to sue for defamation.[6]

In the mid-1990s Russia's economy went into steep decline and social unrest increased, enabling the communist old guard, in the person of their leader, Gennadii Ziuganov, to mount a serious threat to Eltsyn. The ironically named Liberal Democratic Party of the fascist right with which the communists formed a 'Red-Brown Alliance' enjoyed considerable electoral success thanks to their charismatic leader, Vladimir Zhirinovskii. Eltsyn's popularity sank and the result of the 1996 presidential election looked in jeopardy. This left NTV facing a dilemma: did it prolong its commitment to objective journalism, reporting all the president's failings and so inadvertently ensuring the success of his undemocratic rivals, or did it forego its liberal principles and support Eltsyn in the long-term interests of democracy? It opted for the latter, according minimal (and overwhelmingly negative) coverage to Ziuganov and joining ORT in a campaign to 'teach' people the importance of voting (the election result turned on Eltsyn's ability to get his supporters to abandon their summer dachas and vote), whilst associating his campaign with the future and with Russia's children (thereby tacitly tarring Ziuganov with the brush of the Soviet past). With the help of media advisers from America, Eltsyn won his second term.

The advent of Putin in 2000 effectively marked an end to the limited political licence that Eltsyn had granted television. Putin rapidly fell out with Eltsyn's close ally, Berezovskii, the largest stakeholder in ORT, which effectively became the state channel (it was renamed Channel 1, its old Soviet title). The second national channel, RTR (Rossiia) was then assigned the task of integrating local interests with the national perspective. In 2001, the first of several clampdowns on NTV occurred (Gusinskii, too, had now fled to the west to avoid corruption charges) and Boris Jordan, a Putin ally with connections to Gazprom, the state energy giant, was installed as owner. Independent-minded journalists left NTV to join TVS and TV6 which enjoyed the briefest periods of grace as the remaining islands of freedom, before they too were silenced. Curiously, even after 2001, independent voices somehow made their way onto air in the form of controversial talk shows and current affairs programmes such as Lev Shuster's *Freedom of Speech* (*Svoboda slova*) and Leonid Parfenov's audacious *The Other Day* (*Namedni*), but they were terminated in a second wave of clampdowns in 2004. By 2003, the international press monitoring organisation Freedom House had downgraded Russia's rating from 'Free' to 'Not free' (a judgement to which television conformed more readily than the printed press) and has renewed this rating ever since. Of national channels, only RenTV (founded by Irina Lesnevskaia and her son, Dmitrii, and owned until 2005 by a controversial, freethinking, former Eltsyn minister, Anatolii Chubais) retained any independence, although its market share only ever attained 5 per cent. In December 2005, it was taken over by a consortium of companies with close Kremlin ties and since then its inclination to criticise has waned. Its reputation now largely rests on its willingness to broadcast innovative drama and comedy programming (it holds the Russian rights to *The Simpsons* and *The X-Files*, for example).

Putin has seen his unchallenged authority over the media as an opportunity to use television as a propaganda tool with which to promote his agenda of rebuilding popular belief in a militarily strong, self-confident, stable and united Russia. In 2004, for example, Putin launched The Star (Zvezda) a channel devoted exclusively to the Russian army. In 2005, a colossal nation-building effort was mounted in parallel with celebrations of the 60th anniversary of victory in the Second World War. The president never missed an opportunity to exploit the resources of television in his attempt to construct a 'virtual' freedom in which the surface appearances of democratic culture are replicated in meticulous detail but without the substance and structures of democracy to sustain them. In 2005, Putin appeared on *Vremia* in an open-necked, short-sleeved shirt giving an excruciating interview to members of *Nashi* ('Our people'), the supposedly spontaneous youth movement manufactured as a latter-day equivalent to the *Komsomol*, in which he fielded obsequious questions posed with an air of bold informality.[7]

Post-Soviet Russian television has not followed an unbending linear trajectory from freedom to subservience. One complicating factor is the low cultural status that Russian television has endured. Apart from the legacy of the logo-centric Soviet cultural value system, the tide of western commercial imports with which all channels are still compelled to fill large parts of their schedules did little to diminish television's low standing. It was with this in mind that in 1997 Channel Kultura was launched to provide an island of good taste (mainly in the form of screen adaptations of classic literary texts and highbrow discussion shows) amidst a sea of western inspired trash. Vladimir Putin went on record in 2006 to say that, along with most of Russia's oppositional intelligentsia, Kultura was his preferred channel (a statement less ironic than it might seem, given that, since 2002, the channel has been under the guardianship of the Presidential Council on Culture).

The flood of western soap operas, game shows, crime thrillers and romance serials indicated another factor limiting the scope of the television propaganda mission: in general, viewers prefer escapist entertainment broadcasting to news and current affairs. That the value of the western imports extended beyond their relative cheapness is proved by the fact that, when Russian channels did finally establish sufficient income with which to make their own programmes, they invariably replicated the generic formats and formulas of the western programmes that preceded them. Whilst they remain on the surface politically anodyne, the thriller, the game show and the sitcom nonetheless articulate sets of cultural, ethical and other values and worldviews not always reconcilable with the Putin agenda. The increasing importance of entertainment broadcasting is indicated by the rise of the STS channel which concentrates almost exclusively on such programming. Also indicative of this trend is the growth of cable and satellite television. In short, Russia, with its aspirations to be a global market player, is unable to shield itself completely from the consequences of globalisation, including the worldwide penetration of specialist news channels such as CNN and Euronews (Evron'iuz).

Globalisation goes hand in hand with localisation (cf. Roland Robertson's now widely used neologism 'glocalisation') as the homogenising forces of global capitalism generate a counter-trend towards an emphasis on local identities and discourses. The phenomenon parallels television's competing centripetal and centrifugal principles. Accordingly, even as Russian television has come under the sway of global media forms at the national level, so, despite the obtrusive political control exerted over it, regional Russian television has enjoyed a revival and in certain areas plays a vibrant role in forging local identities (Ekaterinburg television, for example, which has over twelve channels, vigorously promotes Ural folk culture).

The scope that Putin's regime has for imposing control on Russian television is further constrained by the rise in the influence of new media. Russia has, so far, eschewed the temptation to follow China's Canute-like path in trying to hold the tides of web-based communication at bay through censorship, partly because it is far more integrated into global structures than China, and partly because Putin adopted the alternative strategy of increasing the presence of pro-government sites on the web. Whilst internet access is low in Russia by comparison with western countries like the UK, it is growing exponentially and those Russians who do have access make more use of the internet than anyone else. One of the many ways in which the convergence between hitherto separate media affects television is through the web forums which many Russian television programmes now host. They serve as a locus for relatively free expression and for the development of autonomous viewing cultures around particular programmes which often sharply contradict the meanings inscribed into the programmes at the production level. Those viewers who enjoy the benefit of internet access are much less susceptible to the Putin control machine than those who do not. The enlightened intelligentsia have always been able to distance themselves from the official propaganda that they are fed by their government. However, there is a key difference: the internet makes minimal distinction between the educated and the non-educated and is potentially a truly democratic source of information.[8]

Our brief survey of the development of Soviet/Russian television has highlighted some of the main themes we will pursue:

(1) the particular importance in Russia of television's competing centripetal and centrifugal tendencies;
(2) the tendency in Russia for television news to converge with the very agenda it is reporting;
(3) Russian television's propensity for embracing post-Soviet paradoxes (for example, the need to adopt profoundly undemocratic means to ultimately democratic ends) whilst also exhibiting clear continuities with the Soviet period;
(4) the continuing problem of television's low aesthetic status and the prerogative to entertain an audience in thrall to distinctly non-aesthetic formats;
(5) the multiple implications of Russian television's susceptibility to the forces of globalisation (its adaptation of global genres to its own cultural paradigms; the boost that globalisation has given to local television's role in forging regional identities constructed though reference to a distant centre located not in Miami but in Moscow);
(6) the enhanced role of audience input in shaping the meanings generated by television (there is a stark contrast between the rigid conformity imposed on news and current affairs under Putin and the range of opinions expressed through web feedback channels and, as we shall see in audience focus groups);
(7) the absence in Russia of a mature, hegemonic approach to the wielding of power according to which dominant discourses, by constantly confronting, internalising and neutralising counter discourses, establish domain over the realm of 'common sense'.

Achievements in the field

Our contention is that we cannot talk meaningfully about Putin's 'control' over television without taking into account the ways in which television generates meaning. Moreover, television differs (though not absolutely; we are confronting an epistemological principle applicable to all human communication) from textual media such as newspapers, literature and film in that it operates in a far less transitive mode. Rather than an identifiable author, director or journalist encoding a discrete text to be disseminated to, and decoded by, a group of readers/viewers, we are dealing with:

(1) a production process involving multiple agents of whom it is difficult to isolate an 'author';
(2) a 'text' whose boundaries are notoriously hard to define (is the television 'text' an isolated programme, a series, a genre, a channel's output, or an evening's viewing?); and

(3) an audience for which television viewing may serve primarily not, as with a novel or a film, as the focus of an intense hermeneutic effort, but as a vague source of relaxation, a mode of sporadic distraction, a stimulus for conversation, the centre of a set of concentric rings of activity (voting in a reality show; responding in an internet forum, applying to participate one-self), or one component in a cultural phenomenon for which the paratextual accompaniments acquire equal importance (a programme cult involving newspaper speculation on plotlines or the private lives of actors).

This brings us full circle back to the issue of the relationship between tele-vision and culture. It indicates the need for a discussion of the theoretical and methodological assumptions implicit in our approach to our subject in the context of a survey of previous scholarship on Russian television.

There is an honourable tradition of television research within Political Studies whose aim is to assess the role television has played in driving, implementing and reflecting political processes. Television is, in such work, subordinate to the concepts and principles of political research. Accordingly, it concentrates on news and current affairs programming. Within Soviet/ Russian Studies, the pioneering work of this kind was Alex Inkeles's study of the mass media in the post-Stalinist Soviet Union (Inkeles 1950). In con-temporary post-Soviet Studies, Ellen Mickiewicz's two books (Mickiewicz 1988, 1997) have made a major contribution to establishing television's centrality to Russia's remarkable post-1985 history. Interestingly, however, in recent work, Mickiewicz turns to questions of the audience reception of post-Soviet news programmes and some of her conclusions are broadly in line with observations we derive from our own research, though her focus is, as we shall see in a longer discussion of her work in our final chapter, on cognitive patterns of audience interpretation rather than the questions of text–audience interplay or viewing mode which concern us.[9] In the UK, quantitative research carried out under the leadership of Stephen White established the extent of Putin's political mastery over national television output, focusing on the impact of election coverage on voters.

Frank Ellis, one of the few Russian media scholars to have emerged from literary studies, portrays developments in the media as moving from the iron grip of censorship to a state of promiscuous availability in which the 'Great Writers' have no place: 'The eagerness with which the Russian reading and viewing public has abandoned Tolstoi and turned to Western videos and Mexican low-budget soaps is a brutal rejection of party-approved culture-behaviour in favour of fun' (Ellis 1999: 137). Ellis is hostile to this trend, viewing 'print based literacy' as 'a form of immunisation against the absurd-ities of the electronic image' (Ellis 1999: 129). As far as 'serious broadcasting' is concerned:

> Grave financial difficulties, the search for new political allegiances, a campaign of intimidation and murder waged by organised crime (often

it seems with the tacit approval of the government) ... and, of course, the enormous challenges of covering the Chechen war, suggest that Russian journalism can only ever at best be an anaemic version of what has long been taken for granted in the West.

(Ellis 1999: 120)

And this was written *before* Putin's multiple media clampdowns.

In Russia, media restrictions have not suppressed objective assessments of those restrictions in the context of comprehensive surveys of developments in the area. Ivan Zassoursky's *Media and Power in Post-Soviet Russia* is the defining work in this category. One of its merits is that it covers economic aspects of the media. This is important in the case of post-Soviet Russia because of the symbiosis between issues of ownership and issues of control; the use of the word 'power' rather than 'politics' in Zassoursky's title reflects this symbiosis. Interestingly, Zassoursky's intimate knowledge of the complexities surrounding post-Soviet media trends (he places television within a widening range of media sources and includes reference to the emergence of the new media) leads him to a less negative assessment of the Russian media than that of most western observers. Elena Vartanova explains features of Russian television less in terms of overt political repression than by reference to its location between fundamentally different western and Asian media models.[10]

Given that 54 per cent of Russians watch regional television, many in preference to national television, it is not surprising that scholars are now turning their attention to this area, although the work has been primarily quantitative and factual. Jukka Pietiläinen's work on media consumption habits in the Russian–Finnish borderlands are seminal here (Pietiläinen 2003).

Recent years have seen more attention in Russia paid to the media, and a Mass Media Centre has been established at St Petersburg University under the directorship of Nina Boikova. The orientation is largely professional and the centre specialises in courses for aspiring journalists. In Moscow, the Moscow Media Law and Policy Institute (MMLPI) was established in 1995 within the Journalism Faculty at Moscow State University. Its purpose is likewise not that of furthering scholarly analysis but 'to assist by means of legal education and research the development of free and independent Russian mass media and to support in all possible ways the formation of a civil society in Russia'.[11]

As far as cultural studies are concerned, in Russia the pages of the cinema journal, *Iskusstvo kino*, regularly include sophisticated analyses of television films and serials. The editor, Daniil Dondurei, is one of the most authoritative contributors. The fact that these analyses appear in a film journal is, however, revealing. One of the few Russian scholars to have devoted their careers exclusively to the cultural analysis of television is Vera Zvereva whose articles on various genres and themes, informed by western cultural theorists such as Barthes and Foucault, have appeared on the page of a web-based entity called Modern Culture (*Sovremennaia kultura*; www.culturca. narod.ru/masscult1005.htm).

Cultural analyses of Russian television in the west have generally been conducted by scholars who have emerged from literary studies and have preferred theoretical paradigms influenced by literary and narrative theory, by adjacent fields such as philosophy, and by the post-structuralist revolution which swept across literature departments in the 1970s. Unsurprisingly, therefore, close readings of the television text predominate. One of the best examples of work produced by this trend is David MacFadyen's book *Russian Television Today: Primetime Drama and Comedy*; Eliot Borenstein's articles on post-Soviet television advertising and the early 1990s talk show *About That* (*Pro eto*); Elena Prokhorova's work on the detective drama; and Nancy Condee's incorporation of television serials in her investigation of Russian nation building are also all highly commendable representatives of the textual approach (see MacFadyen 2007; Borenstein 1999, 2000; Condee 2008). A series of projects funded in 2003–6 by the Finnish Academy of Sciences as part of the 'Russia in Flux' programme apply a range of semiotic and ethnographic methods to post-Soviet media texts and audiences with commendable, if fragmentary, results.[12]

Hilary Pilkington's and Elena Omel'chenko's searching investigations into post-Soviet youth culture touch upon how television viewing habits are incorporated into identity building, drawing on empirical work in the field (Pilkington and Omel'chenko 2002). As sociologists, albeit with a qualitative bent, they are interested primarily in the meaning-making behaviour of their subjects and do not seek to link their findings with details of the source texts.

The dilemma of meaning

This begs the question which will shape the entirety of the present study – that of where televisual meaning is located. The predominance of close readings of individual programmes within Slavic Cultural Studies indicates a predisposition towards the text as the site of meaning. This is hardly surprising and mirrors the state of affairs in television studies generally in the 1970s and early 1980s. But Russian Studies has yet to complete the trajectory followed by Media Studies in the later 1980s and 1990s, a trajectory which led inexorably towards the audience as the primary locus for televisual meaning. Here, partly, no doubt, because of the interdisciplinary nature of Media Studies, there was a recognition that an overemphasis on close textual readings reflected a bias towards the literary provenance of many of the early pioneers of television research (even McLuhan, who did much to establish the unique nature of television as a medium, was, by training and early profession, an English specialist). Television's multiple authorship and viewing modes, its reliance on paratextual adjuncts (magazine gossip and internet discussion), and its seepage into the practices and meanings of everyday life seemed to render even context-sensitive textual exegesis defunct. To do justice to McLuhan, his identification of television as 'cool' (involving high audience participation) rather than 'hot' (relying on transmission to a passive audience) implicitly recognised this fact (McLuhan 1964).

Also subjected to challenge in the late twentieth century media studies revolution were the pessimistic pronouncements of the Frankfurt School about the subjugation of the television viewer to a process of consumerist stultification. Adorno proved little different from proponents of the 'hypodermic needle' theory of television according to which programme makers 'injected' preferred, establishment meanings into willing, receptive audiences. Stuart Hall and his associates at the Birmingham Cultural Studies Centre, whilst sympathetic to Adorno's Marxist underpinnings, criticised his elitist assumptions. Modifying the semiotic paradigm, Hall developed a model in which he distinguished a process of encoding at the television production level from a decoding process at the audience level, stressing that the meanings generated by each process were not necessarily compatible. However, in order not to fall into the trap of over-idealising the viewer's subversive potential (something of which John Fiske, with his notion of the radically open television text was accused), and thus to resist hegemonic consensus building, Hall later identified within the decoding process a spectrum of potential significations, ranging from acceptance of the 'dominant meaning' encoded in the text, through 'negotiated meanings' in which viewers modify dominant meanings to their own situations, to 'resistant meanings' in which they substitute dominant meanings with their own counter-establishment readings (Hall 1980, 1994). David Morley put this model to the test in his study of diverse audience readings of the BBC programme, *Nationwide* (Morley 1980).

The text-based tradition adapted still has an important role to play in television analysis. Influenced by Barthes's literary theory of the 'writerly text', by Bakhtin's notion of the carnivalesque and by de Certeau's theory of everyday tactics of resistance to ideological strategies, Fiske has now redressed, even overcompensated, his earlier omission of the viewing audience (Fiske 1987). In his most recent work, Fiske has responded to criticisms by positing television and audience as interdependent, drawing on Bakhtin's dialogism to locate televisual meaning on the border between text and viewer. He has also incorporated Raymond Williams's oft-quoted insight that television works not in discrete textual units but in a continual flow of programmes, advertisements and publicity which viewers dip into, quite literally, at leisure. He has, like his sociologically influenced rivals, liberated television studies from its subservience to literary models of analysis and inserted it into a broader theory of popular culture (Fiske 2006).

Whilst, in his baffled irritation at the personal experience which occasioned the theory, Williams was himself partly responsible for encouraging the technological essentialism with which some endowed his term, 'flow', in the larger work within which the idea is developed, technology is grounded in cultural practices and power relations (Williams 1974). Flow is a function of the consumerist regime into which television is inserted, not an inherent property of the technology. At the textual level, John Ellis replaced Williams's insight with the intermediate notion of viewing 'segment' – a term which recognises television's transcendence of traditional textual boundaries but nonetheless insists that viewers work with discrete semiotic units. Ellis also developed convincing accounts of the ways in which television represents and engages with time and space, of how it is integrated into everyday life, of how it differs from cinema, and of its relationship to new media forms (Ellis 1992).

Despite its obvious differences from television (its wrapt viewing mode; its inability to transmit live images; its relative lack of intimacy; its emphasis on the visual), cinema has continued to influence television scholars. For example, Richard Dyer's theory of the 'film star as text' (Dyer 1979) has been adapted for application to the television celebrity, whose greater familiarity with the audience eschews the epic distance between actor and viewers implied by film stardom. In recent years, cinema and television have converged within the broader field of globalisation studies (itself boasting cultural studies and social science wings). In television's case, the study of global formats and their adaptation for local markets has proven a popular topic of investigation.[13] It is of tremendous importance for post-Soviet Russian television and will feature prominently in subsequent chapters. The study of formats overlaps with genre theory, the discussion of which we defer until later in this Introduction.

Ironically, if the close of the last century saw the cultural end of Media Studies move away from the text and towards the audience, at almost exactly the same time, the Political Science end discovered the merits of textual analysis and the need to recognise that political messages are inseparable from the form in which they are embodied, inaugurating the new field of Political Communication. We owe awareness of the 'gate-keeping' and agenda-setting functions of television news to scholars in this field. Pippa Norris's work on how television news 'frames' issues in order to impart particular political meaning to events (Norris, Kern and Just 2003) is reflected in our own discussion of Russian news broadcasting. Political Communication has also drawn attention to the importance of editorial choices (of inclusion/exclusion, running order, duration and salience), alongside news values and newsgathering practices, and in relation to the structures and resources of news organisations (Bennett and Entman 2001; Curran 2002; Kuhn and Neveu 2002; McNair 2000, 2003).

The same period saw a convergence between the micro-textual techniques applied by sociolinguists and the ideological concerns of political studies in the emergence of Critical Discourse Analysis (CDA) pioneered by Teun Van Dijk (1991, 1998) and Norman Fairclough (1995). Arguing that discourse is language inflected by power relations, CDA has, indeed, exposed the subliminal workings of ideology, racism and prejudice in the contemporary media climate of suspicion surrounding immigration and, more recently, the terrorist threat. CDA procedures included attention to local semantics, especially lexicalisation and implicature (the denominations used for terrorists; changes in the credibility status of quoted speakers through words carrying different presuppositions), syntactic style (passive constructions to disguise in-group agency), rhetoric (metaphors of 'swamping'), quotation patterns (direct and indirect quotation to (de)legitimate particular perspectives), and argumentation (justification strategies for free speech curtailments). By adapting the methods of Bakhtinian dialogism, CDA analysts have further revealed how different voices are articulated with one another, and how the positions from which these voices speak are accommodated within the morphological systems of particular ideologies. Lara Ryazanova-Clarke (2000, 2005) has applied some of these insights to the post-Soviet media to good effect.

CDA techniques take little account of the visual aspects of television's ideological embeddedness. But the work of Gunther Kress on multimodality (2001) and W.J.T. Mitchell's long-standing interest in the word–image threshold as the site of society's fundamental conflicts and tensions (Mitchell 1994) do much to fill this gap.

Text analysts have thus advanced significantly in terms of their willingness to locate their readings of television programmes in the context of the ideological regimes of which these programmes are part. John Thompson's survey of the media's relationship to modernity also takes into account the importance of institutional and industrial issues (Thompson 1995). The role of genre in mediating between television text and context has increasingly been recognised in this connection. More recently, Jason Mittell has questioned the very wisdom of defining genre, arguing that 'the category itself emerges from the relationship between the elements it groups together [text, industry, audience and historical context] and the cultural context in which it operates' (Mittell 2001: 40, 43). He has proposed instead treating it as 'a "discursive practice" built from the bottom up by disparate micro-instances' (ibid.: 44). His insight will nonetheless inform our own approach to genre.

Mittell's rethinking of genre shows the apparent detachment of most of the approaches outlined from television's empirical audiences. Even those who claim to employ audience-focused methods, such as Tony Wilson, pay little attention to real viewers. Aware of the need to address this gap, Wilson attempts to link his reader-response derived notions of 'horizons of expectations', 'hermeneutic blanks', etc., with data from empirical audience research (Wilson 1993). But he is restricted to drawing on second-hand sources (referring in particular to Morley's work), and then, using deductive reasoning, merely to support conclusions he has reached on the basis of the audience interpretation strategies extrapolated from the television texts. Similarly, post-structuralist theorisations of viewers as networks of textually inscribed 'subject positions', are rarely tested in empirical research. In the absence of empirical 'proof' that our semiotic perspective on a programme is shared by those to whom it is targeted, how can we dispel the impression of a groundless, arrogant subjectivism which, even if it pays lip service to 'the viewer', reflects our own scholarly agendas?

The crisis that this question provoked within television studies took on different connotations, depending upon who was articulating it. Thus, the concern of the Birmingham Cultural Studies scholars was that of white, male, middle-class intellectuals imposing upon an array of class, regional, gender and race positions homogenised meanings with no grounding in lived experience. Hall's Encoding–Decoding model was deployed to great effect in a range of qualitative, ethnomethodological research projects involving varieties of fieldwork borrowed from sociology and anthropology. Rather than applying deductive reasoning to audience data to confirm a priori hypotheses, the Birmingham School researchers were willing to use open, inductive methods which allowed for the generation of new, and unexpected, hypotheses derived from their observations in the field. Similarly, Ien Ang used qualitative survey methods to investigate how women create, from the American soap opera *Dallas*, meanings based around a 'tragic structure of feeling' (Ang 1985).

Well before the 'disappearing audience' crisis had come to light, a media studies grouping known as the 'uses and gratifications' school had been carrying out audience investigations based on the notion that the significance of mass cultural production lies in the empirically measured pleasures and distractions derived from it by real consumers, about whom no preconceived notions of subject positions should be assumed. Employing largely quantitative 'survey' methods, researchers set about determining what proportions of different categories of viewers used particular types of programming for which purposes. But is has been pointed out that in this scheme of things 'what the viewer does with the text is emphasised at the expense of considering the programme itself' and that

> it is a mistake to assert that an audience can perceive a programme as possessing a fixed and unproblematic meaning to which they [sic] *then* 'react' in different ways. Rather, determining the sense of a text and 'reaction' are inextricably and mutually related.
>
> (Wilson 1993: 8)

Nonetheless, the legacy of 'uses and gratifications' concerns is reflected in the theoretically nuanced work of Roger Silverstone and others who have more recently turned their attention to the ways in which television is integrated into the everyday routines, rituals and patterns of behaviour of its viewers (Silverstone 1994).

Ethnomethodology is arguably at its most effective when unencumbered by ideological agendas. Sonia Livingstone's and Peter Lunt's work on the television talk-show audience, for example, combines ethnomethodological fieldwork with insights from social psychology, concluding that, with its strongly participatory focus, this much-derided genre has a role to play in reinvigorating the mediated public sphere (Livingstone and Lunt 1994). Some of the most fruitful ethnomethodological work has been cross-cultural in orientation. Tamar Liebes employed focus groups consisting of three married couples each from a range of ethnic groupings in Israel (Israeli Arab, Russian-Jewish and Moroccan immigrant) to investigate cultural differences in the interpretation of *Dallas* (Liebes 1990). His study did much to counter the view that globalisation was generating homogenised meaning. Of course, this conclusion, along with the programme and audience selection which led to it, all carry deeply political implications, as does Livingstone's optimistic view of the participatory potential of the contemporary public sphere, contradicting the notion that ethnomethodology is somehow ideology-neutral. Ien Ang touched on this issue in the course of articulating her own position on the text/audience problematic, which she believes can be transcended with a theory of television viewing as one component of a unified cultural practice in which a holistic, discursive system 'interpellates people as potential viewers':

> What is at stake here is the way in which television audiences relate to watching television as a cultural practice. ... One cannot deal with this question without an analysis of the way in which television discourse as a complex whole of representations is organised and structured.
>
> (Ang 1995: 21–22)

Ang's intervention highlights other problems with ethnomethodology. Whilst it positions itself against the superficial empiricism of the quantitative, survey-led approach, preferring in-depth, qualitative investigations of individual viewer responses as a means of getting at meaning rather than broad response trends, it cannot entirely escape the brush of positivism. The underlying assumption when conducting focus groups is that, contrary to Ang's insistence on a unified discursive system, the elusive meaning one is searching for is somehow 'out there' waiting to be recorded, albeit in a more self-aware way than through raw quantitative statistics. No amount of acknowledging the bias of the observer can entirely dispel this impression.

There are two other, closely related problems. First, despite the emphasis on the in-depth quality of individual responses rather than the generalised quantity of like responses, ethnomethodologists encounter a difficulty in moving from the particular to the general. For the purpose of conducting fieldwork is implicitly to 'average out' over a range of individual responses, discarding 'rogue' statements and pooling recurrent utterances in order to determine, for example, how working class women *in general* watch soap operas. This is why such care is taken to rationalise the membership of such groups, and why the results of their utterances are 'triangulated' with those of other qualitative methods. No matter how thoroughly contextualised or 'thick' the description on which the process is based (Geertz 1973), the business of extrapolating general conclusions from a range of single utterances is ultimately tainted with the same impersonalised abstraction as that embraced by survey methods.

This brings us to our central problem: what we mean by meaning itself. Ethnomethodological approaches to TV audience research emerged from a reaction against both quantitative surveys and text-based hermeneutics. The problem with the latter is that, adopting an elitist stance derived from literary studies in which the text must be subjected to exegesis by trained experts, it fails to check how the meaning-generating mechanisms it posits correspond to the actual meanings articulated by audiences. The assumption, therefore, is that authentic, verifiable meaning is to be found in and among those who make it: the viewers. But, curiously, this assertion replicates the very elitism that it claims to refute; for just why is it that the primary meaning of television (unlike that of, say, literature and art) must be sought among its users, if not because it lacks the 'high' aesthetic status of those forms and must be assimilated to a set of popular cultural practices best studied within non-aesthetic disciplines such as anthropology? Just as semiotic and literary approaches to television essentialise meaning in a revered text (there is, indeed, a question as to why audience studies of literature and film are not more widespread), so ethnomethodological approaches practice an essentialism of the anthropological object of study.

The obvious answer to the dilemma is to relocate meaning in the relationship between text and audience. But this, too, is easier said than done. The danger is that, in such intermediate approaches, either audience responses are used to authenticate preconceived, primary meanings extracted from a text, or textual features are viewed merely as stimuli for provoking primary meaning making within audiences (Morley 1980; Mittell 2001).

In his ruminations on the humanities, Bakhtin identifies monological, scientific forms of knowledge in which the intellect is faced with a voiceless object (*bezglasnaia veshch'*) that it contemplates (*sozertsaet*) and makes pronouncements about (*vyskazyvaetsia o nei*). (Bakhtin 1986a: 383). Notwithstanding their humanities labels, classic text and audience-based analyses of television each fall into this category. Ethnomethodological accounts tend to abstract such reactions from textual intentionalities, treating them as empirical objects of study, whilst also 'making allowance' for the 'bias' of the observer; semiotic analyses of television are prone to detach meaning-making procedures from both authorial intentionalities and audience responses, elevating the text itself to the status of meaning generator, whilst paying lip service to 'negotiated subject positions'. True, dialogical knowledge locates meaning in the encounter of consciousnesses, on the border between a text, or utterance – and for Bakhtin, a text can only be the living utterance (*vyskazyvanie*) of a subject – and its context (that of the living utterances of others):

> A text lives only in contact with another text (context). Only at the point of this contact does light flare up, shining backwards and forwards,

> bringing the text towards dialogue ... This ... is a dialogical contact
> between texts (utterances) and not a mechanical contact of 'oppositions'.
> (Bakhtin 1986a: 384–85)

Bakhtin recognises that the opposing notions of 'thing' and 'person' (subject)
on which his principles are based represent 'the limits of cognition' (*predely
poznaniia*), that there exists 'degrees of thingness and personhood' (*stepeni
veshchnosti i lichnosti*). He thus makes space for intermediate approaches
which incorporate elements of both dialogism and monological empiricism.
But we are dealing with a fundamental philosophical divide in the way in
which meaning itself is conceived: is it a function of specific utterances in
spatio-temporally contingent contexts, or a realm which transcends such
utterances and forms the ground for all subsequent meaning? The intractable
philosophical dualism of spirit and matter would seem to raise its head here.
With his insistence on the indivisibility of meaning from the context in which
it is embodied, and his anti-idealistic, anti-objectivist notion of the encounter
of two, living consciousnesses, Bakhtin may have succeeded in transcending
such dualism on a theoretical level. But, constrained by the conditions in
which he operated (in which the realm of academic discourse is institutionally partitioned from that of everyday life), his own practical analyses, even
when they situate the discourses of the text in the context of the social discourses they re-inflect, are ultimately hermeneutic exercises in arriving at the
'meaning(s)' of the given text. Ultimately rooted in a mystical faith in
Meaning with a capital letter, they owe more to textual exegesis than to
engagement with real human voices (one explanation of the privileged role
that literature occupies throughout Bakhtin's oeuvre is its status as a figure
for this unarticulated super-realm). Referring at the end of his career to the
humanities as 'the sciences of the Spirit' (*nauki o dukhe*), he is thus able to
declare grandly that: 'The world has meaning ... Each individual phenomenon is engulfed in the element of the first principles of Being' (ibid.: 381).
This is not to criticise Bakhtin. So fundamental is the epistemological gulf
between textual exegesis and empirical analysis that attempts to transcend
the divide tend to end in a declaration of allegiance to one or the other.

Confronting the dilemma: Methodology and the centrality of genre

We adopt three overlapping strategies to address the apparent intractability
of the text–audience divide. Firstly, we ensure that the book's structure
recognises the divide, with separate chapters devoted to textual readings of
particular programmes and audience research respectively. We defer discussion of our fieldwork methodology until the chapter in which the audience
takes centre stage. Suffice to say that it centres on focus groups constituted
with a view to exploring the role of certain differentials in shaping audience
reaction (geographical region, with special reference to the centre/periphery
dimension, age, gender and class), repeated in successive years in order to

gauge changes over time and supplemented with viewer diaries. In addition to compensating for the distortive effect of group dynamics on self-expression (bearing in mind that solipsistic self-expression can, conversely, distort the collective meaning negotiation process), the diaries also allow us to observe viewing habits in a form unmediated by the constraints of oral communication. We cite quantitative data only to furnish a context, or to underpin broad claims made about the relative popularity of particular programmes.

Whilst the balance between the chapters would seem heavily to favour text over audience (six to two), the imbalance applies only superficially. Hence our second strategy: that of a commitment constantly to commute between text and audience. Thus, with one exception, each chapter centring on a particular genre grounds insights into textual features in audience reactions gleaned from fieldwork and/or web forums, and, conversely, refers insights gained from fieldwork to particular textual features. We have tried to ensure that the commutation process is non-reductive (i.e. that we are not merely validating textual insights through audience data, or illustrating conclusions drawn from audience fieldwork by reference to programme features).

However, these compensatory strategies – both ways of attenuating the contradictions resulting from the dilemma we have outlined – are underpinned by a set of theoretical principles through which we address the dilemma head on. Here we must return to the notion of genre. Media genre theorists like Mittell, and Altman (1999), have emphasised the non-essential quality of genre, its constantly changing function as a mode of negotiation between text, producer and audience. In a situation of maximal disjunction between a text producer and his/her disparate audience (that of the modern media), this negotiation acquires an importance beyond that of the role of genre in cultural forms with more restricted, and more stable, audiences. Thus, viewers use generic expectations when attributing meaning to television texts which, equally, however, programme producers constantly repackage in order to appeal to shifting audience 'markets'. In television, genre is, in short, the point at which text and audience meet, the supreme embodiment of Ang's notion of television as 'discursive system' and 'cultural practice'.

Nothing that we have said so far is inapplicable to cultural forms other than television. However, television in its current mode of operation differs from other forms in its emphasis on 'real time', a tendency theorised at length by John Ellis (1992). Even pre-recorded broadcasts (soap operas, serials, series, talk shows, game shows, etc.) stress the 'up-to-the-minute' and the unpredictable (talk and game shows celebrate participants' spontaneous outbursts, or twists of fortune; soap operas incorporate topical issues, following the current calendar; and multi-episode series leave viewers hanging each week on cliff-hangers, mimicking real-time temporality). This principle also applies to the negotiating function of genre. Thus, a long-running talk show conducts its negotiation with its viewing audience *as it unfolds* in viewing time, mutating in response to viewer feedback, viewing figures, the emergence of rivals, etc., 'rewriting' its generic conventions even as it is produced. For this reason, television develops a uniquely self-conscious relationship with its audience. By 'self-conscious' we mean both 'prone to self-reflexive gestures which internalise the sender–receiver relationship' and 'uncertain of its ability to impose itself upon its audience, needing constantly to adjust its mode of address'.

In light of these considerations, our text-based chapters often gravitate towards the point at which texts gesture beyond their boundaries to engage with their audiences, and to internalise that engagement in the form of devices which shift their generic identities. As Bakhtin conceded, in locating meaning on the border of text and context, we can attribute an 'empirical' dimension to 'other' and 'context'. However, we eschew crude positivism by remaining cognisant of the fact that viewer 'data' itself comes in the form of texts requiring interpretation (just as, conversely, textual exegesis must be grounded in a 'data-like' accumulation of multiple instances).

The importance of genre is reflected in the structure of our book. With the exception of dedicated analyses of local television and audience fieldwork, each chapter centres on a particular post-Soviet television genre. In each case, the analysis broaches (though not necessarily centrally) the complex of issues surrounding audience–text interaction and generic self-transformation. A chapter on the talk show focuses on the genre's function in mediating between changing post-Soviet discourses of the public and the private (the role of the studio talk-show audience typifies television's propensity to internalise its relationship with its viewers). Likewise, our chapter on the game show situates changing patterns of audience participation in the phenomenally successful *Field of Miracles* (*Pole chudes*) in the context of local/metropolitan identity shifts associated with the show's status as a variant on the *Wheel of Fortune* global format. Chapters on news bulletins and pseudo-military dramas deal with different aspects of the tension between the need to instil in audiences a sense of documentary authenticity, and the attempt to accommodate them to Putin's nation-building mission. A chapter on 'media events' considers the self-conscious struggle of the televised national celebration to establish a generic tradition in reporting such events in parallel with its efforts to 'manufacture' tradition itself. Our discussion of post-Soviet sitcoms focuses on an adaptation of an American show which internalises viewer debates over the relationship between taste, television and the west.

The state of transition in which these genres find themselves partly reflects their perceived global (usually western) origins, which are still very much a factor in the way that they are viewed. Indeed, a recurring motif in our book is the notion that television meaning in Russia is shaped by the incompletely internalised nature of the cultural forms through which it is conveyed. This carries profound consequences for the hegemonic process of nation building of which they are part. Such partially internalised 'westerness' is counterbalanced by an incompletely externalised ('otherised') 'Sovietness' as the genres become the locus at which the respective values are contested (for example, the perception of a sitcom as a 'copy' of an American format may both lower and raise the genre's cultural taste quotient; and Sovietness in a military drama may increase or diminish its patriotic value).

The genres in question are in a state of flux with respect both to the context to which they are presently conjoined and to their historical contours. This spatio-temporal liminality is an index of the struggle for 'remote control' that the genres host and the text–audience dialectic is key to its outcome. There are a number of different axes along which the audience can be divided, each of which has implications for the assertion of control, and each of which reflects an effort to claim dominion over the meanings of the values of 'the West' and 'the Soviet'. A regional axis designates a greater or lesser distance between a provincial periphery and a metropolitan centre marked positively or negatively in relation to a mythologised 'west'. A generational axis engages directly with the re-evaluation of the Soviet imperial past, the gender axis both with Putin's masculine culture of militarism and with the ideological import of feminism. A class axis intersects with the persistent controversy over the urban intelligentsia's relationship with global culture, and with a provincial *narod* marked in both idealised and negative terms.

What makes this book different?

Whilst our primary allegiance is to Cultural Studies, one of the aims we set ourselves in this book is to institute a dialogue between that field and Political Communication. For, in our view, questions of political communication cannot be considered outside of their relationship with questions of culture, and vice versa. Our objective is to assess the degree to which Putin's regime has established control over Russian television – an area in which political scientists feel quite at home, but a task to which traditional political science paradigms are not entirely adequate, and to which cultural studies can make a significant contribution. This is true if only because most Russians spend more time watching light entertainment and fictional drama than they do the news and documentary broadcasting to which political communication paradigms are best suited. Paradoxically, the more that, for political reasons, Putin replaces controversial, non-fictional programmes with anodyne entertainment and drama, the less appropriate the political communication-derived approaches are to assessing the impact of his policy.

Nor, however, are classical cultural studies apparatuses equal to the challenge we have set. Narratology, post-Lacanian models, phenomenologically inspired viewer-response theory and Bakhtinian celebrations of carnivalesque inversion all have much to offer but ultimately remain in the realm of text hermeneutics. It is no coincidence that the concept of hegemony features intermittently in our discussion. For in its recognition of the need for power to be embedded within the practices and mythologies of everyday life, it bridges the divide between politics and cultural studies. In Jesus Martin Barbero's adaptation of Gramsci's term:

> One class exercises hegemony to the extent that [it] has interests which the subaltern classes recognise as being in some degree in their interests too. This process is based not only on force but on a shared meaning and on the appropriation of the meaning of life through power, seduction and complicity.
>
> (Martin Barbero 1993: 74)

Martin Barbero argues that, within the tension-ridden appropriation process, culture becomes the 'strategic battlefield in the struggle to define the terms of the conflict', and that 'there is no hegemony – nor counter hegemony – without cultural circulation ... no imposition from above which does not imply an incorporation of what comes from below' (ibid.: 99). He perceives mass culture – and especially the mass media – as central to the conflict, cautioning that

> to think of ... mass culture in terms of hegemony implies a double rupture: a break with technological positivism which reduces communication to a problem of media and break with cultural ethnocentrism which identifies mass culture with the problem of the degradation of culture.
>
> (Martin Barbero 1993: 85)

Such a conception of hegemony is well suited to the task of addressing the relationship between Putin's attempts at controlling television and the multitude of serials, game shows, talk shows and sport by which that output is dominated. For it avoids the twin dangers of

(1) judging the extent of the current Russian political class's grip on power solely on the basis of the amount of force (juridical, political, economic and physical) at its disposal; and
(2) dismissing sub-cultural forms such as the game show as 'degraded' forms, peripheral to the exercising of that power.

It is within the realm of the meaning generated by the encounter of official and sub-cultural forms mediated by television that the external manifestations of a hegemonic strategy are internalised, but also resisted by the objects of that strategy. Bakhtin's emphasis on the location of meaning on the border between consciousnesses is therefore a recurrent influence on the mode of analysis we employ. However, we give an empirical 'spin' to the dialogistic apparatus by comparing the comments of actual viewers with the textual features we identify. This gesture has a 'textual' justification in that one of the defining functions of television form as we conceive of it is its tendency to reach out beyond the generic boundaries in which it is embodied and reshape, reinvent and restructure itself in 'live' response to feedback. As Martin Barbero points out (ibid.: 131–37), the supreme examples of this process are to be found in the multi-episode television serial and forms such as the long-running sitcom and the game show, to which we devote separate chapters. Thus, in embracing the methods of audience research, we avoid the worst excesses of positivism to which such research is sometimes prone.

By deploying a theoretical amalgam, we acknowledge that television's reach is too broad to be covered by any single discipline, reconfirming the motivation behind our title 'Television *and* Culture'. However, we would hope that the model we have outlined offers more than merely a catholic hybrid, and that the account of hegemonic meaning around which it is structured is both coherent and appropriate to the task we set ourselves.

A parallel logic operates in respect of our use of the term 'post-Soviet'; rather than positing a temporal amalgam of pre-1991 and post-1991 trends, we define post-1991 Russian television *in relation* to the Soviet television culture that it replaced (without, however, supplanting it) and focus our attention on the meaning packed into the prefix 'post' rather than to the sequence linking the periods it conjoins. At the same time, part of the meaning which the prefix embraces is that of Russian television's location within a global media culture; thus, for us, it is the ongoing interrelationship between the Soviet, the western, the traditionally Russian and the global which defines the post-Soviet.

Questions and themes to be tackled

Our main themes flow from the discussion above. One of the key questions, as reflected in our subtitle, is that of control over television meaning. We will therefore be asking how hegemonic communication operates in Russia, given the centralisation of political power, the absence of intermediary civil institutions and the consequent lack of 'buy in' from a viewing public, itself fragmented by region (Russia's vast geography); age (the chasm separating those whose formative years were lived on either side of 1985); and class (the emergence of a small elite; and the continuing resonance of the *intelligentsia/ narod* dichotomy). On a textual level, Goffman's division of the subject of an utterance between 'author', 'principal' and 'animator' (Goffman 1981) will be key to our discussion of this compromised communicative chain, as will the relationship between the split subject of post-Soviet television and its equally fragmented addressee (implied and actual), and between the official, unofficial and sub-cultural discourses it must mediate. Also pertinent to our treatment of the hegemonic process is television's role as a battlefield on which the struggles to 'fix' cultural value as 'cultural capital' (Bourdieu 1992) and to perform identities (local, national, gender and class) are enacted.

One of the constraints on the use of television for nation building is the fact that viewers are located within a global mediasphere. As well as exploring the extent of this constraint in viewer comment, we also seek to trace its textual dimension through the incessant breaching of generic boundaries that characterises Russian television.

But the centre/periphery structures which the mediasphere phenomenon shapes have contradictory aspects. Russia is a peripheral outpost of the global mediasphere which adapts the genres it receives from the centre for its own purposes (post-Soviet Russia is, indeed, in the unique position of coinciding in origin with the period of rapid media globalisation which began in the late 1980s). But it is also, itself, a centre whose own outposts are prone to deploy global forms against it. An assessment of the balance between these two counter-trends is critical to our project. At every point, we interpose a temporal dimension into our analysis, seeking to identify a Soviet presence in the meaning-making activities of producer and audience, centre and periphery.

The common thread running throughout the book is that of post-Soviet television genre as the supreme locus for the negotiation of control over cultural meaning, genre as a form which constantly overreaches and reshapes itself in response to audiences, at the same time self-consciously internalising that gesture in a perpetual feedback loop.

Structure and content

Seven of the nine chapters to follow are based on particular television genres. The logic of the progression – from centre to periphery – is deliberately ambiguous: on one hand, it cites the rhetorical principle that the most important matters must be treated first; on the other hand, it invokes the narrative convention according to which the endpoint constitutes the climax. The ambiguity is appropriate to our argument: that of a tension between central control and local resistance. Thus, our first chapter deals with news bulletins (the genre in which one would expect the centre's presence to be most keenly felt and the favoured object of analysis for political scientists). There follow chapters on two different varieties of a news subgenre: the 'media event', both of which develop news to the threshold of overt myth making – one on the Beslan terrorist outrage, and another on the celebration of St Petersburg's tricentenary in 2003. Next we treat the talk show – an entertainment genre which nonetheless embraces the realm of social and political opinion making. This is followed by a turn towards the unambiguously fictional, in a chapter on the (pseudo) military drama serial which, however, is related directly to Putin's politically motivated efforts to militarise Russian television culture. We then turn to entertainment proper with chapters on the post-Soviet sitcom and game show, genres traditionally considered bereft of 'serious' political content but, for our purposes, of enormous importance to the hegemonic process in both its manipulative and its resistant modes. Our penultimate chapter looks at local television, and we conclude, in a sense, beyond the periphery altogether – with a dedicated analysis of the post-Soviet viewing audience – in many ways the 'hero' of our account.

1   (Dis)informing Russia

Media space and discourse conflict in post-Soviet Russian television news

Introduction

Russian television news in Putin's second term reached a new nadir in its descent into ideological servitude. With Russia officially designated by international observers as 'not free', Putin's power over the flow of information and the framing of political debate became almost akin to that of his Soviet predecessors.[1] Reporting of the 2004 Beslan tragedy, and of Victory Day celebrations in May 2005, provided two examples confirming that the national media were tacking ever closer to the official, Kremlin line on events, predicted and unpredicted.

There is little need to elaborate on why control over television news is so important to the Kremlin, particularly in light of the central role news broadcasts have played in recent Russian history (see Introduction). However, the persistent fluidity of the political situation (following unpopular welfare reforms in 2005, Putin's own supremacy came under question for the first time) and the fact that Putin felt obliged to assert his dominance so crudely, suggests that classic hegemony has yet to work its magic in post-Soviet Russia; had the values of the forces dominating post-Soviet society penetrated it throughout, there would be no need for the heavy-handed manipulation of news agendas practised under Putin. Indeed, the overarching purpose of this chapter is to challenge the view of Russian national television news as entirely monolithic and uniformly subservient to government ideology.

Another way of accounting for the imperfect functioning of Gramscian hegemony is by reference to Bakhtin's dialogic theory which remains an implicit influence throughout our analysis in this chapter. It would appear to be entirely appropriate to apply Bakhtin's notion of monologism to the situation occurring in Putin's media. However, the term is often misunderstood to mean the silencing of non-official discourses and the erasure of dialogue, when in fact Bakhtin made it clear that the monologism of the centralised state is merely one variety of dialogism – one in which a single voice or discourse has secured a position of authority over that of others and attempts to subordinate them to it. This coincides with Gramsci's notion of hegemony as a constant process of renewed resistance to a dominant discourse which never ceases to incorporate and thereby disarm that resistance. The difference is subtle, but important; for Bakhtin (as for Gramsci), all discourse is dialogic and open, all positions of dominance temporary and constantly subject to challenge. Indeed, as he points out in respect to the seemingly pure monologism of the late Tolstoi, the very heavy-handedness of the assertions of authority betray the strength of the hidden dialogic challenge that they are called upon to rebuff. This was the case even at the height of Stalinism (whose characteristic paranoia can be read in just these terms), but is especially so under the conditions of the proliferating influence of globally disseminated discourses under which Putin's propaganda machine must operate.

Bakhtinian dialogism extends in two other directions of acute relevance to the case in hand. First, Bakhtin makes it clear that discourse is always oriented towards its recipient(s) and is enacted at the threshold at which the voice of the self encounters the voice(s) of the other. In this sense, television is the supremely dialogic form. For, owing to the fluidity of its textual boundaries (it is hard, for example, to say whether the popular meanings generated by soap operas or reality TV shows are located intratextually, or within the readings that they elicit) meanings are negotiated between text and audience in a way that is much less true of traditional, author-centred forms such as the novel, or even film. Thus, when discussing the degree of ideological servitude endured by television news under Putin, we must have regard to the role of viewers, exposed as they are under the conditions of globalisation, to an increasing array of discourses from an expanding range of sources, in negotiating the meanings produced by news discourse, and, just as important, to the efforts of television producers to anticipate, account for and respond to viewer contributions to those meanings. This, too, attenuates the potential effects of Putin's naked propaganda making.

Secondly, unlike popularised versions of the concept which talk merely in terms of multiple references to, and citations of, other texts, Bakhtinian accounts of intertextuality insist that all utterances are essentially re-accentuations of prior utterances, with whose entire context and intentionality they enter into dialogue, and which remain an active force, shaping the discourse in which they are cited. Thus, post-Soviet news broadcasts cannot simply accommodate the passive textual forms of western news making (or, for that matter, those of the Soviet news making which preceded them) to their own ideological agenda. This, too, has profound implications for the ability of post-Soviet news to control the meanings that it articulates.

Dialogism was a key influence on Lotman's notion of semiosphere (Lotman 1990), which, by analogy with Vernadsky's concept of biosphere, he interpreted as the 'semiotic continuum' in which all meaning is created – an organic, but heterogeneous, totality in which different structures come into contact and generate new meaning. John Hartley's adaptation of the notion of semiosphere as 'mediasphere' to account for the particular semiotic continuum from which meanings emerge in the contemporary, globalised, realm of media texts (Hartley 2004) is particularly apt for the purposes of examining the significatory ambiances of post-Soviet news. A section of what follows deals therefore with what, in our turn, we have referred to as 'media space', with particular attention given to the meaning-generating role of generic boundaries, whose instability in post-Soviet television opens up possibilities for considerable activity within that space.

Following Hartley, we have chosen to translate the implicit theoretical assumptions underlying our approach into a set of terminological tools derived from media studies rather than literary analysis. Thus, in following the section on heteroglossic media space with a segment addressing the representational space within which the monological voice of post-Soviet officialdom attempts to (re)assert its control, we adopt the tools of *frame analysis* (investigations of the pre-established narrative models, myths, discourse structures and semantic fields into which news stories are packaged in order to accord them ideologically appropriate significance), *agenda setting* (including running-order hierarchies), and Barthesian *'inoculation' strategies* (the principle by which dominant discourses vaccinate themselves against the seditious potential of oppositional voices by incorporating manageable instances of those voices).[2] At the same time, in a to-and-fro movement between theoretical underpinnings and methodological tools, we re-invoke the Bakhtinian framework by turning to the concept of *chronotope* to capture the temporal constraints on Russian news's ability to manipulate this representational space to its own ends. This, in its turn, returns us to the wider semiotic space in which Russian news meanings unfold, and which complicates, dilutes and subverts the ideological mission to which they are harnessed.

However, it would be entirely misleading to present Russian television news as a hotbed of dissidence, or to deny the ideological manipulation to which it is increasingly subject. A cursory comparison of news output in the mid-1990s and between 2000 and 2007 would reveal that news teams have become increasingly supine in their relationship with the President, and exponentially more obedient to his agenda (a fact explained most obviously by the effective take-over of Channel 1, RTR and more recently NTV, by figures loyal to Putin). A portion of what follows aims to trace the deleterious effects of these changes on the Russian news agenda. Our proposition that all is not quite what it seems is based on the semiotic principle that meaning is shaped not just through a text's intended 'signifieds', but also by the culturally laden signifying forms and codes expressing them, and that forces located at the level of the code are liable to complicate and impede the effectiveness of those operating at the level of the signified.

We focus on three aspects of post-Soviet Russian news 'form' in which we detect these principles at work:

(1) *Media Space* (we focus particularly on generic boundaries, and on that space within the official realm set aside for emergent post-Soviet commercial and celebrity cultures);

(2) *Representational Strategy* (the importance of authenticating inter-texts, myths and narrative structures bearing memories and meanings incompatible with the agendas they serve; the tensions generated by the need to adopt the procedures and forms of democracy as well as to mimic its ambiances);

(3) *Discourse Structures* (ways in which the multiplicity of vernacular discourses which have now entered Russian media space frame and reframe one another and undercut the authority of the dominant discourse).

Our argument is advanced through examples from the main evening news bulletins of the three national channels (Channel 1, NTV and RTR) recorded on a weekly basis from April 2003 to July 2007. It is supported with data analysis of categories of news stories covered, and of voices represented in those stories, during a cross section of the same period (November 2006 to April 2007). For the viewer dimension, we rely primarily on cross-referencing with our audience research chapter, but brief reference is made to web forum commentary contained on the Channel 1 website. Throughout, references to the dates, times and sources of particular broadcasts are given in parentheses in the text.

Media space and generic instability

The notion that the 'objective facts' constituting the content of news bulletins are heavily mediated by the forms and discourses through which they are expressed is rarely contested. One of the dominant concepts within current theories of television news is that of media 'frames': those sets of a priori structures, selections, exclusions and ritualistic gestures which enable news producers to package events according to their implicit agenda, and viewers to identify them as 'news'. In Todd Gitlin's words: 'Media frames are persistent patterns of cognition, interpretation, and presentation, of selection, emphasis, and exclusion, by which symbol handlers routinely organise discourse, whether verbal or visual' (Gitlin 1980: 7). For Gitlin, news frames simplify, prioritise and structure the narrative flow of events (Gitlin 1980). One of the key 'frames' is that of genre. Television, like other forms of cultural production, deals in texts whose definable boundaries and recurring attributes enable them to be categorised into particular types, or genres, each of which carries identifiable worldviews and ideological assumptions. As Fiske puts it:

> Genres are popular when their conventions bear a close relationship to the dominant ideology of the time ... Genre is part of the textual strategies by which television attempts to control its polysemic potential ... influencing which meanings of programmes are preferred by, or proffered to, which audiences.
>
> (Fiske 1987: 112, 114)

Genres imply adherence to sets of rules relating both to formal and content aspects of the texts for which they legislate, with the formal attributes carrying clear ideological weight. Thus, prior to 1991, Soviet news bulletins shared some attributes, formal and ideational (e.g. the ritualised recitation of industrial successes; the avoidance of live reports; and the use of newsreaders as government spokespeople) which would, in western countries, have contravened the rules and ideological remit of the genre. Since the fall of communism, there has been a rapid convergence of generic features between Russian and western news output. The opening sequences of RTR's *Vesti* (*News*), NTV's *Segodnia* (*Today*) and Channel 1's *Vremia* all include montages of busy newsrooms, purposefully engaged journalists, production teams equipped with the latest news-gathering technology, world maps and abbreviated 'headline' summaries of the main items to be covered. These features, absent from Soviet predecessors, have been imported from western sources. Each is preceded by the ticking clock (cf. the chimes of Big Ben at the beginning of ITN's *News at 10*) which serves the dual, and contradictory, functions of reminding viewers of the up-to-the-minute 'liveness' of news coverage, yet also reassuring them of its never-diminished regularity in their daily routines.

Such markers all carry distinct semiotic value which, in turn, and, according to the principles outlined by Fiske and Gitlin, shape the content and control the meaning of the news reports themselves. Thus, the world maps connote the global remit typical of news bulletins. And the images of bustling journalists and technologically advanced production teams contribute towards the construction of news reporting as an autonomous professional sphere, as well as highlighting the value of technology-led, scientific objectivity, none of which would sit comfortably within Soviet ideology.

Continuity with the past underpins the nation-building role assigned to news programming across the world. The retention from Soviet times of the title and signature tune of Channel 1's *Vremia* and the traditional Russian troika in the opening montage of RTR's *Vesti* can be compared in this context to ITN's Big Ben. Also bearing comparison with western equivalents, and an instantly recognisable feature of the television news genre, is the formally dressed news presenter whose authoritative, autocued script and use of standard pronunciation mark him/her as the carrier of official, establishment values. The anchor introduces each item, providing the voiceover for graphic sequences illustrating aspects of the event in question. For important items, there is live reportage from the scene. The framing of the live reporter's voice by that of the establishment in the person of the anchor authenticates the discourse of the latter by separating out a sphere of generalised assertion from a realm of live witnessing. John Ellis has argued that witnessing is one of television's defining functions, tying it to the ever-increasing emphasis on liveness which is its unique privilege (Ellis 2001). During Soviet times, live witnessing threatened the maintenance of ideological control and was substituted by pre-recorded reports. Post-Soviet news operates in a globalised media environment and cannot afford to excise generic features familiar to all those viewers who have had access to CNN or BBC World News. Moreover, the authenticating function of the live report is not lost on post-Soviet news production teams; the 'truths' about the oligarch Khodarkovskii's tax avoidance enunciated in the newsreader's impersonal discourse in 2005, which we deal with below, became far more believable when bolstered by the personalised discourse of the live reporter.[3]

A related generic feature of the live report is the question and answer sequence between the anchor and the reporter. All three Russian national channels have adopted this feature, complete with the informal first-name address mode preferred by the participants. A danger inherent in the anchor–reporter exchange is that its unplanned absence inevitably de-authenticates the anchor's discourse. This happened during coverage of the Beslan School Siege when, following the tragic and unexpected dénouement, *Vremia* briefly suspended live coverage and resorted to brief, unconvincing summaries from the anchor. Post-Soviet national news is increasingly prone to such reversions to Soviet type. Another example is the return of the ceremonial slot when lengthy accounts of official meetings with dignitaries and state rituals are introduced quite openly under the rubric of 'official chronicle' (*ofitsial'naia khronika*). One of several points at which the rhetoric of the official chronicle clashes with that of contemporary global news is where it encounters channel 'brand markers'. All of Russia's channels now feature a company logo displayed on screen throughout all broadcasts, including *Vremia*. Brand marking affects language and discourse as much as it does visual graphics. The standard 'sign off' sequences with which live reports end ('This is Andrei Vernitski, Channel 1, Kiev') are even more prominent on Russian news than in western broadcasts; the reporters list not only their own name but that of the entire on-location news team. And towards the end of the bulletin, anchors now regularly exhort viewers not to switch channels.

The entertainment prerogative also affects the linear trajectory of the news genre. *Vremia*, *Vesti* and *Segodnia* all follow the generic structure of western news bulletins in opening with musically accompanied telegraphic summaries of the main headlines, before proceeding to the detailed accounts, engaging viewers otherwise liable to become distracted, yet also authenticating the news content by conveying the notion of nuggets of essential, indisputable news 'fact' accepted by all sources which must be developed individually by each news programme. Likewise, Russian news bulletins have now adopted the model favoured in the USA and much of Europe of a sequence of up to fifteen short news items rather than the exhaustive, in-depth treatment of five or six items more typical of the BBC. Contentious issues such as the trial of Khodarkovskii on spurious tax fraud charges can then be skirted round or ideologically sanitised; a *Vremia* bulletin concealed the highly controversial verdict as a brief one-minute item listed eleventh in the running order (*Vremia*, 25 May 2005). But it also conflicts with the preponderance of ritualistic 'ceremonial' items; Putin's corruscating speech to leaders of the energy industry following the electricity cuts suffered in Moscow in May 2005 occupied the first 11 minutes of the evening *Vremia* bulletin (*Vremia*, 3 June 2005). Our analysis of categories of news stories on *Vremia* between November 2006 and April 2007 revealed that a full 10 per cent of airtime was given over to 'official items', as compared with 1.5 per cent each for Duma affairs and party politics; 1 per cent each for the environment and education; and 6.5 per cent for economics and financial affairs (see Appendix 1).

The Khodarkovskii issue indicates a running order in which issues are covered in an order of importance convergent with the channel's dominant news values. In Putin's Russia, viewers have come to expect domestic and 'near abroad' issues to appear before properly international issues. Even after the tsunami disaster of December 2004, with which western news bulletins were entirely preoccupied for a week, Russian bulletins swiftly relegated the issue to third or fourth in their running orders.

Genre is, as Fiske establishes, a variety of intertextuality; it 'organises intertextual relations in particularly influential ways' (Fiske 1987: 109). A text belonging to a particular genre is a text which intertextually cites other members of that genre through its structure or content features.[4] And in citing particular generic attributes, a text cannot but cite the entire semiotic context of the source texts. Thus, whilst the producers of *Vremia* may, when adopting features of the western news bulletin, wish to suppress the full context in which those features appear, the generic memory of that context will be activated in the interpretative work of the increasingly tele-visually literate viewer. Notwithstanding attempts to shape the news agenda through the manipulation of the running order, *Segodnia* and *Vremia* cannot altogether censor coverage of ideologically inconvenient issues like global warming and repression in neighbouring Uzbekistan which might, under Soviet control, have been altogether removed from the agenda. This recep-tion-related point, crucial to our argument, is linked closely to the produc-tion-related phenomenon of global networks. Manuel Castells has argued that the dominance of nation-states and their attendant social and political hierarchies has, under the conditions of globalisation, given way to gigantic networks which are non-isomorphic with nation-states (Castells 1996). As Oliver Boyd-Barrett and Terhi Rantanen have suggested, such networks work in tandem with the limited number of large news agencies which control the flow of world news, thus ensuring that news agendas are, to a significant extent, not subject to the control mechanisms imposed by nation-states (Boyd-Barrett and Rantanen 2004).

However, generic 'leakage' into the commercial/democratic space of the western news bulletin is balanced by sporadic leakage into that of Soviet-era propaganda. This occurs particularly during events such as the 1993 con-stitutional crisis and the Beslan siege of 2004. Such phenomena appear to confirm conventional wisdom about a gradual reversion to Soviet type. But this view ignores a number of factors:

(1) in 1993, Russian television's generic transgressions into the field of propaganda were committed in the cause of salvaging western-style democracy from ultra-nationalist assault;
(2) the global context in which Russian television operates rules out the possibility of a mere recapitulation of Soviet propaganda techniques;
(3) as Gary Saul Morson has argued (Morson 1996), Russian culture has tended to favour genres produced at the threshold of objective representation and polemical engagement, which in turn has engendered a form of frame-breaking metatextuality from which news is not entirely free (cf. the 1991 coup, whose outcome was determined partly by a struggle at the heart of the *Vremia* team; television's role in overcoming the 1993 constitutional crisis; and the 2001 clampdown on NTV when the discussion programme *Glas naroda* debated a crisis likely to culminate in the end of the show itself).

Accusations of a return to the days of subservience to the state lose force when considered from the point of view of the field of meanings in which news discourse must operate.

Post-Soviet news and media 'space'

Television genres are especially prone to hybridisation and reflect a multiplicity of generic influences.[5] Thus, the news incorporates elements of the talk show, the commercial, the investigative documentary and even the criminal docu-drama. For example, a *Vremia* report on the unearthing of a foiled assassination attempt on Khrushchev's life employed an elaborate fictional reconstruction of the minutiae of the event (10 June 2005). The fluidity extends to the boundaries between channels (television programmes and personalities cross channels with a dizzying regularity) and national television systems (Russian news relies heavily on CNN and BBC footage), and between television and other media (film, newspapers and the internet).

The fluidity of cultural meaning corresponds closely to Iurii Lotman's notion of 'semiosphere'. In his adaptation of Lotman's term to the context of modern television representations of indigenous Australian culture, John Hartley writes of 'a dialogue between differing domains within an overall "mediasphere", linking rather than separating academic, media, and political narratives' (Hartley 2004: 17). Despite the constraints placed upon it, Russian television news, too, is part of this mediasphere which exerts its own influence on the shaping of news agendas. Thus, in autumn 2004, *Vremia*, *Vesti* and *Segodnia* had little option but to broadcast the same images of youthful, exuberant pro-Iushchenko protestors swelling the streets of Kiev as those flooding the internet and CNN.

However, as Kai Hafez argues, the mediaspheric flow of global news can also be exploited in support of officially approved national agendas (Hafez 2007). The saturation coverage of the 9/11 terrorist attacks, for example, has been a godsend to Russian media attempts to legitimate Russian actions in Chechnia. The sequencing of news items following terrorist incidents in Russia inevitably links accounts of the domestic outrage with reference to (and accompanying western footage of) the global war on terror. The docudrama inspired investigative exposé of corruption and scandal among prominent public figures was exploited to good effect in government-inspired attempts to demonise the activities of Anatolii Chubais, a controversial, liberal-leaning politician under Eltsyn, and now a rich businessman in the energy industry, on the grounds of his accountability for the severe electricity cuts suffered in the Moscow region in May 2005. *Vremia* featured several 'special correspondent' reports casting doubts on Chubais's intentions and honesty, complete with unflattering close-ups of his face (*Vremia*, 3 May 2005 and 5 May 2005).

News, the mediasphere and the internet

But it is the advent of the internet which has done most to broaden the news mediasphere and undermine government control over the media. Many contemporary television genres boast an internet forum or chatroom. Even *Vesti*, the news programme of RTR, the channel closest to the Putin government, runs a lively discussion forum in which opinion extends far further than that expressed on the bulletins themselves. In June 2005, a dispute between Russian and Latvia arose over Latvia's treatment of its Russian population, and Russia's refusal to atone for its previous occupation of the Baltics. Whilst the bulletins followed the official line on Latvian intransigence, one participant in the forum (17 June 2005) suggested quite starkly: 'Acknowledge the occupation of the Baltics, and the mass of negative information on that topic will disappear' (*Priznat' okkupatsiiu Pribaltiki, posle chego ischeznet massa negativnoi informatsii na etu temu*). Amongst other discussion topics on the *Vesti* forum in June 2005 was Putin's recent decree on restricting violence on Russian television which attracted a predominantly scornful response.

The official Channel 1 web forum does not have a separate category for comments on the news. However, word searches for the forms news-(novost), vrem-(vrem-), informat-(informatsi) and politic-(politi) were run in May and June 2007 for the topic of 'General questions' (*Obshchie voprosy*) in the category 'All about Channel One', and for the topic of 'Your news' (*Vashi novosti*) within the category 'Top projects'. Each topic contained multiple threads. On 25 June 2007, for example, there were 165 threads in 'Your news' and 195 threads in 'General questions'. Scrutiny of the messages revealed persistent and often trenchant criticism of, among many other things, pro-Putin bias, the lack of free speech, the absence of serious coverage of controversial issues, the refusal to present the 'Orange' point of view in Ukraine, the suppression of Islam and *Vremia*'s Moscow-centrism. A brief selection of comments from the forum is presented below:

Today there is lots of ideology on the news, aimed mainly at young people ... Those who remember the Communist Party monologues will understand what I mean

They will show whatever Father V.V. Putin (Baten'ka V.V.) allows on the news

Muslims were returning from the Hadja and the Orthodox Church was marking the Christening. The Muslims were only shown for a few seconds ... this is just outrageous [*vozmutitel'no*]

Putin and *Edinaia Rossia* only have to announce one of their run-of-the-mill initiatives and Channel 1 is already trumpeting it at full volume

On the evening news they were doing a round-up of 2004 and they were telling such lies that I won't even begin to describe it

It's impossible to watch the news. For lots of reasons – mainly because of the lies and bias

The first item is always about Putin. It gets on your nerves [*nadoedaet*].

ORT [the previous name for Channel 1] is more of a Moscow Channel

The news is nothing but Edinaia Rossiia and Vovka Pupkin (a nickname for Putin)

I don't intend to talk about the lack of free speech in our media, even in the electronic media now, thinking people already know this ... My dream is to leave Russia now.

You've got to be more neutral, gentlemen, and more literate.

(http://forum.1tv.ru/index.php; accessed 13 July 2007)

Further evidence of widespread suspicion of the range of views and stories covered in Russian national television news, and to some extent, of the degree of objectivity these stories display, will be presented in a later chapter focusing more specifically on audience research.

The Russian news mediasphere fosters a greater level of debate than meets the eye, too, in its approach to what John Ellis calls television's 'working through' function. Ellis argues that television 'attempts to define, tries out explanations, creates narratives, talks over, makes intelligible, tries to marginalise, harnesses speculation, tries to make fit, and, very occasionally, anathematises', connecting this function with what he sees as television's defining feature: its capacity for 'steadying the images' of the contingent reality it inherently deals in (Ellis 1999: 55). He cites the discussion shows, docu-dramas and even fiction films as ways in which news issues and images are 'worked through' (ibid.: 56). An illustrative Russian example is the programme *Vremena* (*Times*) whose title, a pluralisation of the title of the main Channel 1 news programme, *Vremia*, confirms its role in clarifying and explaining 'raw' issues that arise during the week. Its host, Vladimir Pozner, a glasnost-era veteran, is a highly respected, independent-minded journalist. Each programme involves the presentation of an issue of the week and a round-table discussion far more heated than anything encountered on *Vremia* itself, and to which Pozner invites public figures from across the spectrum. One edition on xenophobia in Russia included Anatolii Chubais and Vladmir Zhirinovskii, each critical of the official government position from opposite poles (*Vremena*, 17 May 2005). For Ellis, working through is a conservative, stabilising phenomenon. In Russia, the process is precisely the reverse: images and issues are stabilised and controlled at the outset, and then progressively destabilised the more they are 'worked through'.

'Working through' in Russian television extends and deepens the news semiosphere and thereby weakens the centripetal forces designed to rein in events at the point of entry into the news arena. The Pozner example illustrates a further aspect of the news semiosphere. As indicated before, cultural forms and genres carry within them the 'memory' of their prior articulations. The relative newness of television as a cultural form, the rapidity with which its forms emerge and disappear, and the fluidity of their boundaries with extra-textual realities, accord special importance to intertextual memory. The media persona acquired by Pozner as a result of his earlier glasnost reputation shapes the political space available to him on *Vremena*. Pozner began the edition on xenophobia, for example, with an acerbic comment comparing western 'politically correct' attitudes to anti-Semitism with the tendency in Russia to give tacit approval to racist attitudes and followed this up with a measured diatribe which few would have been permitted (*Vremena*, 17 May 2005).

The fact that, since 2005, control over Russian television, and constraints placed on Pozner's freedom to operate, have both increased significantly does not diminish the truth of the principles outlined in the preceding two paragraphs. Thus, Pozner used the final peroration section of the *Vremena* edition broadcast on 1 July 2007 to return to his favoured topic of the rise of extremist nationalist sentiment in Russia, drawing on his own Jewish background to caution boldly against government inactivity:

> About a month ago someone sprayed in white on the fence of my dacha 'Pozner is a Yid. Get out of Russia!' And they drew two swastikas. I'll survive that, but there are questions. If the authorities and the mass media don't take on the national problem seriously [ne budet vser'ez zanimat'sia natsional'nym voprosom], if they pretend that there is no such politics, then I think that nothing good will come of it in Russia. That's the Times (Vremena) we live in.

Commercialisation

Commercialisation, too, has a bearing on the media space in which post-Soviet news discourse unfolds, and, even under conditions of rigid government control, fosters differentiation. In a two-week period at the beginning of June 2005, issues heading the agenda on all channels included the trial of the one captured terrorist responsible for Beslan; an outbreak of hepatitis in the Tver' region; a change of power in Northern Ossetia; an air dispatchers' hunger strike in Rostov; and the drowning of five sailors in the Gulf of Finland. In each instance, whilst following the official line in broad outline, NTV coverage was subtly different from that of its 'rivals'. Alone among the national channels, NTV paid attention to the change in attitude in the courtroom when local people began to question the Beslan terrorist's guilt and divert their anger towards the authorities who allowed Beslan to happen (*Segodnia*, 7 June 2005). Its idiosyncratic approach to the hepatitis outbreak – devoting one report to rumours about its cause (ranging from terrorism to food poisoning) and showing full screen images of the internet sites circulating the rumours (*Segodnia*, 9 June 2005) – indicates a feel for the extent and importance of media space absent elsewhere. In the case of the hunger strike, NTV included many more interviews with individuals caught up in the dispute (on both sides) than other channels (*Segodnia*, 11 June 2005). Similarly, when reporting the Gulf of Finland tragedy, NTV interviewed local fishermen, taking a much more personalised approach than Channel 1 or RTR who interviewed only officials connected with the search for the sailors. Similarly, coverage of the change of presidents in Northern Ossetia was marked by the use of unflattering close-up shots of the faces of the incoming and outgoing figures, and by reference to criticism from ordinary local people in Beslan that the new president was part of the same complacent clique as the former president (*Segodnia*, 11 June 2005).

Just as post-1991 commercialism brought with it a differentiation of Russian media space, so, too, did the arrival of celebrity culture. The public sphere in the Soviet period was largely synonymous with official space. The news agenda, discourse and style generally reflected the concerns of the communist party nomenclature. Ordinary Soviet people rarely found their way onto television and, as Oleg Khakhordin has shown, they were forced to oscillate between a private sphere in which they expressed their unfettered selves, and a public sphere in which they dissimulated adherence to official models of behaviour (Khakhordin 1999). It is partly for this reason that even now there is a lack of a common 'language' of the public sphere which would facilitate the participation of ordinary people in televised political debates.[6]

Western celebrity culture offers both a means of mediating between the private and official spheres (prominent newsreaders and commentators represent the concerns of ordinary people, speak their language and provide identification points for them, whilst also purveying the concerns that emerge from the official sphere) and, in the form of Russian popular stars, an alternative. However, the infiltration of celebrity culture into Russian news has yet to attain levels equivalent to its West European counterparts. For example, British newsreaders like Natasha Kaplinsky have acquired many of the attributes of media stars in the entertainment sphere. There is little evidence of this in the Russian news, where television journalists retain much of the distant aura and anonymity of their Soviet predecessors (though, briefly, during the glasnost and early post-communist period, the likes of Aleksandr Nevzorov, who presented *Vzgliad*, and even the news-reader, Tat'iana Mitkova, achieved something approaching celebrity status). The tendency has, if anything, increased in the late Putin period when col-ourful, independent-minded news journalists like Leonid Parfionov and Savik Shuster have been effectively silenced.

Nonetheless, aspects of the celebrity sphere have infiltrated Russian news broadcasts and legitimate the presence of the informal style now in evidence at the peripheries of the newsreader's formal script. The newsreaders of *Segodnia*, *Vremia* and *Vesti* all introduce themselves in the style of an entertainment show host ('Good evening, I am. ... Me and my colleagues bring you the news ... '). Whilst their style of dress (and address) still err on the side of formality, that of the journalists and meteorologists is decidedly informal (the latter often concluding their forecast with a 'See you soon'), as are the, admittedly ritualised, exchanges between newsreader and live reporters (who address one another by first name).

In a distorted, but revealing, development of the informality trend, *Vremia* now incorporates at the end of its bulletins a 'commentary' entitled 'However' (*Odnako*), delivered by a prominent figure 'dressed down' in an open-neck shirt or baggy jumper and using highly informal language, but reinforcing rather than challenging official viewpoints. In the post-Beslan bulletins, he delivered conventional nation-building messages expressed in the trenchant vocabulary of a Soviet-era dissident. And, following the Anglo-Russian dip-lomatic crisis precipitated by the murder in London of Putin critic, Alek-sandr Litvinenko, in 2006, he indulged in merciless mockery of the British refusal to accept Russian accusations that MI5 had tried to recruit Russians close to the Berezovskii–Litvinenko circles, in a tone redolent of the Soviet satirical magazine, *Krokodil*:

> Ha-ha-ha, the English espionage experts guffawed. How can that be? English espionage, and with Berezovskii, and Litvinenko? Ha-ha-ha. Yet now our friends from London are no longer giggling. The contacts and the receipt of money have all been documented.
>
> (*Odnako*, 5 July 2007)

Whether this phenomenon is to be seen as an assimilation of 'dissident' rhetoric (indeed, in *Odnako* commentaries delivered in 2001, the same informal style was employed in an appeal for increased attention to freedom of speech), or, contrariwise, as a contamination of the official sphere by the dissident style, is a question whose very ambiguity embodies the fluid status of post-Soviet media space.

Agenda, space and representation

The media space *within* which news unfolds intersects with the represen-tational space which news *engenders*. Prime amongst the constructs that national news bulletins generate is a hierarchical stratification of the geopolitical world map upon which it projects the events it reports. In Russian news broadcasts, a concerted effort has been mounted to recreate the territory of the former Soviet Union as the wider context in which domestic news takes place. As we have seen, running orders place Russian news first, followed by CIS news, and only then by international events. Often, domestic and CIS issues are intertwined, sometimes to stress Russia's affinity with its neighbours, and sometimes to stress the threat that they pose. Appendix 2 details the preponderance of post-Soviet space in an analysis of stories running over more than two bulletins in four weeks spanning 2006 and 2007. A characteristic *Vremia* broadcast led with an account of Prime Minister Fradkov's visit to Tbilisi, featuring a report on Georgian issues from Channel 1's native Georgian correspondent; and followed with the IMF's positive assessment of Russia's economic future; then a report from North Ossetia, home of the manager of the victorious Moscow winners of the UEFA cup. Next, news of Putin's meeting with the new ambassador to Tajikistan was accompanied by a report on heroine smuggling across Russia–Tajikistan borders. The following items covered Boris Nemtsov's criticism of the controversial new Ukrainian prime minister, Iuliia Timoshenko and domestic Russian news relating to crime and educational reform. The bulletin concluded with the only two truly international items – one on the return of winter to the Czech Republic and the other on the mysterious appearance in Japan of metal objects linked by some to 'alien intruders' (*Vremia*, 3 June 2005). In an analysis of stories which ran over two or more bulletins in the period November 2006 to April 2007 (see Appendix 2), those involving the countries of the former Soviet Union scored 132, well ahead of the next two categories – stories featuring the two likely contenders for the Russian presidency in 2008 (Dmitrii Medvedev scoring 32 and Sergei Ivanov 34).

The space of the former Soviet Union is one of several 'frames' which shape and control news meanings and representations. News frames must be established incrementally over a period of time so that their constraining effect appears unforced. The status of the news frame therefore correlates to that of the paradigm in structural analysis – a set of similar items/events/ forms which, when one is cited, the entire set is invoked. Another such frame whose constant deployment offers clear ideological advantage to the Putin regime is that of the corrupt oligarchy. So powerfully resonant is this frame that it only needs to be marginally invoked for the full force of ideological censure that it carries to be sensed. When the story of the electricity cuts which disabled Moscow for several days ran over late May and early June 2005, misguided vitriol directed by viewers against Anatolii Chubais, the director of the energy giant responsible for the cuts, forced *Vremia* to issue a corrective to an earlier, critical report in which it pointed out that no concrete blame had been attached to Chubais.

If news frames constitute the selection axis in news broadcasting, then the running order and sequencing of news items form its combination axis. In a

May 2005 *Vremia* bulletin (28 May 2005), coverage of the rumours linking Chubais to the recent electricity cuts preceded a story on controversial pension reform, but the succeeding item treated Putin's meeting with Roman Abramovich in which he challenged the oligarch over economic problems in Chukotka. In the following item attention turned to joint Russian–American military manoeuvres in Germany. The subsequent report dealt in neutral terms with the verdict in the Khodarkovskii trial. Chubais's purported laxity in the running of his energy concern was linked with the now confirmed guilt of the chief oligarch, Khodarkovskii, via a dressing down for his rival, Abramovich. The oligarch theme acquired the status of a semiotic field, the very imprecision of whose boundaries mean that events close to its peripheries were drawn into its zone of influence.

The security and terror agenda is another such zone. In May 2005 disturbances in Uzbekistan followed accusations of electoral impropriety emanating from Islamic opposition groupings. The *Vremia* bulletin of 17 May opened with the emotive story of the trial of the captured Beslan terrorist and featured images of outraged mothers and relatives (*Vremia*, 17 May 2005). This was succeeded by reports of a terrorist group operating in neighbouring Dagestan. Sandwiched in between this item and a report on the riots in Tashkent was a neutral report on a fire in Kronshdadt. The Uzebkistan story was succeeded by related reports on the influx of Uzbek refugees into Kirghizia, and on the arrest of Islamic protestors outside the Uzbek embassy in London. The running order and the linkage mechanism reinforce the implicit assertion that the Uzbek disturbances are inspired by Islamic fundamentalists. Since 2005, however, following an alarming rise of tensions between Russians and Chechens within Russia, Putin and the national media have worked effectively to de-Islamicise domestic terrorism, redefining extremism as a wide-ranging problem embracing Russian nationalism, criminality and even pro-western liberalism. This shift offers compelling evidence of the discursive instability hidden beneath the superficially ruthless Putin propaganda machine.[7]

Still more ideologically loaded are the juxtapositions with western news stories. Before 1985, news from the west was distinguished by its negativity in contrast with the positive domestic stories of over-fulfilled norms and improving living standards. Now the emphasis is on parallels between western and Russian news stories, with the, still highly polemical, purpose of countering western suggestions that Russia is less democratic or civilised than its neighbours. A striking demonstration of the purchase gained from juxtapositions of domestic with western news stories came during Channel 1 reports on the London bombings of July 2005. On July 10, *Vremia* headlined with the story, the newsreader speaking of 'another strike against civilization' (a phrase used repeatedly in the bulletin), mentioning New York, Madrid, and then Moscow and Beslan in a litany enunciated with clear rhetorical purpose. Following a report on the interrupted Gleneagles summit at which the international dimension of the terror movement was continually foregrounded, *Vremia* ran a story on the unstable situation in Daghestan, completing the legitimation process (*Vremia*, 10 July 2005).

The same segment included a lengthy commentary on the BBC's decision to censor graphic footage of the carnage wreaked by the terror, showing that the legitimation strategy exploits the fluidity of television's textual boundaries to operate across bulletins as well as within them (recent *Vremia* bulletins had featured reports on government decisions to constrain the level of violence on Russian television). Russia is represented as being safely installed in a democratic zone sharing common values.

Representation accomplishes much of its work through the very signifying form it deploys; the realist novel persuades readers of its veracity not just because of its authentic themes but through the manner in which those themes are conveyed (the inclusion of pseudo-documentary evidence, and of authentication codes such as the use of actual dates, names and places; the presence of gritty, everyday dialogue and language, etc.). In representing Russian allegiance to democratic culture, post-Soviet news bulletins are faced with the task of replicating the very structures and forms of democracy. Chiefly, this means embracing the principles of neutrality, balance and free speech. However, post-Soviet TV's very immersion in global forms has laid at its disposal an array of compensatory devices. For example, by relegating Pozner's free-ranging *Vremena* to the margins of the schedules (10.30 pm on a Sunday evening), Channel 1 can not only neutralise the effect of the critical voices heard on the programme but also, to use Barthes's term, 'inoculate' itself against the claim that it restricts free speech. It also deploys 'macro-scheduling' techniques. Oppositional voices are progressively invalidated over a longer period. When the Khodarkovskii scandal was in full swing, approximately equal airtime was accorded to representatives of the prosecuting authorities and Khodarkovskii's own lawyers. As time wore on, the Khodarkovskii position (and that of his western backers) was increasingly suppressed in favour of anti-oligarchic reports. The 'imbalanced balance' principle applies likewise over shorter periods. At the beginning of June 2005, some Russian gas mysteriously went missing in Ukraine and became the source of a major diplomatic incident. On the day that the news emerged, *Vremia* quoted in its report representatives of Gazprom and the Ukrainian government (*Vremia*, 6 June 2005). The following day featured solely a Russian government representative and several Russian politicians expressing dissatisfaction with the Ukrainian response (*Vremia*, 7 June 2005). In overall terms – as demonstrated by our analysis of the numbers of citations of actors in the Russian news compiled on the basis of four weeks coverage spanning the end of 2006 and the start of 2007 – there is an overwhelming bias towards the voices of Putin and his political entourage, with minimal space for *vox populi* contributions, or for critical voices (see Appendix 3).

Restricting the terms and range of the debate enable the semblance of democracy to be maintained even as actual democratic dialogue is suppressed. With its capacity to model and embellish dialogic practices, television is perfectly equipped to foster this illusion and contribute to the marginalisation of dissent. On 23 June 2005, the Russian Duma became embroiled in a complex dispute about the finer points of financial strategy. Both *Vremia* and *Segodnia* headlined with the story and each of them emphasised the virulence of the disagreement between Mikhail Fradkov, the Prime Minister, and Duma representatives critical of his position. Several minutes of heated dispute created the impression of a healthy democratic government, open to scrutiny by a neutral and objective media (*Vremia*, 23 May 2005; *Segodnia*, 23 May 2005). Of course, the issue at stake was highly technical with few significant political ramifications.

A further validation strategy appropriated from the culture of democratic journalism is the use of expert opinion. Reports by on-location special correspondents feature on all Russian news bulletins, usually framed by a dialogue between the anchor and a reporter whose reiteration of the official version of events is authenticated through on-the-ground, eyewitness evidence. During the June 2005 hepatitis outbreak, *Vremia*'s daily reports from its special correspondent in Tver', the source of the outbreak, merely elaborated on and confirmed the reassurances of the government's Chief Medical Officer (*Glavnyi vrach*), creating a circular, self-validating discourse which passed from anchor, through government representative, and back to the anchor via the special correspondent (*Vremia*, 7 June 2005).

Claims to facticity on potentially challengeable issues of political controversy are further strengthened through association with claims to accuracy on uncontroversial matters of scientific fact. News bulletins are the sites for multiple discourses, but overlaying them all is a single monologic discourse of truth which accords them their authority and credibility. A bulletin which reports accurately on a new breeding programme for buffalos, or on floods in California, or a plague of flies in Australia, is more likely to be believed when reporting on presidential elections in Abkhazia, or on Putin's new initiative to develop the scientific town of Akademgorod in Siberia (*Vremia*, 4 June 2005).

Representational authority depends heavily on the extent to which events fit into recognised narrative models fostered through the familiarisation which comes from constant repetition. All *Vremia*'s reports on Kremlin meetings inevitably began with shots of a vigorous President Putin striding purposefully across the Kremlin halls to welcome his visitors, followed by a two-shot sequence depicting Putin engrossed in animated conversation with his guest, succeeded in turn by an extended close-up of Putin as he delivered his diplomatic homily. When national problems and crises arise, the purposeful striding is succeeded by shots of Putin firing penetrating questions at his ministers and exhorting them to take the necessary action. The regularity with which the model was invoked contributes to the myth of a strong, vigorous leader who stresses actions over words.

Other myths and narrative models contributed to the nation-building exercise in which Putin's regime engaged on a massive scale. We have referred in this context to the importance of running orders in which international items are relegated to the peripheries of news bulletins. But even the content of ostensibly international news items reflects Russo-centric bias. In the aftermath of the tsunami disaster of 26 December 2004, reports about Russian contributions to the aid effort and miraculous escapes by Russian citizens dominated *Vremia*. For example, shortly after the event, Putin was shown enumerating Russian actions in support of the victims (*Vremia*, 6 January 2005). On the previous day, the documentary programme *Reporting Profession* (*Professiia reporter*) dedicated a whole edition to the experiences of Russians living in Thailand, focusing its attention on a group of Siberian Russians who had demonstrated the fortitude characteristic of their region in reopening the bars they owned and returning to normality (*Professia reporter*, Channel 1, 5 January 2005). Four days after the London bombings of July 2005, a weekly RTR news compilation programme (*Vest nedeli*) pointed out that it was Putin who persuaded Tony Blair to address the press on behalf of the whole of the G8 (the bomb coincided with a G8 summit chaired by Britain). The rest of the programme was taken up with Russia's impending chairmanship of the G8 (*Vesti Nedeli*, RTR, 11 July 2005).

But nation building is also about ensuring that a nation coheres internally, a task for which RTR has been given the lead role. Its news programme, *Vesti*, is dominated by reports from the provinces. *Vesti*'s evening bulletins generally end with a brief taster of news from a selected local channel. On 7 July 2005, a report from Riazan' on a spate of mobile phone thefts was broadcast. On 10 June 2005, Vladimir was the chosen city. When national crises arise, however, all the news broadcasts are careful to ensure that they embrace regional perspectives. On the day after the tragic end to Beslan, *Vremia* and *Vesti* both featured reports from towns and cities across Russia, with ordinary people expressing their sorrow and outrage (*Vremia*, 4 September 2004; *Vesti*, 4 September 2004). Thus, national unity is performed through the integration of multiple local perspectives on single, dramatic crises, as well as ritualised through the establishment of the regional slot as part of a regular viewing routine.

A third way in which news programmes contribute to Putin's nation-building agenda is through national ceremonial occasions. In 2005, the 60th anniversary of the Second World War victory over fascism was celebrated. This event overlapped with Putin's decision to install the army at the centre of the national identity project.[8] Consequently, the media resurrected much of the style and rhetoric associated with Soviet coverage of similar anniversaries, but inflected it with language appropriate to the new, post-communist era. *Vremia* and *Vesti* bulletins were preoccupied for days before 9 May with lengthy, cheerleading reports on preparations for the event. On the day itself, entire bulletins (but for a rapid trawl through other stories at the very end) were taken up with reports from across the former Soviet Union on the anniversary. What was different from Soviet coverage was the mixing of emotive bombast about 'sacrifices for our great motherland' with the inclusion of the perspectives of ordinary people, and of items of a more mundane nature. One pre-celebration *Vesti* evening bulletin included reports on the temporary travel disruptions suffered by Muscovites in connection with the celebrations, and on the security issues it would raise (*Vesti*, 24 April 2005). Another contained reports on technical problems faced by the parade organisers, as well as human interest stories on the Chief Engineer's father who died in the war; a German–Russian translator with intimate knowledge of Hitler's last days; and old footage of the discovery of Hitler's corpse (*Vesti*, 26 April 2005). The 60th Anniversary was thus capable of generating 'real' events to balance and 'naturalise' the ritualistic, Soviet-style ceremonial rhetoric. Equally, the individualised human-interest stories provided a counterpoint to the anonymous discourse of nation and people which predominated in Soviet ceremonials.

Ritualistic, ceremonial temporality is now inherent to post-Soviet news culture. In addition to the 'official chronicle' segments in *Vremia* we might cite RTR's hagiographic treatment of the Orthodox Patriarch Aleksei II on the 15th anniversary of his ordination (*Vesti*, 10 June 2005). Too easily dismissed as a throwback to the propagandistic Soviet media system, this phenomenon also indicates a mythic approach to time out of keeping with modern news culture. For such an approach, what is worthy of recording is not what breaches norms (disasters, conflicts and all the transitory happenings we come to think of as 'news'), but rather what, through endless repetition, confirms and reinforces them.

Now, however, the remnants of Soviet ritualism must compete with chronologically oriented, western consumer mentalities according to which events, like consumer products, must be packaged to entertain for the moment. By dint of their incorporation of the apparatus and agenda of western news, (most international news is provided by international news agencies, or purchased from foreign broadcasters) *Vremia*, *Segodnia* and *Vesti* are bound to the principles of consumerism, notwithstanding the restrictions applied by the Putin regime. Consumerist culture even affects sign-offs and continuity devices. When breaking for advertisements the *Segodnia* newsreader, for example, exhorts viewers 'Stay with Us' (*Ostavaites' s nami*) and in some cases, 'Stay with us; you'll find it interesting' (*budet interesno*). And the *Vremia* bulletins end with a verbal trailer for the following programme. Undermined by the informal modes of address we have come to associate with the 'selling' of news, ritualism ultimately weakens the representational regime of Russian television news which must strive to accommodate both tendencies.

News as discourse

Norman Fairclough interprets the infiltration of informal styles into news broadcasting as evidence of the 'conversationalisation of public language', pointing to a 'new prestige for ordinary values and practices' (a democratising force), but also, drawing on Habermas, the manipulative tendency to present 'the contestation of relations between politicians and public as simulated relations between people in a shared lifeworld' (Fairclough 1995: 5, 10, 11–12).

Ultimately, as Fairclough argues, the process serves to legitimate power. But this is not to deny the tensions between the competing values of the lifeworlds from which the integrating discourses emanate. They are particularly evident in Russian news broadcasting, where the integration is far from complete, and where the legacy of the Soviet past in which public and private discourses were much more clearly delineated, remains prominent. Channel 1's breakfast news programme, *Good Morning* (*Dobroe utro*), for example, is presented by a couple whose imitations of the informal banter between spouses is choreographed to the extent that the same 'spontaneous' jokes are repeated from hour to hour. The sign offs ('See you soon' – *Do vstrechi*, and, in the case of the weathergirl 'That's about it for now; we'll see you around' – *Eto poka vse. Uvidimsia*) bespeak a proximity between viewer and broadcaster which is not born out by audience response; the practice of texting and e-mailing breakfast news presenters with informal comments is non-existent on Russian national television (though it is used extensively by some local channels). Often, the tension emerges within the linguistic forms themselves. On the *Good Morning* broadcast on Victory Day 2005, one of the presenters comments on a display of formation marching 'That was, speaking in modern terms, a sensation!' (*Eto bylo, govoria sovremennym iazykom, sensatsiia*). The parenthetical 'speaking in modern terms' accords the clash of registers palpable linguistic form (*Dobroe utro*, Channel 1, 9 May 2005).

The informal language of the private sphere can, however, be deployed to powerful ideological effect. On the 25th anniversary of Vysotskii's death this semi-dissident figure of the Soviet period was represented as a national figurehead. Using the popular term '*vlasti*' ('the authorities') when referring to the Soviet government's refusal to accept Vysotskii, the newsreader's script appropriated language from the vernacular critique of Soviet official treatment of the bard for Putin's new official rhetoric of popular patriotism: 'Soviet official authorities [*vlasti*] did not recognise him … People close to him say that the authorities [*vlasti*] simply feared his dynamism and energy' (*Vremia*, 25 August 2005).

Fairclough distinguishes between 'discourse' uses of language of this sort (language in the service of social practice from a particular point of view) and 'generic' uses of language ('the use of language constituting social practice') (Fairclough 1995: 56). Because social practice itself has become more heterogeneous since the fall of communism, since the media have become the site of discourse conflict, and since even centrally controlled television is more porous and open to infiltration by variant social practices than before, we find a multiplicity of speech genres on post-Soviet television. Many of these are generated from within a newly professionalised journalistic sphere. For whilst in the Soviet system journalism was subordinate institutionally to the Communist Party and rhetorically to the all-encompassing language of Marxism–Leninism, in the post-Soviet period it has emerged as a semi-autonomous realm with a profession-specific idiom and set of values which, ultimately, cannot be entirely contained within an official nation-binding rhetoric. Thus, events taking place at a distance from the Moscow news centres are covered by 'our own correspondent' (*nash sobstvenni korrespondent*) or 'our special correspondent' (*nash spetsial'nyi korrespondent*) whose linguistic and pragmatic strategies often mimic the western-style journalistic exposé first introduced under glasnost and now put to work in seemingly pro-regime contexts, but to jarring and contradictory effect. For example, the shaky camera style, the silhouetted interview, the use of vernacular language and the pseudo-dramatic conflicts between reporter and villain were, in Channel 1's weekly programme, *Profession – Reporter*, applied to the issue of the sexual exploitation of young Russians in Cyprus in a shock-inducing manner which left implicit, yet substantive, doubts as to the robustness and adequacy of government counter-measures (*Professia-reporter*, Channel 1, 25 May 2005).

The language and techniques of the exposé are also deployed sporadically in the mainstream news. In July 2005, *Vremia* carried a report on a diplomatic incident in which Georgia suggested that a Russian army officer was guilty of aiding and abetting a terrorist group operating in Georgia (*Vremia*, 25 May 2005). Following footage of the accusation, the newsreader announced, 'We turned to the Ministry of Defence to ask them about the accusation' (the first person pronoun connoting Channel 1's status as an autonomous collective of professionals). The camera cut to a young reporter making a phone call and a close up of his determined face as he asked robustly: 'Georgia has accused one of your officers of taking part in a terrorist act on Georgian territory. What are your comments on that statement?' (*Kak vy prokommentiruete eto obvinenie*). What followed, however, was a long, unchallenged refutation of the accusation. Here the exposé genre had here been enlisted in an attempt to legitimate the official government position. Because the generic procedures were not fully followed through, however, the attempt ran the danger of proving abortive.

Journalism has on occasion become the focus of meta-generic commentary which reinforces its autonomous status. A Channel 1 *Vremia* bulletin in November 2004 featured an item on the reporting of the Chechen wars marking ten years since the beginning of the campaigns (*Vremia*, 15 November 2004). Commentary focused on how reporters from all channels had established unique rituals and jargon (*zhargon*), some of which found its way into reports, and how Russian war reporters stood out from their foreign peers through their disregard for the dangers their profession brought upon them. However, any claim to objectivity was undercut by the remark made by the nationalist journalist Aleksander Nevzorov that all channels except Channel 1 had earlier supported the Chechen rebels (this, two months after the Beslan siege).

The language and rituals of the genres of professional journalism go along with the rhetoric of neutrality and balance. State-owned Russian television accommodates this rhetoric through a discursive deployment of point of view. Towards the end of June 2005, a minor scandal broke out around the financial dealings of the former Prime Minister, Mikhail Kasianov, by now out of favour with the government. The way in which *Segodnia*, still the least politically constrained of the national news programmes, dealt with the issue is revealing. On reporting that Kasianov had been taken to court for the illegal construction of a dacha, the newsreader first asserted 'some say the action is political, others that it is legally motivated', conveying the requisite balance in a distanced, third-person summary mode (*Segodnia*, 7 July 2005). The bulletin then proceeded to broadcast directly words (and images) of the latter group, followed by a rebuttal from Kasianov's press secretary quoted in indirect speech. The impression of balance maintained through the oscillation between rival viewpoints masked a deeper bias embodied in its privileged access to the more persuasive mode of direct speech.

Russian newsreaders' viewpoints are often infiltrated by the terminology and values of the government spokesmen whose words they frame. An instance of this occurred during *Vremia* reports on the London bombings, when the special reporter effectively primed the audience for Putin's assault on the BBC's double standards by asking in an indignant aside to an otherwise factual report, why no footage of Beslan was shown on British television in connection with the bombings. Here, the normal relationship between framing and embedded voices was subtly reversed: rather than the former providing the generalised evaluation of the particularised, partisan speech of the latter, it was Putin's embedded voice with its more measured reference to 'double standards' which evaluated and attenuated the reporter's shriller rhetorical questioning (*Vremia*, 10 July 2005).

Fairclough's discourse model, following Goffman, distinguishes between *author* (the person whose words are spoken), *animator* (the person who articulates them) and *principal* (the person whose position is represented). In cases such as the reports on the hepatitis outbreak discussed earlier, the newsreader animates words authored putatively by the public (it is the 'man in the street' who might react in the spontaneous manner reflected in the words chosen), but of which the government is the principal. Thus, the discourse becomes a circular one in which animator, author and principal (newsreader–reporter–Chief Medical Officer–Government) converge as one.

However, the very expectation of proximity between animator, principal and author in post-Soviet news can mask the introduction of a subtle element of discourse differentiation. *Segodnia* led one June 2005 bulletin with an extraordinarily worded account of challenges to Prime Minister Fradkov issued in the Duma earlier that day, suggesting with unmistakable sarcasm that the counter-criticisms made by Fradkov demonstrate that Russia 'has the most democratic parliament in the world', and portraying the debate as 'a conversation between real men' (*Segodnia*, 23 June 2005). Here, the animator (newsreader) articulated words that might have been authored by a Putin government enthusiast, but whose grossly overstated nature betrayed the cynical standpoint of an oppositional principal. Thus, the NTV newsreader exploited the expectation that journalists now merely mouth the propagandistic platitudes of their masters in order to inject a jarring note of irony which would not have been lost on NTV's audience, still drawn largely from the oppositional-minded intelligentsia. This example is not isolated and news discourse in NTV's *Segodnia* continues to be characterised by a register heavy with metaphor and irony.

Conclusion

The NTV example reconfirms a theme which has recurred implicitly throughout our analysis in this chapter: that no matter how dominant the official line, post-Soviet television continues to serve as a site at which the truth is contested even as it is asserted. Indeed, increasingly under Putin, news broadcasts (like other television output) have formed part of a wider nation-building strategy whose performative aspects (in which the nation is reconfigured even as it is reported) outweigh its constative aspects (in which it is represented as something fixed and pre-existent). It is the notion of a mismatch between what Russian television news 'says' and what it actually 'does' which best characterises the conflicts and contradictions undermining the articulations of media space, representational strategy and discourse structure that we have examined. Thus, the aberrant performativity of Putin's television news machine subverts the performativity of the nation-building mission, indicating the crucial importance of the media phenomena discussed. In disinforming its audience (plying it with a highly restrictive, centrally manipulated, version of events), Putin's television news apparatus dis-informs it (negating the information it disseminates through the form in which it is disseminated). As the empty spaces for subversion inadvertently opened up by the Putin regime's ideological rigidity begin to fill one might even question the blanket pessimism with which each new repressive turn of its media control screw is greeted.

Appendix 1: Percentage of *Vremia* news time by category of news topic (November 2006 to March 2007)

Note that in the following lists, the first number refers to the November 2006 percentage and the second to the March 2007 percentage.

Politics

1. Official messages (9.78%–10.53%)
2. Parliament (Duma and the Upper House) (2.17%–1.05%)
3. Party politics (0.82%–2.10%)

Foreign issues

4. Foreign affairs (22.28%–31.58%)
5. Foreign policy (1.36%–3.62%)
6. Diplomacy (7.07%–2.20%)

Social issues

7. Crime and corruption (5.98%–7.41%)
8. Education (0.54%–1.06%)
9. Health (3.53%–4.23%)
10. Poverty (0.27%–0.0%)
11. Accidents and incidents (e.g. plane and automobile crashes, industrial accidents) (1.63%–7.41%)
12. Religion (1.09%–0.26%)
13. Environment (1.09%–1.59%)
14. Security and terror (8.70%–2.91%)
15. Economics and finance (6.25%–6.88%)
16. Sport, culture and leisure (14.13%–10.05%)
17. Science (1.36%–1.59%)
18. Military affairs – army and defence industry (1.90%–2.65%)
19. Accidents affecting whole towns (shortages of water, power etc.) (3.53%–0.0%)
20. Social welfare (e.g. orphans, maternity allowances) (3.53%–2.12%)
21. Russians, Russian and Soviet culture and history abroad (2.72%–3.70%)
22. Russian space exploration (0.27%–0.79%)

Appendix 2

Table 1.1 Stories running over two or more bulletins between November 2006 and April 2007

Topic	Number of bulletins
Ex-Soviet republics	132
Dmitrii Medvedev	32
Sergei Ivanov	34
Iraq	31
Iran	16
China	19
Sochi Winter Olympics	27
Litvinenko scandal	21
Extremism in society	15
US plan to site missiles in Eastern Europe	10
Global warming	8
Lebanon	8
Ice skating	10
Youth movements	8

Table continued on next page

Table 1.1 (continued)

Topic	Number of bulletins
Demographic crisis	9
Work of intelligence agencies	13
Other international stories	10
Israel and Palestine	8
Dangers of skuba diving	2
Gazprom	5
Space exploration	2
KVN quiz competition	2
Corruption (Vladivostok)	8
Bill Gates	2
US midterm elections	3
Chechnia	25
Russian Day of Unity	4

Appendix 3: Voices in the Russian news

First week of November 2006 (numbers of citations, direct and indirect)

Putin – 7
Gryzlov (leader of United Russia) – 0
Medvedev – 2
Ivanov – 3
Members of 'One Russia' – 0
Russian Ministers and Deputy Ministers – 11
Other Russian high-standing officials – 2
Other Russian MPs – 5
Russian governors – 1
Russian mid-rank officials – 4
Russian opposition members – 0
Russian religious authorities – 4
Russian oligarchs – 1
Russian experts – 5
Russian celebrities and sports people – 3
Russian citizens – 7
Former USSR chief executives – 3
Former USSR Ministers – 2
Former USSR MPs – 1
Former USSR citizens – 0
Former USSR opposition members – 4
Former USSR officials – 1
Foreign chief executives – 3
Foreign Ministers – 0

Foreign MPs – 0
Foreign experts – 1
Foreign citizens – 1
Foreign officials – 1
Foreign transnational companies – 1

First week of December 2006

Putin – 7
Gryzlov – 5
Medvedev – 4
Ivanov – 3
Members of 'One Russia' – 7
Russian Ministers and Deputy Ministers – 6
Other Russian high-standing officials – 5
Other Russian MPs – 8
Russian governors – 0
Russian mid-rank officials – 1
Russian opposition members – 0
Russian religious authorities – 1
Russian oligarchs – 2
Russian experts – 1
Russian celebrities and sports people – 6
Russian citizens – 3
Former USSR chief executives – 0
Former USSR Ministers – 1
Former USSR MPs – 1
Former USSR citizens – 1
Former USSR opposition members – 2
Former USSR officials – 1
Foreign chief executives – 0
Foreign Ministers – 1
Foreign MPs – 0
Foreign experts – 2
Foreign citizens – 4
Foreign officials – 2
Foreign transnational companies – 0

First week of January 2007

Putin – 1
Gryzlov – 0
Medvedev – 0
Ivanov – 1
Members of 'One Russia' – 0

Russian Ministers and Deputy Ministers – 4
Other Russian high-standing officials – 0
Other Russian MPs – 0
Russian governors – 1
Russian mid-rank officials – 4
Russian opposition members – 0
Russian religious authorities – 2
Russian oligarchs – 1
Russian experts – 4
Russian celebrities and sports people – 0
Russian citizens – 5
Former USSR chief executives – 0
Former USSR Ministers – 0
Former USSR MPs – 0
Former USSR citizens – 0
Former USSR opposition members – 0
Former USSR officials – 0
Foreign chief executives – 1
Foreign Ministers – 1
Foreign MPs – 0
Foreign experts – 0
Foreign citizens – 2
Foreign officials – 2
Foreign transnational companies – 0

First week of February 2007

Putin – 5
Gryzlov – 1
Medvedev – 0
Ivanov – 2
Members of 'One Russia' – 1
Russian Ministers and Deputy Ministers – 10
Other Russian high-standing officials – 0
Other Russian MPs – 1
Russian governors – 0
Russian mid-rank officials – 1
Russian opposition members – 0
Russian religious authorities – 0
Russian oligarchs – 0
Russian experts – 0
Russian celebrities and sports people – 2
Russian citizens – 6
Former USSR chief executives – 0
Former USSR Ministers – 0

Former USSR MPs – 0
Former USSR citizens – 0
Former USSR opposition members – 0
Former USSR officials – 0
Foreign chief executives – 0
Foreign Ministers – 0
Foreign MPs – 0
Foreign experts – 0
Foreign citizens – 4
Foreign officials – 0
Foreign transnational companies – 0

2 St Petersburg 300

Television and the invention of a post-Soviet Russian (media) tradition

Introduction

In this chapter we project several themes from Chapter 1 into a new environment: that of the 'media event', a television genre allied to, but not coincident with the news bulletin. Thus, the fragility conferred upon the nation-building project by the performative function it must adopt in television news is further explored through the uneasy relationship between national and media traditions which emerges in the televised official celebration. Moreover, the tension arising from the adoption of pseudo-democratic global forms for profoundly non-democratic national(istic) purposes identified in our analysis of post-Soviet news strategies is found to acquire new complexity in the context of the organised media event. Upon the nexus formed by these two, now familiar, issues we superimpose a topic which will recur as a leitmotif throughout the remainder of the book: that of the importance of the local–global–national axis in its specific, post-Soviet dimension. First, though we should introduce the subject of the present chapter in more detail.

National identities rely upon the traditions that sustain them; nations lacking a sense of continuity with a set of communal rites stretching seemingly unchanged from past to present will not cohere.[1] The purpose of royal weddings, state openings of parliaments, and more popularly inspired phenomena like city marathons is to promote a sense of unity of purpose across the diverse factions making up the modern nation-state. We are encouraged to forget the barriers dividing us on these occasions, but also, as television commentary on the colourful mix of participants in city marathons confirm, to celebrate our mutual differences.

All traditions develop and mutate over time, but in the case of post-Soviet Russia, the 70 years of communist rule which ended in 1991 radically breached the continuity upon which tradition's maintenance is predicated. The architects of official post-Soviet culture have been forced to pick up the threads of a long-lost set of rituals by generating a wave of nostalgia for all things tsarist, whilst, particularly under Putin, preserving and updating those Soviet rituals deemed worthy of retention, several of which, as recent scholarship confirms, themselves date back to pre-revolutionary times.[2]

The Russian media have played a crucial role in developing a sense of tradition appropriate to post-communist sensibilities. The phenomenal marketing operation behind Mikhalkov's 1997 film, *Barber of Siberia*, recalling the halcyon days of life amongst the tsarist military cadets; television coverage of Pushkin's bicentenary in 1999; and the recent centring of a new militaristic patriotism around the Soviet Second World War Victory Day celebration exemplify this trend.

The notion that the modern media should lead the fight to restore traditions to a pristine purity is not unique to Russia. Nor – given the mythical nature of that purity which is demonstrated effectively by scholars like Hermann Bausinger (Bausinger 1990), and Richard Handler and Jocelyn Linnekin (Handler and Linnekin 1989) – is it a paradox. Indeed, Eric Hobsbaum argues that many supposedly age-old traditions are relatively recent inventions intended to shore up imperial regimes nervous about their legitimacy.[3] In describing the provenance of these invented traditions, David Cannadine recognises the media's role in consolidating them, referring to television coverage of the British Queen's coronation in 1953 as central to the myth of quintessential Englishness (Cannadine 1983: 154–55).

Benedict Anderson acknowledges the contribution of the twentieth-century revolution in mass communications to the creation of imagined communities implicitly unified in common experience of national traditions.[4] Daniel Dayan and Elihu Katz, who provide this chapter's main theoretical underpinning, argue that national celebrations have become inseparable from their media representations (hence the coining of the term 'media events'). They posit that media events must satisfy a *syntactic criterion* (they interrupt the flow of daily life), a *semantic criterion* (they deal reverentially with sacred matters) and a *pragmatic criterion* (they invite the response of a committed audience) (Dayan and Katz 1992: 14). With its temporary swamping of the television ether, its sanctification of the myth of Peter's city, and its emphasis on crowd participation, the televised celebration in 2003 of St Petersburg's 300th anniversary meets all these criteria. Dayan and Katz point out that '[i]n the case of media events … organizers and broadcasters resonate together' and that, 'the center – on which all eyes are focused – is the place where the organizer of a "historic" ceremony joins with a skilled broadcaster' (Dayan and Katz 1992: 16). Television's deep complicity in the production of St Petersburg 300 is our main theme.

National traditions require a parallel set of broadcasting rituals through which the former can be expressed, and which facilitate the acceptance of the special ceremonial programmes as part of an organically developing tradition of their own (for example, the use of familiar media personalities for the commentary on state occasions). They must likewise blend with the established broadcasting culture into which they are inserted, just as they enable the occasions they celebrate to be integrated into an officially constructed version of their viewers' everyday routines. This process, too, forms part of our focus.

Post-Soviet Russian television is transforming itself from a communist propaganda machine into something which, despite the growing interference of a centralising government, must at least pay lip service to western-style free speech and consumer choice. In our analysis we inflect Dayan and Katz's notion of the media event with insights derived from cultural semiotics (principally, Bakhtin's concepts of 'carnival' and 'chronotope', supported by Iurii Lotman's work on the semiotics of space). We adapt this model to the task of describing how the St Petersburg tercentenary helps articulate a Russian 'media tradition' which, reflecting the transformation undergone by post-Soviet television, intersects, and enters into tension, with a (re)emergent national tradition in Hobsbaum's sense.

The tercentenary was several years in preparation and was planned to display St Petersburg to the world. The city centre received an expensive facelift and a range of construction projects were timed to coincide with the beginning of the 2003 festivities. The anniversary underwent an elaborate dress rehearsal on the 2002 City Day celebration on 27 May (City Day is a relatively recent post-Soviet innovation) when a gigantic clock on Palace Square began the countdown to the 300-year anniversary and when the dedicated tercentenary Press Centre was opened. Whilst ceremonies celebrating the tercentenary occurred throughout 2002 and 2003, the centrepiece was the intensive schedule of festivities organised for the period 23 May to 1 June 2003 when, controversially, the city centre was made virtually inaccessible and a massive security operation disrupted everyday routine. The festivities reached their climax with a naval parade along the Neva modelled on the launching of Peter's navy and followed by a display of synchronised fountains. Other highlights during the intensive ten-day period included firework displays on Senate Square; pop concerts on Vasil'evskii Island and in Palace Square; a White Nights parade down Nevskii prospect; as well as numerous commercial exhibitions aimed at the international business community. The most significant parade was a carnival procession which took Peter the Great as its theme, and which Mayor Aleksandr Iakovlev used as an opportunity to demonstrate his democratic 'humility' before the people. The historical dimension was further consolidated by a Petrine-era market, a ceremony consecrating the spot at which the city's construction purportedly commenced; a presentation of army cadets to city dignitaries; and a celebration in the style of the revolutionary storming of the Winter Palace of the reopening of a long-disused door to the Hermitage.

Amongst the cultural events were the opening of new monuments to famous St Petersburg figures like Blok and Dostoevskii, and, nationally, the release of Sokurov's cinematic paean to the city, *Russian Ark*, and of the TV adaptation of Dostoevskii's *The Idiot*. Officially approved popular songs were written for the occasion and a city anthem was played incessantly. Politically, the most important events were a three-day summit of G8 leaders hosted by Putin (rehearsed in 2002 through a Bush–Putin meeting coinciding with City Day), several new presidential policy announcements and the organisation of a local Civic Forum hosted by Mayor Iakovlev.

We examine television coverage of the tercentenary, including the lead-up to the occasion and the main week of activities in May 2003. Our analysis, which proceeds by theme rather than chronologically, is based on 20 hours of recordings, consisting of 28 different broadcasts. They were made at an interval of one year: 9 in April–May 2002 (dealing with the celebration of St Petersburg's 299th year) and 19 in April–May 2003 at the height of the jubilee celebrations between 23 May and 1 June. A minority (10) of the broadcasts are from national television (Channel 1 and NTV). The majority (18) are from the local St Petersburg channel, Channel 5, and these include a number of bulletins of that channel's flagship evening news programme *Inform-TV*, along with selections from Channel 5's week-long jubilee special *Telemarafon*. The sources of specific broadcasts are henceforth indicated parenthetically. The bias towards the local is indicative of the emphasis we place on the jubilee as a spur to the regional identity project now discernible across Russia. However, the fact that the trend is part of a centrally managed strategy indicates that the local and the national are being made to work together in uneasy unison. The degree to which the official rhetoric surrounding St Petersburg 300 accorded with popular experience does not form part of our remit, though reactions to the tercentenary from within the intelligentsia reveal deep cynicism.[5] To assess whether this attitude was replicated at large would require detailed study in the field.

Indeed, our methodology in this chapter is situated squarely on the textual rather than the ethnographic side of media studies. The onus is, accordingly, less to corroborate arguments with verifiable empirical data, and more, as in Richard Sennett's account of qualitative research, to aim for 'plausibility' by 'showing the logical connections among [textual] phenomena' (Sennett 2002: 43). Dayan and Katz's theoretical framework is adumbrated on a primary level through careful attention to issues highlighted in the work of Fairclough, John Ellis and other media analysts of a textual inclination. They include

(i)   the placement and sequencing of jubilee broadcasts within the televisual flow, to cite Raymond Williams now famous term;
(ii) the correlation of tercentenary events with post-Soviet news values;
(iii) the structuring of the various discourses and registers prominent during the jubilee;
(iv) the visual rhetoric of the camera shots and montage;
(v)   the relationship between visual image and ideological word;
(vi) the attributes of St Petersburg 300 as television genre;
(vii) its incorporation into post-Soviet viewing patterns.

The primary level textual issues lead us from St Petersburg 300 to post-Soviet culture as a whole, the secondary level at which Bakhtin proves useful. The sequencing of our argument and its themes reflects the intertwining of primary and secondary levels according to a logic in which textual attributes constantly double back on cultural principles and vice versa. Thus, in section 2, St Petersburg historical intertexts (iv) are deemed to invoke a cultural mythology and semiotic space specific to the city. The spatio-temporal dimension of this mythology is related in section 3 to procedures for bolstering national and local identities, including ideological discourse manipulation strategies (iii), and then in section 4 to the notion of an integrated St Petersburg chronotope. The incorporation into this chronotope of event-specific viewing temporalities (viii), news value systems (ii) and television scheduling devices (i), meanwhile, accords it a carnivalesque dimension. The self-reflexive media sphere which is carnival's corollary is shown in section 5 to be a function of the fluidity of the media event's generic boundaries (vii). Finally, sections 6 and 7 demonstrate how, supported by the jubilee's visual rhetoric and word–image relations (v and vi), carnival and self-reflexivity underpin a discourse of participatory democracy incorporated into, yet simultaneously at odds with, the nation-building project.

Mythologising the city

For Mayor Iakovlev's anniversary committee, the jubilee represented a chance to capitalise on the limelight that the city would enjoy in order to assert its influence on Moscow, attract investment and build relationships with the local electorate. This tri-partite addressee was reflected in a prominent jubilee slogan: 'Facing the city, Russia, and the world' (*Litsom k gorodu, Rossii i miru*). The committee's prospectus appropriated the foundation myth of St Petersburg as the embodiment of the will of the first great westernising tsar, Peter the Great, to suggest that the anniversary would provide the city with a new chance to carve out a twenty-first century path by becoming a centre for trans-European cooperation. The city's original construction was described as a 'break-through' (*proryv*) into a new era (the city's ability to defy history lay behind much of the ritual). Iakovlev characterised the anniversary as a second 'break through into the future' (*proryv v budushchee*), marking the 300 years as a new beginning in which St Petersburg shifted again from Russia's margins to become its centre of gravity.[6]

Televisual portrayals of several reconstructions of the Petrine period revealed a consistent emphasis on popular re-enactment.[7] In sequences dwelling on markets set up along the Neva in May 2002 reporters trumpeted the fact that people were not only dressed in Petrine costume, but were, it was dubiously claimed, beginning 'involuntarily to speak in the Petrine manner' (*Inform-TV*, Channel 5, 23 May 2002). Peter's times were thus not merely symbolically represented, but seemingly, and sumptuously, relived.

The twentieth century was treated in a more perfunctory manner, but with significant exceptions: the Hermitage door reopening ceremony which, as ordinary spectators rushed jubilantly towards the Winter Palace, co-opted revolutionary mythology into imperial rhetoric, re-appropriated in turn for the new cult of democratic participation; the incorporation of wartime Leningrad into the St Petersburg myth. Throughout coverage of the festivities, montage sequences juxtaposed aerial shots of parades containing all-Russian contingents with close-up metonymies of the city-specific activities focusing on re-creations of the Petrine period. St Petersburg's geo-symbolic space was thus represented as capable of accommodating the highly choreographed pomp familiar to viewers versed in the well-established television rituals surrounding coverage of Soviet national celebration days (*prazdniki*) alongside participatory, people-centred, Petrine ritual. The Press Centre set up in 2002 was housed in the former Radio Building (*Dom Radio*) which, as the report on the opening of the centre underlined, played a vital role in the 900-day wartime blockade (*Inform-TV*, Channel 5, 22 April 2002). Confirming Dayan and Katz's earlier cited axiom, the media situated themselves at the centre of the ideological complex that they claimed also to represent.

One of the most extensively covered celebrations in 2003 was the presentation of army cadets to the local authorities. In the Channel 5 television schedule, the parade was followed by a documentary on the history of the cadets interspersed with sequences from Mikhalkov's feature film, *The Barber of Siberia*, idealising the 'noble patriotism' of the pre-revolutionary Russian Army. Raymond Williams first coined the term 'flow' to describe the radical break with the notion of text which television represents. 'What is being offered,' claims Williams

> is not a programme of discrete units with particular insertions, but a planned flow, in which the true series is not the published sequence of programme items but this sequence transformed by the inclusion of another kind of sequence, so that these sequences together compose the real flow, the real broadcasting.
>
> (Williams 1974: 151)

Consequently, televisual meaning spans multiple textual boundaries and occupies indeterminate 'semiotic spaces', whilst not dismantling conventional generic units. Thus, coverage of national celebrations constructs around the events a temporary semiotic space transcending the historical fiction/news documentary divide, and at the centre of which the celebration is presented as the core of a network of linked texts and images.[8] As evidence of the interweaving of the factual and the festive, *The Barber of Siberia* and St Petersburg 300, 'peripheral' and 'core' media space, the cadet documentary concluded with a group of cadets conveying festive greetings to viewers (Channel 5, 26 April 2003).

In its tendency to elide traditional lines of distinction, the semiotic space surrounding official celebrations is inherently conducive to the mythical: the myth of Peter, or of the noble Russian army cadets. Television's intimate modes of address and connections with the rhythms of everyday life also facilitated the reactivation of some of the 'apocryphal' myths surrounding the city's lesser-known places. A broadcast called *Planet St Petersburg* (Channel 5, 25 April 2003) took a tour-guide approach in an investigation of the stories behind the names of places such as The Kissing Bridge (*Potseluev most*) and Vasil'evskii Island (*Vasil'evskii ostrov*). The presentation style was quirky, the narrative register vernacular. Frequent reference was made to popular legend, through the use of impersonal phrases such as 'They say that there exists ... ' (*Govoriat, sushchestvuet ...*). And a local report dealt with the reconsecration of a monument marking the point at which Peter reputedly began the building of St Petersburg, now dubbed Point Zero (*Nulevaia tochka*). The reporter concluded her report by speculating that the monument might initiate a new popular ritual in which lovers come to kiss one another, and mothers to tell their sons the story of their native city (*Inform-TV*, Channel 5, 26 April 2005).

Ideology, city and nation

Events like the cadets' parade contribute to a rhythm of special occasions repeated sporadically for the purpose of public ceremony, whereas the Zero Point tradition belonged to the time of ongoing everyday ritual. Moreover, whilst the Zero Point ritual was aimed at furthering a local sense of belonging, the parade inscribed St Petersburg into a national identity project. However, this apparent tension was resolved through the ritual's function in authenticating pseudo-imperial rhetoric. The thematic emphasis on Peter the Great and the construction of St Petersburg enabled the jubilee to be portrayed as a celebration of the Petrine phase in Russian imperial history, according the national a local dimension and vice versa. This is to be seen in the context of the mushrooming of other local festivities celebrating regional contributions to Russian cultural history.[9]

President Putin's Petersburg connections placed him at the core of the local–national nexus. And the specially created St Petersburg anthem converted the city into a metonym for the nation. Several reports covered folk-craft exhibitions effectively bringing Russia's heartland to its edge. Conversely, the White Nights festival initiated during the 299-year celebrations was described in television commentaries as 'All-Russian' (*Vserossiiskii*), installing this quintessential St Petersburg phenomenon at the centre of Russian cultural tradition.

Throughout festivities week, the Channel 5 broadcast day was restructured around the celebrations. Programme interludes were accompanied by jubilee logos. Local news was managed to supplement jubilee coverage. The completion of each part of the city renovation project was synchronised with particular days during the festivities. Thus, within the abnormal television flow which characterised festivities week, reports on 'news events' merged with jubilee coverage, blending the rhythm of regular news stories with the jubilee's exceptional temporality.

The success in melding the celebrations with artificially manipulated news stories was matched by the generation of offshoot, 'unplanned' issues from within the celebrations themselves. One report was dedicated to spontaneous entrepreneurial activity undertaken by ordinary St Petersburgers (*Inform-TV*, Channel 5, 24 May 2003). Such reports accomplish a 'vertical' integration (the integration of the official celebrations with events in the same spatio-temporal paradigm, but of a different semantic order: spontaneous and popularly inspired as opposed to planned and conventionalised). They complement the 'horizontal' integration represented by the renovation reports (located within a similarly 'official' semantic order to the organised activities, but stretching into juxtaposed spatio-temporal paradigms). These offshoot activities infused local identity with ideological meaning: that of St Petersburg as the home for Russian free enterprise.

The fostering of a regional St Petersburg identity in a national context was reflected in local journalistic discourse where a highly subjective tone fostered a sense of communion with an audience distinct from, yet representative of, the nation at large. Newscasters, unusually for post-Soviet television, littered their commentaries with emotive phrases. At one point, concern arose that public access to the parades in the city centre had been curtailed. A newscaster dismissed this concern as 'malicious rumour', articulating the official line, but in the subjective voice of the ordinary person in the street (*Inform TV*, Channel 5, 25 May 2003). As Norman Fairclough has argued, media discourse normally attempts to mediate imperceptibly between the official rhetoric of the state and the vernacular language of the populace (Fairclough 1995: 10–12). During television coverage of St Petersburg 300, however, and as the example just cited demonstrates, the fault lines become more prominent: shrill protestations about the fallacy of unofficial rumours crudely transposed official sentiment into subjective, vernacular discourse.

The most telling instance of 'horizontal integration' was the linking of the jubilee to the political summits when St Petersburg was represented as the point at which, in displaying itself to the world, Russia simultaneously welcomes it across its borders. In 2002, Putin's arrival was reported in a fanfare of pomp. His summit with Bush saturated national and local television. In addition to reports on the business covered, there was extensive national coverage of Bush's trip to the Hermitage which offered a counterpoint to the presidential visit itself (*Vremia*, Channel 1, 24 May 2002). Whilst shots of the US president striding Petersburg's external spaces depicted the world coming to Russia's edge, the Hermitage empowered St Petersburg space to embrace world culture within it. The Hermitage became a key jubilee trope invoked throughout the intermedia text that was St Petersburg 300. This was most powerfully shown in Sokurov's fictional film *Russian Ark*. In this film, a tour of the painterly masterpieces housed at the Hermitage is dovetailed with a dream-like stroll through post-Petrine Russian history, and thus the gallery is portrayed as a Russian sanctuary for European civilisation.[10]

The 2003 G8 summit intensified the jubilee's symbolic significance. Putin's meticulously choreographed speech was staged against the backdrop of the Neva's oft-mentioned 'eternal waves' (*vechnye volny*), a point the Channel 1 camerawork emphasised as Putin faced forwards to 'the world' and the future with the permanent force of Russian history behind him (*Vremia*, Channel 1, 23 May 2003). In his speech, the president stressed both his local origins and St Petersburg's long association with the Russian intelligentsia (an irony given Putin's record in suppressing free expression). Generally, more coverage was given to ceremony than to substance, invoking news values reminiscent of Soviet times in which the immediate and topical was displaced by references to the symbolic import of the event for the 'Great Time' (of unfolding world revolution or of Russian history).

Putin's presence in St Petersburg served other nation-binding functions. On one hand, it turned the space of the city into a microcosm of Russia, stabilising St Petersburg in the eternal time of Russian history. On the other hand, it underlined how Putin had, like Peter before him, literally moved Russia's centre to its edge, projecting it into linear time and the future. Putin also established the city's internal liminality as the point of convergence of metropolitan centre, provincial periphery, and, in light of extensive news coverage given to the restoration of a Muslim mosque, Asian borderland (*Inform TV*, Channel 5, 27 May 2005).

The G8 summit was used as a platform for a raft of concrete policy initiatives (the removal of certain trade barriers; the easing of visa restrictions on travel to and from Russia) crafted with symbolic reference to the city's original role in bringing the country into contact with the world. These initiatives authenticated the saturation coverage through their status as 'real' political news rather than stage-managed ceremonial. Similarly, at the local level, *Inform-TV* issued daily reports on efforts to manage crowd and traffic control which blended the ceremonial aspects of the jubilee with the urgent immediacy of 'hard news'.

Official carnival and the St Petersburg chronotope

The way in which St Petersburg space meshes with the approach to time characteristic of the city's mythology permit us to speak of a distinctive St Petersburg chronotope.[11] Television coverage of St Petersburg 300 actively deployed the chronotope in shaping the meanings it produced. References during commentary on the G8 summit to Peter's creation *ex nihilo*, for example, highlighted the city's perpetual renewal of the temporal cycle (*Vremia*, Channel 1, 23 May 2003). Yet that very perpetuity established an eternal time represented in television's foregrounding of what the Channel 5 commentator on the White Nights Festival called its endless 'suspension of the cycle of day and night' (*Inform-TV*, Channel 5, 25 May 2003). The slogan with which all local coverage of the ten-day festivities opened – '10 days of a new century' (*desiat' dnei novogo veka*) – seemed to reconfirm

St Petersburg's (re)orientation towards the era about to unfold, thus linking the city with the Great Time of imperial history.[12] According to its own myth of origins, St Petersburg is itself a space in which normal temporality is abandoned: it defied linear time, springing from nowhere. The notion of a cancellation of the laws of chronological time emerged in the carnival parades to which the *Telemarafon* special dedicated an entire day and a half (*Telemarafon*, Channel 5, 27–28 May 2003). As Dayan and Katz suggest, the modern national celebration aims to achieve 'charismatic legitimation', balancing its ceremonial function by involving large crowds in 'carnivalistic festivities that are in part spontaneous and self-generated'.[13] As well as emphasising the democratic participation crucial to St Petersburg's contemporary self-image (it is promoted as the city in which Russia embraces the best of modern western practice), carnival, for Bakhtin, invokes a time when hierarchies are temporarily overturned, kings dethroned and new, subversive kings crowned in the ultimate interests of renewing the established order.[14] Appropriately, in reports on a ceremony carried over from 2002 to 2003, we witnessed Iakovlev 'bowing to the will of the people', having his tie ceremonially cut off in a comic, carefully choreographed emulation of revolutionary retributions against French nobility (*Inform-TV*, Channel 5, 27 May 2003).

Local jubilee broadcasts point to the subsuming of carnival time into the official news sphere with its dual temporality of reassuring regularities and transient ephemera. For example, the '10 days' slogan deployed before *Inform-TV* bulletins was later supplemented by constant references to the 'jubilee decade', as though carnival's 'time out of time', when enacted in Petersburg space, implies renewal as constant as time itself. This in turn enabled the renovation projects to be presented as part of a rolling programme in which May 2003 was merely one milestone.

Likewise associated with the linking of carnival time to St Petersburg space was the stress on celebration as an active re-creation of the past in the present. The tercentenary provided the opportunity to renew past tradition by recreating it in a context in which *ex nihilo* recreations are the norm. The Hermitage door ceremony demonstrated that, in facilitating this feat, the carnival chronotope synthesised elements from native monarchist and revolutionary traditions together with 'alien' components (democracy and free enterprise) in the creation of a new tradition based around a city associated with the permanent suspension of conventional value hierarchies. The demotic emphasis also helped to blend the historical re-enactments with contemporary events like the pop concerts in Palace Square and on Vasil'evskii Island, rendered in news bulletins through sweeping panoramas which evoked the temporary occupation of the imperial city's central spaces by spontaneous, unordered masses (*Inform TV*, Channel 5, 23 May 2003 and 29 May 2003).

As a rule, however, central spaces were reserved for choreographed parades, and the margins for spontaneous, participatory activities. The hierarchical structuring of city space was reinforced through a general principle of media events: the authentication of conventionalised activities occurring at the nation's heart via candid reports on rule-breaking acts of celebration perpetrated at the peripheries.[15] The principle reversed that which applies in iconography where stylised images gravitate towards the peripheries, and naturalised figures towards the centre (Uspensky 1976). Accordingly, a news bulletin during the 2002 ceremony described how a trolleybus had been commandeered at the city's outskirts and painted in graffiti images (*Inform-TV*, Channel 5, 26 May 2002). This illustrates what Dayan and Katz refer to as television's use of spontaneous 'visual anecdotes' to 'naturalise' the pomp and ceremony of media events (Dayan and Katz 1992: 88–89).

But it was the temporal trope of renewal which predominated in the media's efforts to forge a new tradition from the tercentenary. Each re-enactment balanced deference to the past with a gesture towards the new. During the spectacular synchronised fountain display which followed the (re) launching of Peter's fleet and which drew inspiration from the famous fountains at Peterhoff Palace, viewers were reminded that this was a departure from recent technological practice. As Dayan and Katz argue, 'the power of [media] events lies, first of all, in the rare realisation of the full potential of electronic media technology' (Dayan and Katz 1992: 15). In the case of St Petersburg 300, radical renewal is central to the tradition itself.

The notion of renewal extended to the logic of human temporality. It is not merely that Petersburg time follows a different pattern from that inhabiting other spaces but that here time *itself* is subject to constant renewal. The ceremonial clock started in 2002 displayed the words 'Petersburg time' (*Peterburgskoe vremia*). 'A new time has commenced' (*poshlo novoe vremia*) was the Channel 5 reporter's gloss on the phenomenon (*Inform-TV*, Channel 5, 27 May 2002). Significantly, the clock doubled as a television screen recording the crowds in attendance. Television imparted twenty-first century modernity to St Petersburg temporality, suggesting that the new time was, like television and the city, ridden with human intentionality.

Television must reconcile the special temporality of media events with the everyday temporality of routine, passing ephemera. Dayan and Katz contend that such celebrations 'interrupt daily life and offer a time-out from the complexities and animosities that characterize it … They … celebrate a golden age which, for a moment, is contrasted with the present' (Dayan and Katz 1992: 152).[16] The St Petersburg 300 approach was to introject events drawn from everyday temporality into a grand narrative. In another instance of media–state collusion, the one-off gift of a free apartment was offered to the families of the first boy and girl born on anniversary day. Thus, childbirth (a routine occurrence in 'small time') intersects with the Great Time of a City's (re)birth (*Inform-TV*, Channel 5, 27 May 2003).

The clock-screen betrayed a profound self-reflexivity, as St Petersburgers viewed television images of people seeing themselves on television (*Inform-TV*, Channel 5, 27 May 2002). One of the values attached to the St Petersburg chronotope is precisely this ability to foster self-admiration from without. Iurii Lotman has traced the notion of a city conscious of itself as spectacle to the façade-like architecture before which Peter the Great paraded with theatrical self-consciousness to foreign visitors (Lotman 1990: 191–202). Because of the city's liminal location, contemporary St Petersburgers are both inside and outside their own city, capable of seeing themselves from the perspective of the western companies to which at the same time they display themselves. Thus, the jubilee was able without contradiction to embody revitalised Russian imperial tradition yet also accommodate western commercial concerns.

Televisual self-reflexivity and the emergence of a media tradition

There is a second, important, level of self-reflexivity highlighted by the clock screen: that of television's consciousness of its own key role in the jubilee celebrations. The opening of the Press Centre, the focal point of jubilee activities, was covered in a deluge of televised events, including a prize-giving ceremony for the journalist considered to have produced the best report on the jubilee preparations (*Inform-TV*, Channel 5, 26 May 2002).

As well as purporting objectively to represent official celebrations, media events offer an equivalent to the 'lost participatory dimension' of the pre-modern popular festival, generating a form of 'diasporic celebration' (Dayan and Katz 1992: 24), a function which accords closely with Bakhtin's account of some modern, carnivalesque literature. The tension is neatly encapsulated in the BBC ploy of using familiar news anchormen (and women) to front its coverage of state occasions, yet allowing them in a temporary suspension of norms to indulge in effusive, vernacular discourse.

The same fusion of medium and event was evident in the St Petersburg television coverage of the city carnival. On one hand, the *Telemarafon* host promoted television's role in allowing the viewer to remain in his/her arm-chair as the cameras brought the carnival into living rooms; the studio's mock living room set, with sofas and a television screen, mediated between viewing audience and carnival. Television events claim to represent national ceremonies in their totalities, 'flattening out' their interactive contours and rendering them as objectified spectacles (Dayan and Katz 1992: 23). On the other hand, the *Telemarafon* studio was decked out in gaudy carnival décor, and the reporters at the parade were shown cavorting with the revellers (*Telemarafon*, Channel 5, 28 May 2003).[17] Television here embraced Bakhtinian carnival logic, according to which the boundaries between spectator and participant are erased.[18] This contradiction can also be explained by reference to St Petersburg television's dual consciousness of itself as a model of/rival to national television (the emphasis on facilitating living room spectatorship of a distant event), and yet also as a key carrier of local identity (the stress on its own festive activities).

Reflecting the absence of established generic formats for ceremonial occasions, the title, *Telemarafon*, highlighted both the exceptionality of the media event and television's heroic role in covering it from beginning to end. Its semi-humorous tone also diminished the official ceremony's sanctity, re-familiarising it and translating the vocabulary of official rhetoric into that of popular culture. For television is 'that which abolishes distance', bringing the normally inaccessible official realm into the intimacy of the living room (Dayan and Katz 1985: 30), and extending the boundary-eroding force implicit in Williams's concept of televisual flow from the multiple texts within television's broadcasting output, to the relationship between the television text as a whole and its audience.

The saturation coverage implied by the concept of 'telemarathon', together with its carnivalesque associations of a breach of norm, sits uneasily with television's 'serious' reporting function. The contradiction demonstrates Dayan and Katz's thesis that in 'destroying the events' "aura", television tries to reinject it through strategies that repeat themselves from media event to media event' (Dayan and Katz 1985: 26). Thus, the party atmosphere fostered in the studio (one such strategy) contrasted with the highly structured organisation of the broadcast day in which regular jubilee updates were given and numerous experts, like army officers for the cadets' parade (*Telemarafon*, Channel 5, 26 May 2003), and cultural historians for the carnival parade (*Telemarafon*, Channel 5, 28 May 2003), were invited to offer advice.

The saturation coverage was driven by both a centripetal logic (all routine events and broadcasts were absorbed into a unifying jubilee frenzy) and a centrifugal logic (the effects of the jubilee were displaced outwards onto peripheral issues). In the prolonged verbal commentaries through which they were often articulated both logics reflect the continued subordination of image to word characteristic of Soviet approaches to media events like Victory Day and May Day (coverage of the progress of the naval parade along the Neva lasted nearly four hours; *Inform-TV*, Channel, 30 May 2003). A generic trait of media events is the interspersal of voice-over with extended periods of silence in which due reverence is shown to anniversary rituals and events 'speak for themselves':

> the voice must be quiet, hushed, reverent, the statements concise, sparse and grammatically simple in order to be interrupted at any point ... one can expect the editorialising function to be performed inside the event and not by the narrator's voice.
>
> (Dayan and Katz 1985: 27)

The carnival coverage in *Telemarafon*, by contrast, featured incessant debate between studio guests and host in which the crowd scenes served merely as the background pretext to unbroken dialogue, suggesting that contemporary Russian television still adheres in part to the very different generic principles of the Soviet media event.

Tercentenary commentary was characterised by fulsome historical accounts; the reopening of the Hermitage door, for example, was accompanied by an unbroken torrent of historical information (*Inform-TV*, Channel 5, 25 May 2003). This marks a stark contrast with, for example, BBC commentary on the Queen's 2002 Golden Jubilee which interwove sporadic historical titbits with pieces of arbitrary trivia (such as the fact that the horses drawing the Queen's carriage were provided by East End undertakers). As well as relieving the austerity of the occasion, this bolstered the mystique of the royal tradition (the arbitrariness represented by the decision to hire East End undertakers marked the tradition's irrational rootedness in the mists of ancient ritual). Whereas Russian television spelled out in words the meaning of the historical re-enactments it reported (that of the new national ideology), BBC ceremonial tradition located symbolic meaning within the visual rituals of the anniversary celebrations themselves.

Russian broadcasting is, however, acquiring many of the authenticating attributes of its western counterparts as it develops its own ceremonial tradition. The studio discussions which dominated the telemarathon were structured around streams of studio experts. For example, guests from the military and academia offered explanations of the pre-revolutionary history of the cadets' parade (*Telemarafon*, Channel 5, 6 May 2003). The advice proffered was demystifying (accounting for the parade's intricacies and historical context), yet also (re)mystificatory (it enwrapped the artificially invented tradition in the discourse of expert opinion). In this way, St Petersburg 300 confirmed the notion that, during media events, television 'reinstates [distance] in the very process of abolishing it' (Dayan and Katz 1985: 30).

Media traditions are sustained by the intersecting discourses and linguistic registers (expert and everyday, political and academic etc.) they purport to integrate into a single organic whole. For example, in one erudite Channel 1 programme, university professors explicated the Orthodox church's role in Petrine Russia, dressing the celebratory attitude to Peter's impact on Russian history in the respectable cloak of academic discourse (Channel 1, 30 May 2003). Another national broadcast devoted to Aleksandr Men'shikov, the city's first governor, blended documentary discourse with overtly fictional techniques, including richly embellished re-enactments of key scenes from his life (Channel 1, 30 May 2003).

Throughout 2003, national television was in fact preoccupied with the tercentenary. Special programmes devoted to prominent St Petersburg figures, such as Dostoevskii and Anna Akhmatova, and showings of films connected with the St Petersburg theme (for example, the 1938 film of A. Tolstoi's historical novel, *Peter the Great*) recurred in the schedules. During jubilee week, the two main national channels featured high-flying talk shows on the St Petersburg intellectual tradition; special editions of popular talk shows such as *The Big Wash* (*Bol'shaia stirka*) recorded in St Petersburg (Channel 1, 24 May 2003); premieres of Sokurov's *Russian Ark* and Dostoevskii's *The Idiot*; as well as the first programmes in a series on the Russian Empire, and one on St Petersburg entitled *St Petersburg from A to Z* (NTV, 23 May 2003). During jubilee week, the breakfast show, *Good Morning* (*Dobroe utro*) featured interviews with prominent St Petersburgers describing their favourite city haunts (NTV, 23–30 May 2003). This exploration of the event from every possible angle, its integration into the fabric of the television schedule and the daily routines of the viewers is one aspect of the 'working through' phenomenon discussed in Chapter 1.

In other respects, St Petersburg ceremonial coverage indicated a media still at the threshold of tradition: hence, the pedagogical approach adopted for many jubilee functions. Among the guests invited into the telemarathon studio during the carnival parade were experts who, in addition to recounting the phenomenon's origins in medieval Europe, lamented the fact that the St Petersburg variant (itself only six years old) is insufficiently participatory, and offered advice on what participants should be doing. This was followed by grandiloquent claims that in watching the carnival 'we witness the creation of history' and reminders that, thanks to TV, viewers could now enjoy the festivities from their lounges (*Telemarafon*, Channel 5, 28 May 2003). Thus, television 'propose[d] a self-portrait' in which it 'exhibit[ed] the very process of its being communicated to them' (Dayan and Katz 1985: 32), fulfilling the dual role of 'teaching' people how actively to celebrate carnival, yet also accustoming them to the role of passive observers of the (re)emergence of a historical tradition.

St Petersburg 300 and the façade of media democracy

Carnival's central role in Petersburg 300 enabled it to feed into the rhetoric of democratic participation. The extent of the carefully fashioned media–democracy symbiosis was apparent in the fact that the first event held in the Press Centre, organised collaboratively by Iakovlev and local television, was a civic forum intended to give St Petersburgers a chance to share in the festive preparations. Crowds assembled throughout the city. Iakovlev began by calling on citizens to exercise their civic responsibility. Encouraging people 'to make suggestions rather than ask questions', he hailed the forum as a democratic experiment and the beginning of a new era linked both to Peter's original project, and to the new democracy in which Petersburg was again transforming the city's rebirth into the rebirth of a nation (*Inform-TV*, 29 May 2002).

The hall in which Iakovlev's administration was filmed had its own audience seated before a screen on which they saw what the viewers saw at home, turning them into a carnivalesque spectacle to themselves and erasing the boundaries between audience and performance. Viewers were constructed as random participants in the democratic project, whilst television acquired the dual function of both the viewing 'eye' of the forum, and its first-person, articulating 'I'. Contrary to its rhetoric of a democratic holding to account, however, Iakovlev gave pat answers to uncontroversial questions, whilst journalists addressed him with deference, conveying little sense of the processes of government.

Throughout, Iakovlev's team sat against a backdrop of banners advertising foreign sponsoring companies. The tendency to portray civic democracy and global capitalism as part of a single utopian enterprise is a feature of media representations of the new Russia, especially those promoted by the 'progressive', Eurocentric intelligentsia traditionally associated with the Petersburg myth. Even as it forged a local identity, the jubilee furnished a microcosm of post-Soviet culture in general.

When the exercise was repeated in 2003, Iakovlev began by asserting that it was because he 'listened to the people's advice' in 2002 that the celebrations had been successful (*Inform-TV*, Channel 5, 30 May 2003). The 2003 forum followed a question and answer format in which ordinary people were described as 'journalists for the day'. However, in one of many mismatches between (global, 'democratic') form and (national, 'authoritarian') content displayed during St Petersburg 300, there was no right to reply to Iakovlev's carefully pre-meditated answers and tendentious points such as the plight of homeless tramps were barely pursued by the 'real' journalists.

In his answers to concerns expressed, Iakovlev portrayed the jubilee as a challenge that it was every St Petersburger's duty to address, eliding the ebullient discourse of civic democracy with the controlled rhetoric of national pride and local tradition. Via the 'civic duty to celebrate', Iakovlev conflated the Great Time of the narrative of nation (that of Russia's democratic destiny symbolised in St Petersburg, the source of this mission) with the immediacy of the news event (the duty to deal with the jubilee's practical challenges).

In 2003, the editing reflected official ideology still more closely. Whilst Iakovlev spoke, the soundtrack of his voice was accompanied not by facial close-ups (as in 2002), but by panoramic sweeps across attentive crowds. The *image* of a pseudo-carnivalesque *demos* merged with the *words* of a pseudo-democratic leader in a media-manufactured word–image ideologeme derived from the city's emergent, and highly contradictory, post-communist mythology.

The 2003 forum integrated pre-recorded montage sequences into live coverage of the question and answer session. When the transport minister dealt with a question about local transport, his answer was accompanied by a pre-edited sequence depicting the innovations to which he referred (*Inform-TV*, Channel 5, 30 May 2003). A journalist's question about the jubilee met with a slick montage of 'ordinary people's' answers. The range of opinions expressed was broad enough to suggest a democratic spectrum (the strongest objections amounted to mild irritation about the disruption to routine), but sufficiently controlled not to contradict the self-congratulatory atmosphere. The montage thus both represented the jubilee, and contributed to the celebratory atmosphere it was intended to generate. Once again, the elision was facilitated by the nexus of symbolic values: St Petersburg as the site of Russian modernity and thus both of democracy and technological advancement, but also of self-display (commentators consistently vaunted televisual feats, like the incorporation of web-based feedback channels).[19] The civic fora, therefore, encapsulated the uneasy reciprocity between an emergent, self-conscious media culture and the centrally managed construction of a national tradition.

Conclusion

Through its co-production of St Petersburg 300, Russian television appeared to reveal its complicity in a government-led effort to revitalise imperial tradition for the post-communist era. The rituals and myths invoked, the discourses employed, and the temporal continuities with the imperial and the more recent Soviet past, all position the St Petersburg narrative at the centre of this mission.

In particular, the saturation coverage on local channels enabled the tercentenary media event to generate a distinctive space–time accommodating a national ideology of renewal in which the pre-revolutionary imperial tradition was synthesised with contemporary, free-market capitalism, Soviet ritual and, in its deployment of carnival logic, participatory democracy. At the same time, the St Petersburg chronotope promoted a local identity project which, precisely by *offsetting* its national counterpart, complemented and *authenticated* it.

Crucially, however, television's role went beyond that of mere facilitator of the invention of tradition. In a parallel process, it established the rudiments of a generic model for the televising of national celebrations. The metatextuality characterising that model entailed the medium inscribing itself into the very participatory process it claimed to describe. In so doing, it confirmed that, paradoxically, it is both much more, and somewhat less, than a passive tool of Putin's increasingly authoritarian regime. On one hand, far from obediently suppressing democratic rhetoric, Russian television actively internalised and eviscerated it, recasting it for incorporation into a hegemonic nation-building project. On the other hand, clashes between the pseudo-democratic, global forms adopted, and the far-from-democratic cause in which those forms were enlisted, and between the patriotic heritage celebrated, and the hesitant, self-conscious media tradition which the celebration inaugurated, meant that the projected outcome of the project might be a diminishing rather than a consolidation of central control over its meaning. As a result, current western concern over the level and nature of state–media collusion under Putin appears, curiously, to represent both a trite exaggeration and a naive understatement of the true state of affairs.

3   Russia's 9/11

Performativity and discursive instability in television coverage of the Beslan atrocity

Introduction

When New York's twin towers fell, news broadcasts struggled to convey the enormity of this strike at the symbolic heart of the world's sole superpower. Since 9/11, however, concrete features have been ascribed to the faces of the perpetrators of the Evil, stories of bravery have emerged from the rubble of the World Trade Center, and 9/11 has been inscribed into the narrative of post Cold War American nationhood, just as it has enabled Al Quaeda to fill the chasm vacated by the evil Soviet Empire. Tales of martyrdom amongst the passengers of the jet that was downed in Pennsylvania, the bravery of fire-fighters who returned repeatedly to the collapsing towers, and the final mobile phone calls to loved ones from those aboard the two jets which crashed into the World Trade Center all now feature prominently in 9/11 folklore.

Since 2001 the 9/11 'brand' has also been exported to other nations. The Madrid bombings preceding the Spanish elections of 2004 have been dubbed 'Spain's 9/11,' just as the Beslan school siege became known as 'Russia's 9/11,' and the events in Britain of July 2005 are now referred to ubiquitously as '7/7'.[1] Paradoxically, an event designed to shake the world's superpower from its consumerist fantasies has itself taken the form of a consumer format! But it is a format with national specificities. In Russia's case the Beslan outrage coincided with a new curtailment of media freedom; one of NTV's flagship talk shows, *Freedom of Speech* (*Svoboda slova*), hosted by the prominent liberal journalist, Savik Shuster, was, in a development not directly related to Beslan, cancelled in the very same month. Shortly before this, Leonid Parfenov's equally controversial current affairs magazine programme, *Lately* (*Namedni*), suffered a similar fate. Some commentators will point to post 9/11 and post 7/7 curtailments of free speech in the USA and UK, but in Russia the imposed constraints were not only much harsher; they were, moreover, happening well before the emergence of any hint that the country was about to suffer a terrorist outrage of this order. Russia also deviates from other 'warriors on terror' in that its nation-building project must navigate between a partially rehabilitated Soviet past and an ambivalently viewed, western-dominated present, and in the intensity with which recent terrorist outrages have shaped that navigation. Writing before Beslan, Ivan Zassoursky suggests that the 1999 Moscow apartment bomb blasts which he refers to as the Russian equivalent of 9/11, 'started the process of the almost instant reconstruction of the Russian mentality' (Zassoursky 2004: 230). Unusual likewise is Russia's television culture, emerging from (and now retracting back into) a controlled environment of mutually reinforcing, state-sponsored voices emphasising the inevitable, the ritualistic and the positive.[2] Russian news broadcasts are still developing a set of generic conventions for the representation of anomalous, unanticipated catastrophes and, despite a sequence of recent disasters exposing media incompetence and/or inexperience (e.g. Chernobyl, the Kursk submarine disaster, the Nord-Ost theatre siege and the apartment bombs – all precursors of Beslan), in the 2004 school siege, they reached a milestone in this process..

Our exploration of how the approach to the problem adopted by Russian news links with, and ultimately complicates, the national identity construction task it has been assigned focuses on certain challenges posed to a media system by its need to collude with a government regime which, authoritarian public image notwithstanding, is beset by profound ideological instability. Our analysis is based on six editions of *Vremia* (*Time*), the main evening news programme of Channel 1, now effectively (along with the RTR channel), Putin's official mouthpiece. The sequence spans the event and its immediate aftermath (the siege itself lasted from 1 to 3 September, with 6 and 7 September declared as national days of mourning). Since our focus is the ideological, post-atrocity processing of meanings derived from Beslan, rather than the spontaneous representation of the atrocity itself, it is the bulletins of 4, 5 and 6 September which we draw upon most. Details of the times and dates of particular broadcasts referred to during the course of our analysis are given parenthetically in the text. Our argument proceeds thematically, focusing first on the key imagery and mythology to emerge from Beslan; then on aspects of the news discourse supporting it, arguing that both seemingly perform the (re)integration of a fragmented nation, before identifying within the representational strategies underpinning this process a tension between the requirement that the events be assimilated to familiar models, and the need to render them in their shocking, chronotopic alterity. We conclude with two brief, but hopefully instructive, post-Beslan epilogues. One draws parallels between the Russian media's culture of terrorism and that of the BBC following the 7/7 London bombings. The other reinforces the paradox according to which the more tightly controlled a nation's media is, the more unstable its war on terror discourse.

Terror and the iconography of nation building

Russia's worst terrorist crisis began when gunmen took schoolchildren and adults hostage on 1 September 2004, at School No. 1 in the Russian town of Beslan in North Ossetia. At 9.30 am, the morning of the first day of the autumn semester, a group of around thirty armed men and women, arriving in a GAZel van and a GAZ-66 military lorry, stormed the middle school, whose pupils were aged from seven to eighteen years. Most of the attackers wore black ski masks and a few were seen carrying explosive belts. After an exchange of gunfire with police, in which five officers and one terrorist were killed, the attackers seized the school building taking more than 1,300 pupils, parents and teachers hostage and traumatising them with the prospect of blowing up the school with the numerous bombs they had wired throughout the building. Their demands seemed to involve the immediate withdrawal of Russian troops from Chechnia. On 3 September, the third day of the stand-off, shooting broke out between the hostage-takers and Russian security forces.[3] The reasons for the shooting and the bloodbath which followed are, to this day, unclear, but it seems likely that unprovoked, precipitous action by the FSB troops surrounding the school may have played a role.[4] According to official government data, 344 civilians were killed, 186 of them children. Hundreds more were wounded. The terrorist attacks were master-minded by Chechen terrorist leader Shamil Basaev and his Ingushetia-based deputy Magomet Ievloiev. President Putin ordered a two-day national mourning period for 6 and 7 September September. The second of these days saw 135,000 people join an anti-terror demonstration in Moscow's Red Square. The identities of the hostage-takers is one of the many contentious issues surrounding the siege, but according to official Russian sources, the attackers were an international group consisting of Arabs, Tatars, Kazakhs, Chechens, Uzbeks and even one local Beslan resident. (The propensity within the Russian media to internationalise terrorist outrages on Russian soil by linking them with the Arab world rather than with Chechnia is well established.)

September 1 marks the day when children throughout Russia return to school after the summer holidays, bearing gifts for their teachers in a time-honoured ritual occupying a sacrosanct place in the Russian calendar, a ritual, moreover, unifying communist past with post-communist present. If 9/11 was an assault on sacred American space (the twin towers of the World Trade Center symbolise the USA's position at the core of global capitalism), then Beslan was a calculated affront to hallowed post-Soviet temporality. The terrorist mission and the Russian media response thus furnished mirror images of one another as Channel 1 acted to annul the traumatic insult to Russia's collective memory by saturating its coverage with melodramatically effective pictures of the very category of Russian citizens (children) whose sacred day had been defiled.

Indeed, Channel 1 lost no time in exploiting the memories of a Soviet Union unified around shared rituals. Reports on reactions to the tragedy on 4 September broadcast from across the former USSR formed part of an implicit effort to reunify the space of the former superpower (*Vremia*, 21.00, 4 September 2004).[5] Putin picked up this thread in his speech to the nation broadcast on the morning after the siege, referring wistfully to a 'gigantic country which had proved unsuited to the modern world,' but whose 'core' (*iadro*) had been conserved and strengthened through the post-Soviet Russian Federation (*Vremia*, 21.00, 4 September 2004). Beslan provided an opportunity to reconstruct (post-)Soviet space. It also served to rearticulate a set of values associated with Soviet time.

Throughout carefully edited coverage of the siege's immediate aftermath, images of headscarved mothers weeping for their children, familiar from Soviet Second World War iconography, were accompanied by the emotional, sometimes even pseudo-religious, words of the newsreader, Ekaterina Andreeva, declaring in a striking break with the journalistic conventions associated with news-reading, 'We weep with you' (*My plachem s vami*), and, in a trope of established socialist realist lineage, claiming Beslan's children as the 'loved ones' (*rodnymi*) of the entire country (*Vremia*, 21.00, 5 September 2004).[6] Thus, when, the following day, Putin addressed the Beslan parents, telling them that 'the whole country suffers, grieves and prays with you' (*vsia strana stradaet, skorbit i molitsia s vami*), his words appeared to emerge organically from the journalistic discourse by which they were framed, masking and 'naturalising' his control over an ideologically subservient media (*Vremia*, 21.00, 6 September 2004).

Another abiding image, used in a recurring continuity montage, was that of distraught parents displaying photo-portraits of their lost children (*Vremia*, 21.00, 5 September 2004; 6/9/04). This image became an icon of post-Soviet culture thanks to the popular missing persons TV show *Wait For Me* (*Zhdi menia*), itself founded on the conceit of an eternally fragmented national family forever in the process of being made whole.[7] The family trope was deployed in a highly individualised manner. The 5 September *Vremia* evening broadcast, for example, headlined with the tale of one injured girl, now 'smiling again for the first time'. It concluded with images of children in their hospital beds surrounded by their teddy bears, elaborating an 'imaginary community', to cite Benedict Anderson's richly productive term, intimately sharing the despair and hopes of each parent in turn (*Vremia*, 21.00, 5 September 2004).[8] The visual rhetoric, with its pathos-inducing close ups of abandoned toys strewn across the disaster scene, was as emotive as the accompanying commentary. The *Vremia* bulletin of 6 September opened with images of siege victims, each separated from the next by the sound of a gunshot. The same bulletin concluded with a montage of images of children recovering in hospital accompanied by the sound of a heartbeat growing in volume to the point where it merged with that of every viewer who now, also, shared the perspective of the wounded child-victim (*Vremia*, 21.00, 6 September 2005). The switching of subject positions achieved a binding of subject (protective parent) to object (vulnerable child), and imagined community of anonymous viewers to individualised victims. The heartbeat metaphor would have been familiar to most Russian viewers, since it was used during Eltsyn's 1996 re-election campaign, when the ORT channel (now Channel 1) ran a highly effective advertisement incorporating an electronic countdown to election day accompanied by the sound of a heart beating and a slogan implying that the infant 'heartbeat' of Russian democracy was at stake. Thus, the heartbeat metaphor acquired in Beslan a metonymic dimension (the heartbeat of real Russian children, maimed by terrorism, was now under threat) which in turn enhanced its performative effect; the onus was on actual doctors and nurses, and by implication all Russians, to preserve the heartbeat of these real children and thereby maintain the nation's life breath.[9]

Vremia made much of the transportation of injured children to Moscow hospitals. The reassuring scenes of children in their hospital beds surrounded by bustling medical teams portrayed the children's arrival in Moscow as a homecoming from the traumas of the front line, aligning centre (the capital) and periphery (the North Ossetian town of Beslan) in an intimate embrace (*Vremia*, 21.00, 4 September 2004). At the same time, Moscow was itself simultaneously depicted as the locus of renewed danger. On 1 September, Beslan reports were succeeded immediately by a follow-up report on an earlier Moscow metro bomb in which the Islamic group responsible was linked with Al Quaeda. The report also contained security advice to Muscovites on using the metro and an interview with Sergei Ivanov (the Minister for Foreign Affairs) who referred to a hidden enemy in a war in which the front line is everywhere (*Vremia*, 21.00, 1 September 2004). This constant oscillation in Moscow's status from (secure) centre to (endangered) front line reminded viewers of the previous spate of terrorist bombings on the Moscow metro, and the apartment bombings of autumn 1999 in Moscow, Volgodonsk and Buinanksk which provided the immediate pretext for the second Chechen war. It thus established Beslan as part of a logical sequence of events, and far from resulting in a sense of inconsistency, consolidated its mediatory, nation-binding function. Moscow was now both the vulnerable 'child' of an entire nation at risk, and paternalistic 'protector' of that nation.

Tales of heroism were quick to emerge after 3 September. Particularly prevalent were narratives of official FSB heroes. In a defiantly nostalgic, but now increasingly common, re-invocation of the self-sacrificing dedication of the secret police, *Vremia* dedicated an entire report to the fate of an FSB soldier whose face had been deeply disfigured by the injuries he had suffered, but who nonetheless declared his intention to return to active service as soon as he had recovered (*Vremia*, 21.00, 4 September 2004).[10] Such narratives were complemented by tales of martyrdom among ordinary people, including the grandfather who perished at the school rescuing other people's grandchildren (*Vremia*, 21.00, 5 September 2004), tales which drew sustenance from the tide of Second World War mythology then rising in anticipation of the 60th anniversary of the victory over fascism. Equally reminiscent of the old Second World War films and documentaries was the demonisation of the hostage-takers. Andreeva's characterisation of the terrorists as 'scum' (*podonki*) in the 6 September broadcast, and her question 'Who are they, these beasts (*zveri*) who shot children in the back?' recall Stalinist depictions of the Nazis (*Vremia*, 21.00, 6 September 2004). Actual events again conspired with the intertextual myths cited in the nation-building project with which they coincided to forge a single master-narrative of Russian identity which transcended the divide between present and past, fact and fiction, objective account and propaganda mission, and which generated, seemingly spontaneously, an image of the archetypal Russian as a victimised but resilient subject.

Russia's refusal to be bowed by Beslan was emphasised in reports on choreographed occasions depicting Putin bombarding his staff with questions, engaging in practical actions rather than verbal rhetoric (*Vremia*, 21.00, 4 September 2004).[11] In his address to the nation, he talked of the need for a 'mobilisation of the country' (*mobilizatsiia strany*), describing the terrorist action as a 'challenge to the whole of Russia' (*vyzov vsei Rossii*) (*Vremia*, 21.00, 6 September 2004).

Vremia struck a balance between this unified national perspective and the need to internationalise Beslan. The first day's report was framed by reports on terrorist activities in Chechnia and Afghanistan and a Hamas bus bomb in Israel, before it moved to domestic issues in a reversal of the usual *Vremia* running order (*Vremia*, 21.00, 1 September 2004). The post-siege analysis featured reports on the identity of the terrorists referring pointedly to '10 immigrants from Arab countries' (*10 vykhodtsev iz arabskikh stran*), along with one negro, Chechens, Daghestanis and a local resident (*Vremia*, 21.00, 4 September 2004). This analysis was complemented by reports on condemnations from CIS leaders and sympathetic western governments, though, in a tactic reminiscent of Soviet tendencies, none of the accompanying calls for a peaceful resolution to the Chechen crisis were mentioned (*Vremia*, 21.00, 4 September 2004). Russia was thus located at the interface between two geo-semiotic spaces with opposing values from Russia's borders through Chechnia to Afghanistan and Egypt (the terrorist 'breeding grounds'); and from Moscow, through the former Soviet republics, to Europe and the USA (the 'terror-fighting' nations). Such a location confers simultaneously upon Russia intra-national coherence and credibility as an international force. Beslan, then, can be said to have enabled Channel 1 to 'perform' Russia's intra-national coherence through a horizontal (re)integration of former Soviet space with the peripheral, contemporary space of Beslan, the space of the centre (Moscow), and that of the civilised world beyond.

The vertical integration of discourse levels

This horizontal integration was complemented by a vertical integration based around a conflation of normally discrete discourse levels. In his account of media discourse, Norman Fairclough distinguishes 'sequential intertextuality' (the combination of different genre and discourse types in linear sequence) from 'embedded intertextuality' (the incorporation or embedding of one genre or discourse type within another) (Fairclough 1995:

88). Later, referring specifically to the news reporting of disasters, he lists the main categories subject to intertextual linking as the discourse of state leaders, that of the victims, bureaucratic–technical discourse (references to the legal issues involved in the post-disaster investigation), scientific–technical discourse (descriptions of crime detection technology), and the discourse of the ordinary witness (Fairclough 1995: 99). The script of a newsreader, whilst providing the horizontal link between discourse types in an intertextual sequence (interviews with victim, then witnesses; account of technical aspects of disaster; speech of state leader; etc.), also embeds within itself elements from each of these discourses. But, given the news script's primary function – that of mediating the values of the official realm to the ordinary viewer – the structure of the embedding process must ensure the pre-eminence of what Fairclough generalises as 'discourses of public life' (discourses spoken by the impersonal, anonymous voices of officialdom) over what he calls, invoking Habermas, 'lifeworld discourses' (discourses articulated from the individualised subject positions of ordinary people) (Fairclough 1995: 164). This can be achieved via mechanisms ensuring the framing of lifeworld discourses by public life discourses. In other words, the 'objective neutrality' of the news script is a function of the clarity with which 'subjective' lifeworld discourses are held in check and framed by public life discourses. As we saw in Chapter 1, Fairclough expresses this elsewhere by reference to the related distinction between *author, animator* and *principal.* Thus, a newsreader might *animate* words of reassurance *authored* by a senior soldier, but of which the government is the hidden *principal.* By placing the words in quotes, and in the absence of a terrorist counter-statement or a clear indication of the government's agenda, the impression is created of an objective account, authenticated by reference to a neutral, technocratic discourse.

Beslan precipitated a breakdown in the principles of embedding, and of the implicit rules by which author, animator and principal are articulated in 'objective' news reporting. When, immediately following the siege, Andreeva embedded within her news script the emotive rhetoric of condemnation (rhetoric later adopted by Putin), she abandoned any attempt to frame lifeworld discourses by public discourse, or to order the voices of author, animator and principal according to any pre-existing hierarchy. For by reassuring the people of Beslan that 'we are weeping with you' (*my plachem s vami*), and then, commenting on the pouring rain in Beslan, that 'nature wept with the people' (*priroda plakala vmeste s narodom*), she integrated author, animator and principal into a single outpouring of nationalist rhetoric (*Vremia*, 21.00, 6 September 2004). Similarly, when referring to the hostage-takers as 'terrorists [who] called themselves suicide bombers (*smertniki*), but when it came to fighting … hid behind children', Andreeva aligned her own status as animator and author entirely with the vernacular discourse of the hypothetical outraged citizen who serves as the statement's principal (ibid).[12] And, in announcing that the terrorists had been 'annihilated' (*unichtozheny*) and 'liquidated' (*likvidirovany*), that they had not escaped 'righteous punishment' (*vozmezdiia*), she synthesised a brutal Russian military idiom and the pseudo-religious language of moral indignation within a minimally marked journalistic discourse (ibid). This, to be clear, is quite different from the mere loss of objectivity often suffered by newsreaders and journalists when such horrific events occur on western soil, following the 7/7 events in the United Kingdom, for example. In such cases, the position of the principal (official government sources) may come to dominate that of the author (the BBC), but the words of the animator (the newsreader) are nonetheless phrased in a professional lexicon which maintains the formal boundaries separating journalist from government (or journalist from eyewitness). The generic integrity of the bulletin as 'objective news' broadcast is thus maintained in a way that it is not in the case of Beslan.

During the unfolding of the Beslan atrocity, *Vremia* displayed a correspondingly anomalous approach to the horizontal, sequential relationship between newsreader and on-site journalist. Channel 1 inverted the norm by which the anchor frames the more subjective voice of the live reporter with the more measured discourse of the newsroom. It is true that on-site reporters were only marginally less partisan than news anchors; the conclusion drawn in one report was that, because of the 'sacrilege' (*koshchunstvo*) against Islam constituted by the Beslan atrocity, 'terror had lost' (*terror proigral*) (*Vremia*, 21.00, 4 September 2004). But it fell to Andreeva to then pronounce the final anathema: 'It is impossible to find any justification for such scum' (*Nevozmozhno naiti opravdanie takim podonkam*), finally exhorting viewers, 'Do not be indifferent!' (*Ne bud'te ravnodushnymi*) (*Vremia*, 21.00, 4 September 2004). Her embedding discourse was thus contaminated by the subjective core of the complex of discourses it was intended to embed, as the process of vertical integration flattened all discourses into the single, undifferentiated voice of wounded nationhood. As we have argued, and will again suggest in our conclusion, the temporary weakening of journalistic codes of objectivity is far from unique to Russian media responses to terrorist atrocity, but the post-Beslan descent into extreme, patriotic emotionalism was of an order unparalleled elsewhere. More importantly, however, and in a further departure from post-terror reporting in the west, we shall suggest that such hysterical excess points to the *insecurity* of the state-controlled media's position in Russian society, rather than its secure enchainment to its governmental masters

The terror chronotope

The integration process coexisted with the need to convey the full scale of the disintegration it reversed, and upon which it was predicated, and the sense of unprecedented horror the outrage provoked. When it first broke, the newsreader referred to its 'epicentre' (*epitsentr*), announcing that the channel was ready to go live to the scene at any point (*Vremia*, 21.00, 1 September 2004). On 4 September, the *Vremia* format was suspended as the programme switched to an extended, heavily edited account of the previous day's events. (On 3 September, *Vremia* was stunned into virtual silence by the tragic dénouement, curtailing its lunchtime edition, which went on air soon after the carnage had occurred, to ten minutes, before ceding the air to an adaptation of Lawrence's *Women in Love*, its pretence at live spontaneity virtually abandoned.)[13]

As Patricia Mellencamp has observed in her account of television coverage of catastrophe, 'television is shock and therapy; it both produces *and* discharges anxiety' (Mellencamp 1990: 246). Indeed, operating in parallel with representations of the siege as connoting sheer, alienating difference was a contrary tendency to reorient them towards the familiar sphere of the self.[14] Within minutes of the first report, it was referred to by the now standard abbreviation for 'terrorist act' (*terakt*) (*Vremia*, 21.00, 1 September 2004). The second day featured the ritualistic roll-call of foreign condemnations; technical maps of the school depicting in precise diagrammatical form the location of hostages and hostage-takers (a ploy tested in coverage of the Moscow theatre siege two years earlier); expert commentaries; speculatory analyses of the terrorists' identity and the siege-breakers' strategies; and witnesses' retrospective accounts (*Vremia*, 21.00, 2 September 2004). All these devices indicated a pre-established set of procedures of which only one needed to be deployed in order for the entire model, or 'visual script', to quote Fairclough, to be invoked (Fairclough 1995: 124). When the critical moment was reached, and in accordance with the visual script for terrorist crises, the rhetoric of 'breaking news' with which the event had been announced was re-invoked (albeit following *Vremia*'s embarrassing time-delay) and the television screen was awash with chaotic imagery, accompanied by breathless commentary (*Vremia*, 21.00, 4 September 2004). In the aftermath of the crisis the roll-call of official statements and foreign condemnations gave way to the leader's address to the nation; as the days proceeded, retrospective accounts of the crisis and its aftermath and analyses of its consequences and significance provided a transition into the post-crisis coverage as the news bulletins gradually returned to normal.

If the *terakt* required a dual mode of representation – as both category-defying shock and pre-modelled media script – then the source of the terror was represented as pure alterity. The hostage-takers generally remained hidden and objectified as the abstract embodiment of evil; at one point, a journalist asked pointedly if the terrorists were 'really worthy of the name of human beings' (*Vremia*, 21.00, 5 September 2004). This was in contrast with ever bolder and ever more acute particularisations of the people's suffering: the close-ups of toys in hospitals, the badly injured boy reassuring doctors of his masculine steadfastness, the grandmother who told of children forced to drink and wash in their own urine (*Vremia*, 21.00, 4 September 2004; 5 September 2004 and 6 September 2004).[15] Images of the terrorists, but for the fly-ridden corpses triumphally displayed at the end of the siege (*Vremia*, 21.00, 4 September 2004), and the degraded figure of one live captive

(5 September 2004 and 6 September 2004), were restricted to archive footage of armed men praying to Allah (2 September 2004).[16]

The deletion of individual agency in respect of the source of the terror found linguistic incarnation in the persistent use of impersonal, third person constructions in which, however, the vague, impersonal origins of the terrorists was mirrored in the equally impersonal, official sources working invisibly to capture them.[17] Apprehender and apprehended formed part of a single representational system in which each was dependent on its opposite, and both were cast into a single 'terror chronotope', a place cut off from the everyday familiar spaces and regularised rituals of news reporting, suspended in an indefinite crisis time devoid of the normal rhythms of cause and effect.

Whilst terror in its essence remained disembodied and unrepresentable, the abstraction of the shady group responsible for the *terakt* was displaced onto the embodied spectacle of the lone captive quivering in humiliation, accompanied by the newsreader's voiceover referring to him in the most derogatory term available – 'bandit' (*bandit*) – and announcing with barely disguised contempt that the man 'offered a prayer to Allah' with every denial he uttered (*Vremia*, 21.00, 5 September 2004). The image of the abased hostage-taker recalled the constantly rebroadcast western images of a humiliated, dishevelled Saddam Hussein following his capture by the Americans. So recently inflated into a demonic figure of awe, Saddam was now depicted being forcibly subjected to a dental inspection as though he were a reluctant child. As Slavoj Zizek comments in this context, 'Enemy recognition is always a performative procedure, which constructs the enemy's true face. Once he is revealed, the omnipotent scary monster turns into a blotch waiting to be erased' (Zizek 2004: 64).

Shreen Hunter (2004) has gone so far as to argue that the demonised Islamic other now occupies the role of the treacherous Jew in Russian racist tracts, whose perpetual gesturing both beyond Russia's borders and to its core is replicated in the paranoid dualism of anti-terrorist discourse: a 3 September *Vremia* report identifying the Beslan hostage takers as Arabs and Caucasians linked with Bin Laden and Maskhadov, then referred to shady Islamist cells (*iacheiki*) at work within Russia's borders (*Vremia*, 21.00, 3 September 2004). These images of international Islamic extremism annulled the moderate Muslim expressions of indignation broadcast on 1 September when a leading Russian imam is heard to curse the kidnappers as 'defilers of Islam' (*Vremia*, 21.00, 1 September 2004).[18]

As the ready availability to Channel 1 of moderate Muslim opinion indicates, Russia has not lacked experience in handling the representation of disaster, from Chernobyl in 1986, to the Nord-Ost theatre siege in 2002. However, two key principles of the managed media event were not adhered to during Beslan. First, the switch to what Daniel Dayan and Elihu Katz call a 'syntactics of interruption' involving 'the most dramatic kinds of punctuation available to broadcasters' was clumsy and incomplete (Dayan and Katz 1985). The regular programming schedule was minimally changed; even the lengthy advertising breaks characteristic of Russian television continued to be aired throughout the crisis, one of the many criticisms made by the *Ivestiia* journalist, Irina Petrovskaia, before the sacking of the paper's editor.[19] Secondly, post-Beslan coverage did not undergo the long 'working through' phase by which, according to John Ellis, 'television provides increasing stability to ... images of disorder ... by parading issues, questions or worries for a time, within slots that are regular' (Ellis 1999: 59). Within a week of 3 September, Channel 1 was more or less back to normal and by November, bulletins rarely mentioned the siege. There have been few paratextual treatments of the tragedy.[20] Because the extremism of the news discourse failed to be matched by the length of coverage sustained beyond the crisis, the imagined community of outraged patriots became harder to sustain.

Beslan and generic transgression

The lack of correlation between the tenor of news broadcasts during and immediately following Beslan itself, and that of subsequent broadcasts, highlighted the degree to which coverage of the crisis transgressed generic boundaries. The extreme rhetorical excesses and emotive photomontages that we referred to earlier subverted the very status of the broadcast as news, as the reporting of the atrocity and the emotions it generated was subsumed into the atrocity itself. The abandonment of any pretence at western-style neutrality betrayed a breach of the frame separating journalist and news team from the event they were reporting which engaged dialogically with both the western news model to whose external forms *Vremia* pays lip service, and the Soviet propaganda model cited intertextually in the programme's retained Soviet-era title and signature tune. Such an approach accorded with the frame-breaking gestures persistently and, often, self-consciously, exhibited by post-Soviet news and current affairs programmes, sometimes in support of, and sometimes in opposition to, government propaganda (see Chapter 1).

In Beslan's case (as with the 1993 assault on the White House, and the 1996 election coverage), the transgression of generic boundaries served the naked interests of the government. However, the effect was in a key sense identical to that achieved in instances of oppositional transgression. For here, too, the transgression indicated a lack of stability in the status of the news broadcast as a *mediator* of state ideology, as a means of grounding the 'truth and wisdom' of government policy in the commonsense apparatus and language of 'objective reporting'. It signalled, in other words, an absence of hegemony in the Gramscian sense. Instead of, as in 'mature' democracies, mediating between the interests of the state and the values of the populace at large, post-Soviet Russian news is liable to 'break free' from its roots within the official sphere to embrace the oppositional values and interests of a wider populace and 'turn against its masters'. More often, of course, as we have seen with Beslan, the absence of a convincing and coherent hegemonic strategy on Russian state television is reflected in its tendency to superimpose in unmediated form upon the vernacular culture of the viewing public the language and values of the state.[21]

Conclusions

The frame-breaking excesses through which *Vremia* enacts its participation in its own object of representation confirm performativity as the common thread running throughout the aspects of Beslan coverage that we have considered; the iconography of a nation 'dismembered' by terrorist outrage and performatively reconstituted; the active reintegration of normally discrete discourse levels; the performance of Russian identity.

We conclude with two brief epilogues from which, however, we might initially draw rather different inferences. First, we might note that BBC treatment of the immediate aftermath of the July 2005 bombings displayed some uncanny resemblances to Channel 1's post-Beslan coverage (which predated 7/7 by almost a year). The Russian emphasis on moderate Islamic condemnations, like that of Channel 1, was intense. And the BBC initially relegated to the margins attempts to link the incident with British involvement in Iraq, or with Islamophobia (a contributor to the first late-evening *Newsnight* broadcast following 7/7 who dared to make these connections was cut abruptly short). Given its earlier willingness to locate the causes of Beslan in Chechnia, the BBC thus unwittingly mirrored the strict, and unashamedly partisan, parameter setting which it had earlier identified in Russian coverage of Beslan. But, conversely, *Vremia*'s own reports on 7/7 projected onto Britain faults for which it was earlier assailed. For example, in highlighting the BBC's decision to excise scenes from the aftermath of 7/7 considered too distressing, *Vremia* merely echoed earlier criticisms of state-led Russian television for its censorious over-reaction to the perceived excesses of NTV coverage of the Nord-Ost siege (*Vremia*, 21.00, 10 July 2005). And the special *Vremia* report on protests from British journalists concerning police reticence in releasing fatality numbers replicated a complaint identical to that made by the BBC during Beslan about Russian government/media collusion (*Vremia*, 21.00, 11 July 2005).

The apparent convergence of otherwise quite distinct media discourses (one that of a mature democracy with a relatively autonomous fourth estate, the other that of a 'managed democracy' in which the managed has now virtually eclipsed the democratic) that this hall of mirrors effect indicates, would seem to caution against overplaying the exclusivity of Channel 1's patriotism, pointing to the emergence of a global 'war on terror' media culture based on an accumulation of televised outrages beamed across the world to audiences ever more accustomed to the generic features of the *terakt* format. But the very mirroring effect that *Vremia*'s account of 7/7 illustrates is also indicative of the manner in which all countries, particularly those in which government and media are bound in close collusion, exploit global terror events to bolster their own domestic agendas. This should alert us to the corresponding danger of understating the very real differences dividing public service stations like the BBC from government mouthpieces such as Channel 1, differences we have already seen reflected in the distinction between a mere reduction in objectivity (BBC) and a complete collapse of the generic norms for news reporting (*Vremia*).

What we also saw, however, was that *Vremia*'s Pavlovian obedience, aversion to alternative opinion and crude propagandising are indicative not of a complete convergence of government and media, but, to the contrary, of a disjunction born of Channel 1's inability to internalise the political positions it is called upon to disseminate. When those positions are themselves riddled with ideological contradiction, the consequences for the reporting of issues surrounding the War on Terror are considerable. This leads to our second epilogue. For, spurred by Putin's post-tragedy speech, Beslan fuelled a wave of Soviet-style patriotic sentiment whose strong anti-Chechen, anti-Muslim element contributed to an alarming, anti-migrant, xenophobic backlash at the grassroots level, and an accompanying increase in hate crime, typified by the inter-ethnic, Russian–Chechen disturbances in the Karelian town of Kondopoga in 2006. This, in turn, has recently precipitated a number of backtracking measures, including a presidential summit on extremism in Russian society in 2006. Putin, his acolytes and successors now all mouth the phrase 'our many-peopled, multi-faith society' (*nashe mnogonarodnoe, mnogokonfessional'noe obshchestvo*) like a mantra, even as multiculturalism has fallen out of fashion in the UK and elsewhere in Europe. The xenophobic backlash has also been responsible for a distinct change of tone within the government-controlled media. NTV, for example, now boasts a weekly programme devoted to Muslim affairs, fronted by a hijab-wearing Muslim woman. Reports on the terrorist activity which continues to plague the North Caucasus are meticulously purged of any reference to Islam and treated as criminal activity. And coverage of inter-faith tensions in western Europe take a distinctly pro-Islamic, politically correct line, as in a report on a Dutch minister's anti-headscarf campaign indicates (Channel 1, *Vremia*, 25 November 2006). Like the words of the moderate Muslim interviewee, the presenter appropriates, and then ridicules, the voice of his opponent, the conservative Christian party proposing the ban. When he reminds us that Holland is called 'the most liberal country in Europe', then refers to it as 'the most immigrant-tolerant people' (*samyi terpimyi k immigrantam narod*), he, too, implicitly subjects the self-identification of the Dutch right to mocking rebuttal: 'now regards [immigrants] with suspicion' (*teper' smotrit na nikh s podozreniem*). This performative enactment of multiculturalist values is in sharp contrast with earlier commentaries on Channel 1's *Odnako* programme targeting virulent criticism at western multiculturalist leniency following Chechen terrorist atrocities.[22]

The servile enthusiasm with which Channel 1 imbibed the new tolerance has on occasion led to inadvertent divergences from the elusive government line, as in a report on the council on extremism, convened when Putin's grip on the media had strengthened still further than in 2004 (*Vremia*, Channel 1, 12 December 2006). During the report a Channel 1 journalist referred with dripping sarcasm to Vladimir Zhirinovskii's presence at a call for vigilance regarding right-wing assaults on foreigners, framing the nationalist leader's comments with a cutting commentary: 'Zhirinovskii was astonished, for, until now, he had been considered the country's most extreme politician. Vladimir Vol'fovich thought a little and decided that extremism was nothing to do with him' (*ekstremizm – eto vse-taki ne pro nego*). The audacious sarcasm is articulated from a position at odds with a president calling for the very restrictions on migration recently demanded more colourfully by the now Kremlin-approved Zhirinovskii himself, indicating Channel 1's embarrassing failure to assimilate the government positions it aspires so slavishly to transmit.

By contrast, a report from the very same bulletin covering celebrations of Russia's Constitution Day concentrated on the actions of the Young Guard, the youth section of the party most loyal to Putin, United Russia (*Edinaia Rossiia*), broaching the movement's struggle to defeat nationalist extremism, and then its contradictory proposal to replace the phrase 'multinational people' with 'Russian people' in the country's constitution. Rather than comment on this glaring inconsistency from the 'politically correct' viewpoint of the now officially multiculturalist regime, the presenter opted for a neutral, non-committal hedging of bets: 'clearly it now remains for the State Duma representatives to decide' (*reshat' teper' predstoit, ochevidno, deputatam gosdumy'*). Russian news presenters either transparently enwrap the regime's guiding voice within western-style, pseudo-neutral discourse, or articulate it in open, Soviet-style polemic, but never engage in the subtle hegemonic mediation between official and popular culture(s) typical of, say, the BBC. The hedging of bets we see here is rather a function of Channel 1's clumsy struggle to process and make sense of a highly contradictory government stance.

Taken together, our epilogues confirm that the full ramifications of the Beslan tragedy point both outwards, towards the wider War on Terror, and inwards, towards the cultural specificities of Russia's own anti-Chechen campaign, but in perhaps unexpected ways. Conventional wisdom dictates that a unified global anti-terror campaign, centred on the post-9/11 USA, and supported by other western nations, has been appropriated for cynical nation-building purposes by an authoritarian, non-western regime desperate to maintain the integrity of an anachronistic imperial state. However, what our analysis shows, is firstly that the so-called 'global' campaign is itself the discursive effect of a decentred process of intercultural mirrorings and exchanges in which each participant articulates a variant of a larger war from which it differentiates itself (the BBC's implicit distinction between understated, post 7/7 British stoicism and American hysteria), yet also cites in the interests of authentication (the term 7/7 is, after all, modelled on 9/11). Secondly,

the invocation of the War on Terror for performative, nation-building purposes appears ultimately to work to a destabilising rather than a unifying
effect. This presents particular problems to a state-controlled television channel
tasked with imposing ideological conformity on the meanings it broadcasts.
The final legacy of the tragedy that was Beslan may yet surprise us.

We need now, however, to explore the extent to which state-imposed ideological conformity is consistent with a television culture which, perforce, embraces
the full range of western-style entertainment genres. The next four chapters
treat key exemplars of such genres, beginning with the ubiquitous *tok-shou*.

4 Promiscuous words

The post-Soviet *Tok-shou* as cultural mediator and hegemonic pressure point

Introduction

We turn now to a television genre which lies on the boundaries between news and current affairs, and the realm of entertainment: the talk show. The advent of the talk show is a defining moment in television history. Though it exists in many different formats, one thing they all share is the (re)presentation of informal modes of talk which contrasted with the arch, stilted tones of the official realm. In the west, the genre emerged in the late 1950s and then gradually infiltrated the schedules, disseminating its influence over neighbouring genres.[1]

Whilst light entertainment genres incorporating spontaneous, everyday speech entered Soviet television schedules in the late 1960s (e.g. pop variety shows featuring the home-grown pop star Alla Pugacheva, and the stand-up comedy programmes of Zhvanetskii and Khazanov which drew on the Russian tradition of oral anecdote telling), the talk show was, because of its dangerous verbal promiscuity and defiance of the dominant rhetoric of the written word, notable by its absence. Variety and comedy shows were in fact recordings of carefully honed theatrical performances (filmed in theatres, rather than studios), reflecting the Soviet view of television as a medium subordinate to 'higher' cultural forms. Indeed, the dominant rhetoric was based on the written word (news broadcasts were measured at the production level in numbers of 'pages').

Live, unmediated talk did occur on Soviet television in the form of the extended interview. Leading cultural figures such as the poets Evtushenko and Akhmadulina would subject themselves to long question and answer sessions whose formal orientation had little in common with the spontaneous and often multi-participant 'chat' that had by now established itself as a staple of western broadcasting. Things changed with glasnost (Gorbachev himself was hailed as the first Soviet leader to dispense with the dreary cadences of official party rhetoric). In programmes like the glasnost flagship, *Vzgliad*, the untrammelled language of rock stars and skinheads began to be heard. With the post-1991 reduction in government subsidies, the economic imperative asserted itself. The new influx of globalised television programming facilitated the emergence of the Russian talk show which was cheap to make, had mass appeal and bore the post-Soviet values of free speech. As a result, the Russian television schedules were soon swamped with a proliferation of what were rapidly dubbed '*tok-shou*'.

Whilst we shall not ignore history, our analysis is primarily based on a cross-section of *tok-shou* broadcast between 2001 and 2007. The analysis is divided into two parts. In Part I, we outline four main themes. We begin by examining the blurring of generic borders between the *tok-shou* and other genres, and on the relevance of the seeping of 'text' into 'extra text' to the construction of the post-Soviet celebrity. This discussion is preceded by a delineation of the varieties of *tok-shou*. While negotiating the 'text–extra text' confusion, we pay attention to the emergence of distinctive post-Soviet generic hybrids which combine talk show formats with models from related genres, some from the Soviet past, others from the west. We then identify a distinctive *tok-shou* 'chronotope' with a bearing on how post-Soviet culture negotiates its relationship with both the Soviet past (marked temporally) and a present dominated by western models derived from the west. This leads to our core theme, that of the *tok-shou* as cultural mediator, for it is the heightened hybridity of the genre which enables it to negotiate the intersection of post-Soviet culture's temporal-spatial axes. The rapidity with which an alien western format transposed itself onto Soviet television is indicative of that format's ability to mediate not only between the Soviet past and a western dominated present, but also between two established television cultures. Moreover, the influx of vernacular speech into an environment dominated by official rhetoric, and the presence of a studio audience as intratextual representation of the home viewership, renders the *tok-shou* the supreme public/private mediator.

Under Putin, television and the official sphere became increasingly synonymous, yet vernacular forms based on adaptations of western models took ever-firmer hold within the media realm. This paradox and its ramifications for the regime's efforts to assert political control and for the emergence of hegemonic consensus is highly significant. Precisely because of its dual affinity with official and vernacular culture, the *tok-shou* furnishes the ideal tool with which to manage 'knowledge' and 'public opinion', to provide authentic, individualised representations of public opinion on topical issues. In a society presenting itself as free-speech oriented, exchanges of opinion in a talk show format bear considerable semiotic value, but they are also fraught with danger. On a macro level, we consider the range of issues and opinions available to the post-Soviet viewer, and the boundaries of the fora in which the exchanges occur. On a micro level, we examine how talk is structured in specific televisual instances. The handling of issues discussed on talk shows reveals how knowledge is categorised and constructed. In this context, we address the ways in which TV experts mediate between post-Soviet official and popular knowledge, and how they interact with celebrity culture as a form of popular knowledge.

In Part II, we conduct a case study based on Andrei Malakhov's *Let them Talk* (*Pust' govoriat!*) (but with a brief detour via Pozner's *Times*), focusing in detail on the cultural mediation issue approached via an examination of the relationship between television 'text' and audience opinions derived from the show's online forum. Our analysis reveals a high level of discursive inconsistency out of step with the Putin agenda and the show's status as a 'safe' entertainment form, and indicative of a 'hegemonic pressure point' in post-Soviet culture.

Part I

Methodological issues: Circulation, genre and cultural meaning

In positing the *tok-shou* as cultural mediator, we penetrate to the heart of the way in which television produces meaning. Genre is fundamental to that meaning in that it shapes audience expectation and serves as the axis around which the circulation of cultural signs revolves. An investigation of generic conventions and generic boundaries and of the differing values attributed to generic forms reveals the prime issues at stake in the battle to stabilise cultural meaning. John Fiske claims that genres 'form the network of industrial, ideological and institutional conventions that are common to both producer and audiences out of which arise both the producer's program and the audience's readings' (Fiske 1987: 111). As Scot Olson puts it:

> [G]enres inculcate what is present across many texts significant to a particular culture, undergirding the authorship of each text. A genre reveals what is ideologically, morally, and narratologically important ... The genre anchors the text to the culture, insuring that it will be meaningful.
> (Olson 2004: 118)

Television's textual boundaries are permeable not only in the relationship between television-as-text and the extra-textual realm of audience discourse, but also through the internal hybridisation that takes place amongst them. Holmes and Jermyn identify television's use of genre as 'slippery', reflecting a post-modern 'self-reflexive and self-conscious interplay between different programme forms' (Holmes and Jermyn 2003: 6). Talk shows emphasise this point forcefully, dividing into a multiplicity of overlapping formats and drawing on other genres.

National television is beset with tension; on one hand, because it requires huge resources, its texts are normally articulated from an establishment position. On the other hand, because the large input of resources demands a mass audience as its justification, it must make concessions to popular taste. John Fiske suggests that not only has the dominant order 'created ... the means of its own subversion', but 'its very existence now depends upon those fissures and weaknesses that make it so vulnerable to the incursions of the popular' (Fiske 1989: 26, 127). It is in the talk show that the unofficial voices of the street are most thoroughly mixed with those of consensus opinion and of the powers that be, in what Wayne Munson calls 'a promiscuous, hall-of-mirrors inclusiveness' (Munson 1993: 5). The relevance of this insight for post-Soviet Russia is self-evident.

Our analytical framework will modulate from section to section, each of which will draw on models relevant to the topic it treats. As the notion of generic leakage brings the discussion into the area of the semiotic 'space' occupied by the *tok-shou*, we will utilise aspects of Lotman's theory of the semiosphere (Lotman 1990). Sonia Livingstone's work on talk show audiences and civil society (Livingstone and Lunt 1994) and Kevin Glynn's Foucault-inspired analysis of the talk show as a forum for the marginalised and the unofficial (Glynn 2000), will influence the section on cultural plurality. Gripsrud's analysis of television and 'common knowledge' (Gripsrud 1999) influences the section on knowledge categories.

Generic variety in the post-Soviet talk show

The Russian word *tok-shou* covers what in English is divided into 'talk show' (programmes in which topical issues are discussed by a moderator and guests plus audience), 'chat show' (in which the host interviews celebrity guests) and 'discussion show' (in which political and social issues are discussed by a panel in response to questions from an audience). The *tok-shou* retains its dual western connotations of free speech and popular entertainment. The conflation of the two terms marks the post-Soviet tendency to assuage the tensions between 'democracy' and 'capitalist consumerism'. This in turn has affected the look and format of the *tok-shou*.

In the early 1990s, serious discussion shows abounded across all channels. One of the most watched programmes was a political discussion show called *Vox Populi* (*Glas naroda*), hosted by Svetlana Sorokina, which aired on Russia's first independent channel, NTV, and in which vital issues were debated before a participatory audience consisting of people in key positions of influence. The very name reflected continuities with the glasnost period, but, like the latter, the show located this voice not in the common populace, but within a liberal elite. One of the most memorable editions was the extended live show that coincided with the Putin government take-over of NTV in June 2001. Politicians and journalists from across the spectrum discussed events likely to lead to the demise of the very format in which the discussion was being held (the show was cancelled in 2002). This exemplified a kind of self-reflexivity peculiar to post-Soviet television; with issues over the ownership and democratic function of television central to early post-Soviet Russia's ongoing political crisis, television journalists frequently found themselves in the position of reporting on events in which they themselves were the key actors (e.g. the dramatic attempt by conservative nationalists to take over the Moscow television tower in 1993). The political talk show served as the point of maximal fluidity between text and extra-text, but in such a way that the boundary across which meanings flowed was foregrounded and, paradoxically, the textuality of the genre reinforced.

Talk is the supreme lubricator of the cultural channels between past and present. The approaching millennium spawned a deluge of media talk which served to blend reminiscing about the Soviet past with the urge to integrate post-Soviet Russia with the civilised world in an act of communal reflection on the passing of an era. An ORT show called *Witness of the Century* (*Svidetel' veka*) which began in 1999 featured one-to-one interviews with prominent people who played significant roles in those aspects of Russia's Soviet past still considered worthy of note and thus eligible for incorporation into the post-Soviet nation-building project.

In the mid-1990s a brand of one-to-one talk show which drew both upon the sudden 'discovery' of informal western modes of media talk and the continuing Russian emphasis on the power of 'the word' emerged. A previously little known figure, Sergei Solov'ev, built his media personality around two such shows which he hosted with considerable skill – *Breakfast with Solov'ev* (*Zavtrak s Solov'evym*) and *Passion, Solov'ev Style* (*Strasti po Solov'evu*). The interviews were filmed in intimate settings, in the case of *Breakfast*, around Solov'ev's kitchen table, connoting the traditional Soviet 'kitchen-table philosophizing'.

A brasher adaptation of western celebrity culture also emerged with *By Myself* (*Ia sama*) hosted by one of the first television stars of the post-Soviet era, Iuliia Men'shova. The title emphasised the hostess's individual star quality, but also the idea that ordinary women are able to assert their rights in this new era of licence. The 'conceits' around which the show was constructed (male guests were sat on an 'accuseds' bench' whilst the female host, guests and audience questioned them on gender-related topics) placed feminist stridency in ambiguously ironic quotes.

In the late 1990s, late night sexual scandal shows made their appearance with *About That* (*Pro eto*) whose title, however, betrayed a residual attachment to 'high cultural' tradition (it refers to a Maiakovskii poem about love). In 1997, after the setting up of the Culture Channel to promote high cultural Russo-centric broadcasting in the face of western-led trivialisation, a spate of shows hosted by writers appeared. *School of Scandal* (*Shkola zlosloviia*) hosted by culture figures, Tatiana Tolstaia and Dunia Smirnova, used a curious mix of the 'cosy' kitchen-table chat and the structured 'grilling' of guests from the cultural world before an invited audience.[2]

The first decade of the new century has seen the consolidation of another trend rooted in Russian tradition. Some of the longest-running Russian shows used formats constructed around an abstract theme reflecting the continuing predominance of verbal–literary culture over the ocular-centric discourse of stardom. An RTR show dealing with controversial issues adopted the title *Short Circuit* (*Korotkoe zamykanie*) in reference to the fact that the discussion generated is guaranteed to produce electric sparks. Two other popular RTR shows still running in 2007 are *Private Life* (*Chastnaia zhizn'*) dealing with 'relationship' issues, and *What a Woman Wants* (*Chto khochet zhenshchina*) in which women put forward issues within the bounds of traditional family values.

In 2004, the most popular post Soviet *tok-shou* was *The Big Wash* (*Bol'-shaia stirka*), based loosely around the notion of an unfettered 'display' of variegated issues mixed together in the tumble-drier of a television studio ('This is *The Big Wash* – anything goes' was the catchphrase). Its host, Andrei Malakhov, acquired a cult status fostered by an active web-based chat room. Each show centred on several discretely treated issues which took the form of a proverb-like axiom: 'To give or to take?'; 'School was the best time of my life'; 'Relaxing is harmful'; etc. The discourse was vernacular and the host addressed his guests in informal manner. The studio was decked in balloons adorned with the show's washing-machine logo and the atmosphere cultivated was pseudo-carnivalesque. The rhetoric was one of eccentricity and convention breaking, but it never strayed into the political realm. Since *The Big Wash* ended in 2005, Malakhov, now a leading Channel 1 celebrity, has hosted several successor shows with similar formats (see Part II).

Political *tok-shou*s became increasingly rare under Putin. One exception was *Basic Instinct* (*Osnovnoi instinkt*) hosted by a newly rehabilitated Svetlana Sorokina. It claimed to refuse to treat those in power differently from ordinary people by positioning audience and guests on benches arranged non-hierarchically across the studio. This, however, resulted in *less* audience input than in programmes like the BBC's *Question Time* in which the formal 'panel plus audience' arrangement ensures that, in a deliberate replication of the structures of parliamentary democracy, the politicians are held to account by their electors. In *Basic Instinct*, the very absence of a structured approach to the handling of the issues meant that, far from ensuring equality of contribution, the politicians and experts prevailed. Nonetheless, because of the range of opinions expressed and Sorokina's independent voice, the programme was discontinued in 2004.

A highly popular programme still running is Channel 1's *Wait For Me* (*Zhdi menia*) which reunites relatives estranged from families who have given them up as missing, often from Soviet times, and always from different corners of post-Soviet space, thus engaging in nation building by linking past with present and centre with periphery.[3] The format integrates documentary footage, interviews 'in the field', and a studio discussion hosted by an avuncular older man and a younger woman and culminating in the live act of reunification accompanied by copious sentimentality. The discussion is rigidly controlled, with audience participation restricted to brief segments, and clear evidence of post-recording editing.

Another index of the generic hybridity to which the post-Soviet talk show is prone is the variety of personae adopted by the programme hosts. In *The Big Wash*, Andrei Malakhov, with his loud clothes and quirky manner, introduced the paradigm of host as performer. *School of Scandal*, by contrast, combined the personae of the two intellectuals engaging in intimate discussions with that of the formal 'interview panel', but through its title, it also cited down-market, 'trash TV'.

In each generic hybrid, the talk component tests out established cultural paradigms in two contradictory ways. On one hand, the free flow of vernacular discourse accorded western-style informality and discursive promiscuity to starchy Soviet models. On the other hand, the prevalence of unconstrained 'chat' is domesticated through native vernacular idioms. Thus, in *The Big Wash*, remnants of the model of television host as master of ceremonies were 'modernised' through the informal manner of presentation and the brash studio set. At the same time, Malakhov's informal chat with his guests betrayed the lingering presence of indigenous discursive traits, such as the propensity for the long anecdotal narrative, what Nancy Dies calls the female 'litany' (a mode also highly prevalent on *What a Woman Wants*), and the rituals by which Russians formally congratulate each other on national celebration days (Dies 1997).

Tok-Shou *chronotopes and the negotiation of abstraction*

The *tok-shou*'s ability to ameliorate the tensions between a Soviet past and a western-oriented present through its promiscuous propensity to flow across generic modes and discourse types presupposes a specific *tok-shou* 'chronotope' (Bakhtin 1981). First, the ability to integrate Soviet intertexts (those belonging to a temporally absent, but spatially proximal 'Self') with western intertexts (those emanating from a co-present but spatially distant 'Other') generates a chronotopic unity of Space and Time, Self and Other. In *School of Scandal*, (and *Breakfast with Solov'ev*), the studio sets connoted the familiarity of the Soviet past, whilst the free-ranging debate reflected the newly permissive orientation towards western values. The act of mediation transformed the domestic intimacy of the setting and discourse mode into the novel and unfamiliar value system of western free speech. This duality was enacted through the show's very structure which was divided between a studio-based interview and a one-to-one conversation in an apartment. As Part II will demonstrate, an awareness of the *tok-shou*'s western origins remains at the forefront of viewer consciousness and this phenomenon has intensified in the wake of the recent cooling of relations between Russia and the west.

The *tok-shou* studio is characterised by high-tech graphics and space age ambiances. Even when the 'interview sofa' is included, it is rarely of the cosy, domestic kind. In *Short Circuit*, the participants were arranged at sharp angles to one another, in an attempt to replicate the theme of sparking conflict. The chronotopic structure of such shows invokes a futuristic, vaguely westernised no-place counterbalanced by the supposed topical urgency of the issues discussed. The balance is weighted further towards abstraction through the restricted nature of the topics discussed and the manner of their

treatment. The seemingly open-ended title of *What a Woman Wants* is a mis-
nomer for a programme which cultivates a highly traditional view of gender
roles, with subjects such as 'Should a man go to any lengths to defend a
woman?' and 'What is male solidarity?' Similarly, the beguiling title of
NTV's *Land of Soviets* (*Strana sovetov*) promised a parody of Soviet rhetoric
but, in the pun that it incorporated, ('*sovet*' can mean 'advice' as well as
'council') delivered a conservative 'women's affairs' programme in which
celebrities dispensed advice about cooking and home decoration.

*Tok-shou*s are generally centred on concepts, rather than personalities:
Short Circuit, School of Scandal, and so on, rather than Kilroy and Donahue. In keeping with the tendency towards chronotopic separation from the
immediacy of time and place, most *tok-shou*s are not broadcast live, though
Vladimir Pozner's political discussion show, *Times* (*Vremena*) is an exception. Instead, elaborate, pre-recorded sequences are edited into the discussion
format, reconfirming the sense of a world closed to unpredictable, up-to-the-
minute reality. In *Wait for Me*, for example, the family reunions are engi-
neered in a highly melodramatic fashion involving pre-recorded, tear-jerking
interviews with the separated parties. Issues are thus 'consumed' as wholes
rather than 'contested' in real time. In *What a Woman Wants*, the hostess
concludes each show with a brief summative monologue which leaves the
received wisdoms on gender issues firmly in place.

The tok-shou *as public/private mediation mechanism*

The assertively bombastic Russian talk-show host(ess) is at odds with his/her
western models who claim to represent the shifting opinions of the populace.
This tension reflects the capacity of the *tok-shou* chronotope to synthesise the
open-ended western talk-show format with the finalising aspects of Soviet-
era media discourse. All talk shows strive to mediate between the popular
and vernacular discourse of 'ordinary people' (or of the celebrity in 'everyday mode') and the discourse of the official realm. This function in post-
Soviet Russia represents a measure of control applied by the official realm to
the vernacular discourse that it is 'admitting'. In Putin's Russia, room for
diversity was constrained, even as the outward forms of democratic discourse were maintained.[4] In a March 2004 *Basic Instinct* show devoted to
security concerns following the Moscow Metro bomb tragedy, four out of six
guests were drawn from government, the security services and right-wing
political circles; the other two were from academia and a human rights
organisation, although even the latter agreed that legislation should be made
more stringent. A December 2003 edition of the show dealing with the fall
of Shevardnadze from power in Georgia included amongst its guests the new
Georgian acting-president, a Georgian 'dissident' figure supported by the
Putin regime; representatives of the Russian government; the extreme
nationalist, Vladimir Zhirinovskii; and the market liberal, Anatolii Chubais.
The weight of opinion, however, was against the new Georgian president

(with Zhirinovskii merely representing an overstated version of the official position), an impression reinforced by the fact that the Georgian president was interviewed only briefly, via satellite link-up. In a *Times* edition from April 2007 discussing the Russian–Estonian conflict over Estonia's removal of Soviet war memorials, the only participant affiliated to the world of politics was Aleksandr Prokhanov, editor of the extreme right-wing newspaper, *Tomorrow* (*Zavtra*); the others were all from the arts, although the ensuing debate was animated. In this sense, Russian television culture resembles the sham imitation of democracy that Andrew Wilson has referred to as 'virtual politics' (Wilson 2005).

In non-political talk shows, there has been an overwhelming preference for guests from the world of entertainment and the media. *The Big Wash* mixed celebrity guests with ordinary people but the latter were selected not for their 'ordinariness', but rather for their quirky eccentricities. As we shall see in Part II, there have recently been signs of a shift towards the representation of a wider range of people in the selection of guests.

A second way in which the public/private mediation mechanism works is through the selection of discussion topics. Shows geared towards, and deriving from, the concerns of ordinary people nonetheless reflect the control exercised by programmers to ensure that boundaries established in the public realm are not crossed. A 2003 *Short Circuit* edition focused on the Soviet claim that 'There is no sex in Russia' – a seemingly controversial topic. But the discussion skirted around sensitive subjects like the growth in sexually transmitted diseases, focusing instead on the 'easier' topics of marital infidelity and pornography.

The *tok-shou* host also plays a mediatory role. Presenters can be chosen to portray a certain disposition towards the matters discussed or to represent a certain segment of society. *Short Circuit*'s sharp-suited male presenter was well matched to the programme's carefully manufactured controversies, as was the rotund, conventionally dressed hostess of *Land of Soviets* to its highly conservative mission. In western variants of the genre, the host performs a related function, by, on one hand, articulating the views of the 'man/woman in the street', and on the other hand, assuming the official consensus viewpoint embraced by the broadcaster in order to put the correct 'spin' on the views expressed. (Oprah Winfrey's ability to reach out to radical Afro-American opinion, yet recast it in moderate, mainstream mode is one illustration.) This function is conspicuous by its absence in post-Soviet Russian television.

Audience participation in the *tok-shou* is minimal. When permitted, it is normally restricted to tightly managed segments accompanied by expansive rhetoric about 'listening to the audience'. Another variant that has recently gained currency is the use of the electronic 'voting buttons' but, in averaging out single-word answers to carefully constructed questions, this hardly corresponds to the expression of popular opinion. In *Windows* (*Okna*), NTV's answer to the Jerry Springer Show, which ran in several seasons between

2003 and 2005, the odd device of the ten second gong limiting contributions at the end of the programme to brief sound bites was used.

The chronotopic 'finalising' phenomenon can be recontextualised as a form of authoritarian intervention into the free flow of opinion. Even in *Windows*, potentially the most anarchic of talk shows, the host, Dmitrii Nagiev, insisted on articulating the 'definitive' judgement on all the disputes he moderates, always grounding his judgemental peroration in a homespun ethics which, through his celebrity status, acquired the validating effects of the public realm.[5]

Precisely because they are oriented towards informal, popular discourse, *tok-shou*s are awash with traditional speech genres and value systems.[6] A *Big Wash* show aired on 14 February 2004 and dedicated to a celebration of Valentine's Day featured numerous semi-formal tributes to 'the fair sex' whose gender values ran counter to the show's contemporary 'feel'. In deploying speech genres deriving from outside the public realm, presenters 'ventriloquate' the voices of their putative audiences, temporarily 'borrowing' their modes of speech and value systems as a means of reassuring them that the public realm to which they belong is not alien. A crude illustration of this principle occurred in a March 2004 edition of *Windows*. One of the guests was a woman who had 'spiced up' her marital sex life by sleeping with a sequence of anonymous men. In articulating his archetypal sexist condemnation, Nagiev descended into the vernacular, describing her as a 'whore' using the Russian curse word (*bliad'*) which was 'bleeped out'. Such behaviour, unthinkable in any western talk show, demonstrates the curious mix of the off-beam with the mind-numbingly conservative which characterises post-Soviet television. When we consider the role a parallel example from the serious realm of political discussion in Part II, we will arrive at the full implications of the phenomenon.

Talk shows also provide the opportunity for the layperson to ventriloquate official rhetoric. By formulating questions to prominent figures on issues in the public domain, 'ordinary' people embrace the discourse of the empowered. In the BBC's *Question Time*, members of the studio audience question public figures on matters of national importance deploying the strategies of parliamentary debate. Even when such opportunities do arise on post-Soviet TV, the lack of a developed civic culture ensures that questions are couched not in the codes of political/public discourse, but in those of the everyday discourses of the vernacular. In an October 2002 edition of NTV's middlebrow *Domino Principle* (*Printsip domino*), a live phone-in on the topic of social deprivation elicited a call from a viewer who, unable to express her frustrations at government policy in party political terms, launched into a vague diatribe against 'the authorities' (*vlasti*). As Nancy Ries has argued, the linguistic conditions for democracy need to be in place before it has any chance of taking root (Ries 1997). The live phone-in, significantly, no longer exists on Russian national television.

The very word 'issue' conveys the notion of a problem with public currency. One of the functions of the talk show is to ensure that general issues are 'worked through' (to use John Ellis's term) in concrete situations, enabling them to acquire authenticity (Ellis 1999). Gender/family relationships feature heavily on *tok-shous*, with several retaining this as their exclusive theme. In a March 2004 edition of *Private Life*, the guests included a daughter horrified by the fact that her mother was having a relationship with a younger man. In the same month, *Land of Soviets* sought advice from a happily married couple on the secrets of a successful marriage, whilst *Private Life* interviewed a woman who justified nine divorces in terms of female sexual freedom. A March 2004 edition of *Windows* included interviews with a father and son who had been secretly writing pornographic fiction at the expense of the wife/mother and with another family in which the husband, an animated film artist, had, to his wife's dismay, been secretly earning money for producing erotic animations. An April 2004 edition focused on a man who had incurred the wrath of local women by buying up all condoms in an effort to combat a decline in moral standards. The comically unlikely narratives are matched by Nagiev's mannered persona and provocative, tongue-in-cheek interventions, and by the (undoubtedly correct) audience perception, confirmed in web forum discussions, that the show is 'not for real', and is performed by actors. *Windows* thus represents one of several examples of the incomplete post-Soviet internalisation of a western format from which distance is established through the adoption of a semi-mocking, deliberately 'performative' stance. To give a more serious example of 'working through', following a summer of inter-ethnic violence at Russia's markets, three autumn 2006 editions of Pozner's *Times* featured discussions of related themes (migration, national identity, xenophobia and criminality).

The treatment of the gender question veers between two poles, both of which exclude the possibility of a meaningful public/private dialogue. In *Windows*, gender problems were represented as the source of sordidly displayed personal narratives. The encounters were melodramatically built in stages, each of which added a new twist. The 'erotic novel' encounter began with the wife's complaint about a graphomanic husband, then proceeded to her concerns for her equally dilettante son, before the husband announced he had finished his novel, only to accuse the son of plagiarising from him, following which the wife then suddenly 'discovered' that both son and husband had been writing pornography. Even in *Domino Principle*, narrative and performative aspects predominated, the latter highlighted visually through the disposition of the presenters in relation to the guests they interviewed: at a distance and in a standing position. The *tok-shou* interview tends to be modelled less on the private conversation than on the stage performance less suited than the 'living-room' or 'village hall' studio to public/private mediation.

At the other end of the spectrum we find *Private Life* in which personalised narratives are eventually superseded by an elevation of the issues discussed to the level of 'eternal values' with currency in everyday discourse. Conflicts between men and women are resolved by reference to 'essential masculine needs' and 'the feminine', rather than socio-economic changes in gender statuses.

Representing celebrity on post-Soviet talk TV

One means of bridging the private/everyday and public domains is through the construct of the celebrity. As Richard Dyer shows, celebrity combines the distance associated with stardom with a sense of everyday familiarity (Dyer 1979). The celebrity is 'just like us, only a little more talented/attractive'. With their privileging of informal speech modes enacted in a performative arena, talk shows provide the ideal vehicle for celebrity.

The model of the TV celebrity as author/creator is a potent residue of Soviet-era literary-dominated discourses. Consolidating her status as the archetypal post-Soviet intellectual, Sorokina, for example, always began each edition of *Basic Instinct* with an account of how she came to choose the theme of the discussion. Pozner concludes every edition of *Times* with a lengthy peroration concluding with a subtle wordplay on the meaning of his show's title (*Vremena*). Several *tok-shou*s presented by figures pretending to literary status are advertised as 'authorial programmes' (*avtorskaia per-edacha*). The splitting of *School of Scandal* into the studio discussion and the kitchen-table rumination actualises the division between the role of the celebrity as the people's spokesperson and creative artist.

But the talk show is also a vehicle for the guest as celebrity. *The Big Wash* and *Domino Principle*, whose quotidian orientation would seem to require an abundance of ordinary people, often opted for guests drawn from the entertainment industries, since celebrity opinion on any issue supersedes that of ordinary people. Even the politically oriented *Times,* which eschews audience discussion, regularly inserts a guest from cinema or literature into its 'fresh face' (*svezhaia golova*) slot: the writer Viktor Erofeev and the director, Vladimir Khotinenko featured in several 2005–6 editions, seemingly to bolster the 'liberal, progressive' side of debates on nationalism and ethnic conflict. In a bizarre, reverse example, the liberal politician, Irina Khakhamada, appeared on the 12 April 2007 edition of Malakhov's *Let them Talk*, to comment on the case of a family 'deceived' by American evangelists into donating their comatose son's body parts to medicine. In a show broadcast on 26 April 2007, guests invited to discuss the case of a man who killed his wife and then had sexual relations with his daughters included Ludmila Senchina (an actress) and Iurii Loza (a pop singer). The construct of the modern, post-Soviet celebrity draws on that of the Soviet-era *intelligent*, by virtue of whose status a pronouncement on any issue automatically acquires value.

Celebrities are rarely interviewed as figures in their own right, although Channel 1's *While Everyone's At Home* (*Poka vse doma*) uses the *tok-shou* format to promote images of traditional family life by interviewing celebrities in their living rooms, surrounded by their families. Even here, the questioning is geared towards soliciting opinions on, and the celebrities' experiences of, abstract, public-domain generalities, and on their work as professionals, rather than the hidden autobiographical depths of their pre-celebrity personas. In the edition of *Private Life* focusing on the mother/daughter/younger lover triangle, an actress who had played the role of the mother in films couched her remarks in the discourse of 'eternal principles' of love and jealousy. In another edition devoted to the theme of gossip, Khazanov, the famous television satirist, referred to the role of gossip in his professional career.

Post-Soviet culture is not disinterested in the private lives of the rich and famous, as the wealth of Russian internet celebrity-gossip sites confirms. Post-Soviet television combines a relatively low cultural status with a set of production values bearing the residue of Soviet official culture (public-sphere oriented, formalistic and favouring the specialist over the vernacular).[7] Influenced by the same market concerns as global television elsewhere, it reserves space for down-market formats like the talk show, many of whose attributes, linguistic and visual, are those we would expect of such formats, but whose discursive boundaries are drawn in such a way that some of the key private sphere concerns normally associated with television celebrity culture remain excluded. Thus, Malakhov's linguistic informality was, until recently, accompanied by a cultural conservatism and an orientation towards the safe and the proverbial. As we shall see in Part II, his most recent project tackles riskier (and more salacious) subjects. In general, however, with its relatively impervious divide between a vast official realm and a smaller yellow press, post-Soviet public discourse has yet to develop the layering effect of mature democracies such as the UK, where 'trash journalism' is only one end of a spectrum which has the establishment broadsheet *The Times* at the other end, with the *Daily Mail* in the middle.

The 'mainstream culture' embodied in the *Daily Mail* has yet to establish itself in Russia. Regional and economic differentials and the lack of a true political consensus make this difficult. Apparently 'mainstream' *tok-shous*, like *Domino Principle* are tarred with the brush of factionalism (male contributors to the web forum for *Domino Principle* – long since discontinued along with the programme – portrayed the programme as a platform for American feminism!). Issues chosen for discussion are condemned to oscillate between the official agenda of a carefully controlled public realm, that of a mythical realm associated with popular tradition, and that of interest groups marked as 'peripheral'.

Talk and the shaping of knowledge

Celebrity experts are used extensively on the *tok-shou*. As Sonia Livingstone and Peter Lunt show, expert opinions often serve as the object of critical scrutiny articulated by the audience and represented by the host (Livingstone and Lunt 1994). The child psychologist who argues that smacking is detrimental to children is subjected to the wisdom of the audience, ably led by the presenter, which dismisses the research as counter-intuitive, exemplifying what Kevin Glynn describes as 'popular knowledge that challenges the sufficiency of scientific rationalism' (Glynn 2000: 11). In Russian talk shows, the holders of scientific knowledge are rarely challenged. A popular science series that aired on NTV in 2004, called *Homo Sapiens*, employed a talk-show format to examine popular scientific and historical phenomena: 'Life as a Game' (involving psychologists and anthropologists) and 'Great Illusions' (including psychologists, hypnotists and magicians), for example. The questioning of experts was designed to elicit information rather than challenge consensus.

The knowledge disseminated on Russian TV is presented as impersonal and unchanging, and the experts as merely its ciphers. An April 2004 edition of *Domino* considered the notion that 'A woman's walk is the mirror of her soul'. Pseudo-experts from the arts disseminating popular mysticism were accompanied by doctors, a dance instructor and psychologists, all of whom confirmed that women can be 'read' through their walk. Contradictory categories of knowledge (scientific, pseudo-scientific, everyday-practical and mystical) were synthesised into a single, undifferentiated category, conferring legitimacy upon the popular forms of knowledge in which superstition, formerly a subversive counterweight to official Marxist scientific knowledge, still abounds.[8] Similarly, *bona fide* scientific knowledge gains in credence from its association with popular wisdom. On one hand, the expert is a modern replacement for the pre-rational shaman, furnishing a layer of mystificatory knowledge and ensuring that the dominant order remains sacrosanct. On the other hand, experts also divest the dark secrets of the world of their sinister aura. In the RTR morning show *Good Morning*, the weather forecast is combined with informally delivered 'cosmological information' about the movements of the planets. Cosmology is a legitimate science allied to meteorology and located in the official sphere, but the relevance of the information imparted for astrologers, frames science with a pseudo-scientific mysticism aligned with vernacular knowledge.

However, televisual meaning is located at the intersection of text and audience. For Russian viewers, the issues that *Domino Principle* treated and the knowledge that it disseminated can be seen as precisely contestatory and counter-cultural. In a July 2004 edition devoted to women earning more than their husbands, expertise was solicited through interviews with laypeople who based their opinions on authentic personal experience. The knowledge that emerged was conservative in western terms, reconfirming that a woman's prime duty was to her husband. However, the mere fact that issues like high-earning women were being discussed as controversies signals that the concerns of ordinary people adapting to life in a marketised economy and to new ideologies were now forcing their way into the official domain.

In the proliferation of female-centred *tok-shou*, the mystification of traditional values through consultations with experts offers support to conservative orthodoxies, but, in the context of the television meaning-making process, subtly stretches official knowledge categories. The very existence of programmes pretending to represent women's desires as different from what men want for/from women extends the boundaries of 'the female realm'. An October 2003 edition of *What a Woman Wants* sought to determine the formula for 'women's happiness' and dispensed the usual mix of weight-loss and beauty tips summed up by the presenter in the form of a 'body of knowledge'. But by framing the section on beauty in terms of the commercial value of good looks (the attractive woman was more likely to succeed), the programme implicitly acknowledged the legitimacy of post-Soviet female desire.

A more radical shift affects the consumer. The RTR morning show *Good Morning*, a mix of news, information and chat, regularly contains a short 'Expertise' segment in which a (male) expert talks to camera on a scientific aspect of consumer information (November 2003 editions looked at microwave cooking, children's soap and baby wipes). The segments were thinly veiled 'infomercials' aimed at the female audience but framed as news material and further naturalised by the scientific jargon in which the information is couched.

The gendering of knowledge forms part of a larger naturalisation process. When two truths are confirmed within multiple discourses, the whole process acquires the form of an intricately linked, organic network: consumerism connects, via news, with science; news connects, via talk, to femininity to form an ideological nexus self-contained yet capable of linking at each of its interfaces with an infinite number of other such nexuses.[9]

As well as presenting consumer issues as news, *Good Morning* performs the reverse gesture, positing news as consumerism. The very idea that hard news can blend with chat, consumer advice and light entertainment constructs news as part of the 'package' that the programme offers its viewers for passive, living-room consumption. The package is wrapped in a pseudo-democratic informality distinguishing it from the stiff, bureaucratic Soviet formalism and infusing it with permissive western values (the choreographed banter between the 'synthetically personalised' male and female presenters of *Good Morning* with which each bulletin begins, and which frames the entire three-hour daily broadcast).[10]

The *tok-shou*s we have examined confirm the genre's role as an arena for the interplay of post-Soviet discourses and speech genres, traditional and contemporary, Soviet and western, private and public sphere-oriented. Above all, it mediates between the discourses of an ever-more interventionist official realm and those of a vernacular origin which persist in asserting themselves, providing the key to the direction of emergent post-Soviet civic culture. We should look now in more detail at a particular example of the *tok-shou*, with a view to determining the extent to which the mediation process can be said to deal in hegemonic meanings, and focusing on its audience-text dimension.[11]

Part II

For continuity, and because it encapsulates the nexus of points we have discussed (mediation, celebrity, genre, the tension between control and 'loose talk'), we have selected Andrei Malakhov's *Let them Talk* as our detailed case study. The programme is broadcast by Channel 1 on Tuesdays and Fridays from 7.10 to 8.00 pm. According to its Channel 1 website listing, it is intended to 'help people solve their real problems by encouraging discussion of these problems on TV'. The additional 'selling point' is the 'subjectivity of the programme's conclusions due to the various voices heard: people involved in the situation, audience members, and celebrities' (www.1tv.ru/). As a source of audience feedback, we have drawn on the show's web-based discussion forum.

The publicity statement will not surprise those familiar with the anodyne brand of popular television for which Malakhov is derided and admired in equal measure. As several audience comments on early editions indicated, the new 'project' is remarkably similar to its immediate predecessors and appears to share the same commitment to downmarket yet respectable, 'talk' about issues which, whilst topical, avoids political controversy. In many senses, *Let Them Talk* is the archetypal Putin-era *tok-shou*, its harmless vacuity an indication of the stranglehold the state now exerts over freedom of expression on Russian television, its garish, verbose informality a sign of the attachment to western-style, market-driven cultural norms with which Putin would have us believe Russia can combine its rigidly statist approach to governance. For this reason, Malakhov's project also provides a test for our conviction that it is precisely at Russian television's apolitical, popular cultural margins that the extent of the mission to 'control' meaning can best be judged.

Much can be gauged from the show's seemingly throwaway title; it is in fact dense with contradictory meaning whose unpacking provides the separate threads of the discussion we wish to pursue. On one hand, it is in line with that of a number of other *tok-shou*s in which the theme of freedom of expression is self-consciously foregrounded: *Freedom of Speech* and *Voice of the People*. On that level, it offers a rather unconvincing message of permissive, unfettered dialogue: 'let ordinary people speak; we won't stop them!' On the other hand, it can viewed by analogy with the 'Let them eat cake!' maxim as an exhortation to the people to avoid serious politics by indulging in uncontrolled, idle talk. A third layer of meaning relates to the context in which the phrase is often used in everyday speech: as a defiant rebuttal to accusations of impropriety: 'Let them say what they like!' In this sense, the title captures Malakhov's willingness to skirt the boundaries of taste and social acceptability, his refusal to be cowed into silence by those complaining of his 'trashiness'.

In aligning these three meanings, we might note that several forum contributors make unflattering comparisons between Malakhov and Vladimir

Pozner, host of the 'serious' political discussion show, *Times*. This, for many western viewers, strangely inappropriate, juxtaposition expresses the themes that our preliminary discussion of the title reveals: the question of genre; the relationship between political repression and popular cultural licence; the construction of celebrity; the failure to generate coherent viewing communities; the continuities and disjunctions between audience and text that the programme reflects; the tendency of post-Soviet audiences to replicate the metatextual attention to rules and boundaries which we find in the titles.

Malakhov strikes the western viewer, accustomed to the careful commodification of celebrity and the genuine panache and polish of presenters like Jonathan Ross or Graham Norton, as shrill, gauche and lacking in the skills needed to manage live studio discussion. The sense of mystery at his success is, however, shared by numerous (presumably reluctant) Russian viewers. In one polemic, a contributor clearly frustrated by his peers' naïve adulation asks ironically what constitutes Malakhov's much vaunted talent: 'Surely not the fact that he can't keep control of the situation in the studio ... Or that precise, grammatical language is absent from his discourse?' The answer comes in a riposte: 'Malakhov is not like all the others. It's interesting to follow his life. He came from the back of beyond [*glukhomani*] and he's a superstar'.[12] The theme of how Malakhov overcame his humble, provincial origins to enter the rarefied metropolitan world of superstardom recurs throughout the discussion threads:

> Malakhov is great [*molodets*]. There aren't so many people who have managed to rise up from nowhere and become a presenter on a central channel. Whatever you think of his style, he's still great!

The emphasis on this aspect of his persona reveals its metatextual function: just as the television celebrity as construct mediates the everyday and the famous, so Malakhov's life trajectory performatively enacts this mediation. His uninspiring 'averageness' within a realm in which metropolitan sophistication is the norm is unpacked as the function of his belaboured progress from dull provincial periphery to star-studded centre. Many Muscovites fail to appreciate this and dismiss his programme as 'oriented towards the statistically average person in the street' (*srednestatisticheskogo obyvatelia*). Unsupportive provincial viewers, by contrast, refer to Malakhov's dubious metropolitan sexuality. In response to praise for his 'metrosexual' grasp of style, a hostile respondent retorts with homophobic bile:

> I was most shocked by his answer to the clearly posed question: 'Are you gay?'; You should have heard him try to avoid the question ... I'm just amazed that a person like this sets the rules and norms of behaviour in Russian show-business.

Malakhov's rapidly acquired over-familiarity with the Moscow 'media set' upsets and impresses viewer in equal measure. During the show, the presenter often addresses his celebrity guests as 'Ty', effectively excluding the ordinary members of his audience. This is indicative of the abortive mediation that he performs: instead of representing the voice of the ordinary person to the celebrity and vice versa, as in the Oprah Winfrey interview, Malakhov is the ordinary person who has undergone a sudden and illegitimate transformation into a celebrity himself, whilst failing to shed the rough edges of his provincial background.

But the unseemly trajectory of Malakhov's career and the incoherent, hybrid persona that he acquires – in answer to the question, 'Is Andrei in life not the same as Andrei on screen?', a fan responds 'Andrei is always different' (*Andrei vsegda raznyi*) – only replicates the lack of coherence in the same Russian viewing audience. The abiding impression gained by the western 'intruder' on these discussions is a sense of disbelief that the contributors are even talking about the same programme. Some defend the programme and its much-maligned presenter claiming that they serve a vital political function:

> Whoever doesn't watch programmes like *Let them Talk* just doesn't want to see the reality of what is happening in our country [*proiskhodiaishchuiu v strane deistvitel'nost'*] and hopes that what happens to the participants of the show won't happen to them; they're naïve.
>
> This is our life, our country and our heroes. If we don't talk about and show all this then we will learn, see and find out nothing.

Others dismiss the trashy insincerity, the collusion between presenter and commissioning channel and the cow-towing to western popular cultural models:

> I am sure that all this sensation and scandal is whipped up [*dutye*] ... The programme is 'bought off' [*kuplena*] – even a fool can see that ... Malakhov don't shame your country [*Stranu ne pozor'!*] Show worthy people or else the viewer will not be able to wash off the shit [*der'ma*] for a long time.

Several viewers refer to the suspicion that the programme is 'made to order' (*zakaznaia*) and is serving the commercial interests of the guests and sponsors. And many reject the notion that Malakhov is doing his country a service by revealing its disgusting underbelly:

> What's the point of drawing attention to THAT? Why show our most vulnerable, defenceless, weak, indecent, dirty places? Nobody is intending to do anything about it anyway!

The differences between viewers are often so fundamental that, despite the programme's resolute apoliticism, they acquire a political hue as antagonisms are translated into the language of liberal progressives and communist apologists:

> My advice to Andrei is to repent [*pokaiat'sia*] for all his journalistic sins ... To ask himself whether what he is doing is moral.
> Advisers like you sat throughout the communist years in the various controlling/checking agencies and hissed: 'Don't allow it; ban it; put him in jail; have him shot!'

At other times, these antagonisms reflect more recent divisions between the renewed patriotism of a revitalised Russian state and a despised westernising minority:

> Some people are interested in seeing famous personalities getting thumped in the mug [*mordoboi*] – that's much more interesting to watch: you don't need to think. Probably Andrei Malakhov went on a trip to America for this. The Americans taught him to do shows like this.
> The head of Channel One should officially apologise on behalf of Malakhov ... for the unacceptable behaviour of their employee. Malakhov is just a grey nonentity [*serost' kakaia-to*] ... I am ashamed for my country!

As this last quote illustrates, we encounter an apparent paradox: Malakhov's very grey averageness emerges as a direct function of the fragmentation within his audience. This fragmentation is, in turn, connected with the generic confusion that the programme, its defenders and detractors, all display. The establishment of clear generic norms, boundaries and expectations indicates an (always provisional) success in stabilising the meaning circulation process. Whilst all viewers accept the designation of *Let them Speak* as '*tok-shou*', the interpretations of the term cover such a multitude of sins (from political discussion to Americanised trash TV) as to render it meaningless:

> With programmes like this we are turning into a pathetic imitation of the American (e.g. the Jerry Springer Show). We shouldn't show such programmes. *What? When? Where?* [the name of an old Soviet-era intellectual quiz show still on air in Russia], *Brain Ring* ... intellectual values must dominate over those of the street market [*nad bazarnymi*]. Let's show executions, catastrophes; let Channel One launch its own version of Nagiev's *Windows*. Let's degrade ourselves together with the whole country.
> I understand your dissatisfaction, but you, too, must understand that this is a *Tok-Shou*!!!

On one hand, *Let them Speak* is compared unfavourably with an example of a different genre altogether (the quiz show) and the accuser, for whom all light entertainment apparently blurs into an undifferentiated mass of American trash, has to be reminded of the show's true designation. On the other hand, equally unfavourable comparisons between Malakhov and the hosts of topical discussion shows such as Pozner reveal an ignorance of the difference between talk show subgenres:

> Personally I'm sympathetic to people and so to the shows they introduce if they have earned my respect ... Malakhov can't be a professional on the same level as Pozner.
>
> Malakhov is a long way from Pozner? ... Don't make us laugh ... Of course, I understand, the programmes of these 'personalities' are on the boring side [*skuchnovatye*] – all you get is news, different problems – politics, economics, education: what a bore!
>
> Andrei is a professional, a genius [*umnitsa*] and just a nice person. And the fact that his programme has recently suffered from problems is not his fault. It's rather a question of who writes the scripts, or whatever they are called.

The suggestion that a talk show should have 'script writers' points to a complete incomprehension of the very purpose of a talk show.

As the exchanges reveal, the instability and uncertainty of meaning that the generic confusion designates is linked to an incomplete internalisation of western models, and an equally incomplete externalisation of their Soviet precursors. *Let them Talk* can be perceived as both a post-Soviet adaptation of the western talk show, and a successor to the more staid Soviet models of light entertainment, or to the author-led, high-cultural discussion programmes exemplified by *Times*. Its defenders can be accused of leading their country into American-inspired degeneracy just as its detractors can be condemned for Soviet-style censorship.

Given the generic confusion, it is hardly surprising that much of the discussion relates to the show's title:

> After 'yellow' (i.e. trashy) editions like that, only people like that will want to go on *Let them Talk* and the intelligentsia won't have the time or inclination.
>
> The format of the programme is as follows: Let those who have something to say talk. There are different kinds of people on the programme, specialists and loads of intellectuals [*sploshnaia intelligentsia*] – why should they have rivals in the studio? There should be two sides.

In another robust defence of the programme's tendency to descend into shouting matches, one viewer argues:

> I agree that the programme's themes are not always interesting and the guests don't always behave with dignity and respect. But, this is a *tok-shou,*

a GAME and there are different kinds of people, each strong in his own sphere of knowledge … That's why you get the disagreements.

The fact that the show's flaws are defended both on the grounds that they reflect the generic tendency to deal in uncompromising portrayals of real life and that they should be seen in the context of the genre's status as mere 'game' is further evidence of the lack of consensus on generic convention, and the consequent drift of definitions.

In much of the metatextualising, the forum contributors get to the heart of the function of the verbal 'free for all' in a society struggling to internalise the meanings and etiquettes accompanying 'free speech':

> (1) Everyone has the right to speak [*pravo na slovo*] … with all due respect to their interlocutors, let them talk [*pri vsem uvazhenii k sobesedniky, puskai govoriat!*].
>
> I say, let them shut up! [*Pust' zamolchat!*]
>
> (2) These are all just actors; you could never show this for real on federal television.
>
> The stories are real and the participants are genuine. Have you ever watched a western talk show? That's just what you have with Andrei Malakhov and it deserves attention.
>
> Of course I agree that everyone talks like this in real life, but that's in life, whereas on the box [*po iashchiku*] they should show positive examples and not negative ones.

The show's most enthusiastic supporters use its unscripted vulgarity and apparent inability to engage in meaningful, structured dialogue on serious issues to outflank those who, pointing to the same traits, tar Malakhov with the 'trash culture' brush; the lack of structure, it is claimed, in fact marks the show's allegiance to democratic politics:

> It is not a political programme but parliamentary deputies take part and the people are given the chance to speak [*narodu predostavliaetsia slovo*] … the people judge … specialists and active viewers are invited … they discuss the problems of the guests, express their opinion and you could call that the 'people's court' [*narodnym sudom*] … everyone decides for themselves and expresses their opinion.

Metatextuality is often seen as a function of aesthetic distance from the object text. Here, however, the viewers' metatextual commentary reflects a deep, literalistic engagement. In the words of one forum participant: 'Constructive criticism will help Malakhov become a leader in this genre'. Others express the hope that 'Andrei is reading our comments', suggesting that the text–audience relationship as represented by the forum is constructed as dialogue and active engagement. The naïvely high significance that the viewers attribute to their comments is seemingly a paradox for a society undergoing a severe curtailment of free speech.

The metatextual commentary is a mark not of the *tok-shou*'s maturity, but rather its status as an inchoate genre still in formation. The programme itself replicates the sense of maximum engagement between viewer and text in the way that it positions its guests and presenter in relation to the studio audience. Malakhov normally stands close to the audience, but with his back to it, at a distance from the person he is interviewing, presenting himself as the ordinary viewer's spokesperson. This point was invoked in response to the accusation that the programme is 'bought' by its guests:

> On our television, it's not the presenter who runs things, it's those behind his back.
> And who is behind his back? The viewers, the audience ... he runs them but doesn't always manage to control them; these are two different things.

Following their interviews, the 'experts' and guests often reseat themselves as the first row of the audience, as if to emphasise the programme's 'democratic' ethos. What often results, however, is the undifferentiated shouting match in which guests, experts and audience members bellow in uncontrolled fashion with Malakhov powerless to assert his authority. It is this which leads many to dismiss it as nothing more than a *bazar* (a negative term connoting a chaotic free-for-all):

> It's time to change the programme's name. 'Let them Talk' presupposes several opinions on one topic. But when only one lot talk and another lot, incompetent and unable to defend their positions are invited on, you get a *bazar*.
> It's a terrible show. They sometimes choose interesting topics, but the discussion is turned into a *bazar*.

These comments point to Malakhov's reorientation away from celebrity guests towards ordinary people (in extraordinary situations). Thus, in April 2007, one programme focused on the family of a Russian boy with a brain tumour, 'deceived' by an American Baptist sect into letting him have an operation in the US, only to be pressured to sign over his internal organs after he had fallen into an irreversible coma following the operation. The following week's edition focused on the life and morals of a professional stripper. The reorientation has had two seemingly contradictory effects. It has fuelled the argument that *Let them Talk* represents a decline into 'trash television'. But it has also strengthened the claim that Malakhov is giving a voice to people who would not otherwise have access to the public realm:

> We're all from that crowd, whether you like it or not. Malakhov is undoubtedly bringing benefit by exposing tricksters and charlatans and

is thereby saving gullible people from ruin. ... the question of taste doesn't come into it.

But everyone has the right to speak [*pravo golosa*] if they've come to the studio. The very name of the show *Let them Talk* – permits them to do this.

In yet another comment, the contradiction is internalised within the attitude of a single viewer who first condemns the programme and its audience, then expresses the desire to appear on the show herself:

They come to the studio to show off [*sebia pokazat'*] ... But I can't take such viewers seriously ... They couldn't care less about anyone [*im po barabanu vsekh*] ... I am soon intending to go to the studio. I may set an example of how to conduct a discussion without interrupting anyone.

The contradiction is reflected intratextually in the choice of 'expert guests'. Whilst figures from the world of entertainment and the arts predominate, there is a growing tendency to invite politicians, even when the 'yellowest' of issues is being discussed. Among the guests for the Baptist theme, for example, was Irina Khakhomada, who stood against Putin in the 2004 presidential election.

It is also apparent that the feeble civic potential that Malakhov's programme displays feeds through into audience commentary. Viewers generally hostile to the show's low-cultural proclivities construct their 'civic position' around this very rejection:

What has amazed me ... has been the reaction of people in the forum to all of this. That I didn't expect. Well done! [*Molodtsy!*]. We've reached a single civic position [*grazhdanskaia pozitsiia*] in response to slops that are being tipped over us [*na oblivanie nas pomoiami*] and the use of us as a means for increasing ratings.

And the perfect, time-honoured rebuttal to those who might suggest that such reactions cannot be attributed to the show itself, but rather constitute its negation, is provided by a supportive contributor alert to the hypocrisy of her opponents:

I understand why certain people are indignant, but ... you can always watch other talk shows. These people are *watching*, becoming indignant, and then writing in here. That I don't understand.

Paradoxically, the parallels between studio audience and forum contributors are at their greatest when viewer alienation is at its height. The curious osmosis of studio audience and web forum contributors is evident in the manner in which the forum arguments descend into the very chaos that the viewers perceive in the studio discussions:

Even here you are trying to shut up those who don't agree with you. A really unique talent!

We're not shutting anyone up, we're discussing a theme on which everyone has the right to express an opinion.

Others go as far as transposing the ubiquitous term *bazar* from programme to web forum. One should not, however, exaggerate either the impact of the osmosis, or the nascent civic function that it occasionally signals. Malakhov's incompetence and intellectual shallowness are as embarrassing as his detractors suggest. Nor does he (or, indeed, the themes he analyses) reveal any consistent philosophy. Here he presents a contrast from the likes of Jeremy Kyle who, however condescending to the dysfunctional guests he torments and preaches to, conveys a set of homespun principles centred on family, self-sufficiency and 'the talking cure'.

Malakhov's chameleon-like inconsistency is a feature of post-Soviet Russian talk television. Despite the almost universal praise he receives from the *Let them Talk* viewers, Vladimir Pozner, a figure of altogether greater stature, is himself often accused by the west-leaning intelligentsia of cynical opportunism. Pozner's role as host of *Times* is relevant here. The selection of guests permitted to appear on the show has become increasingly circumscribed as Putin's grip has tightened. They are now inevitably dominated by Duma representatives, security apparatus functionaries and 'oppositional' figures who are acceptable either because their own opinions are barely distinguishable from the government stance, or because they develop this stance in a direction helpful to the regime's nation-building intentions. One element of consistency in Pozner's position over the years has been his principled objection to xenophobia. Thus, his willingness to accede to the nationalistic agenda by accepting the constraint on his guest list might appear to be an example of political 'chameleonism'. But, even as the constraints have grown, Pozner's own role has tended to become more tendentious. Under the influence of the *avtorskaia peredacha* model, Pozner permits himself a lengthy monologue at the end of each discussion in which he launches his own, eloquently argued, polemic on the matter in hand.

Still more curious was Pozner's behaviour in an exchange between the liberal-leaning writer, Viktor Erofeev and the nationalist politician, Aleksandr Krutov, in a show discussing anti-Semitism. Rather than use his chair's prerogative to prevent such gross insults from flying across the table, Pozner intervened implicitly on the side of Erofeev, from whom the insults emanated.

Apart from giving the lie to the impression that television under Putin has been a morass of trash and official propaganda, these exchanges indicate a high level of discursive instability. The fact that Pozner fails to conform to the model of the western moderator reflects the absence of the hegemonic, consensus position assumed by the western discussion show host able to articulate questions to his guests from the viewpoint of the 'man in the street'. Pozner's apparent inconsistency is a function of this discursive confusion. It confirms the Laclauan model in which hegemonic power is not located within any one group and in which, by implication, the media cannot be a passive tool for a ruling elite. Rather, it is consolidated when 'chains of equivalence' emerge from amidst the clash of 'antagonisms' prevailing in the public sphere (thus the 'moderate, commonsense' view on gender equality might be said to reflect a chain linking feminist, working class, business and middle class professional interests). Both the aggressive dominance of Putin's ruling elite on Russia's Channel 1, and Pozner's inconsistency, are signals of the virtual absence of such chains.

Malakhov's inconsistent, cipher-like flitting from issue to issue, his tendency to address serious social issues in an inappropriate, trash-TV format, is of lesser political consequence, but it is born of the same hegemonic failure. One of the 'benefits' of hegemonic consensus is that it allows for the establishment of stable boundaries between central territory which is contested and politicised, and territory which belongs to the marginal realm of the everyday, ensuring that the very ambiguity of television's engagement with the alternative values of the latter (simultaneously disdaining and embracing them) constitutes part of the strategy by which those values can be appropriated. This is what David Morley means when he refers to 'hegemony as dialogic process connecting/articulating the margins to the centre' (Morley 1999: 152). It is only when one explores beyond the boundaries of Malakhov's project – generically, within the more controversial world of Pozner's *Times*; paratextually, within the hot house of the web forum – that one begins to appreciate the consequences flowing from Russian television's difficulties in embracing this dialogism. For the verbal promiscuity which is the breeding ground for Malakhov's flightiness is poised perpetually to turn from political safety valve into a pressure point threatening the stability of the weak hegemonic process characteristic of post-Soviet television.

5 Unfulfilled orders

Failed hegemony in Russia's (pseudo) military drama serials

Introduction

In continuing our gradual reorientation away from news and current affairs programming towards fiction and light entertainment, we would seem to be moving further from the realm of the political, and therefore from problems associated with hegemonic meaning in its most obvious sense. However, and despite their unambiguously fictional status, the spate of army-related serials to have appeared during the lead up to the 60th anniversary of the Second World War victory would, of all the genres we consider in this book, seem to be closest to Putin's ideological mission to rebuild Russian nationhood. Indeed, it is difficult to discuss such serials without reference to Putin's desire to install a militaristic culture at television's heart by establishing in 2004 a channel devoted to the army (Zvezda).[1] But the more that his regime imposed its authoritarian stamp, the more that resistance seemed to emerge at every point of the meaning-generating process. And it is, paradoxically, those discursive points, where the voice of the ideological centre is strongest, at which the lines of resistance can be most effective.

The scope of this chapter goes beyond the military drama narrowly conceived. Indeed, of the three serials we treat, each deviates from the generic norm: an army setting featuring plots which revolve around military characters, actions and routines. *Penal Battalion* (*Shtrafbat*) is set in the Second World War rather than the present, and features criminals-turned-soldiers. *Soldiers* (*Soldaty*) contains no military action and is closer to a sitcom than a serial. *The Zone* (*Zona*) is set in a prison, though the culture is militaristic and its focus on discipline and the numbing repetitiveness of institutional routine strikes a military chord.

Apart from the shared generic peripherality and institutional environments the serials articulate intersecting thematic patterns (*Penal Battalion* and *The Zone* feature criminals; *The Zone* and *Soldiers* are set in the present; *Soldiers* and *Penal Battalion* are army serials in the stricter sense; and *Soldiers* and *The Zone* possess comic elements). The institution-based genre in its western variant tends to involve 'civil' settings, such as hospitals (*ER* and *Casualty*) and schools (*Teachers* and *Waterloo Road*) in which tensions between professional and personal, official and unofficial, male authority and female ambition are explored. In the Russian variants, the 'private/public' dichotomy is downplayed because the routines are confined to spaces where living is communal; the institutional culture is predominantly male; and the themes of order and national pride are foregrounded. These three qualities define the broader category of what we propose to call the pseudo-military drama (itself a subgenre of the institutional drama).

The serials are linked, likewise, by their popularity. During 2004–6, each occupied the position of most popular programme on Russian television.[2] Each generated much discussion (and, in the cases of *Penal Battalion* and *The Zone*, controversy). Among the programmes that we will not discuss is Channel 1's *Border* (*Granitsa*), on air through 2005. A *strictu sensu* military drama building on the popular docu-drama *Border Guards* (*Pogranichniki*), it features the struggles of the traditionally feted border troops to prevent cross-border crime. So transparently in tune with Putin policy it could have been written by a government hack, it failed to secure a respectable audience and was discontinued.

The failure of *Border* indicates the difficulties that modern states encounter when attempting to transmit ideological messages to visually literate, discerning viewers. The current proliferation of 'reality TV' shows everywhere can be seen as an attempt to accommodate the active role of audiences in shaping televisual meanings by making participation central to programme structure (for example, the audience votes on, and views of, the *Big Brother* 'housemates' are central to the game's outcome). *Border* failed less because of its ideological message than because it omitted to engage its intended audience. Assertive state notwithstanding, television in Russia operates in the competitive sphere where channel differentiation still matters. Significantly, unlike *Borders*, none of our serials was made by Channel 1, or Rossiia, the two closest to the ideological centre (*Soldiers* was a REN-TV product, the other two belonged to NTV).

Another factor hampering the militarisation process is the blurring effect of television's fluid textual boundaries upon the distinction noted in Chapter 1 between *author* (the person whose words are spoken), *animator* (the person who articulates them) and *principal* (the person whose position is represented). Thus, in a pseudo-military serial, the characters who articulate the script (animator), the screenplay writer (author), the commissioning channel (mediating principal) and the government (ultimate principal) coexist in a complex, shifting relationship. The conflation of text (programme) and context (wider cultural tendencies operative at the time of transmission and, later, retransmission), and of text and audience reception, comes into play vigorously. So, too, does the role of generic hybridity (the loosening of borders between genres resulting from the circulation of global formats adapted to native models).

We have already argued that television's function in negotiating the boundaries outlined has accorded the medium a particular form of self-reflexivity.

As we saw in our previous chapter, one of the prime examples is the studio audience, through which television models its external viewing audience within its own programme structures. It is this which accords it its performative tendency to enact both its relationship with its audience and its representational object. We will see this performative tendency at work in a different way in our chosen serials.

We first concentrate on the location of the serials at an intersection of peripheries (geographical, socio-cultural and ideological). This places a particular onus on the role of various sub-cultural discourses in relation to those of an unspecified, but ever-present, centre which dissipates as it attempts to appropriate them: a risk inherent in attempting the performative legitimation of order. The peripheral locus is next linked to the serials' dual function as both metaphors of a larger whole and metonymically displaced parts of that whole which expresses a fault-line in their realist aesthetic opening the way to an unintegrated, anti-realist transcendentalism. The problem is also reflected in their contradictory narrative models (the overarching narrative, and the open-ended 'soap' format) and in the multi-faceted ambiguity over the standpoint from which the action is framed: spatial (the excessive use of facial close-ups), temporal (chronotopic confusions over the associations between institutional place and Soviet past/post-Soviet present) and ideological (nostalgia for Soviet order and dissident oppositionalism). In the concluding section we identify procedures according to which this concealment of sources is self-reflexively incorporated into the narratives and which convert the anonymous, all-seeing Other into an object of viewer voyeurism in its own right, thus disrupting the viewer identification system and its sustaining ideological regime. We link this disruption to the ghost of Stalinism haunting each serial, and to a collapse in the Symbolic Order designed to hold it in check.

The analysis is situated loosely under the umbrella of Gramscian hegemony. However, the methodological vocabulary used is eclectic and draws on Bakhtinian notions of chronotope and multi-voicedness, theories of narrative framing, and accounts of televisual representation. We also refer to reactions to the serials as expressed in web forums, not for empirical 'triangulation' purposes, but because, as in Chapter 4, the meaning-generating structures themselves seep into the wider reception context. In this sense, the subgenre's ability to manage the conflict between (repressive) official and (resistant) sub-cultural discourses renders it a model of the wider encounter of television production and audience reception.

The serials

First, we should provide a summary of the programmes. *Soldiers*, an STS serial, ran over eight series (each of approximately 15 episodes) between 2004 and 2006. Series 1 (on which we will focus) is set in a provincial barracks and traces the stories of a group of new recruits through their compulsory two-year army service, beginning from the day of their call-up, through to their return to civilian life. It deals with themes from military life and features a large cast, with the focus of attention shifting weekly. Its comic features; confined, unchanging setting; and discrete, self-contained episodes have led it to be described as a Russian sitcom. However, this designation ignores the presence of an overarching narrative trajectory and the attempt to broach serious issues.

The source of the comedy derives from the relationships between the new recruits and the officers. Most amusing is the alliance that Lieutenant Shmatkov, who is studying for an exam to gain promotion to Major, strikes up with Sokolov, a well-educated new recruit. Shmatkov coerces Sokolov into helping him with his academic assignments to the point where Sokolov is forced into impersonating him in an oral examination. Whilst the regime is harsh and the officers prone to abuse their privileges, the overall ethos is warm and good humoured (one episode centred on the rituals of the Day of the Golden Spirit when officers agree temporarily to take orders from vengeful NCOs).[3] The overarching narrative tells of the burgeoning love between Ira, a military nurse, and Medvedev, a new recruit. Ira is also an object of attraction for the unscrupulous Major Kolubkov who becomes jealous of Medvedev, finally managing to arrange his wrongful arrest for stealing a weapon, and blackmailing Ira into marrying him in exchange for Medvedev's release. Viewers must wait until the second series for the inevitable happy resolution.

Penal Battalion (Shtrafbat) shares with *Soldiers* an emphasis on male camaraderie. Made by NTV to coincide with the 60th anniversary of the victory over Fascism, it bolsters the mood of admiration for the sacrifices of the Red Army, but adopts a controversial stance on the topic. For it deals with a little-known aspect of the war effort, centring on the many Red Army battalions formed from prisoners offered the chance to 'redeem their guilt with blood' (*krov'iu iskupit' vinu*) by taking on the most dangerous missions. It begins with the story of how Tverdokhlebov, a Red Army officer, miraculously survives his own execution by the Nazis and, clambering from his makeshift grave, makes his way back to his comrades. But, in common with any Red Army soldier 'guilty' of capture, he is arrested; only avoiding jail by agreeing to lead the criminal battalion. He wins over the other battalion members, a combination of hardened criminals and political dissidents, with his blend of harsh discipline (he summarily executes a soldier for knifing a comrade to death), and paternal care (he defends his subordinates against unfounded accusations of disloyalty from the NKVD officer attached to the battalion). As a result, he, too, becomes a target of resentful NKVD suspicion until the officer himself dies in a foolhardy attempt to capture a German food depot.

Each episode features a micro-narrative centring on a military mission, or a subplot among the soldiers (one falls in love with a woman who has lost her husband to the Germans; another, a Jew, a target of racist abuse, begins a relationship with a military nurse; a third brutally rapes a Ukrainian girl but blackmails the Jew into protecting his identity; a Caucasian soldier, misunderstanding an order to capture a German officer, returns with an ordinary soldier, but corrects his error in a lone sortie undertaken against orders). The subplots alternate, attenuating the complex political undercurrents (both anti-Soviet and pro-Russian messages emerge from the action). But the serial's narrative arch proceeds from the formation of the battalion, through to its tragic end, when all are killed but the commander and a gun-toting priest who has attached himself to the battalion, much to the dismay of the NKVD. Controversy aside, *Penal Battalion* ultimately reconciles Soviet Second World War mythology with post-Soviet Russian nationalism.[4] As David MacFadyen puts it, the serial paradoxically helps '*broaden* the definition of patriotism' (MacFadyen 2007: 74).

Although two of its leading characters are Chechen war veterans, *The Zone* offers a shocking exposé of a brutal underworld rather than a nation-building fillip. The script was inspired by an authentic manuscript, smuggled out of an unnamed provincial prison. Apart from its criminal heroes, it shares with *Penal Battalion* a willingness to court controversy; it was moved from prime time to a late-night slot, following a storm of viewer protest (a move, according to some rumours, sanctioned by Putin himself).[5] Like *Penal Battalion*, it generated much criticism relating to its factual accuracy.[6] In his discussion of the serial, David MacFadyen notes that the patriotic newspaper, *Trud*, maintained that the director 'had actively summoned hatred for the forces of law and order, a subversive gesture for which he should be incarcerated' (MacFadyen 2007: 189).

The Zone has a relatively open-ended narrative structure reflected in its 50 episodes. It exceeds *Soldiers* in its attention to the details of the institutional grind (prisoners slurping at food or emerging from behind barely screened toilet areas, arbitrary beatings from prison staff and unauthorised drug-taking sessions). We are swiftly introduced to the prison's harsh rituals and underworld hierarchies dominated by the culture of the *bratva* (or hardened criminal fraternity), each with its unofficially designated leader. A shocking early subplot revolves around Chiga, a prisoner with allegiances to the *bratva*, but who, on the orders of a cynical prison officer, Raevskii, is raped by a group of homosexual prisoners, acquiring the unofficial, shaming label of '*opushchennyi*' (someone who has been 'lowered down') amongst the fraternity. Several prisoners are being held on false accusations, including an economist called Pavlov, the victim of a conspiracy involving higher government echelons on whom the prosecutor (a woman called Kolesnikova who later becomes the senior prison officer) attempts to pin a murder. An American, Denis Warren, has also been framed for a rape and his railings against the *bespredel* (arbitrary mayhem) which characterises Russian justice are ignored.

Each episode begins with a quote from Andrei Tarkovskii's film, *Stalker*, featuring a metaphorical 'zone' (itself a reference to the term used to describe the Soviet camp system) which Tarkovskii defines as 'not a territory, but a test which a human being only survives if he retains his sense of dignity and his ability to distinguish the essential from the transient'. In fact, the action takes place not in the zone itself, but in a holding prison, or SIZO.

The prison staff divide, though not simplistically, into the corrupt and unscrupulous, and the fair-minded and sympathetic. Of the latter group, Bagrov is the most important. The serial begins with the death of the previous prison governor and Bagrov becomes convinced that he was murdered as part of a grand conspiracy. He spends the entire serial pursuing his case, with the detective format enabling each episode to end on a cliffhanger as he inches closer to solving the mystery.

Gradually, comic elements are introduced to relieve the unrelenting grimness of prison life (a female officer with an attraction for a male prisoner who fends off her attentions, until he, too, becomes infatuated; a naïve Georgian hoodwinked into believing that the *bratva* have designated him as leader of the cell and then forced to undergo absurd initiation rituals). For similar reasons, Raevskii and Kolesnikova eventually mellow. First, they become involved in a power struggle which ends with Kolesnikova appointed as prison governor, but at the behest of a sinister superior against whom she rebels. The power struggle leaves Raevskii vulnerable to exposure and he forges a new alliance with Bagrov with whose sister-in-law he has become romantically entangled.

Periphery and performativity

The three serials are situated in the outer orbit of Putin's nation-building project. *Soldiers* is essentially a comedy in which aspects of army life are mocked, but its redemptive story line reinforces official military culture rather than undermines it (cf. the BBC's *Dad's Army* which satirised the puffed-up vanities and muddleheadedness of the wartime British Home Guard, generating nostalgic pride in the stubborn idiosyncrasies which Hitler failed to suppress.) In Episode 6, Medvedev, undertaking military service because he was expelled from his university, is offered the chance by his influential father to be excused from the remainder of his commission. Whilst Ira is partly the reason for his refusal to agree, it is also determined by his desire to prove his masculine worth, and thus that of service to the nation. Significantly, the official website promoting the programme incorporates direct links to the Russian army's official website.

Nostalgia is central to *Soldiers'* appeal. Many episodes are dominated by the reconstruction of time-honoured rituals and army myths (practical jokes, variety shows, meetings with long-suffering girlfriends, etc.). Among the most enthusiastic viewers are older men for whom the serial is a reminder of their own military service.

Soldiers uses a restorative narrative structure to reinvigorate the order myth. In the early episodes, Shmatko's comic exploitation of Sokolov teeters on the brink of corruption. Later, however, he offers avuncular advice to Medvedev when he is subjected to genuine abuse of power at the hands of Kolubkov (Episodes 15–16). Shmatko's position within a 'basically decent' officer corps is restored, Kolubkov's role is diminished to that of the 'one bad apple'. Similarly, when the likeably gauche Kabanov is accused by middle-ranking officers of 'ratting' to the senior officers about illicit gambling, he attempts suicide (Episode 11). Once the true 'snitch' is, revealed, however, Kabanov is welcomed back into the fold. Thus, genuine problems among army recruits (bullying; suicide) are at once acknowledged and attenuated.

Through these narrative contortions, military pride and discipline are realised before our eyes, as doubts which emerge from the revelations about abuse of power, *dedovshchina* and drunkenness, are recast as comedy, and then dispelled.[7] Each micro-plot repeats the overall movement of viewer sympathies: the more we get to know the characters, the more we realise that the deviations from legality are subsumed by the human warmth and good order that finally prevails (the reverse, 'positive' side of the coin to the serial form's de-heroicising tendency). Viewer performance of nationhood mirrors that of the narratives viewed. One female forum contributor describes her changing attitude to Kolobkov, the most corrupt of the officers:

> Kolobkov first seemed the biggest bastard [*poslednei svoloch'iu*]. And only later, when he rushed Irina to the medical quarters and she had a miscarriage, did I really begin to feel sorry for him, because he also clearly loved Irina, but just couldn't express it properly.

By enwrapping the controversial issue in romantic intrigue, it is first atte-nuated, then, in almost cathartic moment of recognition, supplanted by patriotic affection for army service. Another viewer interprets the negative emotions evoked as, ultimately, part of the serial's appeal: 'it is kind [*dobryi*], and although it sometimes makes you suffer a bit [*perezhivat'*], it is about friendship and respect, and it shows that the army is not so terrible after all [*ne tak uzh i strashna*]'; (http://soldaty.tv/forum/index.php?showtopic+6256; accessed 13 October 2006). A female viewer expresses the role of humour in oiling the wheels of the hegemonic process:

> I think this serial is popular because the army is worrying a lot of people. It really hooks them [*tsepliaiet ikh*]. Guys serve, girls and parents wait. And how much concern there is over *dedovshchina*. And it's all there in the serial, and it's even underpinned [*prepodneseno*] by humour.
> (http://soldaty.tv/forum/index.php?showtopic+6256;
> accessed 3 November 2006)

The same performative movement operates in *Penal Battalion*. It is set during the hallowed period of the Second World War. Brutal battles and heroic sacrifice abound, though this familiar epic dimension is diminished by the temporal ruptures and familiarity of the serial form. It revolves around a twist of which we are aware from the outset, one authenticated through historical document (it ends with a roll call of 'real' penal battalions): the fact that the Red Army heroes are not soldiers but criminals. Also difficult to reconcile with familiar war myths is the portrayal of an officer corps in thrall to a vindictive NKVD 'commissar' (the situation reverses the Chapaev narrative in which a heroic commissar keeps an ideologically wayward Cossack in check). Web forum correspondents indicated that the impression at times is of a war won by the Soviet Union's criminal underclass.

> [This] run of the mill anti-Soviet propaganda ... distorts the history of our country and its great victory over Fascism. Primitive lies intertwined with half truths. All the NKVD agents are portrayed as pathological sadists, and the criminals as models to be imitated!
> (http://kino.br.by/film3140.html; accessed 20 October 2006)

> How can someone hate their Fatherland enough to shoot a film like this?
> (www.rutv.ru/forum.html?d=O&cid=386&FID=206&FThrID=144145; accessed 20 October 2006)

The serial anticipates such objections, provocatively addressing itself precisely to those continuing to harbour illusions of Soviet grandeur.

Penal Battalion is situated both at the socio-political and the temporal margins of the (post-)Soviet nation it sets out to (re)construct, though, of course, the mythic temporality of nationhood does not map onto a linear structure of past and present, centre and periphery. Moreover, the battalion members are divided between common criminals and 'politicals'. Whilst Stalin's terror is now received wisdom in post-Soviet Russia, to (re-)insert it into the sacrosanct myth of the Great Patriotic War is a bold gesture.

Although it takes more political risks than *Soldiers*, the rewards that *Penal Battalion* reaps in terms of its performative–cathartic transcendence of those risks, are correspondingly greater. Here, too, the narrative trajectory mirrors that of the transformation. The more that the sullen soldiers subject themselves to the will of their politically loyal, if disenchanted, commander, the more the sense of a purified, truly inclusive, Soviet-Russian nationhood emerges; again, the intimacy induced by the serial format confers authenticity on the eventual loyalty given to his commander by the initially resistant, common, knife-carrying thief, Glymov. Glymov's transformation from murderer to patriotic hero was, however, not universally effective; one forum commentator states: 'Glymov is a murderer. But they make him into a hero ... His "moralising" is just ridiculous [*smeshno*]'. Another, however, enthuses, 'Glymov – acted so well, I can't express it [*slov net*]'. A third indicates that he has but one desire: 'to bring Glymov back to life and see him fight with Tverdokhlebov all the way to Berlin' (www.rutv.ru/forum.html?d=O&cid=386&FID=206&FThrID=144145; accessed 20 October 2006).

The Soviet war myth is here rewritten as a narrative of Russian nationhood. When the deleterious influence of the Red Army higher command is made apparent, Tverdokhlebov and Glymov state that they are fighting not for the Soviet regime, but to save the Russian motherland; at the serial's tragic dénouement, when all but the priest and the commander have fallen in battle, the priest is blessed with a vision of the mother of God which appears above the blood-soaked Russian soil.

That this is no crude effort to recast the Second World War for latter-day Russian nationalism is evident from the prominent role accorded to Tsukerman. This worthy gesture towards racial tolerance is diminished by the condescending portrayal of stereotypical Caucasian bravado, but the two episodes reinvest the hollow Soviet multi-ethnic mantra with truer 'Russian' meaning, at the same time, conducting an implicit polemic with cruder versions of Russian nationalist ideology. The nationalist line resonates in the reactions of one segment of viewers:

> It demonstrated that they fought not only for Stalin (as it says in the text books), but also for their native land, their motherland. The fact that not everything about the plot adds up. … It gives you something to think about. Not like in those glossy Yanky [*gliantsevykh amerikosovovskikh*] films, where your head aches from knowing from the 3rd minute how it's all going to be in the end.
>
> (http://kino.br.by/film3140.html; accessed 20 October 2006)[8]

Shot through with the washed-out colours of nostalgia for a sanitised Russian war heroism, *Penal Battalion*, however, represents nostalgia for an object which, rather than pre-exist its articulation, is constituted by it.[9]

The Zone embraces nostalgia of a different kind. The Tarkovskii quote harks back to an era when spiritual strength was privileged over physical durability, and when dissident and/or underground language was accorded special value. The romanticisation of prison culture, a pre-eminent theme in viewer discussions, is given narrative expression in the story of Vasia, a young man sentenced to four years in prison for manslaughter. When his parents persuade the prison governor to gain permission for him to serve his sentence in the SIZO, they are horrified to learn that Vasia wants to be transferred to a naïvely idealised Zone to serve his sentence 'like a man'. Nonetheless, the persistent use of *blatnye* songs; the awe-inspiring screen presence of Sukhoi, the most hardened of the *bratva* inmates; and the much-vaunted fact that some of the characters are played by authentic ex-prisoners, all add to the undercurrent of romanticism which the serial, despite its naturalistic aesthetics, promotes (yet also subjects to ironic critique; the wife of Pavlov, the economist, remarks upon the prison jargon which has crept into her husband's discourse, at which he announces that he is using it in jest). It shares this contradictory desire to fetishise Stalinist realia whilst exposing their horrors with numerous post-Soviet cultural texts (including

Mikhalkov's *Burnt by the Sun* and the recent TV historical epic, *Moscow Saga*).

Such is the level of viewer involvement in the criminal world depicted that many (male) forum participants adopt the discourse and value system of the prisoners:

> If you sit with a cop [*s mentom*] and drink with him, you're a *kozel* [literally 'a goat' – a deeply insulting term of abuse], but if you're sent something without being asked openly for anything in return, you can take it, as here you're acting in the interests of the collective.

The language of the discussions at times becomes so full of jargon that some (female) participants request a return to normal speech: 'Gentlemen of the criminal world [*Gospoda blatnye*]! Couldn't you speak in ordinary Russian. I've not yet learned the Dictionary of Thieves' Slang [*Slovar' vorovskogo argo*]' www.zona.tv/forum/viewtopic.php?t+484; accessed 30 October 2006). Eventually, the moderator of the threads in which the most abusive comments appeared intervenes; the phrase 'removed by the moderator' (*udaleno moderatorom*) appears more and more frequently, though in these cases, the moderator is merely assimilated to the elaborate metaphorical conceit created by the offending contributors as a 'pig' (*musor*).

The overarching 'detective' narrative ensures that *The Zone*, too, ultimately conforms to type: performing (and thus celebrating) the overcoming of resistance to officially promulgated ideals of an inclusive state. Its late night, NTV scheduling indicates its peripherality to the nation-building mission, also demonstrating how the lack of transitivity in the relationship between television texts and their 'principals' (levels 2, 3 and 4 of our amended version of Goffman's schema) problematises the use of television for Soviet-style, propaganda purposes. But the very distance that lies between *The Zone* and the ideological centre it challenges guarantees its ultimate value to the centre's mission. Hegemony is always dynamic and performative: an ideology remains dominant by constantly having to incorporate resistance to it; if it is not to degenerate into truism, commonsense must bear the residue of the struggle which led to its institution. The path traced in audience reactions to the programme – from controversial Reality-TV shocker to comfortable, armchair entertainment – is enacted through the programme's internal progression. The early episodes are dominated by the homosexual rape; in later episodes, the detective thriller line takes precedence.

The more astute of the forum contributors note the shifting tone and the amelioration of the serial's harsher aspects as shock at the characters' brutal aggression is replaced by respect for their conformity to the implicit rules of the *bratva*: 'Notice how virtually everyone's opinion of Sukhoi changes during the course of the film. First nobody liked him … but now, when he made sure not to touch Taran, he begins to be liked by everyone' (www.zona.tv/forum/viewtopic.php?t+484; accessed 30 OCtober 2006). The 'real time' quality of the long serial generates the audience–text engagement referred to by Martin Barbero: 'Sania is not so simple ... in his role as guardian of the cell he is fair, and he supports Denis, but we'll have to see how he turns out later on' (www.zona.tv/forum/viewtopic.php?t+484; accessed 30 October 2006).

All three serials show evidence of careful political nuancing. *Soldiers* acknowledges all the controversial aspects of life in the modern Russian army: abuse of power, alcoholism, suicide, bullying, homesickness, poor food, racism, sexism, etc. But its comic ambiances draw the sting of the critique. Its legitimating mechanism also works through the principle of balance. Thus, the racially motivated taunting of 'Tundra', the Chukche soldier, is counter-balanced in an episode in which the soldier's Russian comrades rescue him from a racist attack at the hands of skinheads.

Still more subtly calibrated is *Penal Battalion*, which works on a number of carefully overlapped ideological levels. On the surface level, it nostalgi-cally re-invokes war heroism, but it inverts the official war myth by suggest-ing that victory was won by those who had been excluded from Soviet society. Nor does it flirt with anti-Soviet diatribe. Tverdokhlebov, himself a victim of Stalin's repressions, corrects the more extreme anti-Stalinist polemics of the political prisoners, reminding them of the common struggle against the Nazi invaders. In one episode, he captures the Vlasovite general who had earlier condemned him to execution. Rather than dispense sum-mary justice, Tverdokhlebov engages him in a dialogue, permitting the gen-eral to mount a passionate critique of Soviet power, which Tverdokhlebov counters with a reference to the greater evil of betraying one's own country-men. He concludes by giving a pistol to his captive so that he can end his life with honour (a gesture which attracts opprobrium from the NKVD officer). The careful calibration is noted by some viewers: 'The Vlasovite is a traitor, a killer, but he fights for his own principles unbendingly; everyone has dif-ferent shades to their character [unlike] *A zori zdes' tikhie*, in which every-thing is "black and white"' (www.rutv.ru/forum.html?d=O&cid=386&FID=206&FThrID=144145; accessed 20 October 2006).

The underlying subject of *Penal Battalion* is not the Soviet Union, but Russia, which, as Aleksandr Prokhorov points out, existed in a state of vir-tual Civil War throughout the Stalinist period.[10] The superimposition upon the past of a present time frame in which a Russia with Orthodoxy at its head reigns supreme serves as the stimulus for the articulation of the current ideology of soil and motherland. A priest replaces the NKVD officer, ush-ering in a Russian statehood of the present to impose a new order following the collapse of the now moribund order of the Soviets. But, in an audacious appropriation of the latter's myth of origin, it is an order which, far from being superimposed from above, results from a potent synthesis of above and below; Father Mikhail, representative of the new Russian state in its official guise fights alongside representatives of the shameful, hidden underbelly of its failed Soviet predecessor.

Penal Battalion's myth of Russia combines nationalist present with Soviet patriotic past and official Russian narratives of Orthodoxy and native soil with a leftist commitment to ethnic tolerance, purged of its Stalinist negations. The synthesis is naturalised through the Christian myth of resurrection: Tverdokhlebov, symbol of the new Russian order, rises from the soil of his Soviet motherland.

In *The Zone*, the shocking force of authenticity is tempered by a symbolism which projects that shock into the Soviet past (the rude and sullen officials, the queues, the grey, forbidding environment and the communal rituals). This temporal displacement has a narrative dimension. The fact that Bagrov's mission to discover the culprit for Veller's murder is referred onwards to the next episode in a long syntactic chain is matched semantically by the deferral outwards (and upwards) of the crime's elusive source.

Metaphor, metonymy and genre

The level of subversion accomplished by the three serials corresponds to the relationship between metaphor and metonymy within them. In *The Zone* there is no scene which does not take place within the prison compound. There is little account of the home lives of the officers (in marked contrast with the UK prison serial, *Bad Girls*, and other UK institutional dramas), nor the pre-prison lives of the inmates. This complete separation from everyday reality enables the serial to be posited as a metaphor for the latter (as the Tarkovskii maxim confirms); increasing the potency of the critique it mounts. As the director, Petr Shtein, put it, 'Prison is a parallel world that nobody wants to acknowledge, but it does exist' (quoted in MacFadyen 2007: 188). One viewer suggests that the prison setting represents 'that special "zone" in which the essence of the social institution of power as such is revealed'. Another links this with an implicit critique of Soviet totalitarianism to which the thieves' laws (*vorovskie poniatiia*) provided resistance (www.zona.tv/forum/viewtopic.php?t+484; accessed 30 October 2006).

In UK hospital dramas, by contrast, the plots invariably revolve around tensions between home life and official duty. Likewise, *Soldiers* traces an arc commencing in a civilian setting with the pre-army lives of the recruits and ending with their demobilisation. It includes glimpses of life beyond the barracks; one of the officers suffers sleepless nights following the birth of a child and he calls upon Tundra's 'Eastern' healing powers to calm the baby. Shmatko begins a relationship with the daughter of a widow and much of the humour involving him centres on conflicts arising from the clash of female gentility with gruff, military manners. The most telling example of metonymic confusion is also the most ideologically controversial; when Kolubkov marries Irina, an entire episode dwells upon the reverse contamination of the normal sanctity of the marriage ritual (including an excruciating nuptial bedroom scene) by the horrors of military corruption. Thus, the tension between the narrative arc and the comic micro-narrative of each episode carries a significant political charge.

Penal Battalion includes examples of metonymic slippage in the characters' interactions with civilians (Glymov's relationship with a war widow; Tsukerman's love for a military nurse), and in flashbacks to the pre-war period, but the shadow of the war hangs heavy over all the action. In terms of the metaphor/metonymy balance, *Penal Battalion* thus falls between the other two serials – a reflection of its political stance.

The austere settings of the Russian serials also diverge from those of the western institutional drama in their male-centredness and absence of private space. The ethics of mutual responsibility, asceticism, physical rigour and a strong collective spirit are also part of the national myth into which the viewers are successfully inscribed. A female forum participant from Moscow praises the serial for showing 'not only the barracks [*kazarma*], but friendship as well, and mutual support [*vzaimovyruchka*]'. Another female contributor tells her male peers that 'the army will make you into real men, like Medvedev and Kabanov'. A third comments: 'How great it is that there are real men around. Now, when you go off to the army I can sleep soundly knowing that our borders are safe and ... that the serial *Soldiers* helped achieve this' (http://soldaty.tv/forum/index.php?showtopic+6256; accessed 3 November 2006).

But to forego domestic intimacy is also to abandon post-communist individualist values alongside which Soviet-style collectivism must co-exist. Significantly, separate episodes of both *Soldiers* and *The Zone* revolve around the importance of the mobile phone in ensuring private communication with the outside world. Even in Russia, institutional dramas bridge the public and private spheres. Audiences experience their long, drawn-out viewing routines and the gradual process of familiarisation with the initially alien scenes and characters thrust into their living rooms in a manner similar to that in which inmates are inducted into the intrusive rituals and alien mores of institutional life: 'We've already seen the Medvedev–Pyleeva–Kolobkov love triangle, now we are watching a detective story ... The serial is growing and maturing before our eyes. An element of intrigue has appeared and that can only be good.' (http://soldaty.tv/forum/index.php?showtopic+6256; accessed 13 October 2006). The long serial from has, from its inception, played a key role in the operation of hegemony through its capacity for mediating between the producers of mass culture and their target audience, evolving in response to audience reaction, and incorporating within them the 'living reading' made by the people:

> the dialectics between writing and reading ... are the key to how the serials functioned and the best perspective from which to understand the new genre. These dialectics drew in the public and it reveals how the world of the reader penetrated the process of writing and left footprints in the text.
>
> (Martin-Barbero 1993: 130)

The to-ing and fro-ing that this process designates mirrors the 'provocation–pacification' dynamics of the serial's narrative (Martin-Barbero 1993), enabling it to 'sti[r] people up and denounce the atrocious contradictions of society, but in the same process ... to resolve these problems without moving people to action' (Martin-Barbero 1993: 137). Thus, over the wending course of its 50-episode narrative, *The Zone*'s initial uncompromising brutality degenerates into the side product of a detective thriller, albeit with a confused solution.

Subculture and officialdom

As the space where official and everyday discourses converge, the institution is the ideal setting for fictional drama of the Putin period. The serials' ambiguous embrace of sub-cultural themes and language lies at the heart of the hegemonic practice they collectively operate (the ultimate goal of which is to redeploy sub-cultural rhetoric in order to naturalise mainstream culture).

In *Soldiers*, military language, itself a non-standard idiom, is not attributed to any group. The group of mid-ranking officers play an important role in mediating between the senior officers and the soldiers; the use of the euphemism *blin* in place of the curse word *bliad'* abounds in their discourse, but in close proximity to the military phrases 'At Ease' (*Vol'no*), 'Yes, Sir!' (*Est'*), 'Reveiller' (*Pod'em*), etc, and to forms of address such as Comrade Sergeant (*tovarishch serzhant*). The ambiguity mirrors the serial's own ambivalent position between sub-cultural army life and the official military rhetoric to which it ultimately conforms (the officers' quarters are, somewhat incongruously, all adorned with photo-portraits of Putin). MacFadyen describes it appropriately as 'a good example of how funniness and insecure patriotism frequently inform each other' (MacFadyen 2007: 159).

There is an atavistic feel to many of the sub-cultural practices observed. The demonisation of the snitch (*stukach*) is reminiscent of Soviet sub-culture. Now deprived of its totalitarian associations, it merely reinforces the serial's nostalgic dimension, along with the rituals surrounding compulsory military service (the *provody*, or 'seeing off' party, the loyal girlfriend, etc.), all of which provide continuity with the 'best' elements of the Soviet period. This explains *Soldiers*'s huge following amongst the émigré community: 'There is nothing quite like our army. A lot of us have served and understand this. We watch in Germany with great pleasure'; 'The whole of Kazakhstan watches *Soldiers*' (http://soldaty.tv/forum/index.php?showtopic+6256; accessed 13 October 2006). 'Snitching' also features in *Penal Battalion* (one of the characters is blackmailed by the NKVD officer into reporting on conversations within the battalion) and in *The Zone* (Bagrov and Raevskii each summon prisoners to report on fellow inmates; here the practice receives dual evaluation: as a depressing throw-back to Stalinist excesses, and as an activity carried out in support of good order).

In *Penal Battalion*, the political prisoners deploy the language of dissent which, with post-Soviet hindsight, is associated with the perspicacity of the intelligentsia, but 'cleansed' of that group's alienation from the people. This same hindsight renders the NKVD officer's use of Stalinist officialese anachronistic. Tverdokhlebov articulates the patriotic Russian agenda now driving Putin's nation-building mission. But his criminal status, his sympathy for the murderer Glymov, and his refusal to report political subversion lend his rhetoric sub-cultural value. The post-Soviet context reverses the respective positions of Tverdokhlebov and the NKVD: Russian nationalism (official post-Soviet rhetoric) acquires, through Tverdokhlebov's position as a penal battalion commander, sub-cultural authenticity; given the now certain knowledge of its demise, official Stalinist rhetoric becomes associated with criminality in its negative guise.

But Tverdokhlebov's nationalist discourse remains unintegrated with Great Patriotic War rhetoric (he refuses to endorse its dishonest logic of self-sacrifice), with the language of dissidence (the dissident soldiers play virtually no role in the narrative), and with that of the criminal world (Glymov acquires heroic attributes only when he abandons his criminal ways). Rather, these voices test one another, without any one ever achieving precedence. Even the Vlasovite's nationalism is allowed to be heard, albeit framed by Tverdokhlebov's harsh condemnations. It is for this reason that the voice of the priest is added to the mix, to anchor Tverdokhlebov's sullen protestations in a positive discourse of God, nation and duty. But Tverdokhlebov and Father Mikhail never engage in meaningful dialogue. The internal clash of discourses is redeployed by viewers as a weapon in their own battles of opinion with each other. One writes in defence of her positive assessment of *Penal Battalion*:

> The opponents of the serial would make good Kharchenkos themselves [Kharchenko is the NKVD officer in the serial] ... The heroes are the ordinary soldiers, not the senior commanders ... Normal people now see this, while you carry on with your maniacal attachment to the way things were in the past.
> (www.rutv.ru/forum.html?d=O&cid=386&FID=206&FThrID=144145; accessed 20 October 2006).

The Zone foregrounds the role of sub-cultural language. The theme song, delivered in a husky-toned, *blatnoi* style, sets the tone with its references to *etap* and *zona*, and its colloquial use of *pogony* (epaulettes). The value attributed to these forms is, however, unstable. When they encounter the legalese of the staff and lawyers, both discourses are tainted by their association with, respectively, the prejudice and violence of the criminal fraternity and the corruption of the prison officers. Audience feedback reveals a symbiotic process by which the text appropriates from the criminal fraternity sub-cultural discourse which is then re-appropriated by the fraternity of web forum contributors. When Sukhoi is removed from the prison (presumably to be taken to the zone), one commentator from Moscow exclaims: 'Where have they taken him, those bastard pigs [*Musora-tvari*]?' (www.zona.tv/forum/viewtopic.php?t+484; accessed 30 October 2006).

Blatnoi sub-culture hardly provides a credible peg on which to hang a positive agenda. Instead, like *Penal Battalion*, the serial acquires the services of an Orthodox priest. His arrival is motivated by the need to administer the last rites to a dying prisoner. We subsequently learn that he 'discovered' God only after his epic sufferings in the first Chechen war. From a not unlikely synthesis of the myth of the Chechnia veteran and that of the *bratva* jailbird, emerges the altogether improbable figure of the born-again Orthodox Christian. Almost simultaneously, Petiunia Opal'skii, Sukhoi's sinister, drug-taking friend, collapses following an attempt to poison him with corrupted heroin. He, too, re-emerges as a bible-bashing fanatic, now calling himself Tikhon. What 'rescues' these unlikely twists from capitulation to an officially sanctioned osmosis of orthodoxy and order is the ridicule with which Tikhon's conversion is treated (by officers and prisoners alike) and the priest's comic naïveté. Humour in *The Zone* is double edged: it diminishes the serial's radical shock value, yet undercuts the creeping official agenda.

Another measure countervailing the negativity is the prominent role given to 'the economist' (Pavlov), the veterinary doctor ('Aibolit') and Warren, the American, whose alienated perspective, born of their superior education, matches that of the audience. But the fact that it is Warren who articulates the values of democracy and fair play only highlights their absence in a mainstream Russian variety. When Warren dismisses his corrupt defence lawyer and requests legal textbooks, his misplaced enthusiasm is mocked by the *bratva*. With Aibolit inexplicably released, the sinister subplots in which these characters are caught up peter out (Warren, too, is suddenly released; only Pavlov remains, the victim of another unexplained frame-up on the eve of his release), depriving the value systems they carry of the convincing narrative lines they demand.

The narrative drift indicates an overall ambivalence in which competing and official values cancel one another out. This phenomenon is given formal expression through the relentless irony in certain of the characters' discourses. Until the serial's closing stages, all interactions between Raevskii, Kolesnikova and Bagrov are conducted in tones heavily laden with double meaning. But for when he rages with genuine grief at the murder of Bagrov's sister-in-law, whom he loves, Raevskii's lines are accompanied throughout by a sarcastic grin. When the protocol of his actions is challenged by Bagrov, Raevskii parrots back the language of ethics, inflecting them with an irony whose obviousness reveals that he knows that Bagrov knows he is hiding serious misdemeanours. Bagrov responds in kind, using the phraseology of prison procedure, but indicating through his own brand of sarcasm an intent to breach the letter of the procedures in order to enforce their ethical meaning. The on-again, off-again, relationship between Raevskii and Kolesnikova (whose jealousy of Bagrov's sister-in-law eventually lead her to threaten Raevskii with exposure) is conducted via a banter in which each knows that what his/her interlocutor is saying is not what s/he really means. Discerning viewers of *Penal Battalion* note the same phenomenon here, where Glymov's tendency to inflect everything he says with gentle sarcasm bolsters its ideological nuancing. Writing in the *Penal Battalion* forum, one claims that 'it is hard not to notice the irony in the voice of the kulak' (Glymov was a kulak, a rich peasant, before Stalin's collectivisation programme) (www.rutv.ru/forum. html?d=O&cid=386&FID=206&FThrID=144145; accessed 20 October 2006).

Hybrid aesthetics

The Zone's generic hybridity can be compared with that of *Soldiers* which combines situation comedy and serious melodrama. Whilst *Penal Battalion* lacks a comic dimension, it shares with the latter serials a hybridity of aesthetic systems. All three programmes stake a claim to documentary realism: *Penal Battalion* because it is based on historical evidence; *The Zone* since it was inspired by a real manuscript; and *Soldiers* because it depicts everyday army routines. Realist procedures are prominently on display. *Penal Battalion* is shot in a washed-out, documentary-style, monochrome, as is much of *The Zone*. All three serials feature the shabby rituals of male institutional life (slurped-down meals, noisy drinking bouts and scabrous joke telling) and make excessive use of the extreme close-up, depicting lined, sweating faces in grim unmotivated detail.

The expository realist aesthetic is appropriate for programmes setting out to reveal uncomfortable, hidden truths; the (ab)use of Second World War penal battalions; the problems experienced by new recruits. But it sits uncomfortably with the need to re-energise war mythology, generate nostalgia for army service, and reassure viewers that truth and justice will ultimately prevail in a degenerate legal system.

Penal Battalion produces the most significant aesthetic *faux pas*: the Orthodox priest's vision of the Mother of God. The scene represents the final reconciliation between the penal battalion, reputations now restored, the guiding spirit of Orthodoxy, and the new Russian statehood uniting all these elements. But it also represents a spectacularly failed transcendence.

Other films shot within a resolutely realist aesthetic feature similarly transcendent climaxes, include Lars von Trier's *Breaking the Waves*. This is the tragic tale – shot according to the ascetic Dogme code – of a Scottish islander who believes that, by sacrificing her life and reputation amongst her strict, Presbyterian fellow-islanders to a shipload of lascivious sailors, she can mend her husband's body, crippled in an accident on board an oil ship. At the end, and out of keeping with this bleak aesthetic, we see a radiant vision of a church bell tolling above the waves to which her ravished body has been committed. But the divine vision can be recuperated as an ironic counterpoint to the false moral asceticism of the island community which has condemned the girl, and her own naïve faith (throughout the film she addresses God directly in intimate entreaty).

In *The Zone*, the failure of transcendence results from the mismatch between the recurrent Tarkovskii quote and the gradually mitigated brutality. In *Soldiers*, the riotous humour itself works against the grain of the expository aesthetic.

The serial format opens up the possibility that the divide between literalist–realist interpretations and readings elicited by the transcendent elements might have shaped the inner course of the narrative. In web feedback, the divide often takes on the attributes of gender. Contributions to *The Zone*'s forum are dominated by male viewers arguing over the authenticity of technical details (the size and attributes of particular tanks; the rituals of the *bratva*, etc.) Paradoxically, the gist of many is that historical errors reveal the programme makers' disloyalty to the memory of the Soviet war effort. In a particularly robust exchange on the *Penal Battalion* pages, one male proclaims 'My grandfather was a victim of the repressions, but he fought in the war of his own accord, not from fear'. To this, a woman retorts that she nearly died when she read of the claim that 'the order of the Red Star was hanging on the wrong side of the uniform in one scene', that, when she watches films she is 'more interested in the actors' performances than in the details of their clothes', reminding her opponent that there is a difference between 'volunteering to fight for your motherland' and 'being forced to traverse a mine field' (www.rutv.ru/forum.html?d=O& cid=386&FID=206&FThrID=144145; accessed 10 November 2006). Rather than supporting a critical challenge to the war myth, the realist aesthetic is invoked in opposition to that reappraisal. It is left to the few female respondents reading the serial for character and theme to sympathise with the plight of the prisoner-soldiers and accede to the ideological critique. This demonstrates the precarious status of television meaning. The fault line along which its contradictions emerge here is that of genre in its gendered aspect.

Feedback on *The Zone* reveals a range of attitudes to the realist aesthetic, several of which diverge from the textually inscribed readings. Notwithstanding the Tarkovskii quote, intelligentsia viewers evinced repulsion at the sensationalised brutality. Educated female members of the focus groups we conducted in 2006 expressed revulsion at the serial's sensationalised violence. One stated dismissively that 'she has stopped watching on principle [*printsipial'no*]'. Others took it to task for overplaying the expository techniques. Younger male viewers endorse the romanticised prison culture; in one forum 'thread' devoted to 'Mitia Sukhoi' a respondent writes:

Artashonov [the actor who plays him]. He reminded me of Vysotskii a bit. There's an external likeness and an inner one, too, in the way he carries himself. The strength of spirit, the will to freedom [*volia*)]– that's all clear enough. But there's something else as well. I've really become an admirer of his.

(www.zona.tv/forum/; accessed 28 September 2006)

Fewer take issue with the authenticity of *Soldiers* and the serial's 'feelgood', humanism appeals to most. The audience divides equally between male and female viewers, with the more presentable new recruits building a significant fan base amongst younger women.[11] Few comments are offered on the revelatory exposé of abuse, confirming that, during the course of the serial (a genre whose emphasis on slow-burning, routine life itself runs counter to the thrusting, masculine orientation of military myth) this narrative line gives way to the comic subplots, and to the Medvedev–Irina romance. A forum contributor writes: 'In *Soldiers* virtually everything corresponds to reality, it's just that a lot is shown a little more gently. Personally I wanted to join the army after watching the serial' (http://soldaty.tv/forum/index.php?showtopic +6256; accessed 13 October 2006).

Soldiers evokes the nation-building mission most directly, through the links on its official website to army recruitment pages. Viewers, however, see no contradiction between the propaganda function and the claim to realism, which can now be grounded in referential ties to the object of representation. Curiously, the link to army recruitment is not seen as being at odds with the claims to verisimilitude. According to one viewer, in the serial 'army life with all its peculiarities is portrayed. This is life as it naturally is [*natural'naia zhizn'*], and that's why people like it'. Another argues that 'the serial really is powerful propaganda, and that's not a bad thing; on the contrary, every self-respecting man (if his health allows) should serve'. Socialist realist aesthetics have left a powerful residue in post-Soviet viewing codes; one commentator argues that the serial's 'main task' is to 'show the army as we would want to see it' (http://soldaty.tv/forum/index.php?showtopic+6256; accessed 10 November 2006). But the unforgiving aesthetic of the extreme close-up hardly accords with the patriotic cause and *Soldiers*, too, is riddled with semiotic contradiction.

Self-reflexivity

The confusion between aesthetic modes maps onto the tension between the metaphoric and metonymic statuses of the institutional settings. In two of the serials, the self-contained institutional chronotopes foster a brand of self-reflexivity which, far from emphasising aesthetic distance from the socio-political realm, acquires profound ideological ramifications.

In Episode 14, *Soldiers* re-enacts its own, cheery theme song (a gesture repeated in *The Zone*) via a variety concert that the soldiers are asked to put on. Medvedev is the lead singer in a hastily assembled band of recruits who perform the song to great acclaim from an admiring Irina and resentment from the envious Kolobkov. Here, the serial converges with the context which spawned it (that of the rehabilitation of the army as a site of pleasure), and Medvedev merges with his extra-textual persona. This gesture re-projects the programme into a 'light entertainment' genre, reducing the expository critique presented in the Kolobkov line. Kolobkov's 'defeat' at this point in the trajectory of his subplot dovetails with the defeat of the realist aesthetic. The scene also plays self-consciously to the notion of a native celebrity culture based on the values of a distinctly Russian service ethic, a notion borne out in the audience reaction.[12]

The self-contained military celebrity culture is reinforced by the fact that several of the stars of *Soldiers* also appear in *Penal Battalion* (and other war serials) in similar roles. By deliberately employing a number of unknown actors (including ex-prisoners), *The Zone* marks itself out in contradistinction to the other serials. Indeed, for some, it acquires the status of 'reality television' (suggesting that the meaning of this term varies between television cultures), although the notion received short shrift from one web correspondent:

> Quote: 'The creation of the film follows a unique schema: the real events of the Zone will be conveyed to a group of actors who will then rework the material and offer it for the attention of viewers in a non-stop regime' ... This is an advertising ploy. I watch the serial and it is really ... not bad, but the idea that the scenario is handed on by real prisoners I can't believe.
>
> (www.zona.tv/forum/viewtopic.php?t+484; accessed 30 October 2006)

Other examples of self-reflexivity in *Soldiers* simultaneously reinforce and undercut the official agenda. Thus, the Putin portraits adorning staff offices metatextually satirise the propaganda mission of which the serial itself is part. During one episode, the soldiers sabotage the showing of an official army film instilling national pride by substituting the tape with the erotic movie, *Emmanuelle*. One officer jokes that his soldiers prefer pornography to propaganda. *Soldiers* here, too, treads a fine line between light-heartedly mocking (and thus endorsing) the mission of which it is part, and highlighting its sinister context.

The 'divine vision' scene in *Penal Battalion* likewise offers a moment of self-reflexivity whose very impossibility is an acknowledgement of the absurdity of 'tacking on' to a brutal deconstruction of the Soviet war myth a piece of contemporary nation building, and which exemplifies the 'over-identification with official symbols' that Mark Lipovetsky associates with *stiob*.[13] Meanwhile, in *The Zone*, the narrative is sporadically interspersed with black and white CCTV shots of the action unfolding, reinforcing the 'reality TV' association. When Chiga makes an escape attempt, the CCTV footage is used by Raevskii to re-apprehend him. Bagrov is frequently the victim of unsolicited observation by Raevskii and Shvernik (the most brutal of the officers) who thus keep one step ahead of their rival.

In some of the CCTV shots, we see only the observer's hands holding a telltale pipe as he follows the scenes, virtually all of which relate to Bagrov's detective mission. The narrative implication is that the mysterious observer is behind Veller's death, but the shots also precipitate an act of self-reflection on the part of the viewer, who also now gazes voyeuristically at a screen displaying the shocking brutality of prison life. Paradoxically, the hermeneutic object of Bagrov's/our search for the truth converges with the viewing subject of the search, a convergence re-enacted in the generic clash of 'reality TV' and 'detective thriller'.

The parallel between the elusive state machine and the endlessly deferred zone matches the oscillation of audience viewing points: from that of the state 'master criminal' watching events on a screen, to that of the young prisoner who aspires romantically to travel to the elusive zone. Rather than hegemonically 'normalising' sub-cultural perspectives, *The Zone*'s ideological centre of gravity is split into two hypostases which coincide without merging. The implied viewer is left without a stable point of identification. Audiences likewise fail to establish the shared values typical of cult programmes in the west, fragmenting into competing groupings: those so outraged that they want the programme banned; those critical of the political indiscretions; those prone to romanticise the *blatnoi* culture; and those who identify with the 'dissident' element. According to the director of NTV who moved the serial to a late night slot '[it] is too harsh for prime time; we are not only listening to our audience, but acting on their views' (Sergei Varshavchik, 'NTV's *Zona*', *Nezavismaia*, 8 February 2006). *Moscow News* is quoted as claiming that NTV received petitions objecting to the way in which the serial 'defiled the honour and dignity of people who devote their lives to guarding prisoners' (9 February 2006). One individual writes with indignation that he believes the serial is intended to 'set people against those who are implementing our laws' (www.zona.tv/forum/viewtopic.php?t+484; accessed 17 November 2006). However, the Chief Editor of the almanac *Nevolia* is quoted on the web forum as believing that *The Zone* is destroying the romantic illusion about prison that has again taken hold amongst Russia's youth. All that we need to do to disavow them of their false attachment to the 'criminal *bratva*, he claims, is to sit them in front of the television on weekdays' (quoted at www.zona.tv/forum/viewtopic.php?t+484; accessed 17 November 2006). Numerous comments demonstrate the failure of this strategy: 'The most correct [*pravil'nyi*] prisoner is Agdam ... Look at how, unlike others, he doesn't befriend the cops and doesn't rat on his own people'. Yet others raise the status of the serial to the level of political dissidence, referring to the way in which it 'uncovers the essence of the social institution of power as such' (www.zona.tv/forum/viewtopic.php?t+484; accessed 17 November 2006).

Self-contained institutional settings lend themselves to a foregrounding of both the anonymous state-as-Other, and the elusive, unattainable nature of that Other. The authorities to whom the highest-ranking personnel depicted in *The Zone* report are never seen on screen, any more than the upper echelons of the Stalin war machine appear in *Penal Battalion*. The serials thus 'realistically' embody their representational object, whilst ensuring that it remains screened. The contradiction is exemplified in the generic confusion they exhibit, most acutely in the case of *The Zone*, which on one hand employs real prisoners amongst its cast, and on the other hand draws on the most unlikely of paranoid subplots (associating it with the detective thrillers to which it is the antidote), a contradiction evidenced in audience reactions to the serial. Thus, a female blogger fails to understand why fellow correspondents become so concerned about the lapses in realism in *The Zone* 'I've also noticed a load of them, but I watch because of the interesting and dynamic plot'. (www.zona.tv/forum/viewtopic.php?t+484; accessed 24 November 2006).

Stalinism and the collapse of the symbolic

The sinister CCTV monitor which, as David MacFadyen points out, means that 'the actual source of power (and violence) is unnamed' (MacFadyen 2007: 190), is often accompanied by the incongruous sound of a beating heart. The incongruity is linked to a residual difficulty in representing the Soviet past. All three serials are haunted by the ghost of Stalinism from which, as we had cause to discover in Chapter 3, even post-Soviet news and current affairs programming is not yet free. Indeed, in the two contemporary serials, this past's cosy collectivism (*Soldiers*) and dark, enigmatic mystique (*The Zone*) accords it a certain nostalgia. In *The Zone*, the concatenation of illicit desire, repression and awe is evoked in a piece of spatial symbolism which, in its narrative (re-)enactment, provides the serial with its striking, if far from satisfactory, dénouement. During the course of his informal investigation, Bagrov discovers a secret bunker complex underneath the prison, consisting of an ante-room cluttered with the vestiges of the Soviet era (portraits and busts of Stalin and Lenin, communist slogans, etc.), a printing room and a billiard room in which the prison officer who is eventually revealed as Veller's murderer conspires with a mysterious official and an old prison cleaner previously believed to be mute.

The nature of the conspiracy is never made clear, but it entails a money-forging scam carried out with the help of criminals about whose presence nobody knows and overseen by prison officials including Shvernik. The motivation for Veller's murder provided by his discovery of the scam which also involves the apparent abduction of selected prisoners, otherwise destined for the zone, exploited instead as fodder in a sinister psychological experiment requiring them to be injected with a mind-altering fluid. One of the most compelling scenes comes when the terrifying Sukhoi, thought to have vanished into the zone, is revealed to be one of the human guinea pigs, now so broken that he requests to be shot. In the finale, the 'mute' cleaner takes aside Bagrov, whose suspicions are now vindicated, and indicates that 'it is time to tell him about the Zone', hinting that Bagrov himself is now earmarked as the conspiracy's next victim. In this final episode, the identity of the elusive CCTV screen observer, and the mastermind behind the entire conspiracy, is uncovered, as the camera swivels around 180 degrees revealing the pipe smoker to have been the high-ranking regional prison administrator who had earlier feigned support for Bagrov's investigation.

Bagrov's desire to solve the mystery of Veller's death, then, is expressed spatially as his descent into the depths of the prison which, in turn, acquires a temporal aspect: that of the dark, Stalinist past. The baneful Soviet paraphernalia with which the bunker is littered constitute a kind of 'return of the repressed'. Thus, Bagrov's desire to penetrate to the core of the prison mystery duplicates yet masks the viewer's desire to repossess the alternatively seductive and disgusting Stalinist detritus. It is no coincidence that the discovery of the bunker coincides with the return of Sukhoi, the compelling horror of whose criminal demeanour establishes a link between the Soviet past and the *blatnaia kul'tura* of the post-Soviet present. Nor is it accidental that the closing episodes of the serial are overshadowed by the awesome figure of Taran, the senior figure within the criminal fraternity, whose untouchable status, luxurious cell and connections with the external world of business lend him an aura of Stalinesque authority. Viewers, too, are aware of the link between the romanticisation of *blatnoi* culture and nostalgia for the Soviet past. As one puts it:

> Everything should be according to the law, as it was in Soviet times, when everyone was equally poor and decent ... Sukhoi is correct according to the law of thieves, and as far as that of the ordinary people, how can we judge?
>
> (www.zona.tv/forum/viewtopic.php?t+484; accessed 30 October 2006)

When, through the unmasking of the CCTV observer, the viewer–observer of the televised horrors of the post-Soviet criminal present is suddenly thrust into the space of the source of those horrors, the foundation for Russian reality TV's representational 'realism' is revealed to be nothing less than the repressed Stalinist imaginary. The penultimate episode portrays with hard-hitting authenticity a successful inmate riot, led by Taran, including the summoning of the OMON Special Forces by an over-zealous Kolesnikova, and their timely dismissal by Bagrov. The veering from a documentary mode to that of a Byzantine thriller overlaid with dark symbolism replicates in syntactic terms the semantic intertwining of incompatible, but mutually predicated, discursive planes: romanticised *blat*; Stalinist nostalgia; contemporary civic protest; documentary realist; and character-led humanist.

The disjunctive audience reaction to the serial simultaneously reflects and informs the intertwining process. The range of views expressed by the serial's audience is belied by a relative class homogeneity (gender-wise, the viewership is split 56/44 in favour of men); according to a ratings survey, 65.7 per cent of the audience completed secondary education, 20.8 per cent higher education and 13.5 per cent primary education (www.zona.tv/main_chapter/5.html; accessed 24 November 2006). A proportion was too shocked by the naturalistic depiction of prison conditions to watch any further. Others saw it as 'a vulgar caricature of life and reality' and in the choice of a former criminal as one of the characters, 'a mockery of humanity' (*izdevatel'svto nad chelovechestvom*) (http://rostov.kp.ru/daily/culture/doc100688/; accessed 24 November 2006). Many female viewers regard the serial as 'rather truthful' (*dostatochno pravdivym*), exhibiting more distance from the material than the male *aficionados* who adopt the values of the inmates. Such viewers are distinct in turn from two groups of relatively intellectual counterparts, one of which uses the forum pages to display a systematic dictionary of prison jargon, and the other to defend *The Zone* for its sympathetic portrayal of decent prison officers like Bagrov, arguing that 'the system outlives them' (*sama sistema … takikh liudei izzhivaet*) (www.zona.tv/forum/viewtopic. php?t+484; accessed 24/ November 2006).

The closer to Stalin himself that a text ventures, the less it is able to permit the open expression of nostalgic desire. In *Penal Battalion*, it is Stalin's NKVD henchman who is subjected to critique; Stalin and the upper echelons of the Red Army remain unrepresented, enabling some of their aura to be transferred to a Russian-dominated Red Army purified of its Stalinist distortions. *Penal Battalion* has, however, to be viewed alongside a spate of other virtually concurrent serials: the Aksenov adaptation, *Moscow Saga* (*Moskovskaia saga*); *The Kukotskii Case* (*Kazus Kukotskogo*, adapted from Ulitskaia) and the Channel 1 version of Bulgakov's *Master and Margarita*, all of which ostensibly offer soul-searching exposes of Stalin's misdemeanours, recalling the early confessional years of glasnost. But, unlike *Penal Battalion*, two of them (*Moscow Saga* and *The Kukotskii Case*) are glossy epics tracing a family history through the Soviet period down to a present from which the narrative voice looks back to a lost youth. The relationship between 'historical background' (Soviet repression) and 'primary narrative' (the story of the family's romantic peripeteia) undergoes a subtle reversal in which the desire to recreate the lost past (and loves) of the family history is transferred onto the 'lost' historical context. Moreover, unlike *Penal Battalion*, *Moscow Saga* and *The Kukotskii Case* include representations of senior figures in the Stalin regime. In *Moscow Saga*, Beria and Stalin himself are given prominent roles and one of the main heroes of the serial (Dr Gradov) is called upon to treat Stalin for a gland ailment, even as his own children are being abducted to the Gulag. This Stalin cuts an erratic, avuncular figure who, in a later episode, rewards the younger Gradov, now a leading general following his sudden release from the camps, for daring to disagree with the leader's military tactics. When Doctor Gradov, grandfather of the latter-day narrator, gently probes Stalin's neck in close-up, he vicariously realises a desire to reach out from the post-Soviet present and touch the enigmatic body of the monstrous leader.

Stalin is more or less extraneous to the narrative action (in one curious, drawn-out scene he moves slowly from guest to guest at a grand military function, greeting them with a solitary '*Zdravstvuite*') revealing both the hidden fascination which motivates his presence, and the difficulties in integrating him within narrative structures. The 'real' Stalin recedes further into the distance to take up the same slot of 'repulsive object of desire' that he occupies in *Penal Battalion*. The runaway success of Channel 1's *Master and Margarita*, a text with an unimpeachable dissident heritage, is instructive here. Its trenchant critique of Stalin's state crimes (signalled in black and white documentary footage inter-cut with the dramatic plot action) is over-shadowed by lovingly recreated nostalgic realia of the period and by the enigmatic and authoritarian figure of Voland, Stalin's diabolic double.

The problematic with which all the institutional dramas engage can be re-expressed as a breakdown of the Symbolic Order.[14] Partly situated in the realm of the Imaginary, each articulates an illicit object of desire: the enig-matic authority figure behind the death of Veller in *The Zone* (with whom the viewer is permitted momentarily to identify in moments of televisual self-reflexivity); the washed-out heroic past of the Great Patriotic War in *Penal Battalion*; and the nostalgic myth of Soviet army service in *Soldiers*. Each strives to subjugate these desires to a stable, paternal authority in the realm of the Symbolic: a victorious Russian nation, purged of its Soviet distortions (*Penal Battalion*); a benevolent Russian military purified of its excesses, able to reconcile official patriotic discourse with the ordinary language of the lower ranks (*Soldiers*); and a prison regime freed from the deleterious influ-ence of both the *bratva* with its idealised underground myth, and a degen-erate prison regime (*The Zone*). The failure of this process of subordination marks the failure of the serials as realist representations (the reassuring sense of coherence and authenticity that realism conveys involves a suppression of the Lacanian Real).[15] This leaves the viewer in a state of oscillation between a forbidding, elusive Other adrift from any representational system, and an Imaginary, but illicit, object of nostalgic desire. As well as extreme facial close ups, all the serials feature incessant, unpleasant scenes of food and drink consumption whose repulsive nature exceeds any possible motivation in terms of plot consistency or verisimilitude; one officer in *The Zone*, appropriately nicknamed 'Fat' (*Salo*), is seen perpetually with a chicken leg hanging from a mouth dribbling with fat and saliva – indices of the excessive Lacanian Real, obtruding illicitly into the scene of representation.[16]

The failure of the Symbolic Order subsumes the failures identified earlier: that of hegemony (the normalisation of sub-cultural discourses and values) that of aesthetic realism (the articulation of a coherent, self-identical reality), and that of constructing a unified audience fan base. Above all, and in the wider context of the unsuccessful *Border*, it confirms the failure of the state's attempt to deploy the pseudo-military drama in its nation-building project. To use a military figure of speech peculiarly appropriate to the present argu-ment, it constitutes an example of a remotely issued 'order' which remains singularly (and, some might say, thankfully), unfulfilled.

6 Laughter at the threshold

My Fair Nanny, television sitcoms and the post-Soviet struggle over taste

The curious absence of the post-Soviet sitcom

If epic military dramas like *Penal Battalion* found a natural (albeit awkward) place within the Putinesque patriotic environment, and if deeply Russian, light-hearted semi-comedies such as *Soldiers* reinforced television's potential for authenticating that environment's ideological underpinnings, it would be difficult to say the same for the alien format of the western sitcom. The television sitcom has, indeed, been a long time in coming to post-Soviet Russian television. The reasons for this form part of the subject of the current chapter, but suffice it to say for the time being that those attempts at a home-grown, native version of this distinctly foreign format which did appear on Russian television prior to 2004 proved in the main to be short-lived failures. Whilst American and British imports such as *Friends*, *Cheers*, *Fawlty Towers*, *I Love Lucy* and *Grace under Fire* had enjoyed considerable success throughout the 1990s, the genre did not, as Dana Heller points out, have an established lineage in Russia.[1] Early attempts at Russian versions of the sitcom were, perhaps not surprisingly, short-lived. The first two – *Family Business, Funny Business* (*Semeinoe delo, smeshnoe delo*) and *Strawberry Café* (*Klubnichnoe kafe*) – aired in 1997. The former centred on a family which had lost all of its savings in a pyramid scheme and included an array of social types from the New Russia. The latter, something of a cross between a sitcom and a soap opera, focused on the tribulations of several generations of a family of café proprietors. Each opened to great interest both at home and in the west but, despite efforts to tailor the format to Russian tastes and cultural traditions (efforts which Heller analyses in detail), failed to secure a loyal audience and were removed from the schedules after less than a year.

A second, concerted effort to establish the sitcom in the Russian viewing consciousness was made in 2002 with *Friendly Family* (*Druzhnaia semeika*), based on the US show, *Married with Children*, and involving a successful Moscow family with materialistic aspirations to improve their lot still further. Again, despite the domesticating features, which included a highly mannered acting style inappropriate to the genre, but familiar to Russian audiences, it lasted only a few months. Two years later, an NTV show called

FM and the Guys (*FM i rebiata*), centred around a radio station set up by a group of fashionable young Muscovites whose petty disputes, trials and tribulations, amorous relationships and subversive attitudes to their superiors, provided material well suited to the sitcom format. It aired in 2004 but, owing largely to its restricted target audience (young, 20-something urban sophisticates), it, too, was removed after a few months. The Channel 1 show, *Simple Truths* (*Prostye istiny*), shown in 2004 and 2005, was likewise targeted at a youth audience (this time, teenaged schoolchildren), and though it also embraced many of the key features of the sitcom genre (a defined locale, an open-ended structure capable of generating an infinite number of new narratives, a focus on comedy of character and situation), it failed to establish sufficient momentum to acquire a permanent place in the schedules.

These failures are in one sense hardly surprising. Other than news programmes, a very restricted number of talk shows and the odd enduring game show success, such as *Field of Miracles* (*Pole chudes*), Russian television has, since the fall of communism, been characterised by a complete lack of stability; channels have repeatedly changed hands; shows have switched channels, along with stars, with an alarming alacrity;[2] few programmes of any genre have lasted much beyond a year; the inability of the sitcom to take root in post-Soviet television culture is matched by that of the soap opera (in its British, rather than Latin American, manifestation) and the fact that the two genres share the same emphasis on open-ended narrative structures involving ordinary people in stable, everyday, family environments – neither at a premium in Russia's period of emergence from the ravages of communism and robber capitalism – is hardly coincidental. Russian television culture, moreover, lacks a tradition in situation comedy, which is not the case with the game show and the quiz, preceded in Soviet times by the popularity of the *viktorina*. Irina Petrovskaia's comments in *Izvestiia* on the failure of *Strawberry Café* seem pertinent: 'I don't think the sitcom is organic to the Russian mentality. And the laugh track is absolutely horrific. I think even the Americans must hate it' (quoted in Stanley 1997: 1). Television humour in Russia has meant primarily comedy of the virtuoso, stand-up variety, as exemplified in the legendary status achieved in Soviet times by Arkadii Raikin, and more recently, Dmitrii Khazanov and Mikhail Zhvanetskii, as well as by the annual youth variety quiz show KVN. Political satire has a long and noble lineage in Russian culture, as does the puppet show, which helps explain why NTV's *Puppets* (*Kukly*), an adaptation of the British *Spitting Images*, enjoyed considerable success until the political environment became too oppressive to sustain either NTV in its path-breaking, independent manifestation, or political satire of the savage kind practised by the makers of *Puppets*.[3]

The arrival of *My Fair Nanny*

Nor, then, is it surprising, that the first really successful Russian situation comedy should be adapted from an American format to which, on the face of things, it adheres closely. *My Fair Nanny* (*Moia prekrasnaia niania*) began showing on the STS (CTC) channel in early 2004 and by the middle of the year had become the most popular entertainment programme on Russian television. Its success has been quite phenomenal and even as late as 23 December 2005, the RusKino website was listing it as the third most watched serial on Russian television, after RTR's eagerly anticipated adaptation of Bulgakov's legendary novel, *The Master and Margarita* (then in its first week on television), and Channel 1's equally high-profile adaptation of Dostoevskii's *The Idiot*, released to great acclaim to coincide with the celebration of St Petersburg's tercentenary in 2003. On the same website, Anastasia Zavorotniuk, who plays the role of the Nanny, was listed as the second most popular actor in Russia (www.ruskino.ru; accessed 23 December 2005).

My Fair Nanny (MFN) was based on the popular American CBS sitcom *The Nanny* which premiered in November 1993 and ran for six seasons throughout the 1990s, starring Fran Dreshcher in the lead role. The first episode established the basic situation around which subsequent episodes were based; a working-class girl from the Queens District of New York is sacked from her job as a hairdresser by her boss, who also happens to be her boyfriend. Fran (the character takes the name of the actress who plays her) finds herself in the rich Manhattan District selling cosmetics. By chance, she calls at the mansion of the recently widowed Maxwell Sheffield, a sophisticated English Broadway Producer, who is seeking a new nanny to look after his three children, a pubescent girl prone to teenage crushes, a mischievous 10-year-old boy with a wicked tongue, and a neurotic 8-year -old girl already in therapy. She ends up being offered the job and soon endears herself to the children, and to Maxwell's prim and proper English butler, Niles. However, Sheffield's snobbish female associate, C.C., takes exception to Fran's vulgar manners and uncultured speech, and to the obvious attraction that Maxwell begins to feel for the Nanny, who now establishes herself as the rival to C.C. for the producer's never openly acknowledged attentions, and an ally to Niles and the three children in their attempts to mock and antagonise the loathsome C.C. The humour, a combination of verbal gags (mostly at C.C.'s expense), comedy of character (with Niles, Fran, her still louder mother, the children and C.C. the main objects of fun), and of situation (revolving around differences of class and culture between Fran and the rest of the household), is accompanied by frequent canned laugher.

The third episode of the CBS sitcom is entitled 'My Fair Nanny' and entails a contemporary updating of Shaw's 'My Fair Lady' as Maxwell attempts in vain to educate Fran in the speech and manners of his peers in time for a party to celebrate his eldest daughter's coming out as a high society debutante. It is from the title of this episode that the Russian version takes its cue. Launched with the collaboration of its American owners, Sony Pictures, MFN replaces Fran with Viktoria Prutkovskaia (Vika), an uneducated Ukrainian hairdresser likewise fired from her job by her boyfriend. Maxwell Sheffield becomes Maksim Shatalin, a famous producer of musicals on the Moscow stage (played by Sergei Zhigunov). Niles is substituted by Konstantin (Boris Smolkin), and C.C. by Shatalin's scheming financial adviser, Zhanna Arkad'evna (Ol'ga Prokof'eva). Vika's mother (the ever popular, now deceased, Liubov' Polishchuk) is the archetypal provincial *khokhlushka* who wants nothing better than for her daughter to acquire a rich, metropolitan husband and sees in the handsome, if ambivalent, Shatalin the perfect match for her Vika. Like Sheffield, Shatalin has three children – Masha (a teenager with her mind on boys and parties, but rather more outgoing than her American counterpart), Denis (older than his US equivalent, but equally mischievous and sharp-tongued) and Ksiusha (who lacks the neuroses of her source, but is every bit as 'cute'). MFN follows its American source likewise in incorporating a 'canned laughter' track.

Global formatting is now an established feature of twenty-first century media culture and MFN appears to offer little more than one more example of the unstoppable tide of popular western light entertainment programmes to have swamped Russian television since 1991, albeit more recently in forms lightly adapted for their domestic audiences.[4] Russian versions of familiar game shows such as *Who Wants to Be a Millionaire* (*Kto chochet stat' millionerom*; *O schastlivchik!*) and *The Weakest Link* (*Samoe slaboe zveno*); 'reality TV shows' like *Big Brother* (*Za oknom*) and *Survivor* (*Poslednii geroi*) and drama series like *Sex and the City* (*Bal'zakovskii vozrast. Ili vse muzhiki – svolochi*) abound, and meet with varying degrees of success; the first series of the Russian *Sex and the City* was panned by critics and shunned by all but a handful of viewers for its complete unsuitability to Russian cultural tastes and traditions.[5] The initial failure of *Bal'zakovskii vozrast* reflects the greater challenges faced by global exporters of contemporary drama serials than those of game shows, quiz shows and reality TV shows, whose appeal to the competitive instincts and prurience of television viewers is more universal than the more culturally nuanced fictional serial. The sitcom would seem to fall into the same category as the contemporary drama serial in this respect, since the genre is reliant on the universality of a set of familiar settings, character types and plot situations which do not transpose easily onto a culture beset by socio-economic instability.

Methods

Any attempt to understand the phenomenal success of MFN would need to pay attention to those (seemingly superficial) ways in which the programme deviates from its source. In our reading of the programme, we will use these differences to demonstrate how, despite (and, at times, because of) its apparently slavish obedience to its US model, MFN is located at the threshold of a series of key semiotic 'flashpoints' in post-Soviet Russian culture: those of *genre* (the programme's ambiguous position on the boundary between the finite serial and the open-ended sitcom); *aesthetic taste* (its espousal of borderline 'vulgar' humour and its feisty heroine); and *class* (the accompanying

divide between the metropolitan sophisticate and the provincial parvenue).
These flashpoints map in turn onto tensions of *realism versus aspiration*
(Vika's life offers both a compendium of the challenges faced by ordinary
people in post-Soviet conditions and a model of hope for escape); of the
public sphere/private sphere divide (Shatalin's celebrity status acts as an
incentive and a barrier to his nascent feelings of attraction for Vika); of
gender and sexuality (on one side, the resourceful, scheming, yet intellec-
tually limited Vika, prepared to 'use' sexual charm in the interests of economic betterment, on the other, the educated, yet gullible, Shatalin and
Konstantin); and of *national identity* (arguments over whether the programme is authentically Russian; questions as to the reasons for making the
main heroine Ukrainian).

When unpicking the nexus which these multiple mappings generate, we
will have recourse to tracing a series of thematic patterns and continuities
which accord the tensions, ambiguities and conflicts concrete value: the
importance to the plot of the construction of mistaken or usurped identities
(related in turn to a distinction between laughs derived from conscious 'gags'
in which one of the characters is complicit with the audience, and laughs
derived purely from comic situations in which the viewers remain 'a step
ahead' of the characters); the role of the threshold as a space in which
character conflicts are initiated; contrastive shots of inner and outer space;
the absence/omission (or near absence) of key topographies and biographical
trajectories. In gathering together the threads of the nexus, we will show how
these phenomena also serve as the sites of the key 'laughter points', thus
enabling us to link the humour on which the programme's success is predicated with the semiotic tensions to which it gives unwitting expression.
Thus, as is so often the case with popular cultural texts, the very 'cosy light-
heartedness' and innocence of the surface meanings of MFN alerts us to the
presence of conflict and paradox beneath.

Our argument is grounded in the analysis of several key sources: the full
range of MFN episodes from the five series of the sitcom broadcast on STS
(issued on DVD in 2005); the complete series of the American *The Nanny*,
also issued on DVD by CBC in 2005; several web-based chat-rooms dedicated to MFN and perused over a one-year period (from December 2004 to
December 2005) when the programme's popularity was at its peak. There are
two justifications for the inclusion of the audience response material. First,
as our Introduction established, the meanings of televisual texts are notoriously difficult to locate within precise textual boundaries. For example (and
this is especially pertinent to MFN), what is most significant about many
television shows resides in the active fan culture which emerges around them.
Audience research thus becomes an essential tool for assessing how textually
inscribed meanings are calibrated through viewer reaction – the general
reason, and one particular to the case in question. Secondly, however, in the
case of MFN, one of the textual 'themes' explored relates to questions of
cultural taste, and it is precisely the perceived 'lack of taste' (or otherwise)

which forms the central debating point in audience discussions of MFN. Moreover, these discussions reveal confusion over whether the lack of taste is 'intentional' and part of the object of laughter, or whether it resides in gullible viewers foolish enough to like the show. One might say both that the viewer feedback foregrounds an issue central to the textual thematics and that the text foregrounds an issue of importance to post-Soviet television culture. In this sense, as we argued in our Introduction, the empirical data becomes a 'master threshold': that of the televisual meaning situated between text and audience, official realm and popular taste, and, indeed, between text-based and audience-based approaches to television studies. Because of the importance of audience reactions to MFN (it is, after all, this which determines its status as a cultural phenomenon worthy of study, and which distinguishes it from other, run-of-the-mill Russian adaptations of global formats), and because of its metatheoretical capacity, we will structure our analysis around the issues of character and plot important to audiences, focusing our argument on the phenomenally popular Vika Prutkovskaia.

We begin by considering some of the recurrent plotting devices in MFN, dwelling in particular on the role of mistaken and usurped identity and their links with economic and class anxieties, and with the interplay between the show's aspirational and realist aspects. We examine in this context the generic conflict between the show's dual status as an open-ended sitcom and a serial with a finite, overarching narrative trajectory, drawing here, as throughout, on references to the American source and to the audience data. We single out Vika's central role in driving the narrative, focusing on her Ukrainian origins, the features distinguishing her from her US counterpart (and thus on the two aspects of national identity with which she engages), her cultural status and aesthetic taste, and her gender, before discussing the ways in which the 'border conflicts' identified are given spatial expression. We use this as a bridge to a conclusion in which we attempt to place MFN in the broader context of shifts in post-Soviet television culture towards a more dynamic model in which viewing audiences shape the meanings generated by programmes produced according to global formats in ways both more active and unpredictable than previously, yet also, by virtue of that very openness and unpredictability, closer to the pulse of the tensions driving post-Soviet Russian culture.

Identity shifts as plot driver

Several early episodes of MFN are minimally adapted transpositions of episodes of *The Nanny* shown previously on CBS. One, for example, repeats almost scene for scene, and gag for gag, an American story line in which the nanny ends up enthusiastically volunteering to direct the play put on by the youngest daughter's school. Having allocated the main role to her protégée (Shatalin's daughter) and having displeased the school's snobbish headmistress, Fran/Vika is eventually replaced by her boss but ends up saving the day when she persuades the daughter to return to the stage after she has been alienated by her father's over-zealous attitude to direction (MFN, Series 1, Ep. 3).

The Russian series soon acquired its own momentum and, with that, its own scriptwriters and plots. As is the case with many popular comedy genres, mistaken, or usurped, identity is the mainspring of many of the narrative situations. Several episodes of MFN involve Vika reluctantly agreeing to stand in for one of the Shatalins (a situation which echoes the establishing master-narrative in which Vika is hired by the Shatalins in the absence of a 'true nanny'). Thus, in one episode, Vika agrees to attend a school parent's evening in the guise of the poorly performing Denis's father (MFN, Series 1, Ep. 5). Predictably, Vika ends up having to take the role further than she would like. In a later episode, she is persuaded by Masha to stand in for her for one night at the hospital at which she works, so that Masha can meet her new boyfriend (MFN Series 1, Ep. 8). By coincidence, Shatalin is admitted to the hospital with appendicitis the same night, and to her embarrassment, Vika is asked to shave his nether regions in preparation for the operation. Elsewhere, Vika is mistaken for Zhanna by a prominent Georgian figure in the entertainment business with whom Shatalin hopes to do business and who, true to national stereotype, begins to take an amorous interest in her. Vika is forced (by both Shatalin and the avaricious Zhanna) to prolong the illusion, even entertaining her admirer at Zhanna's apartment, with comically disastrous consequences (MFN, Series 2, Ep. 14).

Characters constantly and consciously usurp the role and identity of others. In one episode, Vika falls for a rich man she meets in the supermarket who promises to make a large investment in Maksim's productions. When it transpires that the man is a kebab-selling charlatan, Vika resorts to dressing as a businessman so that she can subvert the fake business deal the kebab-seller has set up with Maksim in a nightclub (MFN, Series 3, Ep. 4). Here, gender ambiguity serves as a cipher for class tensions, disguised as comic farce. In another episode (MFN, Series 1, Ep. 4), a potential rival to Vika in the form of an attractive female 'image maker' for Shatalin turns out to be a lesbian, but Vika's sense of relief dissipates when the woman attempts to seduce her. Apart from offering a rare example of the treatment of female homosexuality in Russian culture, the episode confirms the function of gender transgression as a vehicle for conveying the tensions and ambiguities of social structure (had she not been a lesbian, the image-maker could have put paid to Vika's matrimonial aspirations).

Identity-shifting dominates MFN to a greater extent than *The Nanny*, where the comedy relies more on differences between the Sheffields' effete, high-class manners, and Fran's sharp-tongued Queens' humour and honest materialism. In an incident within an episode which found particular favour with female contributors to MFN's web forum, Konstantin pretends to be Shatalin, mischievously telling the besotted Zhanna who has her eyes closed in anticipation of a kiss that there is nothing which excites him more than hearing her grunt like a pig; Zhanna, naturally, dutifully obliges (MFN, Series 4, Ep. 2). Konstantin spends much of another episode as Shatalin, following another 'stand-in' at a parents' evening, and is forced to fend off the amorous approaches of a teacher who is convinced that she should have the leading role in Shatalin's next musical (MFN, Series 4, Ep. 4). In one episode, Vika is excluded from the action altogether as she takes a well-earned holiday on the Black Sea, only to be temporarily replaced in the Shatalin household by her mother and grandmother, whose still more rambunctious Ukrainian provincialism and overt fortune-seeking upset the balance of relationships in the household.

The uncertainties and shifts of class allegiance and identity drive much of this comic chaos. Class was equally central to *The Nanny*, where the juxtaposition of pseudo-aristocratic English old money and the vulgar materialism of the upstart nanny from Queens struck a chord with post-Reagan America in which the post-war New Deal settlement, backed by a patrician Republican establishment with roots in the East-Coast WASP community, had been shattered by the new monied classes created by Reaganomics. One of the attendees at the eldest daughter's 'coming out' party in Episode 3 is specifically described by the elitist C.C. as 'Old Money' and is heard boasting that she can trace her descendants to 'The Mayflower' generation. The fact that MFN reflects such class uncertainties through dramatic identity shifts rather than sharp-tongued gags at scenes in which the entire social cast is brought on stage at once, indicates the still greater fluidity characterising the socio-economic shifts taking place in post-communist Russia.

Sexual tension as the language of comedy/conflict

Viewers rarely express their opinions of MFN in socio-economic terms. Indeed, many of them praise it precisely because it offers a light-hearted break from the concerns of the world outside, and for its innocent family-centredness. Thus, one web correspondent from Zakholust'e describes it as 'The coolest serial! [*Samyi prikol'snyi serial*] Suitable for all ages; my whole family watches with great interest' (www.ruskino.ru/movie/forum; accessed 17 March 2006). Another suggests that 'it has been created especially to enable you to take a break from problems at work, or family problems' (ibid.). However, female viewers are consistent in including among their reasons for watching MFN its status as a modern-day Cinderella story in which a young provincial woman enters a world of wealth and glamour to find the Prince Charming who will rescue her from adversity. One Muscovite praises the show as 'a wonderful serial. It really raises your spirits. A lot of the phrases you hear on it have become quotations, and the girls all dream of "meeting a man like Shatalin"' (ibid.) Another (from Ussuriisk) 'hopes that Vika will eventually marry Shatalin' (ibid.) A third from Zaporozh'e is more expansive: 'Niania has made viewers tormented by taxes, poverty and unemployment [*izmuchennykh nalogami, bedenezh'em, bezrabotitsei*] look at the world in another way: suddenly there is cause for optimism … and one can even believe that men like Maks really exist!' (www.ruskino.ru/movie/forum; accessed 12 April 2006).

There have been many such aspirational programmes on post-Soviet Russian television, following the early successes of Latin American soap operas like *Just Maria* (*Prosto Maria*) and *The Rich also Cry* (*Bogatye tozhe plachut*) in which a maid from a poor background falls in love with a rich male from among the family entourage of her employers. The detective series, *Cinders* (*Zolushka*), was one of the great successes of the late 1990s. MFN's proximity to this model is amongst the reasons for its success; it is a 'realistic', domestic version of the 'illusory' Latin American dream. The fact that the class tensions are inscribed beneath the surface of the Cinderella myth and released only at the point at which the sexual tension between Vika and Maksim comes to a head helps to explain the programme's comic appeal. Laughter and the release of tension are intimately connected.[6] The link is foregrounded in a scene from one episode in which Vika is watching a Latin American television soap in which the poor girl marries the man of her dreams. She is reprimanded by Maksim who, however, becomes rapidly drawn into the action of the soap himself (MFN, Series 3, Ep. 4).

The sexual tension between Vika and Maksim provides most of the plot situations in MFN. Underlying them all is the question which underpins the Latin American soap plots: will the girl 'get her man' and will there be a marriage? Typically, MFN plots follow a pattern in which Vika 'upsets' Maksim in some way or other, they are reconciled to the extent that they are forced to recognise their mutual attraction, but then recoil from consummating the attraction. For example, in one episode from the second series, Vika accompanies Masha to a kissing competition, the prize for which is an appearance on a pop star's album cover. Masha persuades a reluctant Vika to enter the competition herself which, to her surprise, she ends up winning. When Maksim learns of this, he severely castigates Vika. In making her 'angry' response, Vika decides to demonstrate her kissing skills on Maksim who, at the point of losing control of his feelings, stops just in time (and to Vika's disappointment), asserting with a prolonged pause before the predicate to his sentence 'You are my … nanny' (MFN, Series 2, Ep. 3). The accumulated tension – comic, sexual and social – is concentrated in that pause (the predicate could, of course, have been 'love', 'fiancee', etc.).

Maksim alternatively plays the disinterested male, insensitive to Vika's true feelings, or the rival to one of Vika's many male rivals, forced to admit his hitherto unacknowledged jealousy. In one episode, he masks his jealousy with an employer's concern that his nanny is staying out too late at night, thereby compromising her ability to look after his children (MFN, Series 3, Ep. 5). The strength of Vika's own commitment is often placed in question, through her interest in other rich males, her own decisions to reverse the identity shifts which force her into the role of Maksim's partner, or by comparison with her mother's more openly articulated desire to 'marry her off' (the mother deliberately refers to Shatalin as her 'son-in-law', much to his embarrassment). In one episode (MFN, Series 3, Ep. 2), Vika's mother inadvertently interrupts Maksim as he is about to declare his love for Vika; so tentative is the commitment on both sides that the intervention scuppers the whole 'deal'. Vika's mother represents class tension in its literal form, whilst Vika and Maksim transpose the language of social conflict into the more subtle language of sexual tension.

The two languages are mutually translatable. The early episodes of the first series are dominated by Shatalin's anxiety over the potential impact of the loss of his newly acquired nanny on the proper upbringing of his children; as the series progresses his fear becomes a function of his growing feelings of attraction for her which, in turn, enhances her power over him. But, when, at the end of a riotous episode set in a downmarket nightclub, the heroine throws a cake in Shatalin's face in frustration at his unwillingness to respond to her advances, he reminds her that he pays her wages. The 'not quite-ness' of their mutual affection mirrors the 'not-quite-ness' of the Shatalin family, and the 'not-quite-ness' of the challenge to social norms that Vika's relationship with Shatalin represents (MFN, Series 1, Ep. 10).

As a sitcom, MFN centres its comic effects around a combination of situations in which the characters are the unwitting victims of mistaken identities or other such unanticipated circumstances, and verbal gags in which one or more of the characters consciously mocks one or more of the others. In MFN, Zhanna is the most frequent target of the gags, most of which are delivered by Konstantin, or by Denis, Maksim's son. On one typical occasion, the acerbic Konstantin, in response to Zhanna's frantic assertion that she will die of embarrassment unless she gets her way, enquires if he can hold her to her promise (MFN, Series 4, Ep. 5).[7] Zhanna and Maksim are rarely the active subjects of verbal gags. Vika and her mother find themselves almost equally in the positions of 'objects' and subjects – itself an expression of the social tension at whose cutting edge they are situated.

The gag functions as an instrument by which social control can be exerted. The witticisms meted out to Zhanna by Denis and Konstantin are motivated by a desire to put this social parvenue in her place; Zhanna's role as a calculating member of the new Russian business class intersects with the threat represented by her aggressive femininity. At the end of a poignant episode, Shatalin irresponsibly proposes to Vika to spite his visiting mother who is concerned about her son's relationship with his vulgar nanny. Vika, now furious at the deceit, and attired in her wedding dress, throws a pink negligee at Shatalin who, on enquiring why it is so 'transparent', is told that, since this is what she would have worn on her wedding night, he should 'go and torture [him]self with regret' (*Vot i muchites!*). Vika's 'put-down' enables her to reassert the control over her social/sexual aspirations which she momentarily loses in succumbing to the false dream of the wedding (MFN, Series 4, Ep. 11). The comedy of errors, meanwhile, functions as an indication of the precariousness with which social control is maintained and its propensity to disintegrate into chaos.

Realism, aspiration and the question of genre

The comparison of MFN with its Latin American soap predecessors requires several qualifications:

(1) the generic distinction (MFN is a sitcom and not a soap);
(2) the language/cultural difference (MFN is a Russian-made adaptation of a foreign format with adjustments made to take account of the new domestic context);
(3) the chronological gap (Latin soaps were at their height when the Russian economy was in its most precarious and chaotic state; MFN came to the fore in a period of relative economic stability and emergent social mobility).

These differences have a clear bearing on the status of the show as alternatively aspirational and realistic. Whereas the Latin American soap heroine always 'gets her man', the budding romance between Vika and Shatalin must remain forever frustrated so that the sitcom format can continue to generate the tension that drives it. This brings the show closer to the territory of the real in which dreams are never realised. The cartoon animated re-enactment of the show's first episode with which each episode opens establish a mythic subtext of recurring patterns which conflicts productively with the aspirational narrative arc ending in Vika's marriage to Shatalin.

Aside from her good looks and acting talent, Anastasia Zavorotniuk's popularity is explicable in terms of the sheer 'ordinariness' of the role she plays: Vika is the archetypical provincial girl living with her mother in Moscow; her Ukrainian accent, lack of sophistication, short skirts and heavy make-up are all reassuring to an audience seeking the familiar and the down-to-earth with which to balance the hopes and dreams of social (and sexual) betterment they share with her. Also calculated to integrate MFN with the real everyday lives of its viewers is the setting of some episodes around familiar dates in the Russian calendar: one, for example, takes place on 8 March (International Women's day – still a big event in post-Communist Russia).

Recent economic changes are reflected subtly in MFN. An indicative episode opened with Vika administering a curt reprimand to a penniless tramp (*bombzha*) asking her for money on the Moscow metro, and then taking home a baby seemingly abandoned by a feckless provincial mother laden with shopping – a familiar sight on the Moscow metro for years (MFN, Series 2, Ep. 14). The fact that Vika, herself a mere provincial girl, feels able to moralise about begging, and to 'adopt' a poor child, marks a difference separating her from the urban poor. Social stratification is gathering pace, rendering defunct the earlier crude separation of an impoverished mass from a corrupt elite. Also significant in MFN, and concordant with audience sensibilities, is the association of wealth and privilege with the education and good taste of the urban intelligentsia; Shatalin is a well-read, tastefully dressed producer of musicals, not a grasping New Russian. This *kulturnost'*, interestingly, adds both to the aspirational function he fulfils, but for the same reason to his realism (it is precisely such men whom young women like Vika aspire to 'catch'). Vika thus represents the average Russian female hoping to find herself a good-looking, cultured man of standing. Whilst appreciated as a 'family' show, MFN's most ardent admirers are overwhelmingly female and it is Vika who is the point of identification for them.

Genre, the public/private threshold and the role of metatextuality

A feature shared by MFN and *The Nanny* is the regular inclusion of guest appearances by well-known television personalities. However, in MFN, celebrities invariably play themselves rather than fictional roles, as is often the case in *The Nanny*. And the television shows with which they are associated are often worked into the plot. For example, in one episode (MFN, Series 3, Ep. 1), Zhanna's brother takes a liking to Vika and bets with his sister that the nanny is intelligent enough to win a TV quiz show to which he has access. Vika wins through a combination of luck and native wit, much to the dismay of Zhanna Arkad'evna. In another episode, the entire Shatalin family win first prize in a family quiz show (MFN, Series 2, Ep. 7). The show centring on 8 March celebrations includes guest appearances by a number of comedians, including famous stand-up artist, Mikhail Zhvanetskii, who presents gifts to the female members of the Shatalin household. Naturally, Vika does better out of this than Zhanna Arkad'evna (MFN, Series 3, Ep. 2). One early show involves the Shatalins having to accommodate the monstrously precocious boy who stars in a television shampoo advertisement. He is simultaneously 'put in his place' and 'humanised' by Vika (MFN, Series 4, Ep. 8).

Such plot lines dovetail with the self-reflexivity discussed earlier. During the episode in which, against their better instincts, Shatalin and Zhanna Arkad'evna end up following a Latin American soap to which Vika is addicted, Vika herself dreams first of receiving a TEFI award for her role in a Russian TV series, and then of appearing as a star guest on the popular talk show *Domino Principle* (*Printsip domino*). The foregrounding of celebrity is indicative of the shifting boundary between private and public space in the new Russia. Ordinary people rarely if ever found their way onto television until the Gorbachev era, other than in the most choreographed contexts. Private personas were, as Oleg Khakhordin has argued, maintained separately from the public masks adopted in the Soviet official sphere (Khakhordin 1999). It is consistent with the breakdown of this barrier that Vika should encounter and, albeit temporarily, attain the status of television celebrity herself. In this sense, individual textual instances instantiate the basic plot situation around which the programme is structured: that of the illicit intrusion of an ordinary provincial girl into the world of a famous media figure. But, at the same time, the repetitive nature of the sitcom genre familiarises Anastasia Zavorotniuk, facilitating her intrusion into the sitting rooms of her 'ordinary' viewers. The intimacy with which fans relate to her are reflected in the second-person singular terms of endearment by which she is addressed in the web forums: 'Nasten'ka, you're a pure delight! How I want to get to know you. You're a miracle. Happy Women's Day to you!' (*Nasten'ka, ty prosto prelest'! Kak zhe ia khochu s toboi poznakomit'sia! Ty chudo! S prazdnikom!*) (www.ruskino.ru/movie/forum; accessed 13 April 2006). 'Good on you, Nasten'ka! You're cool!' (*Molodets, Nasten'ka! Ty kruta!*) is another characteristic comment. In one exchange, a male corre- spondent even chides a female contributor for her naiveté in addressing 'Nasten'ka' (Zavorotniuk) directly in the hope that the actress will reply (www.ruskino.ru/movie/forum; accessed 17 March 2006).

But the very peculiarity of the nannying profession is that, conversely, it brings the public world of work into the heart of the domestic sphere. The fact that the threshold is breached 'from the opposite direction' (i.e. Vika's intrusion from the private realm of the ordinary person into that of the public celebrity replaces Vika's intrusion from the public world of work into the private realm of the Shatalin household) brings the two spheres into still greater contact, 'evening out' and thereby naturalising the act of intrusion.

The boundary confusion is bound up with the audience's confusion over the show's generic status. Most early respondents to the web forums referred to it as a '*serial*' (serial), assuming that the narrative situation would even- tually be resolved through Vika's marriage to Shatalin. Later respondents, particularly self-appointed male aficionados, reminded others that the pro- gramme is a sitcom, with all the open-endedness and lack of gravity that this entails.[8] The confusion is in turn connected with that over Vika's status as both an aspirational point of identification, and a comical object of fun. The respective statuses of the serial and the comedy are themselves reversible: the comedy is both 'earthy reality' (cf. Bakhtin's genealogy of realism, traced through carnivalesque comedy) and 'cosy fantasy', just as the serial is both romantic whimsy and serious narrative. Audiences divided roughly evenly between those who praised MFN for the relief it provides from everyday cares (it is consistently lauded for being a family show), and those who see in Vika an authentic representation of their own concerns, and thus an ambassador of televisual realism.[9]

The conflict can be resolved by reference to the particularity of television realism. The very 'cosiness' which established MFN as a refreshing break from the ubiquitous fare of sex and violence brings it closer to the domes- ticity of their own daily routines. The number of fans who stress the context in which they watch MFN ('with all the family', 'on the sofa with my husband', 'in the kitchen', 'every evening, if I can') indicates a convergence of viewing situation and text. Here the televisual self-reflexivity becomes particularly relevant. For when Vika appears on television, encounters celebrities, or watches soap operas, she negotiates the divide between her own celebrity status and that of her viewers as ordinary people for whom, nonetheless, the public sphere is no longer remote. Vika Prutkovskaia, who meets celebrities, converges with Anastasia Zavorotniuk, the embodiment of celebrity.

Such cosy intimacy between celebrity and audience indicates a profound difference between the semiotics of television representation and that of other representational forms. The role of the metatextual 'mise en abime' brings this to the fore. In its classic interpretation, the mise en abime or 'in-text' functions either to stress the authenticity of the surrounding text (an image of a painting, coded as 'art' within another work of art highlights the verisimilitude of the surrounding scene, now coded as 'reality') or its vertiginous, modernistic self-reflexivity (the film within the film which codes the surrounding text as the aesthetic artifice in which it locates its claims to authenticity).[10] In television, by contrast, the device foregrounds the phatic link between text and audience, character and viewing situation/routine and it is on the strength of this link that it bases its claims authenticity and 'realism'.

Aesthetic taste as metathreshold

One of the keenest topics of debate on MFN web forums is that of the heroine's cultural standing. The vociferous group of detractors justify their views by reference to Vika's uncouth Ukrainian accent, 'loud' voice and behaviour, and provincial manners. Her garish, provocative clothing also attracts condemnation, as does her propensity for sexual vulgarity; references to jokes 'beneath the belt' (*nizhe poiasa*) and to her *poshlost'* abound. Vika's shallow obsession with finding a rich husband and her lack of education indeed feature prominently; in one episode, the entire narrative revolves around Vika mistaking an authentic Pushkin manuscript for one of Shatalin's shopping lists (MFN, Series 2, Ep. 2). The show's popularity is adjudged a poor reflection of the cultural level of its viewing audience.[11]

In an extension of the argument over MFN's cultural status, several comparisons are made with the 2004 adaptation of Dostoevskii's *The Idiot*, and with Chekhov, Tolstoi and Bulgakov, accompanied by reminders that much of what we now consider serious art was rejected as such at the time it was produced. In response, others point out that MFN is intended not as high art, but as light entertainment.

The fact that such a debate has arisen at all is a further reflection of a confusion of generic boundaries. Comparing MFN with *The Idiot* is odd because it requires a sitcom to be measured against the standards of a classic adaptation. As we have seen, forum contributors sometimes remind their interlocutors that the programme is a sitcom and explain, then argue over, the definitions of 'sitcom'. The confusion also reflects a tension between 'high' and 'low' art in post-Soviet culture generally, a tension which comes to the fore in attitudes to television. Whilst contemporary western culture is characterised by an organic shift in the relationship between 'high' and 'low' and a productive exchange of values expressed in the convergence of 'art house' and 'mainstream' (cf. the work of directors like Lynch and Tarantino), in post-Soviet Russia the encounter takes the form of a pitched battle in which bold incursions from one field into the other are not necessarily succeeded by convergence and exchange. The representation of the Kul'tura channel in *Iskusstvo kino* as a fortified outpost of good taste within a hostile desert of trash culture indicates this conflictual mentality. So, too, do the aspirations of essentially mainstream popular cultural texts such as MFN and the Akunin adaptations, to the status of 'high art'. (MFN's very title, though derived from a particular episode of *The Nanny*, requires cognisance of the George Bernard Shaw literary intertext.) The tension is given its quintessential expression in Pelevin's *Generation 'P'*, in which the advent of the trash culture of Pepsi and Coke is presented as the apocalyptic 'end' of Russian literary culture within a novel, itself written by a former advertising copy writer who, nonetheless, draws his apocalyptic imagery from none other than Dostoevskii.[12]

Another index of the tension at the heart of post-Soviet culture traceable through reactions to MFN is the (mis)application of high cultural metalanguage. Much commentary on the show centres, for example, on the identification of acting techniques appropriate in an appraisal of a serious theatrical production, but at odds with the sensibilities embraced by popular television genres, to which audiences in the west relate quite differently.[13] Televisual form has yet to be integrated into post-Soviet Russian aesthetics and jarring interpretations of MFN which result either in unjust rejection of the programme for failing to meet high cultural standards, or over-egged claims for full aesthetic status are linked to this problem.

The taste issue is, as we have seen, aired intratextually. A series 5 episode begins with Shatalin rebuking Vika for watching a 'rubbishy' Hollywood film about a bank robbery and ends with Vika herself being held hostage in an armed raid on a shop, albeit by a highly idiosyncratic robber (MFN, Series 5, Ep. 3). In another episode from the third series, Vika signs up for a part in a Shakespeare play about which she is embarrassingly ignorant, raising suspicions amongst the remainder of the cast that she has slept with the director to secure her part (MFN, Series 3, Ep. 4). In an episode from series 2, Vika's ignorance of haute cuisine leads her to raid Shatalin's expensive cellar for wine to use in her cooking, only to find herself locked in with Zhanna Arkad'evna, who launches a tirade against Vika's cultural ignorance (MFN, Series 2, Ep. 12).

The vitality of the debates over the 'taste question' in MFN result from a difference over how to read this internally foregrounded 'bad taste'. There are three approaches. The first, common to many male forum contributors, is to make no distinction between the external *poshlost'* of the (female) viewers and that which the show itself embodies. In this reading, the metatextual function of the 'inner' *poshlost'* is merely unwittingly to reveal the essential *poshlost'* of those viewers who defend the show; Vika becomes a cipher for the materialistic shallowness and vulgarity of her fans who are consigned to the same cultural desert to which Vika herself belongs.[14] The second approach which finds favour among younger, female viewers is to excuse Vika's *poshlost'* as part of her 'honest, down-to-earth approach to life', and to accuse her detractors of elitism and snobbery. Such an interpretation illustrates the 'metatextuality as televisual realism' phenomenon (Vika's *poshlost'* highlights the phatic ties between show and fans).[15] The third reading is to posit MFN as a satire on shallow-minded post-Soviet materialism. (Paradoxically, the more 'intellectual' viewers embrace both this approach and its polar opposite: that of MFN as a cultural scourge.) Here, Vika's excessive vulgarity provides the essence of the show's comic effect.[16]

The taste threshold encapsulates the issue of authenticity at stake in all the other cultural divides that MFN foregrounds and reveals the uncertainty over what constitutes good taste in the post-communist cultural landscape. The same attributes feature in opposite arguments. Fans and detractors, for example, perceive the show's cosy, light-hearted family orientedness as representing either a refreshing break from US-inspired sex and violence, or as the root of the shallow *poshlost'* and *tupost'* with which they associate Vika Prutkovskaia. MFN thus serves as the battleground for the struggle to establish the boundaries of post-Soviet taste. So sharply drawn are the lines of conflict that correspondents do not hesitate to accuse their rival contributors of illiteracy and thus prove that they are on the side of culture and good taste.[17]

MFN, taste and the discourses of national identity

Mapped onto the tension over taste is a still more virulent conflict over national identity. Again, the same qualities are cited in support of opposing viewpoints. For example, fans repeatedly cite the programme's eschewal of excess as an antidote to the tide of US-produced (or, worse still, inspired) excess.[18]

Fans are not deterred by the knowledge that MFN is produced with the support of an American company and is based on a format which aired on US television well before the fall of communism. Some wilfully ignore the existence of the precursor; others claim that the Russian version is better than its US equivalent, citing the superior acting skills of its stars and its relative lack of vulgarity. There are even those who present MFN as the true, authentic variant of the format, dismissing *The Nanny* as an irrelevant aberration.[19] In this, they illustrate Lotman's thesis about the stages by which cultures enters into dialogue with another. Having imported texts which 'keep their strangeness' in stage one, a receiving culture's own texts are, in stage two restructured under the influence of the imported texts which themselves undergo restructuring as a result. This is a precursor to stage three in which the importing culture assumes that the imported texts 'will find their true heartland over here' (Lotman 1990: 147). Only in stage four does a receiving culture become a transmitting culture in which 'imported texts are dissolved in the receiving culture which begins to produce new texts' according to 'an original structural model' (ibid.). The insistence of MFN fans that the show is the true variant of the Nanny format corresponds to Lotman's stage three. And the gradual domestication of the story lines (the construction of narratives around native celebrations like Army Day, and around local character types such as the lascivious Georgian producer, or Vika's *khokhlushka* mother) indicates that stage three requires input from both 'producers' and 'readers'.

But MFN is also targeted by a nationalist movement for which Vika's *poshlost'* and stupidity, along with the show's crass humour, 'alien' canned laughter, and shallow characterisation, signal the degeneration of Russian society. This self-appointed cultural elite is overwhelmingly male, just as the majority of MFN fans are women. Throughout 2004 and much of 2005, MFN's main rival for top spot in the audience ratings was *The Idiot* which became the symbolic flag of Russian high culture around which the critics of MFN rallied, adding a cultural dimension to the political and gender axes. For a period, MFN forums became sites in which viewers could parade their knowledge of the achievements of Russian culture in a litany of references to Dostoevskii, Chekhov's comedies, Gogol's humour and the plays of Fonvizin, all of which MFN, naturally, fails to live up to.[20]

But in response, anti-nationalists lay claim to the very cultural sophistication regarded by their 'simplistic' nationalistic opponents as rightfully theirs. The xenophobes, it is pointed out with condescension, simply do not understand the generic rules and boundaries of the American sitcom, which the west-leaning anti-nationalists proceed painstakingly to distinguish from the serial. Thus, MFN features at the heart of yet another threshold: that of the arrival of television at the peripheries of high cultural discourse.[21]

Vika's grating Ukrainian *govor* is repeatedly mentioned by those who dismiss the programme for its vulgarity. The most virulent comments combine extreme irritation at her provincial manners and accent (though some are more repelled by the fact that the accent appears to be 'put on' than by its Ukrainian gutturals), with disgust at her grasping materialistic attitude to securing a husband, and the American-inspired trashiness of the humour.[22] Thus, anti-western sentiment is grafted onto an elitist anti-provincialism. But, equally, fans cite the warm, endearing familiarity of Vika's status as a *khokhlushka* as chief among her charms. The programme has a particularly large following in Ukraine and amongst Ukrainians in Russia. For them, Vika's Ukrainian provincial speech and manners make her 'one of our own', and lends the show its homely, domestic feel. The actress who receives the most praise, even from the show's harshest critics, is Liubov' Polikovskaia, who plays Vika's still more Ukrainian-sounding mother, and who is treated as a national (i.e. Greater Russian) treasure. However, there is a distinction between Russian fans who cite Vika's provincialism as evidence of the show's non-western Russian-ness, and Ukrainian fans who defiantly claim her as a representative of Ukrainian authenticity, appropriating the term '*khokh-lushka*' as a rallying point for young Ukrainian fans seeking role models: 'She is a *khokhlushka*, but she is at least our *khokhlushka*' is a familiar refrain.[23] Thus, the Ukrainianisms are transposed simultaneously, but con-tradictorily, onto two varieties of anti-western, nationalist discourse: that which associates them with American vulgarity, and that which associates them with the domestic authenticity of Russian culture. They also inform a discourse of localism (provincial and/or Ukrainian) posited against the metropolitan centralism of official Russian identity (of which the Shatalins are, in part, an embodiment).

Sporadically, accusations of a more overtly political nature are made against MFN, as when Vika's Ukrainian origins are posited as belonging to an official nation-building project in which nostalgia for Russia's former status at the centre of a multi-national empire which included Little Russia (Ukraine) plays a central role.[24] In this sense, the programme's Ukrainian dimension shapes both an official, trans-Russian nation-building discourse, and the liberal, anti-nationalist discourse by which it is challenged at the level of the audience.

Spatial thresholds and MFN as reflexive model of television culture

The location of MFN at the threshold of a range of cultural nexus estab-lishes it as a lightning rod for many of the tensions besetting contemporary Russian culture: the decline of 'high cultural' values; the existence/non-existence of social mobility; shifts in gender relations and in the nature and scope of the public sphere; the status of western cultural imports; the fate of Russian national identity; and the positioning of the metropolitan centre with respect to provincial and ex-Soviet peripheries. Several tensions are modelled explicitly within MFN. Vika's appearances on television shows and interactions with media celebrities are ridden with an ambiguity which cor-respond to the ambivalence towards Zavorotniuk's star status; the crass tas-telessness with which the show is credited by its critics finds resonance in portrayals of Vika's own *poshlost'* and ignorance; in one episode she admits to not knowing the name of the current prime minister, complaining that 'they change so quickly' (MFN, Series 2, Ep. 2). Even the national identity issues are foregrounded, as in one jibe about the parlous state of the Ukrai-nian economy intended to highlight Vika's mother's obsession with finding a rich (Russian) husband for her daughter (MFN Series 5, Ep. 2).

The close correlation between viewer reactions to MFN and aspects of the show itself secure its metatextual status. Moreover, the threshold function highlighted by this correlation is in turn modelled through the show's inter-nal, represented space. The opening animation sequence which recapitulates the plot of the first episode depicts a traversing of social space up to the point of the threshold which is never fully crossed; Vika's journey across town from the cheap hairdressing salon from which she is evicted ends at the door of the Shatalin residence. The transition from the recurring animation of the credit sequence to the particularised action of the individual episodes marks the transition from the aspirational dream of betterment to the 'reality' of constant frustration.

The threshold separating the Shatalin household from the world outside forms the conduit through which the characters who temporarily 'disrupt' the equilibrium are admitted: the celebrity actors; Vika's 'dubious' new boyfriends; her quintessentially provincial mother and grandmother; and the odious Zhanna Arkad'evna. In contrast to the animation sequence, the traversing of the threshold is represented from viewpoints within rather than outside the household: many narrative sequences are initiated by Konstantin's movement across the living room to answer the doorbell, as the audience, along with Vika and/or Shatalin, wait in anticipation to discover who has arrived. This shift – from the 'outside' viewpoint of the stylised frame text to the 'inside' viewpoint of the inner authentic text – itself marks Vika's temporary intrusion into the 'illicit' inner space of the Shatalin sanctum.

The action in MFN tends to be limited to two rooms: the living room and the kitchen (with occasional scenes in Shatalin's study, still fewer involving scenes outside the home and, rarest of all, scenes within Vika's bedroom). This claustrophobic intimacy is a generic feature of the sitcom. The staircase to the upper floor is rarely used by the adults, but the children, by contrast, and sometimes Vika, are often seen descending and ascending it, mediating between the inner, private sanctuary of the bedrooms and the semi-public space of the living room. This corresponds to their mediatory role in the narratives: they are Shatalin's offspring, yet allies of Vika in all disputes between her and her employer; in one episode, Vika supports Masha's frustrated attempts to persuade her father to let her date a boy whose intentions Shatalin believes are suspect (MFN, Series 2, Ep. 11); in another all three children plead with Shatalin to re-appoint Vika after he has sacked her following a dispute (MFN, Series 1, Ep. 2). In only two episodes do bedroom scenes occur, one of which involves a drunken Vika getting into Shatalin's bed by mistake (MFN, Series 5, Ep. 6). This is in contrast with British family sitcoms such as *My Family*, *One Foot in the Grave* and *Fawlty Towers* in which scenes of the married couple in bed are a staple source of humour. The whole point of MFN is that the characters are forever on the threshold of establishing a family, a threshold that, were it to be crossed, would remove the source of the comedy. Moreover, the Shatalins' intimate space differs from that of standard sitcoms through its function as a forum for the encounter of the private realm of the metropolitan intelligentsia and the 'public' realm of media celebrity, work and provincial parvenues. Vika's status as a provincial intruder and domestic employee, and that of Shatalin as a media celebrity encapsulate this related threshold function.

Also significant is the movement of characters across, and beyond, the Shatalin space. Zhanna Arkad'evna's role as an outsider, rival to Vika for Shatalin's affections and representative of an aggressive new female business class, deprives her of the right to a stable position. Her arrival regularly provokes a flurry of acerbic gags and, unlike the other characters, she rarely sits but rather stands or perches on the edge of the sofa. Her trademark tic-like fidgeting when standing complements her constant striding across the space of the household, often in comic pursuit of, or pursued by, other characters. The kitchen space is reserved primarily for Konstantin and Vika, and when Zhanna intrudes, often to 'pick at' the food Konstantin is preparing, she is usually swiftly ejected. Equally, however, she attempts to appropriate the space of Shatalin's study – the threshold between work and home; here it is Vika who is made to feel unwelcome and who is herself often ejected for impeding the spurious business deals on which Shatalin works under Zhanna's influence.

The threshold transgressions within MFN's represented space are mirrored by the threshold-crossing action of the camera as representing tool. A feature of every episode (a production 'tic' acquired from *The Nanny*) is the insertion towards the end of each narrative of a view looking up at the elegant stone walls and windows of the Shatalin apartment block, succeeded by a shot from within the living room (usually depicting the characters on the sofa). From occupying an intimate, inner viewpoint on the Shatalin family crises, the viewer is suddenly called upon to assume a subject position external to the action, as s/he is (re)constructed as a temporary intruder into the inner living space of the media celebrity, a mere 'provincial' aspirant to the material and social privileges enjoyed by the urban sophisticate.

Indeed, the key to MFN's success is its position at the metathreshold of text and audience, a threshold onto which the tensions afflicting post-Soviet culture are transferred. Vika's (un)popularity is a function of her role as an emblem of television culture in its negative connotations (MFN as the ultimate in American-inspired vulgarity) and its positive manifestation (MFN as the epitome of the earthy authenticity of the provincial parvenue) whom, of all cultural forms, only television can accommodate. It is no coincidence that Shatalin is not a television personality but a producer of upmarket musicals, an activity under threat from TV. This authenticity is measured not by conventional standards of representational realism, judged against which the highly ritualistic sitcom format falls well short, but rather by the degree of participatory interpenetration between text and audience, evidenced by the numerous web respondents who in solidarity with their heroine adopt her trademark expression of surprise '*ochumet*" ('Insane!'), often with her elongated provincial vowels emphasised (*aachumet'*).[25] The semi-irony with which this gesture is made indicates the ambiguity of the stated belief in Vika's authenticity, but this, too, is part of the pleasure taken in the show's location at the threshold of (fictional) text and (actual) audience.[26]

MFN foregrounds the movement towards a more dynamic cultural model characteristic of early twenty-first century Russian television. Just as Vika, the Ukrainian parvenue from the peripheries of the Russian-Soviet colossus, has penetrated the metropolitan, media-soaked centre, so the peripheral genre of the American-inspired sitcom has forced its way to the foreground of a television culture whose flagship remains the staid, high-art output of Channel Kul'tura, beloved of President Putin. It is no surprise, then, that the programme should become the focus of a virulent exchange of opinions about aesthetic values and US cultural imperialism. In its capacity as vital, local variant on a successful US global format, MFN situates itself at the crossroads of Russian cultural development, importing the semiotic values of the periphery into the space of the centre which, notwithstanding Putin's baleful influence, must undergo an inevitable transformation in response.[27]

7 (Mis)appropriating the western game show

Pole Chudes [*The Field of Miracles*] and the double-edged myth of the *Narod*

Introduction

Our discussion of audience reactions to *My Fair Nanny* brought to light a theme which has surfaced periodically throughout our book, and which will dominate the remaining chapters: the intersection within contemporary Russian television of global television forms, nation-building agendas and local meaning-making practices. If we add to this mix the function of a Soviet past both nostalgically recalled and disdainfully rejected, we have in place all the elements which, in their infinite permutations, account for the complexity of post-Soviet television culture. In Chapter 7, we explore one such permutation: the Russian domestication of a global game show format in which the regional audience dimension, rather than, as in *My Fair Nanny*, merely shaping the meanings that the show generates, is incorporated into the format itself as part of a nation-building gesture centred on a mythologised folk culture. As a consequence, the generic status of the programme, *A Field of Miracles* (*Field chudes*), based on the global *Wheel of Fortune* format, is, over a period of time itself transformed from within by the practices of its audiences. In this sense, it bears close comparison with the prison serial, *The Zone*, analysed in Chapter 5.

It is worth noting that the progression from Chapter 6 (where we see regional audiences shaping the meaning of national programming) to the present chapter (featuring the restructuring of a global format around the role of the regional audience) recapitulates the audience–text movement we pursue in the book as a whole, and within each chapter. Indeed, the fact that, at the end of the chapter, we consider the response of viewing audiences, regional and metropolitan, to *The Field of Miracles*, reconfirms the 'to-and-fro' form that the audience–text dialectic inevitably takes.

It is in keeping with the dialectic that, when the mythologised *narod* around which *Field of Miracles* is based encounters the 'real folk' constituting our focus groups, the nation-building strategy comes under pressure and fragments along both centre–periphery and class axes. For this reason, we suggest, the myth of a unified *narod* proves to be a distinctly double-edged sword in the hands of the nation-builders who wield it.

Field of Miracles first appeared on Russian television screens in 1990, shortly before the collapse of the Soviet Union and the emergence of the new Russia. It is thus one of the few programmes to span the Soviet and post-Soviet periods (and, other than *Vremia*, the only such programme to feature in our book). This is significant for our purposes since it highlights the fact that, in a sense, the arrival of the *national* in post-Soviet Russia coincided with that of the *global*; the Russian nation-state began to emerge even as it was penetrated by the all-consuming force of globalisation (Rantanen 2002: 3). In the case of the new Russia, then, the relationship between the global and the national becomes particularly fraught and we should bear this in mind when considering the role of *Field of Miracles* in national identity construction. For instance, the show's lineage explains why it differs so radically from another Russian version of a global game-show format: *Who Wants to Be a Millionaire?* (*Kto khochet stat' millionerom?*), which first appeared in Russia in 1999, when Russia had already established itself as a nation-state, but one more or less subject to the laws of global enterprise. Unlike the latter, from the beginning *Field of Miracles* was driven by a subversive, anti-imperialist impulse, as its (still) Soviet producers appropriated the format illegally in a deliberate act of defiance towards the globalising impulses of its legal owners. As we shall also see in Chapter 8, television format piracy in a post-Soviet context is liable to generate a unique set of meanings.

Precisely because it was illegally pirated, the Russian version of *Wheel of Fortune* was, from the very beginning, subject to radical change and adaptation. Crucially, the game element was progressively overshadowed by an emphasis on ritual as *Field of Miracles* was employed to promote a post-Soviet national identity; national holidays, national symbols and national mythology all featured heavily in the programme's newly constructed ambiance. But the success of *Field of Miracles* ultimately owed less to this carefully managed, 'top-down' *national* strategy than to the popular spirit injected into it by its *local* contestants, gathered from across post-Soviet space, a popular spirit eventually, and problematically, reincorporated into the national strategy. We discuss the related tension between the programme's nation-building agenda and traditional folk rituals such as gift giving in the light of Marcel Mauss's understanding of the phenomenon as 'contractual exchange' (Mauss 1954: 3). This reveals another contradiction pitting the programme's commercial element (advertisements and shopping) against the avowedly non-commercial practice of gift giving. Although *Field* is a scrupulously edited television commodity, its contestants are seen by viewers as ordinary people whose gift giving is motivated by genuine generosity and whose (often long, drawn-out) stories are authentic. In this, it differs from shows like *Windows* (see Chapter 4) or *The Hour of Trial* (*Chas suda*) both of which appear to be written and enacted by professionals and are perceived as inauthentic.[1]

Local rituals and nation-building strategies converge in *narodnost'*, and it is by invoking this concept that the programme makers attempt to resolve any contradiction between the two. The definition of *narodnost'* ranges between folklore, popular spirit and nationhood and all these elements are put to work in *Field* (a more detailed discussion of the term is given below). Drawing on a combination of Antony Smith's understanding of national identity and Benedict Anderson's and David Morley's view of identity as a fluid cultural construct subject to negotiation by groups, we suggest that *Field* is situated at the intersection of a 'top-down' national identity construction process, *and* 'bottom-up' representations of ordinary, provincial, people (Smith 1991; Anderson 1991; Morley, 1992). For although the idea of making local people the show's focal point was that of the presenter, these people have, by and large, been permitted to represent *themselves* in their own words rather than enact idealised images of workers and peasants to support state propaganda, as in Soviet televisual appropriations of *narodnost'*. This tension belies deeper conflicts between the national and the local which come to light in the re-fragmentation process mentioned above, a process in which, as we shall see, the global is appropriated for opposing purposes. Thus, the local can exploit the global against the national, just as the national can assert its supremacy over the local by associating it with derided global tastes and values.

In revealing how global formats might serve to negotiate between the abstract universalism and the concrete localism required in equal measure by national identity projects, *Field* participates in a process underlying the construction of the modern nation. Writing in the context of the fragmentation of another East-European communist state, Slavoj Zizek comments:

> On the one hand 'Nation' designates the modern community delivered of traditional 'organic' ties, a community in which ... the traditional corporate community is replaced by the modern nation-state whose constituents are ... people as abstract members ... On the other hand ... 'national identity' must appeal to the contingent materiality of 'common roots' ... In short, 'Nation' designates both the instance by means of which traditional 'organic' links are dissolved, *and* the 'remainder of the pre-modern in modernity'
>
> (Zizek 2006a: 20)

As we shall see, it is in the ultimately failed attempt to appropriate *narodnost'* as the embodiment of nation in Zizek's sense, that *Field* exposes the contradictions to which Zizek points.

Our analysis is underpinned by Bonner's notion of 'ordinary television'. She uses the term 'ordinary' interchangeably with 'everyday', 'familiar', 'routine' and 'mundane' (Bonner 2003: 29). 'Ordinary' television programmes are thus concerned with the mundane aspects of everyday life, with domestic concerns, familial relationships, personal appearance and so on. The mundane had no space on the Soviet television screen, and *Field* was considered quite innovatory in inviting ordinary people to take part as game contestants and studio viewers. The differences between the 'ordinary' in *Field* and the 'ordinary' in the original *Wheel of Fortune*, as well as between *Field* and other post-Soviet game and talk shows which have embraced 'ordinary' values, are to be located in *Field*'s consistent association of those values with folk culture and rituals. In exploring these differences, we will locate the programme not only within a broader post-Soviet television context, but also in relation to other national adaptations of the *Wheel of Fortune* global format. For the purpose of this study, we watched *Field* regularly over two years (2004 and 2005). We base some of our insights on editions of the programme viewed sporadically through the 1990s (including the earliest period in 1990 when it was hosted by Vladislav List'ev).

Our analysis comprises three components treated in the following order:

(1) a comparison of *Field* with *Wheel* aimed at establishing in broad, quantitative terms the differences between the Russian format and that of other nations;
(2) an analysis of the structural specificities of *Wheel* and its contradictory role in the nation-building mission;
(3) the ways in which those contradictions are played out in audience reactions explored from the perspectives of class, location, age and gender. (For a full account of the focus group methodology employed in all our audience research, see Chapter 9).

Field and *Wheel*: Subverting the game show genre

Wheel has been successful throughout the world. According to Albert Moran, there were two ways of purchasing the original US game show format: (1) by acquiring the US version of the show; (2) by buying the syndication rights from the format owners, King World (Moran 1998: 31). Some countries, such as the Philippines or Columbia, chose the first option because it involved minimal production costs beyond those incurred in providing translation for non-English speaking audiences (Moran 1998: 19). Other countries, such as Germany, France and the Scandinavian states, opted for making their own versions from the syndicated format (Skomvand 1992: 91).

A still cheaper means of acquiring the *Wheel* format was, of course, through illegal piracy. In the late 1980s and early 1990s, when Mikhail Gorbachev's *perestroika* and *glasnost* required new approaches to the mass media, Soviet television began to abandon the rigidly ideological approach to programme making which had seemed to serve it so well up to that point. While new original programmes were created, there was also an insatiable market for foreign television products, especially in the area of entertainment. During the search for new formats, the well-known television journalist, List'ev, discovered *Wheel*. On 25 October 1990, he presented the Soviet Channel 1 audience with a new game show identical to *Wheel* and pirated at a time when Soviet television did not pay for licenses and copyrights (Iakubovich 2004b).[2]

Soon after, List'ev asked Iakubovich to replace him as presenter, and the first Iakubovich show was broadcast on 1 November 1991. Since 1991, Iakubovich has been the show's only host. In December 1991, Iakubovich and List'ev discussed the programme's future and Iakubovich suggested reorienting its focus from the game itself to the contestants' personal stories (Iakubovich 2004b), thus reducing the possibility of a successful lawsuit against the programme producers on copyright issues (the Russian format was now to differ considerably from its western original). The title of the show was changed from *The Wheel of Fortune* to *The Field of Miracles*. The new title alludes to Aleksei Tolstoi's famous children's story *The Golden Key, or Buratino's Adventures* (*Zolotoi kliuchik, ili prikliucheniia Buratino*), in which the fox Alisa and the cat Bazilio fool Buratino by promising the innocent boy that a tree of fortune would grow from one golden coin thrown onto the field of Miracles in the Country of Fools. The reference to 'fools' has not diminished the constant flow of participants to *Field*. In fact, the generous prizes on offer reaffirm the fool's positive status in Russian folk tales: it is usually he who gets the prize and marries the princess.

It is helpful to compare *Field* with the generic format of *Wheel* and its other adaptations. In the original US programme, contestants play four rounds of the game in groups of three. The host asks a question. The answer is usually a word, all the letters of which are covered with blank squares. If the participants do not know the answer immediately, they have to guess it letter by letter. Each participant rotates the 'wheel of fortune' and is given the chance to suggest one letter. The first person to say the whole word is the winner of the round. Three winners take part in the final round, which determines the game's overall victor. Michael Skomvand explains the programme's success as follows:

> American critics have argued that one of the main appeals of the US *Wheel* is that it is precisely pitched at a level of difficulty at which the majority of its audience will enjoy the sense of superiority of being just a fraction quicker than the contestants at solving the puzzle.
>
> (Skomvand 1992: 93).

In *Field*, contestants in groups of three are likewise posed questions and offered a chance to rotate the wheel of fortune. However, the questions are exaggeratedly easy. Participants tend to forget them in the course of telling their stories and Iakubovich will often hint at the answers on the grounds that the game will otherwise never end. For instance, in a December 2004 edition, the contestants were told in advance that the questions were going to require them to spell out the names of famous world capitals such as Paris (17 December 2004).[3] Sometimes, the game's 'intellectual' element is almost completely withdrawn; in a programme dedicated to International Women's

Day (5 March 2005), each woman contestant was given a present for every letter that she guessed correctly.

In his analysis of *Wheel*, Skomvand observes that 'there are ... two distinct phases in the show: the game phase and the consumer phase. The game phase is structured by its two components, the board and the wheel, signifying the two elements of the game: skill and luck' (Skomvand 1992: 93). The consumer phase includes 'shopping', i.e. 'the phase in which the contestants spend their own hard-won money on the merchandise, and where the merchandise is portrayed by camera and voice-over' (ibid.: 97). But in addition to these, *Field* has two more phases:

(1) a *ritual phase*, in which the contestants introduce themselves, presenting their stories, songs, and gifts to the host and the studio.[4] The ritual aspect of the show is different from the 'conversationalization' that Bonner refers to as a typical feature of ordinary television (Bonner 2003: 50), in that *Field*'s contestants tend to indulge in monologues directed at the camera;
(2) a *bargaining phase*, during which the host negotiates with the contestant who wins the 'Prize' sector on the wheel by offering him or her money instead of the prize (this can also be considered a sub-phase within the consumer phase).

Adding the two phases to the scheme suggested by Skomvand, we have calculated the time spent on each activity in a representative *Field* edition (i.e. one without a special theme) broadcast on 23 December 2005.[5] Times are expressed in hours, minutes and seconds and as a percentage of the total.

Comparing *Field* with US, Scandinavian, Northern European and Danish versions of *Wheel*, several differences can be noted:

(1) the total running time of *Wheel* is, on average, half that of *Field* (the length of *Wheel* varies between the Danish version of 25 minutes and the pan-Scandinavian one which is 32 minutes);
(2) the time of the game phase on *Field* is only half or less than that of *Wheel*. The shortest game phase is to be found in the Northern

Table 7.1 Pole (Russia)

Game	17 mins 39 secs	26.88%
Talk	4 mins 22 secs	6.65%
Ritual	15 mins 50 secs	24.12%
Prizes/Bargaining	11 mins 43 secs	17.85%
Shopping	1 mins 21 secs	2.84%
Juice Ads	1 mins 52 secs	19.59%
Ad Blocks	12 mins 52 secs	
Total	1 hr 5 mins 39 secs	

European version, (45.33 per cent of the total time), and the longest is in the Danish one (57 per cent);

(3) together, the ritual and talk phases in *Field* occupy the longest period of time (we have incorporated the personal stories and remarks included within the talk phase in Skomvand's analysis into the – essentially oral – ritual phase of *Field*). Thus, talk in *Wheel* takes between 17 per cent and 19 per cent, considerably less than the 24 per cent attributed to ritual in *Field*;

(4) in *Wheel*, shopping occupies between 6.60 per cent (the US version) and 21 per cent (Northern Europe) of the total time, while in *Field*, shopping occupies a mere 2.84 per cent, in contrast with the 18 per cent of time devoted to bargaining;

(5) during the period of study *Field* regularly promoted one sponsor – the juice company My Family (Moia sem'ia) – during the show. Advertisements for the juice were built into the body of *Field*.

The relationship between host, contestants and audience

Surface variations in the amount of time dedicated to particular game elements (in particular the weight attributed to the ritual phase in *Field*) are a surface indicator of more profound structural and cultural differences. This applies in particular to the relationship between the host and contestants. Comparing the relationship between the host, hostess, contestants and audience in *Wheel* and its European versions, Skomvand remarks on the contrast between the American 'cheerleader' style of presentation and the 'low-key' European approach. The most striking difference is in the involvement of the hostess: in *Wheel*, she remains mute throughout the show, but in the Swedish and Danish variants, she engages actively in conversations with the host and contestants (Skomvand 1992: 96). *Field* takes the American approach to its conclusion; there is only one presenter – Iakubovich – and the female presence is reduced to a handful of mute helpers who emerge periodically to reveal letters from the mystery word or to bring in presents.

Based on stereotypes of gender and family, the style of Iakubovich's behaviour towards contestants is familiar in the extreme. For instance, at the special edition dedicated to Women's Day in 2005, the producers created a 'lips' sector on the wheel of fortune: those contestants – all female – whose arrow landed in the sector were permitted to kiss Iakubovich. The sexual undertones co-existed with a gender stereotyping of woman as 'housewife' (*khoziaiushka*) and 'mother'.[6] Male contestants are often represented by the prey they have hunted and bring as presents (fish, rabbits, etc.); women appear as gatherers with their pickled mushrooms and berries. Both genders are seen primarily in their family roles: fathers, mothers, grandfathers, grandmothers, housewives and so on. Many contestants bring their children and grandchildren to the show with them. Children are expected to sing a song or recite a poem for which they get a prize. Boys and girls are usually treated with special respect by Iakubovich who acts as a universal grandfather.

Iakubovich's familiarity with adult contestants often borders on the patronising and the pejorative. He mocks participants by undermining their intelligence, asking them how many years they completed at school, saying that he hopes they still remember the alphabet and commenting on their behaviour. One of his favourite tricks is to mimic foreign contestants. For example, a Vietnamese student, accompanied by his sister, brought some Vietnamese presents and sang a song to celebrate the beginning of the Year of the Rooster (27 February 2005). He was also asked to say a few words in Vietnamese, so that Iakubovich could parrot them back to him. A half-Russian, half-Cuban female contestant was made to say something in Spanish for Iakubovich to mimic (28 January 2005). Such 'friendly ridiculing' is double-edged, appealing to popular xenophobic stereotypes, yet also gently undermining the host himself. Indeed, in their turn, the contestants treat Iakubovich as a jester whom they love, but whom they can also tease, dress up in costumes and force to dance.

The relationship between the presenter and participants is similar to that of the *shut* (street clown) and the crowd: the *shut*'s status confers on him the right to mock the crowd, but the crowd takes the opportunity to make fun of him in return. One television critic referred to this aspect of the relationship between Iakubovich and the contestants as a 'people's theatre' (*narodnyi teatr*), noting how, for viewers, it renders the programme an antidote to contemporary reality shows, in which people are competitive and nasty to one other (Petrovskaia 2002). Another commentator describes Iakubovich as 'the country's favorite plump and velvety teddy bear' (*pukhlyi i pliushevyi liubimets vsei strany*) (Grymov and Lysenkov 2000). This comparison with the Russian folk-tale bear has become an essential part of Iakubovich's image.

Because the programme's appeal is based on Iakubovich's charismatic personality and celebrity status, he was prevented from leaving *Field* in 2002 when he publicly announced that he was planning to quit (Iakubovich 2002). Iakubovich's carefully cultivated persona has also coloured his career outside *Field*. The image of the Russian fairy-tale fool, kind yet stupid, was ascribed to him when he co-presented the New Year's show *Blue Spark* (*Goluboi ogonek*) in December 2004. In May 2005, Andrei Makarevich attempted to teach Iakubovich how to dive on his show, *Three Windows* (*Tri okna*), dressing him in a wet suit and soaking him with water, reconfirming him in his familiar role.

Identity construction: *Field* and nation building

The tension between nation building at the level of the state and the ordinary, local practices in which it must ground itself appears to dissipate within the myth of the Russian *narod*, which can conveniently mean both 'nation' and 'people'(Perrie 1998: 28). It is for this reason that state television under the Soviet regime, and now increasingly in the post-Eltsyn period, has referenced the myth so widely, and nowhere more so than in *Field*. The programme is undoubtedly exploited as part of the Putin regime's nation-building campaign. This applies particularly to editions broadcast to coincide with national holidays, such as Victory Day and International Women's Day. The nostalgia for the Soviet past that such occasions recall has been a key feature of post-Eltsyn Russian culture (Barker 1999: 19; Borenstein, Lipovetskii and Baraban 2004). In *Field*, this nostalgia is also manifested in the host's general attitude and in the geographical provenance of the contestants.

As someone who grew up in the Soviet Union, Iakubovich publicly admits to feeling nostalgic for the country and people of his youth, to having lost 'some strange nation ... the nationality of the *odessit*' (*kakuiu-to strannuiu natsiiu ... natsional'nost' odessit*) (Iakubovich 2004a). As a former member of *The Club of the Merry and Quick-Witted* (*Klub veselykh i nakhodchivykh*), or KVN, Iakubovich here refers to the myth about the city of Odessa, famous for its special sense of humour, which best manifested itself in the presentations of the KVN team from the University of Odessa. Iakubovich himself writes humorous monologues and short stories. He mourns Soviet culture in this iconic and idealised view of Odessa and attempts to reconstruct the 'country of his youth' in the studio of *Field*.

Using such popular emotions as nationalism and nostalgia for the Soviet past, *Field* promotes official holidays, reinforces state rituals, reinstates traditional values and shapes national identity. The special holiday editions are made in accordance with the rest of the festive schedule. For instance, on 9 May 2005 the two central channels broadcast all Victory Day events live and ensured that all programmes on the day conformed to the theme. For such editions, the *Field* producers select contestants with appropriate backgrounds. For example, on International Women's Day in 2005, all the contestants were women; on the May 2005 Victory Day show, all the players were Second World War veterans; on the December 2005 New Year's show, they were selected from people who had to work on New Year's Eve. *Field* is particularly generous to contestants on these days. The studio is usually decorated in keeping with the theme: on Women's Day it is adorned with flowers and balloons; on Victory Day it is decorated with scaled-up pictures of the medals and awards issued during the Great Patriotic War, and a war-period car – even the girls bringing the presents into the studio and opening the letters in the game wear military uniforms. The theme is also reflected in the manner that Iakubovich presents contestants. On Victory Day, he introduces them not, as habitually, by their area of residence, but by the front they fought at during the war. In a radical departure from the game-show format characteristic of Russian television's propensity to overlay the conventions of a global television genre with practices derived from its pre-televisual, oral cultural tradition (see our discussion of the *tok shou* in Chapter 4), they are also invited to tell their war stories and to bring their war paraphernalia into the studio.

In the festive editions, the competitive element is reduced even more substantially than usual. During the Victory Day 2005 edition, the final contestant was offered a prize of 600,000 roubles merely for agreeing to play the final round (10 May 2005). As soon as he announced his willingness to play, Iakubovich withdrew the offer and revealed the word behind the white squares: 'victory' (*pobeda*). All the other contestants were war veterans and all were rewarded in recognition of their role in securing the great victory. Here we see a clear example of a nation-building gesture conceived overtly, and dialogically (in the Bakhtinian sense), to undermine the ethos of a global form, from within that form itself. In the post-Soviet context, the gesture serves to authenticate the *narodnost'* to which the programme lays claim by grounding the official strategy in a populist rejection of the western competitive spirit.

The festive editions of *Field* also indulge in the hybridisation of global and Soviet generic traits observed in Chapters 1–3. Thus, on such days, the programme acquires the characteristics of popular Soviet variety shows, incorporating performances by famous singers, dancers and musicians. On the 2005 Victory Day show, Iakubovich surprised the female contestants by inviting the favourite singer of each of them into the studio to perform.

The geography of the participants' origins maps out a patent nostalgia for the former Soviet Union. Contestants are selected from across Russia and the republics of the former USSR, and, remarkably, even from former socialist countries, like Vietnam. Ukraine, Moldova, Belarus, Uzbekistan and Kazakhstan are represented on a regular basis.

Narodnost' in question: The ordinary, the traditional and the commercial

But if the nation-building purposes to which *Field* is put are to coalesce around the myth of *narodnost'*, then the popular, demotic aspect of the myth must also be invoked. It is here that the consistent 'ordinariness' of the contestants comes into play. In a Russian context, ordinariness is often associated with provinciality and it is clear that the overwhelming majority of the contestants hail from beyond Russia's large metropolitan centres. Applications to participate on the programme from ordinary people are rigorously judged according to this criterion. The *Field* website states that a person wishing to become a contestant on *Field* needs only write a letter with a short autobiography, attach a photograph and send an unusual crossword to the studio. The competition is tough as organisers claim to receive between 500 and 1000 applications a day and the decisions are made with the socio-geographical considerations very much in mind. At this level, then, the nation-building aspect of the *narodnost'* myth (the desire to use it to re-invoke Soviet space and certain of its ideological associations) and the demotic aspect (the requirement that it be grounded in the provincial, the ordinary and the non-competitive) exist, conveniently, in a relationship of mutual complementarity. However, the coherence that this complementarity brings with it comes under pressure at other levels.

Thus, as 'ordinary' contestants who value television exposure as a special gift (Bonner 2003: 92), the contestants in *Field* are particularly keen to have their turn at the wheel. However, unlike the unfettered, excruciating individualism displayed by exponents of the 'fame syndrome' on western reality TV shows, the self-promoting aspirations of *Field* contestants are channelled into predictable sequences so strictly ritualised that any residual spontaneity is drained from them. The contestants invariably introduce themselves and their local town or village; tell their story; send their regards to families, neighbours, colleagues, local authorities, sponsors and friends; and, most importantly, unpack presents from their family and local community for *Field* and its host. Sometimes the sequences resemble fairy-tale narratives. Thus, far from regretting that she never had a chance to answer the quiz question because the word had been guessed before her turn, one female contestant from Moldova tells of her delight at making it to the studio after a protracted journey full of obstacles: having run out of money she had been offered help by her local TV station which even gave her a lift to the train station (23 December 2005). Another female participant on the Victory Day 2005 show summarised her passion for the programme and Iakubovich: 'So what if I don't win anything; I get to see you' (*Mne hot' i nichego, zato ia vas vizhu*).

To celebrate their successful journey to *Field* many contestants play musical instruments, dance, and sing songs and couplets sung with or without an accompaniment (*chastushki*) in praise of Iakubovich. In one *Field* edition, an older man sang *chastushki* accompanying himself with a *garmon'* (a traditional Russian musical instrument) until Iakubovich silenced him by putting his hand over the man's mouth (23 December 2005).

As part of the process by which the incursion of the ordinary into the sphere of celebrity is re-channelled into the straitjacket of an artificially manufactured *narodnost'*, the contestants are required to bring gifts to *Field* and Iakubovich. Their presents usually include various local artefacts, foods and drinks, such as paintings by local artists, national and regional costumes, knitted items, homemade pies, pickles, local spirits and so on. In one show, a female contestant from a textile town brought a set of sheets, a bath robe and a hat for Iakubovich; a male contestant from Uzbekistan brought presents from his three 'mothers' (his father has three wives), a male wedding costume and a national hat (*chelma*) (10 May 2004 show). The 'ordinary' desire for fame is thus exploited as part of a carefully manufactured display of ethnographic variety which, at the mercy of the idiosyncrasy of its exponents, however, often degenerates into an accretion of ever more obscure and/or off-beat objects: dried fish, home-baked pies, knitted washing cloths (*mochalki*), a tank of golden fish, some holy water, a cake, some ice-cream, strawberry preserve and a figure made of local semi-precious stone (17 December 2004).

Iakubovich justifies the receipt of gifts by reference to the Russian hospitality tradition and the habit of going to visit people with your own food. He recalls how his mother once brought to their friends' a very heavy goose cooked in a cast-iron baking dish. By comparison, he admires the easy spontaneity of people who bring their own gifts to *Field* as though they were merely visiting a relative. The genuinely intimate domesticity of the 'ordinary' gift-giving gestures must thus coexist uneasily with two other functions: the nation-building emphasis on an artificially manufactured *narodnost'*, and the consolidation of the aura of modern, televisual celebrity created around the figure of Iakubovich.

There is, though, a third function to be accommodated in this uneasy hybrid. For *Field* is, perhaps above all, a successful television commodity widely used for product promotion and placement purposes. Shopping and advertising are intrinsic parts of the show. Contestants can buy merchandise with the points they earn; they are also often given commercially produced presents: household equipment and other goods. Iakubovich masterfully uses *Field*'s image as a programme for the *narod* to promote products to its large viewing audience.[7] One of *Field*'s sponsors, the producer of My Family juice, is constantly present on screen. Each contestant is offered a glass of juice and asked to comment on it. With the camera focusing on the juice brand, each participant praises the quality of the drink while Iakubovich repeats again and again: 'This is what the *narod* says! The *narod* likes it!' (*Eto* narod *govorit!* Narodu *nravitsia!*) When the arrow on the wheel ends up pointing at a sector labelled 'My Family', the contestant wins a prize from the juice company.

The television camera confers temporary celebrity not just on the contestants, but also upon local companies and local authorities who take the opportunity to promote their interests by sponsoring contestants, or by giving them presents to pass to Iakubovich. In a symbolic illustration of the programme's incoherent, hybrid function, these gifts become mixed up with the berries, fish, meat, animals and plants presented by the contestant's intimate family or friends. This curious mix reveals a tension between capitalist and traditional economies, between individualist consumerism and primitive forms of gift-exchange which co-existed with the exchange of 'courtesies, entertainments, ritual, … dances and feasts' (Mauss 1954: 3), all of which feature in *Field*. In the Russian context, gift-exchange is rooted in pre-Petrine *podnosheniie*, a gift-presentation practice accompanied by the expectation of some kind of return. Thus, the gifts brought by *Field* contestants are matched by the commercial presents given to them by Iakubovich. In primitive economies 'it is groups, not individuals, which carry on exchanges, make contracts, and are bound by obligations; the persons represented in the contracts are moral persons – clans, tribes, and families' (Mauss 1954: 3). Accordingly, *Field* contestants act primarily as representatives of their local community and family. This brings to light the encounter of standard game-show competitive individualism with the collective spirit of *Field* in which it is more important for the contestants to represent their local community than to win the game. This collective spirit has been identified by Dana Heller as a feature of Russian television culture in general. Heller notes that, by comparison with Americans, Russians prefer 'television formats that emphasize group interaction, sociability, and teamwork' (Heller 2003).

Narod and intelligentsia (again!)

It is in the meanings attached by viewers to the *narodnost'* myth propagated in *Field* that the contradictions underlying the nation-building strategy that it has been commandeered to fulfil emerge with most force. It would seem that the ultimate failure of the strategy has much to do with its emergence in reactive response to organic changes to the programme's original 'pirated' status and to the role of its decidedly 'ordinary' contestants. In this sense, of course, it offers further confirmation of the 'dialectics between reading and writing' which, for Martin Barbero, attains its apotheosis in television (see Chapter 5). But rather than appropriate popular reaction in a unifying, hegemonic strategy, what we find with *Field* is an appropriation from above which fosters a split in popular reaction from below.

The split is apparent even in the programme's audience ratings. Since its appearance, its popularity has been concentrated overwhelmingly outside Moscow. This is evident from a random selection of audience ratings between 2003 and 2006 taken from Gallup surveys conducted in Russia (see Table 7.2).

The discrepancy between Moscow and the rest of the country was confirmed in our focus groups findings which, however, in addition to this geographical difference, reveal a split by class. For, not surprisingly, *Field* appeals mostly to working-class people. In summer 2005, three retired female participants with incomplete secondary education in Perm claimed to regularly

Table 7.2 *Pole*'s rating in Russia and Moscow

Week	Rating/audience share (Russia)	Rating/audience share (Moscow)
11–17 August 2003	7.8%/26.8%	4.9%/17.6%
2–8 February 2004	11.8%/27.6%	7.8%/18.5%
14–20 March 2005	10.5%/27.5%	7.6%/19.1%
13–19 February 2006	7.8%/19.9%	Below 100 most watched programmes; no statistics

Source: Rezultaty isledovanii, Reitingi SMI: Televidenie at www.tns-global.ru/rus/data/ratings/tv/russia/top_100/_20030804_20030810/index.wbp, www.tns.global.ru/rus/data/ratings/tv/moscow/top_100/_20040202_20040208/index.wbp, www.tns.global.ru/rus/data/ratings/tv/moscow/top_100/_20060213_20060219/index.wbp, www.tns.global.ru/rus/data/ratings/tv/russia/top_100/_20060213_20060219/index.wbp (accessed 17 July 2007).

watch and enjoy *Field*. Their male counterparts and the working-class participants of younger age groups all confirmed watching it from time to time. These results drastically differed from the data received in 2004 when 40 focus group participants with (or in receipt of) higher education were interviewed. None of them openly admitted to liking or watching *Field* on a regular basis, either in Moscow or in Perm and Voronezh. Overall, educated members of the intelligentsia found the programme to be 'belittling', 'offensive' and 'patronising'.

But, what is perhaps more interesting is that there is a further subtle divide within the intelligentsia. The most vehement rejections of the programme were to be found among educated viewers in Moscow, in particular older ones. Still more significant is the fact that the objections were often expressed overtly in terms of a regional 'superiority complex'. Typical is one comment from a retired Moscow participant with higher education: 'They should have closed the program down a long time ago! *This is a spectacle from the province!*' (our emphasis). Here we see a class-inflection of the global–national–regional axis similar to that which emerged from our discussion of the struggle over taste in Chapter 6. As with *My Fair Nanny*, a globalised format is associated with regional 'trash' in an assertion of national pride to which an educated, metropolitan elite lays claim. Conversely, the degree of hostility to *Field* is markedly less among educated viewers outside that metropolitan centre. Here, Iakubovich's nation-building efforts are recognised by educated viewers, but the recognition is tinged with an irony betraying the lingering influence of the class perspective. For instance, in the summer of 2004, one male photographer from Perm sarcastically linked *Field* to the Soviet concept of internationalism, highlighting its 'political flavour': 'Iakubovich should be awarded with a medal of People's Friendship ... He helps to create a nation and link communities to each other, as in "say hi" to my uncle in ... And "this is from the head of our Kolkhoz"'.

This tolerance laced with irony pervaded the group of Perm professionals with higher education. They tended to relate to Iakubovich affectionately, but condescendingly, as a 'people's clown and jester'. Their attitude was characterised by a sympathetic understanding, underpinned by a disinterested distance. One woman in her forties in this group described Iakubovich as follows: 'The *narod* loves him. They all try to get into the program. They all want to kiss him and give him their presents. They all want to dress him up. They treat him as a god'

However, within this group, certain of the older viewers went further and expressed a partial identification with the programme, even referring to the contestants as 'we' and claiming that they reflect 'our', Russian (rather than a global, western) mentality. Here, then, the same class inflection is seen to reconfigure the global–national–local axis in a different way, one more compatible with the unifying concept of *narodnost'*. The regional intelligentsia associate a global format with national pride, which they relocate from the metropolitan centre to the provincial periphery. But, combined with the overarching, two-way professional/working class divide, the three-way split within the professional class grouping which this reconfiguration completes (hostile-metropolitan; tolerant-ironic provincial; identificatory provincial) merely confirms the failure of the *narodnost'* project to which *Field* has been progressively wedded.

There is a further fine distinction to be made within the professional-intelligentsia grouping. For the attitude in Moscow is not exclusively hostile. The liberal media elite associated with the widely respected, and semi-oppositional, radio station, *Ekho Moskvy*, it would appear, approve of the rootedness of *Field* in the folklore of the common people. In response to his listeners' questions about whether *Field* should cease to exist, Matvei Ganapolskii, an *Ekho Moskvy* presenter, stated: 'While Iakubovich is there and his moustache is puffed up, while the *narod* is dancing, singing and bringing him gifts – let the programme carry on. I think it should be for ever, like *Blue Light* [*Goluboi ogonek*]' (*poka est' Iakubovich i toporshchatsia ego usy, poka narod pliashet, poet, i darit emu podarki – pust' eta peredacha idet. Mne kazhetsia, eto dolzhno byt' vechno, kak vsiakie golubye ogon'ki*) (Petrovskaia 2002).[8] Comparing *Field* with *Blue Light*, Ganapolskii inadvertently describes it as a popular Soviet-style entertainment programme rather than a western-style game show. The television presenter Aleksei Lysenkov also endorses *Field* as a 'people's project' (*vsenarodnyi proekt*) (Grymov and Lysenkov 2000). On several occasions, the television critic and journalist Irina Petrovskaia warmly compares *Field* with popular folk tales, such as *Red Riding Hood* (*Krasnaia shapochka*) and *Kolobok*, referring to the programme's generous spirit and folksiness (Petrovskaia 2002). Marina Golub, an actress, accepts that the *narod* loves Iakubovich (Golub 2001). By associating *Field* with the folksy and the warm-hearted, the liberal media elite internalise elements of the *narodnost'* strategy foisted upon the programme by its state-sponsored makers, but inflect that strategy with a mild condescension derived from their position within the metropolitan professional class whose compliance in the strategy is conspicuous by its absence.

Conclusion

Our account of the conversion of *Field* into a vehicle for the promotion of a mythologised *narodnost'* demonstrates that what was intended to unify a nation shattered by the collapse of Marxism–Leninism, then exposed to the divisive flow of global imagery, ironically ends up fragmenting it still further. The fragmentation occurs along the horizontal centre–periphery axis, the vertical class axis, and (as the last example showed) at the intersection of the two. The fact that the unifying strategy is itself mounted on the back of a pirated version of a globalised television format only intensifies the contradiction.

In a sense, of course, what we see with *Field* is little different from what we find in other, western, instances of the commodification of tradition for nation-building purposes. What is, perhaps, of particular interest in the case of *Wheel* is that the commodification comes up against a set of profoundly non-commercial traditions and rituals that, far from belonging to a mortified past, are alive and well in the real, everyday practices of ordinary, provincial Russian people. For this reason, they become bound up with class and regional prejudices in a way that subverts their incorporation into the nation-building strategy. On one hand this indicates that the Russian culture of the ordinary and the everyday retains ties to the communal, ritualistic ways of life which remain resistant to the global media culture with which its western equivalent is imbued (hence what sometimes appears to be the complete symbiosis of media phenomena such as *Big Brother* and the ordinary discourse and behaviour of its mass audience). This explains the ultimate failure of Russian national television to appropriate the global game-show format and harness the everyday ritualistic behaviour of the *Field* contestants to it for nation-unifying effect. On the other hand, and paradoxically, it reveals that, deprived of organic ties to the nation-building centre (Russia's weak sense of nationhood accounts for Putin's panic-stricken, authoritarian reining), local regional culture has retained more autonomy than its western counterpart. Whilst it might therefore offer resistance to national appropriations of global culture, and as the immediate and phenomenal success of *Field* as an adaptation of *Wheel of Fortune* attests, 'the Russian ordinary' is curiously susceptible to global influences unmediated by a national hypostasis. It is to the complex ramifications of the global–national–local complex for Russian regional television itself that we now turn.

8 Russian regional television

At the crossroads of the global, the national and the local

Introduction

Chapters 6 and 7 have demonstrated the importance of the regional perspective on Russian television genres intended for a national audience. And, as we saw in Chapter 2, regional television itself is eminently capable of serving the post-Soviet nation-building mission. Indeed, in each of these chapters, albeit in rather different ways, we have observed a tension between the global television forms to which post-communist television is bound, the national agenda it is called upon to implement and the local contexts in which that agenda is put to work. It is to a consideration of the interaction of these three phenomena within regional television proper that we now turn. In the light of Tehri Rantanen's thesis that, in the 1990s, the global merges with the national and complicates the relationship of the latter with the local (Rantanen 2002), we aim to determine to what extent Russian television at the regional level is shaped by the influence of the global and/or the global/national, and to observe how differently global trends may affect local television depending on whether their influence is direct, or mediated by national television.

According to a survey conducted by the Public Opinion Foundation, 53 per cent of Russians consider themselves 'permanent viewers' of regional and local television and 31 per cent are identified as casual. Only 14 per cent do not watch regional and local television. Of all regional programming, viewers watch the news mostly (90 per cent), films (37 per cent), music (20 per cent), entertainment programmes (19 per cent), educational programmes, serials and programmes on social and political issues (18 per cent each). Significantly, 67 per cent of viewers claim to trust local television more than its national counterpart.[1]

Despite its obvious influence, regional television has been under-researched in both Russia and the west. This is partly because of the sheer number and variety of television companies which sprang up in the 1990s and 2000s throughout the country. The precise number of television companies functioning currently is unknown even to official licensing bodies because there is no mechanism for recording the companies that shut down or stopped using their broadcasting licence.

As Olessia Koltsova (2005) points out, the diversity of the post-Soviet regional media reflects the composition of the Russian Federation which currently consists of 85 'subjects', each with its own administrative and political system, ethnic composition, etc., and with varying levels of independence from the centre.[2] Koltsova distinguishes three media configurations: 'monocentric' (when one dominant media actor defeats others by force); 'pact' (when one media player compromises with others); and 'conflict' (when 'resources are distributed relatively evenly, and no one can dominate) (Koltsova 2005: 171–77). Her analysis helpfully exposes the limits of such concepts as 'a national media system' and demonstrates the 'internal diversity and fluidity of the country's media landscape' (ibid.: 183). However, her study is limited to the analysis of situations as portrayed by the main actors and journalists themselves. In addition, Koltsova does not differentiate between television and other media, and finds no place for audience research (ibid.: 100).

Our own approach complements Koltsova's by filling some of these gaps. First, in conducting one case study – an in-depth analysis of the Perm *krai* based on three field trips to Perm undertaken between 2004 and 2006 – we can accommodate those inner tensions inherent to any given media situation which no general classification model can fully describe. Secondly, we attempt to provide an in-depth picture of the particular situation pertaining to television by comparing three leading regional and local television companies: Perm GTRK, Rifei and Ural-TV. The comparison is informed by

(1) an analysis of television programmes from all three channels recorded selectively during the three years of research and intensively during the week 22–28 June 2006;
(2) interviews with leading television producers and journalists (Veronika Dukarevich, Broadcast Manager of GTRK Perm; Irina Shcheglova, Sales Manager at Rifei channel; Valerii Sergeev, Director of GTRK-Perm; Galina Tsvet, Director of Ural-TV; and Anna Vodovatova, Rifei channel presenter and local celebrity);
(3) audience research consisting of viewer diaries completed for two weeks twice a year and six focus groups differentiated by age and class and prompted with questions about preferences amongst regional channels, programmes and presenters.[3]

Our findings reveal a complex picture featuring tensions between state-owned and private television companies, media elite and audiences, national and local television networks. Some of them contravene Koltsova's assertions that 'common people' have almost no influence on the media (ibid.: 100), demonstrating how ordinary Perm viewers take part in shaping the local television landscape.

In the west, local media have recently moved to the forefront of academic debate. Meryl Aldridge (2007), for example, argues that, as most Britons are still surprisingly attached to their locality, local communications media are becoming essential in delivering local news to the viewer. Aldridge emphasises the proliferation of local newspapers and the development of local and 'community' television (Aldridge 2007: 21). The local mass media are thus linked to the development of democracy on a 'community' level. In the context of increasing centralisation under Putin, it is appropriate to ask if local television can play the same role in post-Soviet Russia. Whether, in light of Geoffrey Hosking's argument that the community has traditionally served as a basic organisational structure in pre-Soviet and Soviet Russia, and that only recently have 'community'-based structures begun to disappear, independent television networks are capable of resisting the formation of the 'power vertical' (Hosking 2004).

Our discussion is loosely informed by the notion of *mediasphere* employed in Chapter One. The concept, we recall, is characterised by overlapping, heterogeneous core–periphery structures which provide a mechanism for developing new information resulting from communication between texts at different points in the structures. Moreover, within the overarching global mediasphere a single point can be located at the core of one structure and the periphery of another. Thus, the post-Soviet Russian news texts examined in Chapter One are peripheral in relation to the western-generated news flows by which their meanings are shaped. But the producers of those news texts, Channel 1 and Rossia, also form the core of a national structure (located within the larger global mediasphere) with the All-Russia State Television and Radio Broadcasting Company (Vserossiiskaia gosudarstvennaia televizionnaia i radioveshchatel'naia kompania, or VGTRK) at its summit. The meanings of the texts produced by that company's regional offices, and by the multitude of independent regional and local television companies likewise situated at the periphery of this national structure, are in turn both shaped by, and shape, those produced at the national core.

At the next level of the mediasphere, regional television itself operates on a core–periphery basis. Thus, texts broadcast by the leading regional television networks form a core for the smaller, local television companies whose peripheral texts generate meaning in relation to that core, and to those of the national and western structures. It is, in general, at the boundaries demarcating the points of intersection of these multiple core–periphery structures that semiosis occurs, and where the complex interrelationship of local, regional, national and global is best studied. As we have already observed during the course of the book, in the post-Soviet, globalised media environment, national media systems are constrained in their ability to control meanings both by the intercultural flow of texts washing over them, and by the intensification of local identity formation that is globalisation's direct product. For a nation in which a heavy burden of responsibility is placed on the media for propaganda purposes, the ramifications of this phenomenon are considerable. Nowhere are they more evident than at the most peripheral point in the structure of the national media system tasked with implementing the propaganda agenda. Our study of Perm regional television should therefore enable us to draw conclusions about the national television environment of which it is part

Perm

Perm is one of those few Russian cities with a population of around a million known as 'mega-cities'. It is located in the western Urals and is the centre of the Perm *krai* which covers 160,236.5 square km and has a population of 2,820,000 (see www.perm.ru/region/; accessed 29 June 2007). As Federico Varese (2001) shows, the area is characterised by strong links between the mafia, local authorities and business structures, all of which put pressure on the regional media. Perm is not unique in this: the corruption of local authorities and the media is a common post-Soviet problem. Moreover, the regional authorities exercise an authoritarian approach to the media similar to that applied by Putin's administration on the national level. In a letter written to President Putin in November 2006, Perm journalists demanded the removal of Governor Chirkunov for consistent infringement of citizens' rights, lack of managerial competence, and anti-constitutional activities, including censorship (see 'Zhurnalisty potrebovali ot Putina uvolit' Permskogo gubernatora', Lenta.ru: Новости: http://lenta.ru/news/2006/11/10/ letter1/14.11.2006; accessed 29 June 2007). This letter mirrors the accusations made by foreign and Russian journalists against Putin himself.[4]

The Perm mass media comprise seven local television companies, eight radio stations, thirty-two newspapers and five internet sites providing news and business information about the city. Perm television is not as developed as that in Tomsk, Ekaterinburg and some other cities, but its structure, diversity and complexity reflect the general development of the media in the country as a whole.

We begin our analysis with an overview of the history of Perm television, focusing then on three current tendencies in its development, each illustrated by a case study drawing on readings of the television texts, interviews with the media elite and audience research. The first tendency – that of the preponderance of the national over the local and the global – is demonstrated by Perm GTRK, a regional representative of VGTRK on whose hierarchical structure it bases its management style, and an example of the neo-Soviet media model as described by Sarah Oates (2007).[5] The second trend is represented by the independent local Rifei channel which operates on the principles of community television. Its influence is restricted to Perm but its news programmes are the most watched of all regional and local TV programmes where they are available. Rifei's television production mechanisms are based on horizontal structures and the involvement of local community in the shaping of the news. In Rifei's texts, the local dominates over the national and the global. The third trend is illustrated by the Ural-Inform TV network in which the emphasis on commercial interests and advertising obviates the national dimension and facilitates the virtually unmediated intrusion of the global into the local.

A brief history of Perm television

Soviet television was controlled by the State Television and Radio (*Gosteleradio*) in Moscow. The national *Gosteleradio* network included 52 stations in the former Soviet republics and 78 regional stations broadcasting primarily programmes supplied from the centre and regional news bulletins. However, a basis for diversification emerged as, during the 1970s, regional stations began to produce more of their own programming, albeit within the strict requirements of *Gosteleradio*, and despite unease about the prospect of local republican television going 'off message' (the issue of foreign-language broadcasting was also contentious from the beginning).

Perm regional television dates from 1956 when the construction of the Perm Television Centre began. On 8 June 1958, the presenter Anna Shilova introduced the first Perm broadcast, which included films for children, a live concert from the Perm television studio and the film *Carnival Night* (*Karnaval'naia noch'*, Ryazanov, 1955).[6] From the very beginning, the focus was on regional and local stories. Perm claims to have invented the genre of 'television newspaper' producing a programme entitled *With a Camera around the Native Land* (*S ob'ektivom po rodnomu kraiu*). In 1960, the programme was awarded the Diploma of the First Degree at the All Union Television Competition. Later, it was renamed and appeared as *Evening Perm* (*Perm vecherniaia*), and then *Evening Perm Region* (*Prikam'e vechernee*). The First National Channel began to broadcast in Perm in 1962. The Second National Channel appeared on Perm television screens in 1965. Since then national television has dominated the regional schedule. The contribution of Perm television to national programming was minimal. The highlights were an issue of the New Year variety show *Blue Light* produced for the First Channel in 1964 and a children's film entitled *Three Days from Ivan Semenov's Life* (*Tri dnia iz zhizni Ivana Semenova*) (K. Berezovskii, 1966), which received the main prize at the First All-Union Festival of Television Films in Kiev in 1966.

Perestroika brought changes to Perm along with the rest of the country. Following national trends, Perm television also aspired to become more transparent and flexible. The programme *Direct Line* (*Priamaia linia*) was created to provide time on-air for dialogue between members of the municipal and regional authorities, and the public. There were new programmes for young people, including an alternative television show entitled *Tonight* (*Segodnia vecherom*), the programme *Open Microphone* (*Otkrytyi mikrofon*) and *Tele-Day* (*Teleden'*). The first entertainment show of a 'new kind' *An American Girl* (*Amerikanka*) was produced by Veronika Dukarevich who was then a young and promising journalist of the *Vzgliad* presenters' generation. Her chat show *Private Life* (*Chastnaia zhizn'*) was one of the three

programmes in the country nominated for TEFFI 1998 (see www.tefi.ru/ru/
tefi/tefi-vict1998/; accessed 29 June 2007). Now Dukarevich is a leading
producer and manager at the state-owned Perm GTRK.

Dukarevich herself describes the period of the early 1990s as a 'wild out-
burst of capitalism'.[7] New television companies emerged to compete with T-
7 which was the successor to the Perm branch of Gostelradio. To establish a
new television company, it was necessary to apply for a broadcasting licence
to the regional Licensing Commission which was formed of regional and
federal representatives. Broadcasting licences were given out on a competitive
basis. The applicants had to formulate their broadcasting conception and strategy. As a result, throughout the 1990s several kinds of broadcasters appeared
in Perm. Firstly, federal companies received their licences to broadcast in the
region, including NTV, STS and TNT. Secondly, independent regional and
local companies were founded, such as Rifei and Vetta, Eastern European
Telegraph and Television Agency (Vostochnoevropeiskoe telegrafnoe i tele-
vizionnoe agenstvo). They usually bought licences to broadcast on the frequencies of national channels. Rifei was established in 1991 on the REN-TV
frequency. Vetta was founded in 1991 and has been broadcasting ever since
on the frequencies of the Kultura channel. The commercial Ural-Inform TV
was founded in 1995. Its network partners are Petersburg-Fifth Channel
(Peterburg – piatyi kanal) and MTV-Perm. These companies are the main
players on the Perm television market, the turnover of which in 2004 was
about 4–6 million roubles a month shared by five to six major TV companies.

The state has several means of control over regional television at its disposal, including legislation (laws on the mass media, advertising and licensing
have all been passed since 1991); licensing of the electronic media; and pricing
for signal transmission. Regional governments also put financial and administrative pressure on regional and local television broadcasters. The regional
and local governments can support television companies through commission and non-budgetary means, such as preferential pricing for electricity
and utilities, loans not subject to repayment and mandatory subscription by
regional government agencies to 'necessary publications'.[8] The following
sections of the chapter look in greater detail at the types of companies that
survived and succeeded in these conditions in the late 1990s and early 2000s.

Perm GTRK: Neo-Soviet television

Organisational structure

The largest national network of regional television stations undoubtedly
belongs to VGTRK. Its structure is vertical with the top leadership based in
Moscow. On 8 May 1998, Boris Eltsyn signed a decree 'On improving the
work of state electronic mass media', as part of which VGTRK was formed
as a holding to include all the regional TV companies owned by the Russian
Federation (Zassoursky 2004: 32).

Under Putin, the government made further steps to increase control. The centralisation of VGTRK was realised in two stages. In 2002, the Law on State and Municipal Unitary Agencies came into force. It affected all 89 regional state broadcasting companies, which were transformed into VGTRK's unitary affiliations. In practice, regional GRTKs still had independent licences to broadcast and could enjoy relative freedom. Perm-GTRK used its own brand known as T7. VGTRK did not interfere much in programming on the regional level. However, this changed in February 2004 when the Russian government issued a decree on the reorganisation of VGTRK through the affiliation of subsidiaries. This decree affected all regional GTRKs which were turned from unitary affiliations into incorporated affiliations of VGTRK. This meant that the national channel Rossia gained full control over all national and regional affiliates. Regional branches were turned into '"re-transmitters" of Moscow-produced content'. This had consequences for the content of regional broadcasting:

> VGTRK management had decided to cut all types of broadcasting in the regions, except news. This decision caused an inevitable reduction of GTRK broadcasting volume from 900 – 1,200 to 590 hours, the closure of whole subdivisions and departments and the dismissal of hundreds of employees in each of the 89 companies. Accordingly, cultural, children's and educational programming was cut, especially in regions with local language broadcasting.
>
> Quoted in 2005 'Internews' report on the Russian media.
> See http://internews.ru/internews/publications/tvproducer.html;
> accessed 7 September 2005·

In her interview, Dukarevich stated that 'no one in Moscow wanted to have control over the regions again but as soon as it was introduced it started working very quickly'. As a regional affiliation, Perm GTRK is now strongly controlled from the centre. For instance, since 20 March 2006, Perm GTRK's schedule has been sent to Perm from the Moscow headquarters. As a result of restructuring, the Kudymkar branch of GTRK, which broadcast for the autonomous Komi-Permiatskii district, completely lost its autonomy and became part of Perm GTRK. In addition, Perm GTRK had to reduce its staffing from 450 to 350. Among the presenters, journalists and correspondents who appear on the Perm GTRK screen, there are now 24 men and 15 women. Some of the best correspondents have left for Moscow. The 'brain drain' problem was also identified by one of our focus group participants, the professional photographer in his forties: 'They suffer from a brain-drain. The best people leave for Moscow. They are paid better there and there is more space to be creative.'

Dukarevich who is, in general, very optimistic, finds it hard to see the latest structural changes in a positive light, illustrating her attitude with an 'old joke': 'If you are being raped, try to relax and enjoy it.' The freedom of reporting which the journalists enjoyed in the 1990s and early 2000s has gone and has been replaced by direct daily instructions from the Perm GTRK director, Mr Sergeev, who came into television industry from government with no media background. We witnessed an example of such pressure during the interview, which took place in her office on 7 July 2006 between 10 and 11am. While we were talking, a message from Mr Sergeev informing staff about the 'theme of the day' popped up on her computer screen: 'Gasification: drawing people's attention to gasification, monitoring whether it improves people's life, telling viewers how gasification has affected individual citizens'. Dukarevich explained the reasons for this agenda: *Gazprom* was installing a major pipeline through the Perm area, so the regional authorities wanted to highlight how they had negotiated the diverting of some gas from the pipeline for the people of Perm. At our request, Dukarevich also read out themes from previous days: 'Gasification: monitoring the whole chain'; 'Gazprom – regional/local authorities – people'; 'Advertising and the law', 'the Russian postal service', 'the law on advertising in action', etc. It should be noted that it is not surprising that Gazprom is a popular topic on the GTRK agenda, as it is a major shareholder of the Rossia channel.

The relations of Perm GTRK with the regional and local authorities are contractual and financial. Perm GTRK is, for instance, sponsored by the authorities to cover all governmental social initiatives. When regional or municipal authorities conclude a contract with Perm GTRK to report on a governmental social project they stipulate that Perm GTRK should make an 'explanatory' (*ob"iasnitelnuiu*) or educational programme, elucidating the purpose of the initiative to the viewers. The practice of providing reporters with news agendas and telling them to 'educate' the people is highly reminiscent of the Soviet period.

Perm GTRK is financially dependent on two sources. About 40 per cent of its funding comes from Moscow VGTRK, and 60 per cent from contracts with local and regional authorities, commercial contractors and advertising. Moscow also conducts monthly checks of the programmes produced in Perm. They choose two random days in the month, during which all the programmes must be recorded and sent to Moscow. With plans to move to satellite transmission, Moscow will be able to monitor regional programmes at any time.

Programming: News bulletins

Perm GTRK transmits on two channels which are both part of VGTRK: Rossia and Kultura. Daily, twelve stories from *Vesti Perm*, the main news bulletins produced by Perm GTRK and commissioned by Moscow VGTRK, are broadcast on Rossia to a potential audience of three million viewers (as noted in Chapter 1, Rossia has been given the task of representing Russia in its regional dimension). The overall daily broadcasting time of *Vesti* is two and a half hours. On Sundays, short *Vesti* bulletins are included in the national morning show *Dobroe utro* between 9.20 and 10am.

The main trend in changing the GTRK regional news format has been a move away from global news formats to national and neo-Soviet news formats. This involves the compliance of the regional news bulletins with the national *Vesti* format and increasing the length of news stories from three to between four and five minutes. In his interview in 2004, Sergeev commented: 'We are now creating a news factory and make our news bulletins in tune with *Vesti* [produced in Moscow].' The Perm *Vesti* bulletin opens with a picture of Russia's map and a *troika* similar to that which opens the federal *Vesti*. Then an anchor appears in front of the screen bedecked with iconic pictures of the city of Perm, including the Perm Opera and Ballet theatre and the Fine Arts Gallery. Here, then, the local serves as an undifferentiated cipher for the national.

The unification of the regional news according to the national format is also reflected in the studio settings and the selection of anchors. The Perm GTRK studio setting is designed in Moscow to match the national *Vesti* setting. The presenters of *Vesti* are chosen on the same criteria as federal presenters. As Sergeev underlined: 'The rhythm and speed of their speech, their presentation – everything should be as in the centre, like in Moscow. We don't have any minority languages represented here. Rossia is a Russian-language channel.'

Perm GTRK news bulletins have the second biggest audience after Rifei. Among our focus group participants most Perm GTRK viewers were older people, aged over 55. It seems that many still watch the Perm GTRK news by habit since it used to be the only channel available to them. Younger Perm professionals also watch it sometimes, as well as the regional cultural news. Several female viewers remarked on the professional presentation style and proper, accent-less, pronunciation of the GTRK presenter, Shilov.

Perm GTRK principles of newsworthiness recall those of the Soviet period (it even identifies itself as 'the channel of social optimism'). Following the federal format, regional news bulletins invariably open with stories about the government. Dukarevich states, 'as part of Russia, Perm GTRK has an obligation to tell viewers about the movements of the president and to cover the activities of the regional authorities'. On 29 June 2006, Perm *Vesti* started with a report on Governor Chirkunov's plans for the development of the region, followed by an interview with a regional Duma Deputy. This was followed by a story on the relationship between Moscow and the region in relation to gasification. Other stories included reports on the festival in the regional Tatar centre opened by the governor, a plan to build a new housing complex in the town of Chusvoi and the local effects of the new alcohol licences introduced by the federal government. Virtually all these stories were covered from the government's perspective and/or featured government officials in a positive light.

Another news programme produced by Perm GTRK but shown on the Kultura channel is *Perm Express* (*Permskii ekspress*). It is less formal, and has a more conversational and regional flavour. However, it follows a similar, 'top-down' format, and is subservient to the regional government, but with a greater slant on business news. On 22 June 2004, *Perm Express* began with a story about the Gazprom conference in Moscow. This was followed by a report on a business fair in Perm, some new trends in the development of mobile phones and an interview, conducted by Sergeev, with Mr Deviatkin, a member of the Legislative Assembly, who wanted to introduce an oath for deputies. The point of the interview was not to question the deputy's ideas but rather to 'educate' the viewer by explaining them. This 'neo-Soviet' approach is also used in Sergeev's talk show *A Cutting Question* (*Vopros rebrom*) whose title, like so many of those discussed in Chapter 4, fails to live up to its provocative connotations, functioning merely to endorse government decisions and policies.

Other Perm GTRK programmes

Perm GTRK has slots on the Kultura channel from 8 to 9am on the 29th frequency (available to the viewers of the Perm *krai*) as well as from 6 to 7am and from 9pm to midnight on the 12th frequency (available only in the city of Perm). Forty per cent of these programmes are live. Locally produced programmes include the conversational/informational *Good Morning* (*Dobroe utro*) and *Culture's Territory* (*Territoriia kul'tury*); the educational *All Left Home* (*Vse ushli iz domu*); the patriotic *Russia's Shield* (*Shchit Rossii*); and the commercial *Simple Stories* (*Prostye istorii*).

The breakfast show *Dobroe utro* (*Good Morning*) uses the global format that has arrived in Perm via the national, as it is modelled on the federal channel's breakfast show (see Chapter 1). Although the breakfast show setting is designed locally, its approach follows the pattern of *Vesti*. The format involves two presenters, male and female, who introduce daily themes ranging from the likes of 'food in the street' and 'physical culture' to 'building bridges with Europe', etc. Throughout the programme, viewers can put questions by phone to a specially invited guest in the field (phone-ins, as we noted in Chapter 4, are now virtually absent from national television). The presenters try to maintain a less formal style than that of the *Vesti* anchors. However, like their national peers, they often lack the spontaneity required by the conversational format.

Ironically, whilst local TV producers and reporters mourn the loss of freedom resulting from tightened control over the VGTRK, the little freedom they have is used to pirate other national TV formats. For instance, Perm GTRK runs the project *Territoriia kultury* (*Territory of Culture*). The project includes the regional news bulletin *Novosti kultury* (*News of Culture*) blatantly pirated from the federal *News of Culture* (*Novosti kul'tury*) bulletin produced by Kultura. The programme updates the viewer on classical music concerts, ballet and opera shows, exhibitions, newly published books, news from theatres and museums, etc. Meanwhile, the federal Kultura managers are oblivious to the piracy, placing in doubt either their ability to maintain control or their general attitude to piracy. Just as it was impossible to pirate a piece of a Communist party document because the canon according to which it was written presupposed a strong element of mimicry (Yurchak 2006), so Perm GTRK personnel proudly insist that they have pioneered the regional *News of Culture*, without even thinking that such obvious plagiarism could be considered an act of piracy. In neo-Soviet conditions, the subservient agent continues openly and innocently to apply national templates to local contexts as it did under Soviet orthodoxy.

Even though the talk show *7 Inches* (*7 piadei*) is not such an act of obvious plagiarism, it resembles the format of *Night Flight* (*Nochnoi polet*), a talk show on Kultura. In both shows, there is one host and one guest with (though in *7 Inches* the hosts alternate). There are also similarities in the studio décor – both are decorated with mirrors – and the trademark camera work of *7 Inches* – showing the reflections of the host and guest in broken mirrors – is similar to the technique used in *Night Flight* when the camera focuses on the reflections of host and guest. However, whilst *Night Flight* offers intimate 'conversations' between the presenter, Andrei Maksimov, and the guest, usually a famous actor or writer, a shortage of local celebrities necessitates a shift to a topic-based approach in the Perm variant: *7 Inches* centres on themes such as 'whether we should punish our children', 'the use of technology in linguistics', 're-interpreting Pushkin' and 'male mid-life crisis'.

Perm GTRK's Soviet-style, 'educational role' must now be applied to new, post-Soviet groupings, such as housewives. Thus, in *Simple Stories*, Tatiana Listratova and Elena Lebedeva play the roles of two housewives, discussing new government policies with a glass of fruit juice at the kitchen table. For instance, on 22 June 2006 they talked about new medical equipment ordered by the government in a dialogue straddling the border between Soviet-style propaganda cliché and popular western-style advert.

Documentaries are more expensive to make than live shows and require sponsors whose agenda dictates the format and content of the piece. Documentaries produced by Perm GTRK in recent years include *Russia's Shield*, a documentary about the Russian national festival of patriotic TV programmes held in Perm; a film about the *Lukoil* company; and *Perm – the Cultural Capital of Volga Area* (*Perm' – kul'turnaia stolitsa Povolzh'ia*). The titles reveal the sponsors: Perm regional government, *Lukoil* and other government and business structures. However, even under such financial and political pressure, GTRK journalists occasionally manage to produce documentaries which do not follow the agenda of their sponsor. On 22 June 2006, the channel broadcast a programme about Perm soldiers who served in the same company in Chechnia. They were attacked by Chechens and many of them died. The soldiers are interviewed standing near the graves of the lost friends. Eschewing both black and white political messages and gruesome details, this was an extraordinarily honest and humane piece of filmmaking.

Another minor outlet for free expression is the only remaining children's programme, *All Left Home*, in which the presenter, Ksiusha, chats to children who ring her in the studio.

Rifei: 'Community television'

As Geoffrey Hosking (2004) has argued, Soviet and pre-Soviet communal structures of living are disappearing in post-Soviet Russia, but, especially in the provinces, people are discovering that some of the functions previously exercised by traditional communities such as the *krugovaia poruka* ('circular surety' or 'joint responsibility') and the *domovoi komitet* (the committee which managed whole apartment blocks) can be fulfilled by local television. 'Community television' serves a range of purposes, such as maintaining communication on the local level; supplying information about local accidents and developments; creating a local network of viewers; and affording them the opportunity to deliver their own messages and take part in creating their own television texts. Unlike the hierarchical structure of the 'village commune' or 'communal apartment', community television provides for a more democratic mode of communication based on the principles of *krugovaia poruka*. It offers a range of interactive techniques, such as the phone and the pager which constitute tools for 'DIY citizenship', in Hartley's words (Hartley 2003). Thus, community television's horizontal structures challenge the centralising, 'top-down' forces of state-sponsored, vertical structures.

The concept of 'local celebrity' helps understand the impact of 'community television' on local viewers. As we saw in Chapter 4, celebrities perform a mediatory function through their familiarity and accessibility to the viewer, and because their appearance on the television screen is 'regular'. For local television personalities, this function is intensified because of the greater relevance of the issues they cover. Local celebrity presenters derive sense from local environments, events and communities, and reflect local trends, fashions and systems of value (Marshall 1997: 12). As we saw in the case of Malakhov in Chapter 4, they also provide a basis for identities constructed in opposition to the metropolitan images of the super-glam and super-rich. In the post-Soviet context, the global phenomenon of television celebrity liberates the local from the dominance of the national.

In the words of one young Voronezh male focus group participant, provincial viewers prefer local and 'everyday life' (*zhiznennye*) stories, 'news about *our* city', and 'local crime updates' to 'political' ones. National news, particularly election campaign coverage, is trusted to a far lesser extent, a point confirmed by focus group participants in other provincial cities. Workers in Perm felt particularly disconnected from the national and international news stories but watched the local news on a daily basis. Their channel of preference was Rifei.

In Perm, Rifei is a community television channel. It was founded in 1991. Since then, it has been among the five most popular channels in Perm. It transmits on REN-TV frequencies (REN-TV is the largest private channel of national/federal significance.) Rifei is independent from REN-TV and the latter has no influence on Rifei's programming. The need to coordinate Moscow and regional scheduling causes some tensions between REN-TV and Perm Rifei, but, so far, Rifei has managed to keep a licence to broadcast for 18 hours per week and to fill those hours with programmes produced or purchased exclusively by Rifei.

Another key to Rifei's independence is that it remains free from governmental structures. The current Rifei director, Boris Prokhorov, a former general director of the newspaper *Local Time* (*Mestnoe vremia*), avoided extensive coverage of the last mayoral election in 2006. The election was dominated by a clash between the municipal authorities and the *siloviki* and Rifei was the only channel to support neither and to cover the election only in news bulletins. Some Rifei staff attributed this to Prokhorov's lack of experience and inability to secure a place for Rifei in the election campaign. However, it also meant that Rifei remained unfettered. Rifei's motto, formulated at a brainstorming session in 2003, is 'to be accessible and to be trusted by the people'. This strategy has brought success and in the two years between 2004 and 2006 alone Rifei's staff increased from 100 to 130.

Programming: News bulletins

As a poll of the 18–54 age group conducted throughout May 2006 by TNS Gallup shows, Rifei's news bulletins are among the most watched by Perm viewers. These findings are confirmed by our focus group data. Perm professionals with higher education and their contemporary workers aged 35–55, as well as older viewers with higher education, all prefer Rifei's news bulletins over others. Retired Perm viewers with higher education watch it at least once or twice a week. All viewers aged 35–55 watch Rifei news between three and seven times a week. In 2006, professionals with higher education admitted to watching *only* Rifei's news, although one of them added that even Rifei's news bulletins were becoming a bit 'toothless' (*bezzubye*). In 2005, Perm workers also confirmed that they watched almost exclusively Rifei's news because they found it the most 'truthful', 'interesting' and 'trustworthy'. They called it 'our Rifei', emphasising that they watch mostly local news because they want to know what is going on in Perm.

Rifei's news bulletins are dominated by the local agenda but their format is influenced by global trends. Thus, the newsworthiness of the stories is based not on their 'educational' aspect, as in the case of GTRK Perm, but on their relevance to the local citizen. For instance, on the day when the governor presented the plan for the development of Perm *krai*, which unsurprisingly made the lead story in the GTRK Perm news bulletin, Rifei's news bulletin commenced with a story about a car crash in the city centre. The focus then moved to the governor's initiatives. The following stories covered a government plan to fight illegal casinos, a census in the countryside,

the renovation of a local monastery and the international festival of university theatres held at the University of Perm. Rifei also differs from Perm
GTRK in its concern with basic community issues, such as housing, transport, food, environment and the elderly, and in its focus on the consequences
of the reported news for individuals. For instance, the story about the census
centred on one village where a few people were interviewed in their own
homes. Another bulletin which began with a story about private bus drivers
and how much they charge elderly citizens was followed by an account of the
illegal sale of watermelons along suburban roads.

Rifei's other programmes, such as *Fun Bucks* (*Veselye baksy*), *Your Health*
(*Vashe zdorov'e*), *Parallels* (*Paralleli*) and *Autobahn* (*Avtoban*), follow the
same principles, providing the community with locally relevant information,
news and advice as well as general entertainment. One programme in particular, *On Duty in Town* (*Dezhurnyi po gorodu*), is essential to Rifei's identity
as a community television channel which helps solve local problems, acts as
a monitor of, and commentator on, local developments, and recreates the
semi-formal atmosphere of a 'neighbours' council'. On air since February
2002, it is also the most popular programme on Perm television. Its presenters, Anna Vodovatova and Igor Gindis, have become local celebrities.
Vodovatova in particular has attained cult status. Local newspapers write
about her personal life. Viewers discuss her in their live journals. Assessing
her own success as a presenter she says that she has attracted a primarily
female audience because she looks normal, just like most of her viewers, and
because she projects the same image in real life as on screen: 'We are not
virtual. We are "*svoi*" ["part of the local community"]'. One of our focus
group participants, a woman in her late fifties with higher education, said
that she liked Vodovatova for her informal and relaxed manner. Most others,
including males, agreed. A retired factory worker told us that he enjoyed
watching *On Duty* because of Vodovatova and Gindis. In the group of
workers aged 35–55, everyone agreed Vodovatova and Gindis were the only two
presenters on Perm television whose voices they would recognise immediately.
They referred to them as 'Rifei voices'. A professional woman in her forties
pointed out that, unlike Vodovatova, Gindis has a Perm accent, which she
objected to. This, however, did not stop viewers like her from watching *On Duty*.

Trust is central to the success of the *On Duty* formula. A male lorry driver
proudly said that he had travelled across the country and watched a lot of
local TV everywhere but had never seen a programme like it. The best thing
about it for him was that it helped solve people's problems: one just needs to
leave a message on the *On Duty*'s pager – he remembered the number by
heart – and the programme team would highlight the problem. They would
also return one month later if the issue had not been solved. The lorry driver
was convinced that this was an effective way of putting pressure on local
authorities.

The *On Duty* formula is as follows: one presenter gets into a car decorated
with a little red flag. The driver takes the presenter around town to report on

minor local problems, such as broken and leaking pipes, sewage, the state of a city tip, a broken tree lying on a road, dead pigeons in a central fountain, broken public toilets, street lighting, broken traffic lights, even a stray cow tied to a garage and found by the owner thanks to *On Duty*.

Often there are additional stories about local trivia. The reporter carries a pager, enabling viewers to send messages about issues of concern to which the reporter immediately reacts by visiting the relevant site. Vodovatova recollects that initially the initiative attracted little interest. Slowly, the programme started receiving 10–15 messages a day. By 2006, this had grown to several hundred. Each week the person who sends the best story receives an award.

Humour is an essential element of *On Duty*, whose goal is not only to identify problems but also to amuse and entertain the viewer. As Vodovatova puts it: 'How can you tell a joke about hot water being turned off? But you have to. You must show it in an amusing way'. To make their stories more entertaining, they started using video clips from old Soviet comedies, extracts from cartoons and video clips as references.

Vodovatova sees the fact that *On Duty* fell victim to piracy as a further sign of its success. At TEFI-Region 2002, an issue of *On Duty* was shown to all the competitors as part of a Rifei news bulletin. It was well received but did not get the TEFI. Later the team received letters from Kirov, Khanty-mansiisk and three other cities in which colleagues from other regional channels admitted that they had 'pirated' (*slizali*) the format. Recently, the idea of *On Duty* was also stolen by the Perm branch of TNT which has created a youth show, one of the rubrics of which is presented by 'a female reporter on duty in the rubric' (*dezhurnaia po rubrike*). Rather than solving everyday problems, however, and in marked contrast with Vodovatova, the pretty, young presenter travels around town to advise young people on the coolest things to do.

Ural-InformTV: The globalisation of the Russian provinces

If Perm GTRK reflects a preponderance of national and regional issues, and Rifei's focus is almost exclusively on local community issues, Ural-Inform TV brings in almost unmediated fashion global news, commercial products and viewing modes to the Perm *krai*. By encouraging interactivity using the latest technological tools, it installs western-style viewing modes at the heart of provincial Russia and although the context is limited to commercial advertising, the mode itself is perhaps more durable. The channel claims that it wants to encourage viewers to develop their 'active standpoint' (*activnaia zhiznennaia pozitsiia*) and to engage them in public discussion of local/regional issues. However, the claim is largely rhetorical and currently the channel offers little more than commercialised infotainment modelled on western-style formats. The programming is targeted at male viewers aged 29–45. As its current director, Galina Tsvet, who joined the channel in 2002, put it, 'We have no old grannies among our viewers. Our main audience is men, businessmen, managers'. Indeed, judging by our focus group data, Ural-Inform TV has not yet managed to attract professionals or workers of any age.

Ural-Inform TV was founded in 1995 and is a subsidiary of Uralsviazinform, a large telecommunications company, which also has branches in Kurgan, Ekaterinburg, Tiumen' region, Iamal, Salekhard and Cheliabinsk. It should be noted that the spread in Russia of mobile phone networks – the basis of Uralsviazinform's success – has been phenomenal. Benefiting from this success, Ural-Inform TV owns a new television tower covering most of the city suburbs: Krasnokamsk, Ust'-Kachka, and Dobrianka. The channel transmits on the frequencies of TVK, TV3, a film channel and the music channel MTV which, along with TV3, is Ural-Inform TV's business partner.

Ural-Inform TV is a commercial channel created to promote Uralsviazinform's services. This explains the channel's strategies and television products. According to Tsvet, it promotes an interactive approach using the latest technologies supplied by the channel founders, such as a television voting system capable of processing 1,000 votes a minute.

Programming

Ural-Inform TV produces 19 programmes, including *Ural Portal* (*Ural'skii portal*), a show whose adaptation of global tools to local circumstances betrays a distinct awkwardness. It consists of a mixture of stories presented by Ioulia, an overweight woman with a Permian accent, and Vlad, a middle-aged man who maintains an intellectual look by wearing trendy spectacles. As if conscious of their own incongruity, they close each show with apologetic sign-offs such as, 'We may have been on the screen for too long … ' or 'We hope to see you next time if we may … '. Attempting to appeal to businessmen and managers working on the international level, they select news stories and reports focusing on international business developments, especially in the sphere of communications. Certain clichés associated with cutting-edge television, such as contemporary electronic music played in the background and swift-montage editing techniques, are often used in excess.

Each section of the show tends to promote a particular product. The 'Super Model' (Super model) section is designed for fashionable consumers: it tells viewers about the latest mobile phone models. The 'Advice for Novices' (*Sovety dlia chainikov*) section is full of advice for various consumers. The endless stream of commercials is interspersed with jokes and humorous pieces of advice, for instance on how to read a person's character based on the mobile phone s/he owns, and so on. The 'Virtual Recipe' (*Virtual'nyi retsept*) rubric updates viewers on news about computer games.

Some lifestyle shows are made for single and married urban professionals. These include *To Stay in Shape* (*Byt' v forme*), *Family Pie* (*Semeinyi pirog*) and *The Formula for Happiness* (*Formula schas'tia*). The latter adopts a western-style chat show format. A successful family is invited to share its recipe for happiness. In one show broadcast in 2006, a family of two dancers with a baby talk about their life together: the wife loves to cook and the husband likes the way she looks. He gives advice to men on how to dance on a disco floor. Traditional stereotypes are dressed up in glossy wrapping for urban professionals. The children's programme *Special Action* (*Osoboe deistvo*) targets professional parents and their children by interviewing small children in a sand pit. They ask children to define certain words associated with working parents' lifestyle, such as 'meeting'. To involve older children, a humorous competition for the 'fastest' mobile phone has been introduced: mobile phones are lined up on a table then called from other numbers. They start vibrating and the phone which moves furthest from the start line wins its owner a prize.

News bulletins (one at 7pm and the other at 9pm), too, follow the commercial agenda. Most stories involve reports on new kinds of foreign and domestic phones, new mobile phone devices and trends, etc. These are complemented by news relating to Uralsviazinform: reports on shareholders' meetings, celebrations of its financial achievements, etc. Ironically, the off-beat impression created by such bulletins, along with that of the other examples of Ural-Inform TV programming we have discussed, suggest that, for all its globalised ambiences, the channel lies still further from the western televisual norm than either Perm GTRK or Rossia.

Conclusion

Our analysis in this chapter has confirmed the complex relationship between the global, the national and the local noted in the two preceding chapters, and in Chapter 2. By focusing on television produced (and consumed) at the local level, it has foregrounded the inherent contradictions in the functioning of the very concept of nation, contradictions expressed with particular force, and carrying particular implications, in the centralised Russian nation which the Putin regime has been attempting to use television to forge from the detritus of the collapsed Soviet Union. Here we might re-invoke Zizek's comments (quoted in Chapter 7) on the modern nation's dual embrace of the organic and the abstract. For it is in this light that we can view the clumsy efforts to impose on Perm GTRK a programming model originating at the national level, so that the local forms and meanings produced by regional programmes replicate those of their national counterparts. Thus, the specific local issues covered in Perm Vesti bulletins legitimate and 'concretise' the abstract image of the Russian nation produced by Moscow VGTRK, but, in their slavish replication of the forms, and modes of control, adopted by their national counterpart, also contribute to the artifice of a harmonious community of centre and regions.

However, the fact that the homogenising measure involves the replacement of global formats adopted at the regional level by neo-Soviet formats imposed from the national centre indicates that the post-Soviet Russian national artifice is itself a 'local' response to global forces perceived as emanating from a centre located firmly in the west (Russia's experience of globalisation differs from that of many other developed nations). And if we recall that these neo-Soviet formats are derived from a project that itself represented an earlier form of globalisation (the attempt to unify a nineteenth-century empire through the imposition of an abstract, Marxist model), the global–national–local triad acquires a further layer of complexity. Here, Zizek's 'organic links' turn out to be derived from the superimposition upon the modern/pre-modern model of a secondary structure in which the equivalent to the 'pre-modern' is constituted by what served as the 'modern' in the first place.

The contradictions are further epitomised in the widespread phenomenon of programme piracy in which a practice conceived as counter-cultural under the new global disposition is filtered through the image of former Soviet control strategies. The result is a form of miscommunication in which what is perceived as 'loyal obedience' at the local level is simply ignored at a national level which, in its desire to compete on the global stage, must begin to pay lip service to global norms (significantly, international copyright law was adopted in the late Soviet period).

In the example of Rifei, by contrast, we detect an effort to employ global phenomena such as the roving television celebrity to restore the 'organic', local community ties suppressed (but, as Hoskings points out, never eradicated) under both the Soviet and the post-Soviet Russian regimes. Through programmes like *On Duty*, the channel succeeds in creating a genuine grass-roots alternative to the dead weight of central control, one in which global television practices such as the live phone-in, long since abandoned on the national screen, thrive and develop organically. The growing popularity of such programmes, and of Russian local television generally, offers a fascinating parallel with viewing habits in the neighbouring post-Soviet country of Belarus, geographically still more peripheral to the 'ex-colonial centre' than Perm, but whose neo-totalitarian approach to the media (responsible for references by some commentators to Russia's own authoritarian turn under Putin as 'Belarusisation', see Iu. Latynina, 'Kto ubil Aleksandra Litvinenko: mneniia', http://grani.ru/Politics/Russia/m.114865.html; accessed 14 September 2007) has caused viewers to turn away from both local and state television, and to tune into Russian national television, now considered more palatable and less rigidly controlled.[9] This illustrates:

(1) the radical non-linearity of the post-Soviet mediasphere (from one point within its area of influence Russian national television is accorded the negative qualities of a controlling centre, whilst from another it plays the role of freewheeling alternative to another such centre, itself intended as a peripheral replica of the first);

(2) the paradoxes of post-Soviet consciousness (Belarusians seeking to escape the iron hand of a regime modelled on the old colonial master turn to the television channels of ... that old colonial master);

(3) the unpredictable consequences in post-Soviet space of globalisation's disrespect for national boundaries.[10]

It is the unmediated transposition of global formats into local contexts that we witness in Ural-Inform TV, rather than the mediation of these formats through robust local codes and practices, which produces the cultural forms most alien to the western models from which those formats originate. An edition of *Ural'skii portal*, for example, is likely to strike the western viewer as far stranger and more incomprehensible than the self-confidently Russian version of *The Nanny* analysed in Chapter 6. From this, we might surmise that the centre–periphery model of the post-Soviet mediasphere within whose orbit our analysis in this and other chapters has been conducted, even one which allows for multiple intersecting and overlapping centre–periphery structures, is not entirely adequate to our task. For the linearity implied by this model fails to allow for the bizarre 'leapfrogging' effect that we see in the case of Ural-Inform TV in which, avoiding mediation by the national, the global penetrates to the heart of the periphery to generate new, hybrid forms with intensely local properties. It also fails to accommodate the temporal dimension according to which the forms and ambiences of the Soviet past can be revitalised for the present in the service of (a) national stances against globalising western imperialism; (b) a new homogenising project subordinating the regional to the national; and (c) local attempts to regenerate the community ties in danger of being lost under pressure from both national and global influences. The post-Soviet mediasphere might be more usefully compared with the phenomenon of 'rhizome' identified by Gilles Deleuze and Félix Guattari:

> Unlike trees or their roots, the rhizome connects any point to any other point, and its traits are not necessarily linked to traits of the same nature; it brings into play very different regimes of signs. It is composed not of units but of dimensions, or rather directions in motion. It has neither beginning nor end, but always a middle from which it grows and which it overspills.
>
> (Deleuze and Guattari 1987: 21)

Viewed in the context of the post-Soviet mediasphere as rhizome, Russia's assertion of (very real) control over the output of its regional media loses some of its restraining force. And when we factor in the role of the regional audience, for which, as we have seen, programmes like *On Duty* mean much more than the average *Vremia* broadcast, the potential for restraint seems to diminish still further. It is to a fuller consideration of Russian television audiences, a growing presence in this book, that we must now turn.

9   Television through the lens of the post-Soviet viewer

So, then, to our elusive protagonist, the audience. In contemporary Russia, as we have seen in earlier chapters, the elitist view of television audiences is widespread. Aleksandr Oslon describes viewers as people who 'gobble down' (*khavaet*) whatever they are offered (Oslon 2003: 12). Marina Davydova portrays the viewer as a drug addict incapable of selectivity. Olessia Koltsova completely writes off the influence of viewers on the mass media:

> The ... 'common people' hardly have any strategies of influence on mass media at all, since its only resource – information – is temporary, casual. These agents are the weakest; they cannot get access to the mass media on their own, to say nothing of influencing the interpretation of the situation created by them.
>
> (Koltsova 2006: 100)

As we indicated in our Introduction, western media theory has tended to fall into the opposite trap by idealising the potentials of the 'active audience', or by abstracting television audiences from the actual viewing process. One of the first scholars to avoid such pitfalls is Ron Lembo, on whose work this chapter draws. Lembo developed a sophisticated apparatus for considering how audiences create meaning from television by focusing on the variety of precise viewing modes by which they interact with the medium within their daily routines:

> Television use involves a complex process of meaning-making, one that is mindfully and emotionally constituted in a variety of ways, ranging across the three components ... the turn to television ... interaction with programming imagery per se, and leaving television and fitting it back within daily life.
>
> (Lembo 2001: 112)

Based on the degree of mindfulness and engagement with television, he identifies three main uses of television: 'discreet', 'undirected' and 'continuous'. Each is a combination of several viewing modes including simultaneous, narrative- and picture-based. His findings are based on a study of a group of Californian viewers, all of whom were of working age and employed; he was particularly interested in the use of television after work and the role television plays in helping people 'change gears' between work and home.

The most interesting and in-depth analysis of post-Soviet Russian audiences has been produced by the US scholar Ellen Mickiewicz who, like Lembo, studies the complex processes of meaning-making by observing real viewers in the field, painstakingly analysing how they unravel actual television stories. Mickiewicz, however, focuses on cognitive strategies rather than practical viewing modes. Her methodology involves an analysis of 16 focus group interviews in Moscow, Nizhnii Novgorod, Rostov and the Volgograd region conducted in January 2002. She is particularly interested in the views of the post-Soviet generation, of those born around 1980. Focusing on discursive practices, she examines how viewers detect channels, how good they are at recognising concealed trade-offs in news stories, how they read election stories, how they remember Soviet television and how they reacted to the closure of the T-6 channel. She comes to some revealing conclusions. Post-Soviet Russian viewers are sophisticated: they are capable of recognising concealed trade-offs, they use the powerful tool of heuristics, they can see that different values are attached to various policies, and they would like to see more diversity of viewpoint (Mickiewicz 2008: 205–6).

However, Mickiewicz also acknowledges that post-Soviet viewers can be complacent and xenophobic. Her approach, which provides a vital second reference point for our own research, does not attempt to explain the reasons behind the contradictions. How could it be, for instance, that viewers who recognise the hidden agenda behind election stories nonetheless voted for those who manipulated them? And why were viewers sensitive to the rigidities displayed by state-controlled channels so indifferent to the closure of independent channels such as TV-6? Nor can these questions be answered by the data available from large-scale television audience research, such as the surveys conducted by the Levada Centre and Public Opinion Foundation (Fond "*Obshchestvennoe mnenie*") (FOM). Large quantitative surveys cannot reveal why people think as they do; they are designed neither to disclose nuances nor to analyse the complexity of viewing practices and interpretations.

Synthesising aspects of Lembo's approach with issues raised in Mickiewicz's research, we aim here to explain some of the complexities and contradictions by analysing viewers' social practices alongside their discursive strategies. One of our main findings is that post-Soviet sociality creates a unique viewing culture, the specificity of which can be comprehended only when the social is analysed against the discursive because the two overlap and complement one another. We begin by outlining our methodology. We then differentiate viewing modes by age, education, gender and location, identifying several specifically post-Soviet viewing practices. Finally, we provide three case studies based on focus group discussions of national and local news bulletins, and two popular serials. These reveal some powerful themes which both divide and unite audiences.

Methodology: Focus groups and viewer diaries

Our methods include distributing viewer diaries and conducting focus group discussions. Viewer diaries were mainly used to take snapshots of viewing practices and reveal the typical. The viewer diary consisted of several sections:

(1) data about the viewer (gender, age, education, occupation and residence);
(2) television and other video equipment owned by the viewer;
(3) the daily length and content of television viewing (by channel and by programme);
(4) viewing process (whether the viewer was engaged in other activities simultaneously with viewing, whether the viewer chose television programmes to watch or not, whether the viewer watched television alone or with somebody else and so on);
(5) the most interesting and memorable programmes of the day/week;
(6) comments.

Some viewers left extensive comments which also contributed to our understanding of viewers' individual tastes and specific attitudes. Focus group discussions provided discursive data for examining specific topics, individual views and experiences, and for finding out *why* a particular issue is 'salient, as well as what is salient about it' (Litosseliti 2003: 1, 11).

Our research took place over a period of three years, between 2004 and 2006. Viewer diaries were distributed twice a year in 2004 and once in 2005 and 2006 to observe seasonal and annual changes. Overall, we collected 168 diaries. In the course of the project, we conducted 22 focus groups in two metropolitan and two regional Russian cities: Moscow, St Petersburg, Perm and Voronezh. Each focus group session consisted of four to ten people and lasted two to three hours. Sessions were audio-recorded and subsequently transcribed. In St Petersburg, Perm and Voronezh, we organised the groups through the University of St Petersburg, the University of Perm and the University of Voronezh, but only a subset of the participants were university students or lecturers. In Moscow, focus groups were organised with the help of *Obrazovannye media* (the former *Internews*).[1] All groups were combined according to the need to produce data comparable by age, gender, education and location.

Our focus group questions varied depending on the year. In 2004, we asked about television programming, entertainment shows, presenters, viewers' self-identification with television characters and personalities, and some specific questions about popular serials and talk shows. In 2005, we asked what viewers made of news bulletins, how they interpreted the representation of specific political events, and how they rated patriotism and objectivity in relation to news reports. We also showed extracts from post-Soviet serials to provoke discussion. In 2006, we combined both groups of questions with a discussion of one serial.

Location and age

Chart 9.1 indicates that each year we organised a minimum of six focus groups with the purpose of mapping out data by location and age. Location and age were constant throughout our three-year study and provided the basic matrix for analysis. The choice of the four Russian cities made it possible for us to compare viewers in the metropolises with viewers in the two large regional centres. We factored in location and age by running same-age focus groups in metropolitan and regional cities. Each year groups of young people aged 18–30 were interviewed in St Petersburg and Voronezh, so as to compare the attitudes and viewing habits of young people. Parallel-age focus groups were also conducted in Moscow and Perm. Each year there were a minimum of two groups in Perm and two groups in Moscow: one group aged 35–55 and the other aged 56+. Thus, we achieve a comparison by location for three age groups (18–30, 35–55 and 56+). Other factors, including gender, class and continuity, were superimposed onto the location and age axes.

Location and gender

Gender was one of the most difficult factors to follow consistently since men were less inclined to participate in focus groups. It was hardest of all to bring retired men into focus groups in Moscow partly because the average life expectancy of women is 72 and that of men is only 58. Thus, in 2005 and 2006 we conducted a single-gender focus group of older women in Moscow.

In 2006, we focused on how gender difference might be revealed in the attitudes of younger viewers. We organised one group of younger male and one group of younger female participants in both St Petersburg and Voronezh.

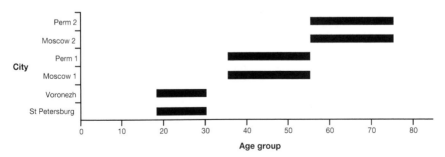

Figure 9.1 Focus groups by age and location conducted in 2004, 2005 and 2006.

Location, age and education

To reveal differences in the viewers' attitudes and viewing modes according to their educational background, we selected only university-educated focus group participants to take part in all the groups in all four cities in 2004. In the case of Voronezh and St Petersburg, the participants were either university-educated or in higher education. In 2005, all the focus group participants were school-educated and involved in manual labour, i.e. working as factory workers, nurses, shop assistants and so on. However, our results from 2004 and 2005 are not completely comparable, firstly because there was a one-year gap between the two rounds of focus groups and secondly because the topics of focus group discussion differed slightly from one year to the next. Thus, in 2006 we ran four focus groups in Perm (instead of two, as in previous years), pairing a group of professionals with a group of workers of the same age (35–55), and a group of retired lecturers and teachers with a group of retired workers. In Moscow, we reconvened the group of professionals with higher education from 2004 and the group of retired people from 2005. In St Petersburg and Voronezh, we formed male and female groups of young people consisting of both university- and school-educated people.

Continuity

During our fieldwork we reconvened the same focus groups in Moscow and Perm in order to observe temporal changes in the attitudes of the viewers. In Moscow, the group of university-educated professionals was convened twice in 2004 and 2006, and the group of elderly women was organised twice consecutively in 2005 and 2006. In Perm, in the third year of our research, we reconvened all four groups conducted in the city in the two previous years. In 2006, many of the focus group participants in St Petersburg and Voronezh were those who had already taken part in the focus groups in

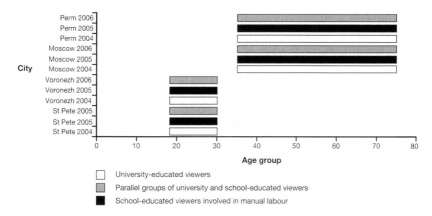

Figure 9.2 Focus groups by age, location and class conducted in 2004, 2005 and 2006.

the two previous years but this time they were grouped not by education but by gender.

Social aspects of viewing culture: Post-Soviet viewing modes

Watching television is one of the top three most popular activities among people in Moscow. Outside metropolitan cities, television is even higher on the list of priorities, as people have less money and there is less entertainment to choose from. Mickiewicz explains such popularity by the fact that television is still free in Russia while most other forms of entertainment have become relatively expensive (Mickiewicz 2008: 14). However, this does not reveal whether viewers are manipulated as easily as is suggested by some Russian scholars and as easily as the government would like them to be. What viewers actually get out of television depends on how they are engaged with it, but before we look at this, let us consider some statistics.

According to FOM, 32 per cent of Russian viewers have the television switched on most of the time (http://bd.fom.ru/report/map/tv/520_15868/tv020115; last accessed 22 May 2008); the figure according to Irina Poluekhtova is 34 per cent; (Poluekhtova 2003: 376). They are 'continuous users of television', in Lembo's terminology, and, as such, they are supposed to be the least critical and most prone to manipulation. Meanwhile, 58 per cent of Russian viewers turn on the television only when they intend to watch a programme, and 47 per cent of viewers plan what they want to watch in advance. Most of our focus groups' participants watched television daily between one and five hours. Independently of age, location and education, the most watched channels were Channel 1, RTR and NTV (in

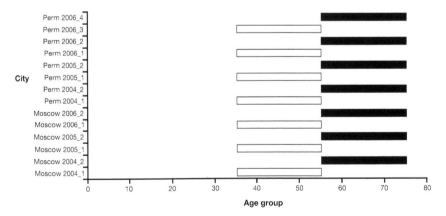

Figure 9.3 The recurrence of the focus groups by age and location conducted in 2004, 2005 and 2006.

Notes: Each colour indicates one group. If a focus group gathered more than once, the colour is repeated accordingly. The colour does not reflect the composition of the group.

different order depending on location, age and education). Among young viewers in St Petersburg MuzTV was particularly popular. In St Petersburg and Perm, local television channels were among the most watched. All these numbers are helpful but they do not tell us how exactly viewers are using television, why they choose a particular programme, whether they discuss it with others or not, whether they believe what they see or not, and so on.

In answering these questions, the keyword is mindfulness, which Lembo defines as a 'most important interior dimension of social actions and activities' (Lembo 2001: 122). Greater mindfulness is characterised by selective, critical and narrative-based viewing, when viewing is separated from other activities. Less mindful viewing is associated with continuous, habitual, image-based and simultaneous viewing, when viewers find it difficult to separate watching television from other activities. Lembo identifies a connection between low mindfulness and the potential power of television 'to standardize people's mindful experience' (ibid.: 135). Lembo distinguishes three uses of television depending on the level of viewers' mindfulness:

(1) 'Discrete' use, in which viewers separate television viewing 'as a distinct activity that occurred regularly'. Approximately one-third of the viewers Lembo interviewed used television in this way. They typically watched entire programmes and exercised the most control (ibid.: 216–17).
(2) 'Undirected' use of television contains elements of selectivity and focus but, on the whole, 'it exhibits a more diffuse, fragmentary, and open-ended sociality compared to discrete use'. Viewers 'moved back and forth between periods of attention to these more mindful involving activities and television viewing'; 'they were no longer able to maintain the distinction between television viewing and other discrete activities' (ibid.: 220–21).
(3) 'Continuous' use: the television is turned on all day long, and off just before going to bed (ibid.: 226). In Lembo's research, one-third of viewers were continuous users.

In addition, Lembo cautions us about 'simultaneous viewing', which is usually associated with the continuous use of television but the two do not have to come together.

> In simultaneous viewing people tend to focus their mindful attention on shorter scenes or segments of a program and are less concerned with coming away from what they watch with such elaborated meanings intact … content, it seems, to 'catch' the meaning of what is on in bits and pieces.
>
> (Lembo 2001: 206)

How well, then, do Lembo's findings apply to the post-Soviet Russian context?

Simultaneous viewers: Television as glorified radio

Continuous simultaneous viewing is the dream of any authoritarian state because it implies unquestioning acceptance of government propaganda. The number of simultaneous viewers in the USA (one-third of the total) is roughly the same as in Russia (32–34 per cent). Stereotypically, housewives are the main 'simultaneous' consumers of daytime television. Our respondents included two very typical examples: 40-year-old, university-educated Tatiana and 44-year-old, university-educated Veronika. They both kept television switched on all day long most days. On average, Tatiana's viewing time was twelve hours per day. Only on one day, when she was away, did she not watch television. She described television as a 'background noise' that she listened to (*prislushivalas'*) while doing other things, such as cleaning the flat, preparing food, having meals, assembling new furniture and doing various chores. When she heard something interesting, she would 'tune in'. Then she would 'switch off' again until another 'interesting' moment that would grab her attention. Although both women live in Perm this is not a regional phenomenon. Among retired people in Moscow, for example, there were a number of continuous viewers. Tatiana's and Veronika's continuous use of television is clearly sound rather than image-based. The fragmentary, distracted nature of such use would seem to render its practitioners particularly vulnerable to ideological manipulation.

Undirected users of television: Elusive mindfulness

The degree of viewers' mindfulness is directly linked to their critical engagement and, therefore, to the amount of control they exercise over meaning construction. However, it is often difficult to measure mindfulness with any precision because the boundaries between continuous and undirected use of television, as well as between undirected and discrete, may shift. The majority of Russian viewers fall between continuous and undirected use: over 70 per cent of viewers tend to watch television for several hours after work, as Lembo puts it, to shift gears from work to home. The typical examples of such undirected users in our focus groups were Lena, a 42-year-old female physician from Moscow, and Vera, a middle-aged factory worker (*operator*) from Perm. They both kept television on in the morning before work and after work in the evening. Vera, for instance, watched television for over five hours a day on average. Like Tatiana and Veronika, these women combined viewing with preparing food, getting ready for work and chilling out.

University-educated men of working age tended to watch television for a few hours in the evening to relax, like many Californians described by Lembo. They were occasionally engaged in other activities, such as reading or working on the computer, but, on the whole, they were undirected users. Victor, a 33 year-old university educated manager, and Igor, a 39-year-old physician from Perm, watched programmes that they chose themselves as well as those chosen by other family members. Their degree of attention varied depending on who made the choice. For instance, Igor remarked that he was very attentive when watching programmes he chose himself including football, the news, and serials, such as *Officers* (*Ofitsery*) and *Soldiers* (*Soldaty*). When he watched television with his family, he paid less attention.

The working class men differed in that they were characteristically unengaged in other activities while watching television and did not switch channels as often as their university-educated contemporaries. Most of them were either discrete or undirected viewers, such as Nikolai, a 39-year-old metalworker, who enjoyed watching television after work to relax but finished watching most programmes. Interestingly, school-educated male viewers were more focused and mindful than university-educated male viewers because the latter switched channels more often (perhaps reflecting greater access to cable television).

Elite simultaneous viewers

In Lembo's study of American viewers, continuous simultaneous viewing, likewise widespread in Russia, is associated with distracted, fragmented and uncritical viewing. But, crucially, in Russia it also plays a very different role, due to the low cultural status television has habitually held here. This is best represented by the group of university-educated Moscow professionals, part of the metropolitan elite. They watched television least of all but many enjoyed simultaneous viewing as a way of acknowledging that television was a 'waste of time'. Dmitrii, a 35-year-old who is university-educated and worked for the British Council in Moscow, remarked that he would rather see the television set used as a bookshelf. Nevertheless, he watched television for just under an hour per day on average in 2004, but noted that many programmes had been chosen for him by his wife or mother. He usually read and/or ate while watching television.

Two female participants in this group were simultaneous viewers who did not rate television highly and treated it as a means of relaxing and staying informed. One was Irina, a 46-year-old former television scriptwriter and director. She watched television for about two-and-a-half hours per day in the winter of 2004. In the summer of 2006, she watched less (between one and two hours a day), which is a typical seasonal change attributable to the summer dacha phenomenon. The second was Ira, a 45-year-old lecturer/manager, who spent a similar amount of time watching television, usually late at night while doing other things.

Ira's boyfriend, 48-year-old geologist Aleksei, could not talk about television without irony or cynicism. His viewing pattern was curious in that he watched television *only* when not at his girlfriend's flat. During the first week, he viewed only a couple of DVDs with his girlfriend. Then he got excited about the serial *Ofitsery* (*Officers*) when on a five-day expedition in Plesetsk, where he and his five colleagues regularly sat around the television over dinner. As soon as he returned home, he stopped enjoying the drama and ceased watching. Discussing serials at our focus group, he said that in 'their circles' (*v nashem krugu*) 'no one talks about serials'. Aleksei thought of television as something worthless and low-cultured, but he also secretly enjoyed it when there was an excuse to watch it without being responsible for making the decision to turn it on. In Russia, then, the usually passive simultaneous viewer turns into an active viewer, a critical and engaged interpreter of the television message.

Stiob-*viewing*

The attitude adopted by such viewers does not, however, equate to the 'oppositional' stance identified within Stuart Hall's typology of viewing modes. Rather it combines elements of both acceptance and resistance in a complex synthesis best characterised by the uniquely (post-)Soviet notion of *stiob*, which Aleksei Yurchak defines as:

> a peculiar form of irony that differed from sarcasm, cynicism, derision, or any of the more familiar genres of absurd humour. It required such a degree of overidentification with the object, person or idea at which [it] was directed that it was often impossible to tell whether it was a form of sincere support, subtle ridicule, or a peculiar mixture of the two
>
> (Yurchak 2006: 249–50)[2]

Stiob viewers acknowledge their over-identification by, on one hand 'enjoying' a programme in the passive, uncritical way it was intended to be enjoyed, but on the other hand sporadically, and ambivalently, transcending this mode by smirking, smiling, or commenting, in groups and individually. Such viewers tended to be university-educated men and women aged between 18 and 55.

A typical *stiob*-viewer was Vladimir, a 44-year-old photographer. He frequently switched between terrestrial and cable television channels including Channel 1, Rossia, NTV, RBK, Explorer, National Geographic, Fashion TV and others. A simultaneous viewer, he was often distracted from what was on the television screen; his comments on programming drew on disjointed impressions of different shows which in most cases he did not finish watching, distancing himself from both the narrative and characters. In Lembo's terms he could 'continue *looking at* the people or the characters who are located in the social action depicted in images, and observe from a distance what it is that they do'; he could 'then see others, not as intersubjectively based social actors, but as *images*.' (Lembo 2001: 239) Lembo remarks that this type of image-based viewing produces indifference. In Vladimir's case, however, it led to the kind of double-edged (or backhanded) endorsement of the officially intended meaning. For instance, when in 2004 we discussed the game show *Pole chudes*, Vladimir over-identified in semi-mocking fashion with its presenter, Iakubovich, whom he described as 'a Soviet hero deserving of a medal for his contribution to improving people's friendship'.

Stiob-viewing appears to be genre-specific, with the news or old Soviet films providing particularly fertile territory for its practice. Describing the news as it was presented in the former Soviet Union, Nikolai, a 40-year-old Perm worker, enthused: 'In those years, we listened to news about virgin lands, BAM, and new construction sites. Communists ahead! That was patriotism! And what now … ?' From a position at once inside and outside Soviet discourse, he does not appear to be sure whether it was good or bad that news stories were so exaggeratedly optimistic. This ambivalent nostalgia for Soviet optimism crept into various comments on news and films. On the one hand, viewers were critically aware of its mendacity, on the other hand, they contrasted it wistfully with the gloom and pessimism of contemporary reality.

Often, as in the previous example, viewers would begin their comments in *stiob*-mode, and then finish with a straightforward endorsement of the intended meaning. An example of the reverse shift – from serious to *stiob* – emerged in a discussion of the Soviet television series *The Place of Rendez-vous Cannot Be Changed* (*Mesto vstrechi izmenit' nel'zia*). A nurse from Moscow commented on the depiction of the Soviet city and citizens after the war: 'The serial reflects the life of Soviet citizens as it was after the war … Everything is so celebratory [*prazdnichno*]. Everyone has little push-chairs [*koliasochki*] and is eating ice-cream,' The use of diminutives (*koliasochki*), with their part-endearing, part-condescending tonality, is characteristic of *stiob*'s inside–outside effect.

Non-switching attentive viewers

Mindful, focused viewing without channel-switching usually implies the ability critically to engage with the content of the programme. However, it can also be the result of habit, as was the case with most of the retired viewers in Perm and Moscow. The older generation became familiarised with the remote control only later in their life, but they also spent the greater part of their lives having the choice of only two or three Soviet television channels, and, even now, they rarely have access to cable television. Vera, a former industrial designer, was a typical viewer. She watched television for a few hours every day but switched channels only to watch a particular programme. Similarly, 62-year-old Nina (who was still working) rarely switched channels at all. For several days in a row she watched only Rossia, switching channels only twice throughout the evening on seven days out of twelve. Retired people saw switching channels as disruptive and confusing; they complained that, like the commercials to which their Marxist upbringing had left them inherently hostile, it fragmented their viewing.

Older people also 'made an effort' or 'tried' ('*staralas*', as Valentina, a 68-year-old retired dentist in Perm put it) to concentrate on what they were watching. Valentina, for instance, talked on the phone and did chores *only* during commercial breaks. It was usually important for her that it be quiet in the room and she was selective: she would study the television guide and choose what she wanted to watch in advance, usually several hours' worth every day. Similarly, Sergei, a 66-year-old lecturer in Physics at the University of Perm, watched television attentively, without switching channels.

Retired people also tended to view more than one news bulletin a day. Aleksandra, an 82-year-old who completed only seven years of secondary school, watched the news on all channels (although her analysis of news stories lacked clarity during focus group discussions; for her it was the act of viewing which was important to her daily routine). In both Moscow and Perm, older viewers could list the news bulletins on three national channels in order. Vera, a 69-year-old, proudly claimed:

> I watch all the news. Firstly, I watch the *Euronews* at 7am. At 7.35 I watch TVTs. Then, I watch First Channel and *Vesti* [on Rossia]. In short, I watch it all. And NTV, of course. It is like a conclusion to them all.

Nina, a 62-year-old from Moscow said that she starts watching Rossia at 6am, followed by the news from the regions, then *Vremia-Moskovskoe*, and so on. Thus, in post-Soviet Russia, there is no contradiction at all between mindful viewing and the passive reception of television messages.

Multi-tasking viewers

Equally, however, the variety of simultaneous viewers in post-Soviet Russia is greater than that described by Lembo. In addition to the highbrow university-educated metropolitan elite for whom simultaneous viewing offers a way of negotiating television's low cultural status, we encountered many simultaneous viewers among the young and university-educated in Voronezh. Many combined their simultaneous viewing with a high degree of mindfulness and were capable of analysing not only the story but also the way it was presented by different channels. This marks the most sophisticated type of 'critical' viewing.

The activities that these viewers were engaged in while watching television were unusual. For instance, Maria, a 17-year-old student, wrote '*konspekty*' (the concise interpretation of university lectures in the form of notes) or undertook other kinds of university study. Despite multi-tasking, she watched certain television programmes attentively and left detailed remarks on them. Aleksandra, a 19-year- old 'multi-tasking' viewer, used television continuously and habitually. She considered it 'a background to her other activities', like reading, emailing and tidying up. In theory, she should have been a disengaged, image-based viewer but in fact, she was sophisticated and engaged in her comments. Her interpretation of news stories throughout the fortnight which she volunteered without prompting was narrative-based and critical. She watched the news on different channels and wrote on Sunday, 2 July 2006, that the main story was the legitimacy of the Ukrainian presidential elections. On Monday she compared the presentation of the news story on different channels, noting that on ORT and RTR it was reported in the style of Russian propaganda, whilst NTV and Ren TV 'tried to show' the events from both sides. On each of the following days, she entered her comments on the progress of the story. Aleksandra's engagement varied according to what she was viewing. Just like other female students in the group, she regularly watched the news.

By comparison with other age groups, university-educated young people were much better adapted to making sense from disrupted, fragmented and image-based viewing. In particular, they displayed a remarkable capacity for extracting and critically assessing narrative-based meanings from main news stories.

Enjoying food and entertainment

The viewing modes of school-educated young Voronezh participants were similar to those of their peers in Perm. Compared to their university-educated contemporaries in Voronezh, they were less prone to simultaneous viewing. They were mindful viewers, paying 70–100 per cent attention to programmes they watched. Another difference between the two groups of young Voronezh viewers was in the choice of programmes. If university-educated viewers watched the news, analytical and cultural programmes, talk shows, films and so on, school-educated viewers watched mostly serials, chat shows, comedy and films. Olga, a 21-year-old tailor, never combined television viewing with other activities and insisted on silence when watching. Her use of television was predominantly undirected and routinised. Each day she watched chat shows, the reality show *Dom-2* and the serial *My Fair Nanny*. Anna, a 22-year-old vacuum operator, likewise laid great stress on silence.

Gender differences in the school-educated group were greater than those among the university-educated and were mostly expressed through programme choice. The latter tended to watch 'gender-neutral' programmes, such as the news, socio-political programmes and Kultura channel shows. School-educated participants opted for more gender-specific entertainment shows, such as the serials *My Fair Nanny* and *Karmelita* (favoured by women) and the serials *Bandit Petersburg (Banditskii Peterburg)* and *Mole 2 (Krot 2)* (preferred by men).

School-educated young men in Voronezh habitually watched television while having meals. Dmitrii, a 21-year-old single shipping clerk and a typical viewer, usually had his meals or packed/unpacked for his frequent trips while viewing. His routine included serials, comedy, films, chat shows and criminal updates. Untypically, however, he regularly watched business news on RBK.

University education, then, reduces gender differentiation in viewing choices and promotes more sophisticated tastes in television consumption. Moreover, working-class young people in Voronezh had more in common with work-ing-class viewers in Perm than with their contemporaries in Voronezh, sug-gesting that class is more significant than region or age. University-educated viewers are, on average, more analytical in their approach to television and are less likely to be manipulated by it, though the differences are less stark than might be expected.

Focused, mindful and sceptical

Young, university-educated St Petersburgers shared the highbrow view of television expressed by Moscow professionals but there were more 'discern-ing' viewers among them. There was one young married couple in this group: 23-year-old Olga and 26-year-old Maksim. In the course of a fort-night in 2004, Olga watched 0.4 hours per day and Maksim 0.31 hours. Their viewing patterns were almost identical: repetitive and highly selective. On eleven days out of fourteen, Maksim watched the two-minute daily weather forecast. Olga joined him on five days. In 2006, Maksim's viewing pattern was less regular and, in addition to weather forecasts, he watched sport (it was the World Cup) and music channels. Although these two par-ticipants are not typical in that they watched less television than most, they represent a tendency towards discrete viewing in this group. Only one woman, Maria, a 22-year-old linguist, engaged in regular simultaneous viewing. However, this did not prevent her from being attentive when she watched her chosen programmes.

School-educated participants in St Petersburg did not leave sufficient com-ments to allow us to evaluate their simultaneous viewing, but they all watched television on a regular basis for a few hours a day, mostly in the evening, which identifies them as undirected users. Their choice of programmes included serials, talk shows, Kultura channel, local news and reality shows.

Comparing St Petersburg students with their Voronezh contemporaries, we find that Voronezh students watched more television, often simultaneously with other activities, while among St Petersburg students there were no simultaneous viewers. The explanation of this regional difference may lie in the fact that St Petersburg offers more entertainment opportunities outside television than Voronezh. However, simultaneous viewing did not prevent most Voronezh viewers from engaging thoughtfully with television.

Our survey of the distinctive features of post-Soviet viewing modes suggests, then, that mindfulness does not necessarily bring with it a critical attitude to viewing content. Mindfulness depended considerably on age: elderly viewers were more focused and discrete while younger viewers tended to 'multi-task' more, except for young St Petersburgers who watched hardly any television at all. Retired viewers described this as a legacy of their Soviet upbringing: they were 'educated' to pay attention; indeed, a crucial difference between post-Soviet viewers of all kinds and their American counterparts is a propensity for *self-reflexive awareness* of viewing modes and patterns adopted.

Equally divergent from Lembo's findings is the observation that post-Soviet simultaneous viewers tended towards heightened scepticism. Simultaneous viewing offered a means of watching television, whilst drawing attention to the medium's low cultural, 'unworthy' status. This mode was central to *stiob*-viewing whose elusive hybrid of 'inside and outside' seems, likewise, to be a characteristic (if not peculiar) feature of post-Soviet television culture.

Another explanation for the prevalence of simultaneity, of course, is to be found in the crowded living conditions in which many post-Soviet audiences are forced to watch television. This leads inevitably to a heightened role for collective viewing, to whose further details and ramifications we now turn.

Collective viewers

Living conditions matter in considering viewing modes because of the opportunities for discussion and collective evaluation they afford (Lembo 2001: 168). *Stiob*-viewing, as we have seen, draws heavily on collaborative modes of meaning-production. In this section, we consider viewers' sociality in more detail.

Mostly our focus group participants watched television at home or in their dachas. On a few occasions, they watched it at friends, at relatives, at work (the Moscow nurse Oksana told us that there was a television set at the hospital where she worked), or on business trips (geologist Aleksei from Moscow and lorry driver Sergei from Perm). In one case, Moscow lecturer/manager, Irina, watched five minutes of a talk show in a shop while her boyfriend was looking for something.

Households each had at least one colour television, and often more than one. Some had as many sets as viewers, like that of Boris, a 56-year-old Muscovite, where four people had access to four television sets. In most households, television sets were located in the living room, kitchen and bedroom, although it should be added that in small Russian flats, living rooms can often be used as bedrooms and vice versa. In these multiple spaces, our focus group participants combined solo viewing with collective viewing involving friends, colleagues and neighbours.

Interestingly, however, results on collective viewing differed between focus group discussions and viewer diaries. When asked during discussion, most middle-aged and older viewers said that they rarely watched television with other members of the family. University-educated Moscow professional Vladislav perceived that television fragments his family: 'We have four television sets, one in each room. So, we often watch television in separate rooms.' Marina, also from Moscow, commented: 'I have two television sets. I also have a granny and a son. Granny tells me about serials and my son watches MuzTV. Awful music! I leave them and go outside to read books.' A retired school-educated Perm viewer describes a similar situation: 'There are four of us and we share three television sets. My grandson has got a computer. … We all watch television in different rooms.' Among the retired Muscovites, three old women all said they watched television separately from others: one from her husband; another from her son; and the third from her daughter.

Young viewers in both St Petersburg and Voronezh were more willing to admit to sharing television with their family members. Igor from St Petersburg remarked that they watched old Soviet films together, because the films were 'familiar to parents and interesting to children'. His contemporary Dmitrii added that they watched the news as a family. In the St Petersburg female group in 2006, Larisa said that they usually watched television while having dinner: during the monitoring period, dinnertime coincided with the serial *Do Not Be Born Beautiful* (*Ne rodis' krasivoi*). Another family usually gathered to watch the reality show *The Factory of Stars (Fabrika zvezd)* which was voted one of the best TV programmes of the year in 2004 (www. levada.ru/press/2005011401.html). A St Petersburg female student commented that in her family they watched two kinds of programmes together: travel and the news. Other families watched sport events together, the Olympic Games, the World Cup as well as entertainment programmes of Soviet origin, such as *Blue Light* (*Goluboi ogoniok*) and KVN.

Most young participants also said that they discussed programming with other family members and friends. Young St Petersburg men talked about sport, the talk show *To the Barrier* (*K bar'eru*), news stories and their coverage on different channels. Among the programmes discussed, young women also mentioned specific news stories, such as Beslan and 9/11, the serials *Moia prekrasnaia niania* and *Doctor Zhivago* (*Doktor Zhivago*), sport programmes, music and Soviet films.

Thus, in a fascinating paradox, viewers too young to have experienced Soviet reality acknowledged the value of Soviet programming and viewing patterns more readily than their parents, for whom collective viewing was now tainted both by the negative aspects of the Soviet past, and the deleterious, low-cultural consumerism associated with western-influenced television programming in the present ('I leave them and go outside to read a book'). However, in viewer diaries people were more willing to admit to collective viewing than in discussion. Perm school-educated viewers of all ages and classes repeatedly owned up to watching and discussing television with their family members, friends and co-workers. Young viewers in St Petersburg and Voronezh, it emerges, often watch and discuss television with others, as do all Perm professionals. Even the Moscow professionals who in discussion claimed they watched television separately (if at all!) admitted in some instances to collective viewing in their diaries. Natalia discussed the news, a talk show, a serial and a concert with her mother, and the World Cup with her son; Maria talked about the cancellation of privileges for retired people with her parents. Irina mulled over the Moscow Cinema Festival with her daughter and the rock group *Time Machine* (*Mashina vremeni*) with the daughter of her tailor. Half of the retired Moscow and Perm participants watched television with other members of the family at least once during the fortnight, discussing Zhirinovskii, the latest Parfenov show and the old Soviet singer, Zykina.

Young women seemed to chat about television more often than males, reflecting the greater acceptability of the medium for the female gender noted in Chapter 6. Typical was Alisa, a 19-year-old from St Petersburg, who, in the course of the fortnight, analysed the news with her relatives; shared her 'strong feelings' about a reality show with a friend; had a chat with someone about a common friend who was acting in a serial; talked with colleagues about the talk show, *The Domino Principle* (*Printsip domino*); offered a piece of advice from *The Land of Soviets* (*Strana Sovetov*) to her mother; told her husband about an interesting programme; discussed the recipes and the guests' behaviour on a culinary show with her female friend; and chatted with friends about television in general. Alexandra from Voronezh, who lives with her parents, sharing two television sets in the kitchen and the sitting room, usually watched television with her parents in the sitting room. She chose about one-third herself; another third was chosen by her mother, and a third by her dad. With her mother she watched the talk show *Wait for Me* (*Zhdi meni*), the serial *The Street of Broken Street Lamps* (*Ulitsy razbitykh fonarei*), and occasionally the news, opera, films and *Goodnight, Children!* (*Spokoinoi nochi, malyshi!*). Aleksandra's father chose the game show *All or Nothing* (*Pan ili propal*), which father and daughter found 'primitive' and 'limiting'. She also watched with her father the news, the news of culture, local news and *Basic Instinct* (*Osnovnoi instinct*). In this family, then, viewing choices were democratic, confounding expectations of patriarchal authoritarianism in respect of rights to the remote control.

In Russia, it is still common for several generations of family members to share one flat and this inevitably increases the likelihood of collective viewing. Indeed, the absolute majority of our focus group participants were primarily collective viewers who collaboratively monitor, evaluate, compare, question and sometimes subvert what they are seeing. Collective viewing with older family members also helps explain how Mickiewicsz's young Russian viewers could express nostalgia for Soviet programming that they cannot actually remember, particularly since Soviet films and shows of Soviet origin unite families in front of the television set more often than other programmes. Here, yet another of the fascinating contradictions in post-Soviet television culture emerges: for the very same collective viewing of old Soviet programming which underpins Putin's attempts at a partial rehabilitation of Russia's glorious past simultaneously raises the audience's critical faculties and shifts control over the meaning of the message towards the viewer.

Four case studies

Case study one: National and local news

How, then, are the contradictions relating to control over televisual meaning reflected in viewer responses to particular forms of programming? One of the key factors in establishing such control relates to the ability to separate the plausible from implausible, the believable from unbelievable, the real from unreal, and the true from the untrue. To find something believable, especially in a news story, viewers must trust what they see. In 2005 and 2006, we included in our focus group discussion questions about news coverage to reveal how trustworthy Russian viewers find national and local news bulletins. The results revealed interesting differences, the most pronounced of which had to do with location and level of education: the further away from the metropolitan centres viewers were, the more mistrustful of national news coverage they became. Outside Moscow and St Petersburg, both genders found local news more believable, real and relevant; they felt alienated from national and international news stories. The differences between university-educated metropolitan and regional viewers were less evident, however (the intelligentsia was almost uniformly sceptical), and our analysis below draws primarily on discussions held with school-educated viewers in 2005.

Greater trust of local news is, of course, to be expected; local news stories are easier to test against reality and the objects of the news are familiar and relevant to everyday life. Discussing the differences between national and local stories, young Voronezh viewers distinguished between 'political' and 'everyday life' (*zhiznennye*) stories. The former included primarily stories concerned with national politics and, in particular, election campaigns – viewers found these least trustworthy. The latter included local news, i.e. stories about everyday life in the region.

Workers in Perm felt similarly disconnected from national and international politics but very keen on their local programming. It is significant in this context that on 8 July 2005, the focus group participants had generally not heard about the London 7/7 bombings of the previous day. Only one woman knew about them because she *happened* to watch the news. Perm workers were, however, avid and proud viewers of local programmes, such as *On Duty in Town*, discussed in the previous chapter, which they described as trustworthy and useful. One male participant remembered the programme's phone number which he cited during our focus group discussion.

Despite being in the capital, school-educated female viewers in Moscow admitted to being 'passive viewers' of national news bulletins (they would watch only if their television sets happened to be on) but said that they would start properly following a story if they had heard something interesting. During the Beslan events, two nurses at a local hospital watched the news even at work. Otherwise, they all expressed more interest in local news. When asked to what extent they trusted the news, Oksana said: 'I think that no one will tell us all the truth anyway, so we have to cut off a certain part of the story.' They gave two examples: one had to do with a report on the government's promise to increase nurses' salaries by 25 per cent, which never materialised in real life; the other was about inconsistencies in Beslan reports on different channels.

Older viewers in both Moscow and Perm watched national news bulletins more often and clearly wanted to trust what they saw. Anna from Perm said: 'We try [to trust it]. We trust it.' Anatolii added: 'But not always'. Anna interrupted again: 'But we still try. But not always.' Galina joined in: 'We have been brought up to trust [the news]. So we do.' Anna then interjected: 'Of course, we analyse whether it is correct or not. To start with, we trust though.' Anatolii summarised: 'Then you make your own conclusion, using your own experience ... They say one thing but in reality, things are different. Understand? We have lived life. We are no longer so naïve' (*My uzhe ne takie lokhi*). Again, we are struck by the level of critical self-reflection accorded these relatively uneducated viewers by their Soviet experiences ('we have been brought up to trust ... so we do'). Nothing better exemplifies the post-Soviet condition.

We must, however, now attend to the question of how, in this context, the patriotic agenda promoted by all state television channels on behalf of the Putin regime has received such seemingly uncritical support.

Case study two: Patriotism and anti-western sentiment

The first point to note is that the majority of our focus group participants wanted the news to be both objective and patriotic, seeing no contradiction in this whatsoever. They distinguished 'patriotic' from 'pro-government', emphasising that to be patriotic does not mean to be skewed or untruthful. School-educated viewers aged between 35 and 55 in Moscow and Perm (2005) defined patriotism with reference to their own education in the former USSR. Patriotism in both groups was associated with sentimental *nostalgia for the pride* they used to feel for their country and sadness caused by the loss of it. According to the Levada Centre, 67 per cent of Russians regretted the collapse of the USSR in 2004 (www.levada.ru/press/2004122904.html). We are dealing, thus, with a form of meta-patriotism: pride about pride in a country which no longer exists.

In Moscow and Perm, viewers aged 55 and over shared the same nostalgia and complained about a lack of information in the media about the former Soviet countries. Galina in Perm summarised this sentiment in the form of a fairy-tale: 'Once upon a time there was the USSR. [*Zhil byl Sovetskii Soiuz*]. They all lived well and amicably. Everyone did something. Now we know nothing about each other.' This idealised memory was interrupted by Anatolii who added with irony that it was also the time when they were all poor and ready to give their lives for the fatherland while now the situation is different. The feeling of regret for the lost country and Soviet past does not completely overshadow the memory of actual Soviet reality but the two seem to coexist.

Sentimental nostalgia for the Soviet past is often expressed through the familiar binary of 'us' and 'them', Russia and the west. Young university-educated St Petersburg viewers thought that Russia was either under- or misrepresented in the media abroad. As a result, they supported the creation of the patriotic Star (*Zvezda*) and Russia Today channels as good initiatives of Putin's government to promote patriotism and the image of Russia abroad. In addition, they were critical of westernisation and, in particular, of Americanisation, which they associated with commercialisation, blaming it for lengthy commercials and unethical programmes, especially those for children. This argument was voiced in different cities by all age groups. Retired university-educated participants in Moscow were outraged by the overflow of 'stupid' American cartoons as much as the university-educated Voronezh viewers aged 18–30. A Voronezh university student Svetlana accused American cartoons of doing moral damage to Russian children:

> Firstly, American cartoons are made in brighter colours that irritate the eyesight. Secondly, our Russian/Soviet cartoons are harmless with their teddy bears and dolls. In American cartoons, they would show a cur- vaceous female cat, which walks in such a way that you can appreciate all her female forms ... And this is made for children!

Viewers also blamed western influence for the influx of poor quality reality shows, celebrity culture, vulgar jokes (like those on MTV), tasteless sitcoms with the 'stupid laughter behind the screen' and so on. The government's patriotic agenda has successfully tapped into the sentimental nostalgia per- petuated by post-Soviet television programming and, indirectly, into the anti- western feeling generated by its commercialised successor – but at the price of lowering the overall value attached to the medium, and thus of reducing its effectiveness as a propaganda tool.

Case study three: Penal Battalion

The serial, *Penal Battalion*, analysed in Chapter 6, creates similarly ambiva- lent post-Soviet meaning from Soviet-era nostalgia. To initiate discussion about the serial in focus groups conducted in 2006, the moderator showed an extract from the serial and watched it with the participants. The chosen extract included the last scenes from *Penal Battalion* starting with the priest's blessing of soldiers before their final battle and ending with the priest seeing a vision of the Virgin Mary.

Although *Penal Battalion* split viewers by location, education and age, most focus group participants found it truthful and convincing because it represented Russian values and portrayed former Soviet patriotism in a positive light. University- and school-educated Perm viewers aged 35–55 (2006) described it as '*our* serial' because it is part of 'our history' and is made in Russia. Here, too, it is important to distinguish representation of the former Soviet Union from representations of Soviet patriotism, and from projections of post-Soviet patriotism onto the Soviet past. For instance, in response to the scene with the priest, physician Andrei from Perm did not think that the presence of a religious uniform looked out of place. He also endorsed the scene with the vision of the Virgin Mary: 'Nothing strange in this vision. Very believable. I have a grandfather who was in a penal battalion – he told me stories – you'd get a gun and three bullets and go ahead. This is the truth.' Yet, Andrei's account of his grandfather's experiences contained no reference to religion at all. University lecturer Elena explained the contradiction:

> The Priest could be used in the serial as an allegory – it did not have to be a priest – someone else could have taken this role instead. I even thought that the priest stood there for our whole country, for the people, Russia, motherland, mothers, children.

Her comment confirms that support for the portrayal of the priest is tied closely to Russian Orthodoxy's central role in post-Soviet nation building. It is in keeping with this phenomenon that young viewers in Voronezh, male and female (2006), should also underline the serial's truthfulness and, like Andrei in Perm, suggest that 'it was a time when anything could have happened; people used to worship and baptize children secretly'.

Moscow professionals were most critical of *Penal Battalion* which they found to be contrived, unbelievable and burdened by theatricality (*teatral'shchina*). They doubted the truthfulness of the priest scene which they attributed to the modishness of religion in post-Soviet Russia, an argument they also applied to the prison culture the serial celebrates. They criticised the actors' work. They regretted that a good idea (the portrayal of a penal battalion) was turned into *lubok*, which they described as 'a picture with a sign, almost a caricature, embarrassing to look at', that a serious topic should be made the subject of a serial intended for mass consumption (*shirpotreb*).

Case study four: **Do Not Be Born Beautiful**

Like *Penal Battalion*, *Do Not Be Born Beautiful* (*Ne rodis' krasivoi*) was hugely popular. Unlike the former, it is an adaptation of a foreign telenovela, it concerns the contemporary post-Soviet world, and it glamorises the fashion industry. Based on the Columbian telenovela *Yo Soy Betty, La Fea* (shown in the US and the UK under the title *Ugly Betty*), it was produced by Amedia in 2005–6. The plot resembles that of the original and tells of how Katia Pushkariova, a plain, but clever, girl starts her business career at the Zimaletto company which specialises in fashion design. Like the Columbian Betty, Katia achieves success in both her career and private life thanks to her ability, persistence and single-mindedness. To provoke discussion in our focus groups in 2006, the participants were shown the opening scene when the unattractive, unkempt Katia is interviewed for the position of secretary, walking into the swish company building and meeting her future boss for the first time.

The popularity of the serial was confirmed by our focus group responses, although, unsurprisingly, most of the enthusiastic responses were from women (men also watched it but almost always with their female family members or girlfriends). However, the interpretations of the serial given by women of different educational background were strikingly diverse. Viewers aged 35–55 in Moscow and Perm tended to agree that they enjoyed the serial but talked about it with faint irony. In Perm, female professionals remarked that it was a 'glamorous' (*glamurnyi*) serial made for younger female audiences. But they approved of its guiding concept: 'At least, it shows business in a positive light and lacks violence.' University-educated Ira from Moscow commented: 'It is a wonderful serial, about nothing. But you can't stop watching it. It is like reading women's fiction – you read it and later you can't remember what it was about.'

Young female viewers in St Petersburg (2006) generated a revealing argument. Half of the group were university students and the other half were school-educated. The latter interpreted the plot straightforwardly as a 'Cinderella story' about a clever but awkward girl who turned into a beautiful woman, and married the rich and handsome company manager. The story was similarly interpreted by retired females in Moscow, viewers in Perm and even some Moscow professionals. However, the St Petersburg university students and graduates thought that the supposedly 'ugly' protagonist was, in fact, more attractive at the beginning of the serial than at the end. They were angered by the representation of an intelligent, educated girl with experience of working for a German bank as an ugly duckling who turns into a swan by dressing as a conventional sex object, characterising the intended message as appalling and vulgar. On the one hand, then, they reflect the influence of western-style feminist opposition to the portrayal of women as sex objects. On the other hand, they associate the vulgarity of the portrayal with the serial's western provenance, confirming post-Soviet television's function as the stimulus for a complex and contradictory process of intercultural meaning production.

Conclusions

To conclude, then, government attempts to use television as a vehicle for nation building and the instillation of patriotism meet with a deeply ambivalent response from post-Soviet audiences. This multi-levelled ambivalence is expressed through

(1) differentials between discrete categories of viewers (provincial male workers deploy markedly different interpretative strategies from metropolitan female professionals, for example);
(2) contradictory positions occupied within single viewer categories (viewers may adopt anti-western, or anti-Soviet stances towards one issue, then pro-western, or pro-Soviet attitudes towards another);

(3) interpretative strategies that are split from within (for example, *stiob*-viewing which manages to be both inside and outside official culture).

A particularly interesting, and potentially subversive, instance of the third kind of ambivalence is to be found in the meta-level approaches to television news management adopted by older viewers brought up under the Soviet propaganda machine ('we try to trust because we were educated to trust').

The ambivalence is compounded by a pronounced propensity (born of need) for collective viewing in post-Soviet homes. This encourages critical talk about programming content and style, but it also underpins the Soviet nostalgia industry to which television of the Putin era is a prime contributor, meaning, in turn, however, that the patriotism promoted by the regime is often at one stage removed from patriotism per se: it is patriotic nostalgia for an earlier, purer form of patriotism.

A recurring theme in our book has been a further aspect of the contradiction that defines post-Soviet identity: the double-edged sword that is post-Soviet television's stubbornly low cultural status. This phenomenon bolsters (albeit indirectly and no doubt unintentionally) the Putin regime's anti-western agenda (the low status attributed to contemporary commercial genres is tied inextricably to their perceived western provenance). But it also erects an inconvenient obstacle in the path of the patriotic propaganda machine (how can audiences be expected to treat with seriousness messages conveyed via a medium which fails to command respect?). Finally, it accounts for the inversion of the norms in viewing modes identified by Lembo: in post-Soviet Russia, the 'simultaneous viewing' usually associated with uncritical, passive attitudes to television is, by contrast, practised by a sceptical group of viewers whose deliberately cultivated distraction is in part a way of signalling active rejection of the dominant message carried by the Putin media machine, though in part just a way of masking a guilty interest in a phenomenon of low cultural status.

What we find, then, with respect to our protagonist is neither the complete capitulation to ruthless state control mechanisms portrayed (or at least implied) in many western accounts of the Russian media environment, nor the brave resistance to manipulation depicted in romanticised western depictions of the 'semiotic guerilla', but rather something altogether more subtle, and more complex: something perhaps best conveyed in the subtitle of our book: a submission (which can only ever be partial) to a control (which must always remain remote).

Conclusion

In order briefly to recapitulate the key points raised in our book we might remind ourselves of its (calculatedly) ambiguous trajectory. On one hand, it has pursued a path from centre (commencing with those television genres closest to the official sphere) to periphery (ending with light entertainment genres, and with the relevance to our concerns of the regional perspective and of Russian television's viewing audiences). On the other hand, we have claimed that without giving due attention to the interaction of text and audience, and to these 'peripheral' genres, any assessment of official culture's control over the meaning-making activity around television is likely to remain partial and off-target. This ambiguity has been replicated micro-cosmically within each chapter.

Chapter 1 placed the authenticating myths called upon to implement Putin's nation-building agenda in the context of the news broadcast's unstable generic boundaries and a global 'mediasphere' which, along with the complexities of the programmes' discourse structure, and the disjunction between the performative and constative aspects of Russian television news, constrains the effectiveness of the implementation process. Chapter 2 traced tensions between competing local and national causes for which the myths of St Petersburg are invoked, between the timelessness of the historical tradition and the novelty of the media tradition which it inaugurates, and between the celebration's centralising political purpose and the rhetoric of participatory democracy that the St Petersburg myth embraced. Chapter 3 linked the performative reintegration of a fragmented nation facilitated by Beslan to a dual need to both familiarise and defamiliarise the event that produced it, associating this contradiction with generic tensions. Chapter 4 highlighted the benefits to, but also the dangers for, the Putin regime of the post-Soviet talk show's ability to mediate between official and sub-cultural discourses. Chapter 5 further discussed this mediatory function in its reading of the pseudo-military serial, arguing that the genre's ability to amend its narrative structure in response to viewer reaction rendered it a model of the wider encounter of television production and audience reception, but also recontextualising the encounter in terms of a Soviet/post-Soviet temporal dimension.

In applying the mediation principle to the first of our light entertainment genres, Chapter 6 recounted how the most popular post-Soviet television comedy, adapted from an American original, hosts overlapping cultural struggles (of class, gender, region, nation and taste), opening the programme out onto the wider controversy over television's own status. Chapter 7 further pursued the taste and global format issues by exploring the paradox through which the *Wheel of Fortune* game-show format has been appropriated by the metropolitan centre as a marker of deleterious US influence, but by regional viewers as a means of asserting local identity against a distant, elitist centre. It thus provided the lead in to Chapters 8 and 9 which treated in the round two issues which ran throughout each chapter as subtexts: the relationship of the local–global–national axes to the official agenda foisted upon national television, and the role of audience reaction as alternatively formative of, and disruptive to, that agenda.

Without in any way challenging the coherence, authenticity or accuracy of parallel research of a strictly empirical orientation, we have, throughout the nine chapters, implicitly distanced ourselves from the conclusions such research tends to reach regarding our central concern: the extent to which the authoritarian government in whose grip Russia once more finds itself can, in the post-communist, global era, be said to be in control of the meanings generated by television. Notwithstanding the undoubted effects of the ever-increasing pressure applied to the media under Putin, we have argued that the regime's capacity for exerting power over televisual semiosis is relatively weak, owing to the absence of a fully developed hegemonic process as described in our Introduction. This was reflected as a series of abortive, or problematic, mediations: between the official and the vernacular realms, between Soviet and post-Soviet chronotopes, between the levels of global, national and local culture, and between the dimensions of audience and text.

However, in positing genre as the site on which these failed mediations are enacted, we have attempted to avoid lurching from an over-emphasis on the authority and influence of text producers, to attributing excessive semiotic 'empowerment' to television audiences. In fact, we found little evidence among our post-Soviet Russian viewers of the subversive readings celebrated by John Fiske in his work on audience reception. Suspicion, mistrust, disengagement, deviations from intended messages all abound, alongside examples of complete conformity with 'dominant' codings, yet counter-cultural strategies of the sort that Fiske (and, indeed, Morley, in his notion of 'resistant' viewing) had in mind were few and far between; the *stiob*-viewing we identified in Chapter 9 is defined precisely by its partial endorsement of official cultural rhetoric. Conversely, and equally contrary to the romantic 'viewer as semiotic guerrilla' theory, we have located many of the disjunctions and tensions at the level of texts coded resolutely in line with the nation-building mission which Putin has assigned the newly compliant Russian media.

Indeed, the common thread running throughout the book is that of post-Soviet television genre as the supreme locus for the negotiation of control over cultural meaning, genre as a form which constantly overreaches and reshapes itself in response to audiences, at the same time self-consciously internalising that gesture in a perpetual feedback loop. In this way, we have, albeit only partially, addressed the intractable theoretical dilemma raised in our Introduction: that of the epistemological conflict pitting text-based exegesis which brackets the 'real' viewer out of existence, against positivistic data analysis which, even in its self-conscious, qualitative variant, tends towards the reductive averaging out of individual readings and the relegation of text to the function of mere stimulus for audience activity.

At the level of textual analysis, and precisely because of their remoteness from the political centre of gravity, it was, we discovered, light entertainment genres such as the drama serial and the sitcom that appeared to deviate most significantly from the official line. Paradoxically, however, this remoteness establishes such genres at the threshold of the very hegemonic process which might consolidate the centre's power over televisual meaning: hence, the far superior nation-building power of politically controversial serials like *Penal Battalion*, as compared with controlled artifices like the St Petersburg 300 celebrations. This example illustrates Morley's notion of 'hegemony as dialectical process'; it also foregrounds the recurrent theme of performativity: the value to hegemonic logic of the perpetual need to perform the overcoming of resistance to the centre, yet the concomitant instability and precariousness this need transmutes to it: the dissonance between what Russian television 'says' and what, via the forms it adopts, it 'does'.

One of the apparent perils of researching television lies in the transience of its favoured forms, a phenomenon encountered in extreme form in Russia. Unlike Dostoevskii's *Crime and Punishment*, it seems likely that in as little as five years time, few will even recall, let alone watch, *The Big Wash*, or *My Fair Nanny*. Moreover, authoritarian tendencies notwithstanding, the Russian political scene itself remains consistent only in its mutability. By the time this book goes to press, Vladimir Putin, already no longer Russia's president, may have retreated still further into Russia's political shadowland, and there will undoubtedly have been yet more twists in the unfolding drama that is the history of the post-Soviet media. Finally, with the rapid convergence of television, in which the national dimension remains a force, and an increasingly globalised new media, viewing modes and audience demographics will, within the same five-year period, have changed beyond all recognition. This multi-faceted ephemerality, however, provides the ideal environment in which television's orientation towards the performative, along with the unfolding of the hegemonic process to which that orientation is ideally suited, might manifest themselves. For this reason, it is hoped that, whether Russia is by then edging painfully towards civic democracy, lurching back into xenophobic authoritarianism, or carving out some as yet indeterminate 'third way', the insights we have gleaned from our admittedly wafer-thin cross-section through that complex and contradictory process will still carry significance.

Notes

Introduction

1 These themes are considered with respect to Soviet television in McNair 1991.
2 Our necessarily brief summary of developments in Soviet television is based on more detailed accounts provided in McNair 1991, Mickiewicz 1988 and Hopkins 1970.
3 For a fuller account of Zakharov's film, and of the role of the literary adaptation in Soviet television culture, see Hutchings 2004: 129–32.
4 For an account of television's role in unseating the 1991 coup leaders, see Bonnell and Freidin 1995.
5 For a full account of this event and television's role in covering it, see Mickiewicz 1997.
6 It is not part of our brief to tell the complex story of the multiple changes in ownership and political orientation which Russian television underwent during the 1990s. The story is told in full in Zassoursky 2005.
7 Andrew Wilson gives an excellent account of the extent to which this virtualisation process has stymied the development of a democratic culture in post-communist Russia (see Wilson 2005).
8 See the closing chapters in Zassoursky (2005) for an elaboration on this and other aspects of the internet in early twenty-first century Russia.
9 See Mickiewicz 2008, and her chapter 'The Conundrum of Memory: Young People and their Recollections of Soviet Television' in Beumers, Hutchings and Rulyova 2009: 125–137.
10 See Vartanova's paper 'Post-Soviet Media Model as Euro-Asian Model' read at the 'Media and Change' conference held at Moscow State University in October 2005.
11 See www.medialaw.ru/e-index.html for details of the work and mission of the institute.
12 The academy allocated 8.2 million Euros to the programme which ran from 2003 to 2007. It consisted of 30 separate projects with over a hundred researchers from various fields of research. The programme included cooperation with a Russian funding partner – the Russian Foundation for the Humanities.
13 See in particular, Moran and Malbon 2006.

1 (Dis)informing Russia

1 Freedom House, an international organisation dedicated to the monitoring of press freedom around the world demoted Russian from 'partly free' to 'not free' in a report issued on 11 February 2004. Reported in 'Bush says he wants to keep ties

with Putin', *Washington Post*, 12 February 2004. The assessment has been repeated in every year since 2004.

2 For Barthes's explanation of the principle of 'inoculation', see Barthes 1972.

3 Khodarkovskii was imprisoned, tried and sentenced to seven years imprisonment for tax fraud in November 2005 in a process which had far more to do with the political challenge the oligarch represented to Putin, than with standards of financial probity.

4 Jim Collins argues that intertextuality plays a special role in television:

> There is no other medium in which the force of the 'already said' is quite so visible as in television, primarily because the already said is the 'still being said.' Television programming since the fifties has depended on the recycling of Hollywood films and the syndication of past prime-time programs. The proliferation of cable channels that re-present programs from the past four decades of television history marks the logical extension of this process, in which the various pasts and presents of television now air simultaneously
>
> (Collins 1992: 333–34)

5 Thus, Jane Feuer writes of television's 'greater tendency to recombine across genre lines' (Feuer 1992: 158). See also Turner 2001.

6 On the few occasions in post-Soviet participatory talk shows such as *Domino Principle* (*Printsip domino*) when ordinary people were permitted time and space to express their frustrations with government, they did so using vague, homogenising terms such as *vlasti* (the authorities) indicating their alienation from the political process, rather than the engaged idiom of party political dispute: left and right, conservative and progressive. Later in Putin's presidency, such discussions became notable by their absence.

7 For an analysis of this instability see Hutchings, Miazhevich, Flood and Nickels (2007: 43–70).

8 For a detailed analysis of television coverage of the 60th Anniversary of Victory in the Second World War, see Hutchings and Rulyova (2009: 135–157).

2 St Petersburg 300

1 Anthony Smith identifies 'common myths and historical memories' as one of the key prerequisites for national identity, defining the nation as signifying 'a cultural and political bond, uniting in a single political community all who share an historic culture and homeland' (Smith 1991: 14).

2 See Barker 1999 and Gunther and Dobrenko 2000. An early expression of the longing for tsarist times was Stanislav Govorukhin's 1990 documentary film, *The Russia We Have Lost* (*Rossiia, kotoruiu my poteriali*).

3 Hobsbaum writes that the invention of tradition occurs 'when a rapid transformation of society weakens or destroys the social patterns for which "old" traditions had been designed ... or when such old traditions are eliminated', a description which characterises post-1991 Russia precisely. See Hobsbaum and Ranger 1983: 4.

4 Anderson notes amongst other things in this regard, that this revolution 'made it possible and practical to "represent" the imagined community in ways that did not require linguistic conformity' (Anderson 1991: 139).

5 In an interview with the journalist, Anna Kachkaeva, Elena Afanas'eva, a commentator from the *Politbiuro* journal, expresses a lack of surprise that television showed only the 'triumphal' aspects of the tercentenary, pointing to the imperial (*velikoderzhavnoe*) tone of Russian television in general (Kachkaeva 2004).

6 Iakovlev's comments, along with the jubilee slogan, were to be found on the St Petersburg administration website throughout 2003 www.300.spb.ru/jubilee/index_ru.htm; accessed 24 June 2003).

7 The 'City Day' celebrations date from the renaming of Leningrad as St Petersburg in 1991. The annual jubilees are just one example of the 'jubilee mania' which, as Maia Turovskaia notes, is connected with post-Soviet culture's need to re-establish a sense of the continuity of national tradition (Turovskaia 2003).

8 For Lotman, space is inseparable from the production and reception of meaning, since meaning is itself bound up with boundaries, principally the (shifting) boundary between language and what lies outside language, text and extra-text. This dimension of space Lotman calls the 'semiosphere' (Lotman 1990).

9 Another example was the celebration in Voronezh in 2003 of 1,000 years of Russian written culture (*pis'mennost'*), for which the city claims to be one of the earliest sources.

10 In her review of the film, Birgit Beumers argues that 'the Hermitage functions as the ark of Russian cultural heritage' (Beumers 2002). In the film, the Hermitage contains a door opening onto the 900-day blockade, indicating how Sokurov, too, re-inscribes the Leningrad myth into that of imperial Petersburg.

11 Bakhtin defines the chronotope as a concept in which 'spatial and temporal indicators are fused into a ... concrete whole' (Bakhtin 1981: 84). The concept is inherent to semiosis itself, connected, as it is, with the whole notion of embodiment of abstract concepts in spatial form. For Bakhtin 'every entry into the sphere of meaning is accomplished through the gates of the chronotope' (Bakhtin 1981: 258).

12 According to Bakhtin, language is not only marked by the *presentness* of each moment but also, potentially, by the perspectives of centuries, a concept he called *great time* (Bakhtin 1986a: 84).

13 As Dayan and Katz suggest, the modern national celebration legitimises through its controlled ceremonial function and balances this by being charismatic to the extent that it involves crowds in carnivalistic festivities that are in part spontaneous and self-generated (Dayan and Katz 1992: 23).

14 Bakhtin writes, 'What is suspended [in carnival] is first of all hierarchical structure and all the forms of terror, reverence, piety, and etiquette connected with it – that is everything resulting from sociohierarchical inequality' (Bakhtin 1984: 122–23).

15 BBC coverage of royal celebrations invariably balances reporting on the official events in London with sequences depicting unorthodox behaviour in the regions (the northern landlord who, 'on this special day only', keeps his pub open beyond legal opening times).

16 They also suggest that to mesh these 'time-outs' with routine temporality, media events are framed by a 'latency' stage (in which the occasion is pre-signalled so that viewers can reshape their routines around it) and an 'evaluation' stage in which the meaning of the occasion, once it has passed, is mulled over at length, ensuring that it can be fully integrated into the viewer's own value systems (Dayan and Katz 1992: 185).

17 In their account of the British Royal Wedding of 1981, Dayan and Katz note that

> a clear distinction is made between those television people who were part of the event ... and those ... who were out of the event ... To be 'in' and not ... 'out', in the desolate limbos of television studios, is a mark of added prestige ... of participation in the event's mana
>
> (Dayan and Katz 1992: 26)

18 Bakhtin writes that 'carnival does not know footlights ... does not acknowledge any distinction between actors and spectators. Footlights would destroy a

carnival, as the absence of footlights would destroy a theatrical performance'
(Bakhtin 1984: 7).

19 As Dayan and Katz point out, 'Media events provide media organizations with
an opportunity to test new formats and embark on technical experimentation'
(Dayan and Katz 1992: 194).

3 Russia's 9/11

1 For example, in a report on the website of the UK's Channel 4, Jonathan Miller
describes Beslan as 'a byword for horror: Russia's 9/11'. See Miller 2005.

2 As we saw in Chapter 1, news broadcasts under Putin now exhibit uncanny
resemblances to their Soviet antecedents, with images of combine harvesters
reaping record harvests, 'official chronicle' segments detailing the rituals accompanying Kremlin state visits and obsequious interviews with Kremlin officials. The
Soviet concept of news chimed with Marxist–Leninist theories about the long,
inevitable march towards world communism and the notion that what is worthy of
reporting are not the anomalous dramas which interrupt progress, but the predictable achievement of milestones along the way. Such an approach fits uncomfortably within a consumer economy in which viewers expect news to entertain
and surprise.

3 For a detailed, eyewitness account of the siege told from the viewpoint of a family
caught up in it, see Chivers 2006: 143–60.

4 An enquiry into the reasons for the tragedy which reported in December 2005
attributed some of the blame to mistakes made by local authorities. A vigorous,
year-long campaign led by the mothers of Beslan victims did much to pressurise
the commission into reaching these conclusions which, however, fell short of
attaching responsibility to central government. In a more recent, and highly significant, development, the mothers of Beslan have been prosecuted under the
Putin regime's new legislation on the prevention of extremism, a darkly ironic
turn of events from which liberal opposition leader and former world chess
champion, Garri Kasparov, has also suffered.

5 Among the first live reports on reaction to the siege were those from correspondents
in Kiev, Kazakhstan and, most significantly, Grozny.

6 For an analysis of the role played by images of the family in Stalinist rhetoric, see
Clark 2000: 784–96.

7 The show, among the most popular on Russian television, involves a team helping
families across the former Soviet Union to relocate relatives missing, often since
the Soviet era, and reuniting them in a display of sentimentality before an audience itself consisting of people looking for loved ones whose photographs they
display to the camera.

8 For the notion of 'imagined community' see Anderson 1991.

9 Another Eltsyn campaign advertisement involved images of children's drawings
culminating in the suggestive slogan 'Children are our future', implying that the
opposition represented the interests of those imprisoned in the past. With Beslan,
the abstract image of the child's precarious future is now realised as actual,
wounded Russian children.

10 The televisual rehabilitation of the secret police under Putin (himself an ex-KGB
officer) has gained pace in the context of the president's efforts to burnish the
image of the Russian military forces generally (cf. the establishment of Zvezda, a
TV channel dedicated to military affairs, and Channel 1's *Special Forces* (*Spets-
naz*), which celebrates the achievements of undercover forces on Russia's borders),
and to militarise the national identity project.

11 The portrayal of Putin as a man of action has, as we saw in Chapter 1, become
part of his televisual iconography.

12 Nomenclature for the hostage-takers oscillated without distinction along a spectrum ranging from *terrorist*, through *boevik* to *bandit*. By 3 September, these terms were being used in contradistinction to the positively loaded term 'rescuers' (*spasateli*).

13 Of all national news sources, only the newspaper, *Izvestiia*, gave a full account of events at Beslan, including misjudgements made by the forces attempting to break the siege. The editor was sacked soon afterwards as the paper was brought into line with official versions of what happened.

14 Mary Ann Doane sees the shock of catastrophe and the banality of mere information conveyed in familiar packages as representing television's two poles: 'Information and catastrophe coexist in a curious balance ... Television produces both as the two poles structuring the contemporary imagination' (Doane 1990: 236).

15 With each successive post-Beslan bulletin, the focus became more local and individualised, when, based on the experience of post 9/11 coverage, one might have expected a broadening outwards to the general circumstances in which the siege took place.

16 No images of the corpses of victims of the siege were shown either during or after the crisis. This is in marked contrast with the Nord-Ost theatre siege, when NTV was roundly criticised by official sources for the gory detail of its coverage.

17 For example, reports on government positions on the identity of the terrorists were introduced with phrases like '*soobshchaetsia, chto*' and '*predpolagaetsia, chto kto-to vyshe stoit za terroristami*' (the latter phrase illustrating how both the source (*predpolagaetsia*) and the object (*kto-to vyshe*) of the search are deliberately impersonalised. Such linguistic practice confirms Mary Ann Doane's view that catastrophic events, unlike crises, which are attributed subjects, 'are ... subjectless, simply there, they *happen*' (Doane 1990: 223).

18 For Russian demonisations of Islam in the context of the Chechnia conflict, see Russell 2005: 101–16.

19 In a blistering full-page assault on all the national television channels, Petrovskaia lambasted Channel 1 in particular for its minimal coverage on 3 September 2004, and for following its *Vremia* bulletin by an episode of the D.H. Lawrence adaptation, *Women in Love*! (Petrovskaia 2004: 7).

20 This is in contrast to long-term American and British media responses to 9/11 and 7/7 which generated a stream of paratextual documentaries, interviews and special reports.

21 The 1993 and 1996 examples are less clear-cut, since they involved an unmediated convergence of 'text' and 'extra-text,' state and populace, in which it was not certain whose interests were best served. (Eltsyn was either 'the best chance that the popular democratic movement had', and therefore worthy of reluctant media support, or a cynical manipulator of a media fooled into thinking that he supported democratic reform, or an obstacle to Russian national interests supported by a western-funded media.) The *Glas naroda* example is complicated by the fact that here television arguably reached out not to a wider populace but to the relatively small group of liberal intellectuals who constituted its viewership.

22 In 2002, the presenter, Maksim Sokolov, noted sardonically that 'the charm of modern European multiculturalism [*multikul'tural'nosti*] consists in the fact that immigrants show not the slightest desire to acquire European culture, customs and morals and live as a state within a state' (3 April 2002).

4 Promiscuous words

1 For a full history of the talk show in the west, see Timbey 2002.

2 The programme's mainstream success led later to its switch from Kul'tura to NTV (such channel switches are now a common feature of Russian television culture).

3 According to statistics produced by a Russian audience research organisation, in the week 26 June 2006 to 2 July 2006, *Wait for Me* achieved a highly significant 23.3 per cent share of the viewing audience when it was broadcast (www.tns-global.ru/rus/data/ratings/tv/russia/top_100/_20060626_20060702/index.wbp; accessed 30 July 2006).

4 See Chapter 3 for our discussion of the sham democracy promoted in the 'Civic Forum' held in St Petersburg held in connection with the city's tercentenary.

5 Nagiev is a well-known actor who starred, for example, in the controversial Chechen war film, *Purgatory* (*Chistilishche*, A. Nevzorov 1998).

6 For the importance of speech genres in structuring, and imparting value to, linguistic discourse see Bakhtin 1986a.

7 As the focus group data we produce elsewhere demonstrates, educated Russians in particular have a low regard for the medium and profess guilt at watching it. According to statistics produced by FOM (Fond obshechestvennogo mneniia), Russia's main opinion survey agency, in June 2006, 64 per cent of those questioned said that they watched television every day, a relatively low number compared with other developed countries (http://bd.english.fom.ru/report/cat/societas/mass_media/televidenie/TV_news/ed040633; accessed 27 July 2007).

8 This is to be contrasted with much western television in which, as Jostein Gripsrud argues, non-rational, popular forms of knowledge take precedence over formal, academic knowledge, and where 'a spectre of [negative] stereotypes specifically related to "academics", "intellectuals" etc.' reigns supreme (Gripsrud 1999: 47).

9 Such networks bear comparison with Foucault's understanding of power as 'a multiplicity of force relations immanent in the sphere in which they operate and which constitute their own organization ... as the support which these force relations find in one another, thus forming a chain or a system' (Foucault 1978: 92–93).

10 For the 'synthetic persona', see Fairclough 1995.

11 It is in the relationship between the post-Soviet television text (produced within the official realm) and that text's audience (located in the unofficial realm of the everyday) that the success or otherwise of its hegemonic function can be gauged. The fact that, to a greater or lesser degree, the *tok-shou* internalises this relationship within its structure (host plus studio audience) makes the genre vital to our concerns.

12 See www.1tv.ru/; accessed 5 May 2007. All subsequent quotes from the programme's web forum are cited from the same source.

5 Unfulfilled orders

1 The channel began broadcasting on 22 February 2005, on the eve of the day dedicated to celebrating the 'Defenders of the Motherland'.

2 At its peak in August 2004, *Soldiers*, which began broadcasting earlier that year, obtained a viewer share of 16.8 per cent. By 2006, it was among the three most watched serials of all time on Russian television. *Penal Battalion*, shown in autumn 2004, secured a rating of 47.8 per cent for its third episode, making it briefly the most popular programme on air. *The Zone* began showing in January 2006. In its first week, it gained a 19.1 per cent viewer share (nearly a fifth of all viewers). It reached the position of seventh most popular programme among Moscow viewers. These statistics are taken from data provided by TNS, represented in Russia by TNS Gallup Media, TNS Gallup AdFact and TNS Marketing Information Centre, and by the journal *Kommersant*.

3 Thus, one 2006 posting on a thread of the web forum of the official site devoted to 'my favourite episode' from a correspondent nicknamed Iaroslav praises the episode as 'just classic' (*prosto klass!*). Another, named Nate, describes the episode as

the most 'amusing' (*prikol'no*). See http://soldaty.tv/forum/index.php?showtopic +6256 (accessed 22 September 2006).

4 In one particularly ferocious and long-running web forum debate, a (male) correspondent berates a (female) viewer of the serial for failing to see that the serial is a piece of anti-Soviet propaganda, an example of 'brainwashing' (*promyvaniia mosgov*) trying to suggest that Red Army soldiers were somehow not keen to fight for the Soviet motherland and did so only out of fear. See www.rutv.ru/forum.html? d=O&cid=386&FID=206&FThrID=144145&page=2 (accessed 29 September 2006).

5 The controversy over *The Zone* even played itself out within Russian jails. One prisoner wrote to the programme's web forum complaining that:

> according to the programme makers, there are only animals serving their sentences, whereas the staff, according to the authors, are all drunkards, cowards, traitors, cannibals and bribe-takers. I'd like to know who the consultant was. ... Anyone with any sense can see that, to put it mildly, what they show on *The Zone* does not correspond to reality.
> See www.zona.tv/forum/viewtopic.php?t+484 (accessed 13 October 2006)

It was thus, not, a cowardly NTV, fearful of censorship from above, but rather a viewer protest from below which prompted the rescheduling of *The Zone*.

6 Arguments raged over the historical accuracy of *Penal Battalion* (perhaps because of the political implications of the errors). Participants went to the lengths of citing real historical documents to prove their point. However, it is often prisoners' wives who provide the factual correctives in the forum for *The Zone*:

> I'm sorry, but when you go to a meeting with a prisoner in a SIZO, there's a sign at the entrance telling you to hand in mobile phones, arms and so on. It is not possible for there ever to be any weaponry in the isolation unit.
> See www.zona.tv/forum/viewtopic.php?t+484 (accessed 13 October 2006).

7 *Dedovshchina* is the informal system of subjugation of new Russian army recruits to soldiers of the last year of service, NCOs and officers. It involves mental and physical bullying, similar to the US practice of 'hazing'.

8 Web commentary on *Soldiers* evinces the same propensity to claim the serial as uniquely Russian: 'In the first place it is life-like [*zhiznenno*], in the second place topical [*aktual'no*] and in the third place ... patriotic, i.e. it is done in our style ... Our mentality, Our humour ... Our people watch it and recognise themselves' (http://soldaty.tv/forum/index.php?showtopic+6256; accessed 3 November 2006).

9 Zizek defines nostalgia as melancholic desire for 'an object ... lacking from the very beginning, [whose] emergence coincides with its lack ... a purely anamorphic entity which does not exist in itself' (Zizek 2001: 143).

10 See A. Prokhorov, 'N. Dostal: *Penal Battalion* (*Shtrafbat*, 2004)', www.kinokultura. com/2006/13r-strafbat.shtml (accessed 28 September 2006).

11 The official website for *Soldiers* includes threads in which female viewers discuss the respective masculine charms of their favourite characters (http://soldaty.tv/ forum/index.php?showtopic+6256; accessed 13 October 2006).

12 A number of fans single out the generic specificity of *Soldiers* as the reason for its success, noting that there is nothing like it on western television (http://soldaty.tv/ forum/index.php?showtopic+6256; accessed 10 November 2006).

13 Unpublished paper given at Russian Studies Seminar, University of Manchester, 23 November 2006.

14 For differentiation of the Symbolic, the Imaginary and the Real, see Lacan 1977.

15 In Zizek's provocative inversion of 'common sense', what we have come to accept as 'realistic' and self-identical, is in fact the fantasy which we collectively inhabit in order to conceal and repress what is truly 'Real':

> The Real is ... the disavowed X on account of which our vision of reality is anamorphically distorted; it is simultaneously the Thing to which direct access is not possible and the obstacle which prevents this direct access, the Thing which eludes our grasp and the distorting screen which makes us miss the Thing.
>
> (Zizek 2006a: 26)

16 They are what Zizek terms 'the excess of Stuff over symbolic network (the Thing for which there is no place in this network, which eludes its grasp)' (Zizek 2006b).

6 Laughter at the threshold

1 According to Heller 'the sitcom claims no place in [Russian viewers'] stock of popular memory' (Heller 2003: 3).
2 The case of the Russian variant of the quiz show *Who Wants to be a Millionaire* is paradigmatic. The quiz crossed to and fro between NTV and Channel 1 in the early years of the twenty-first century and at one point there were two programmes showing, each following an identical format, but with different titles, one called *Who Wants to be a Millionaire* (*Kto khochet stat' millionerom'*) and the other called *O, Lucky One* (*O, schastlivchik*).
3 For an analysis of the role of satire in post-Soviet Russian television, see Dunn 2004.
4 For an overview of global television formats, see Moran 1998.
5 The second series, which ran in 2005 and 2006, however, was more successful and attracted a loyal following.
6 As Steve Neale and Frank Krutnik suggest, 'The true butt of humour is always repressed' (Neale and Krutnik 1990: 76).
7 Neale and Krutnik distinguish the 'gag', a discrete, self-contained joke (verbal or visual), from the 'comic event', which is driven by the narrative context (Neale and Krutnik 1990: 43–61).
8 A *My Fair Nanny* detractor who argues that the programme is cheap, repetitive and unoriginal is rebutted as follows,

> Let's begin with the fact that this is not a film but a comedy serial, a sitcom [*sitkom*], and the action limited to two rooms is completely natural in this context. And as for the fact that the scenario was pinched from the Americans ... in this respect your 'Idiot' is no better since it was pinched from Dostoevskii [*sodrali u Dostoevskogo*].
>
> (www.ruskino.ru/movie/forum; accessed 17 April 2006).

For a textual explanation of why the same viewers might gain pleasure from programmes as ostensibly different as *The Idiot* and *My Fair Nanny* in terms of a shared propensity for the sentimentalism they each derive from Latin American soap influences, see Klioutchkine 2005.

9 A Kiev viewer writes, 'I really like the serial because you can laugh to your heart's content when watching it, and switch off from the reality of being for a time'. Another, by contrast, comments

> At last they're showing how people really live, how they interact [*obshchaiutsia*]; they've showed real conversational speech and that simplicity of existence [*prostotu bytiia*] which is so lacking in cinema ... It is life in the here and now. Just like it is in any normal family.
>
> (www.ruskino.ru/movie/forum; accessed 17 April 2006)

10 For an account of these two functions, see Lotman 1992.

11 One critic describes the programme as a 'vulgar, stupid little soap serial with a curvy madam in the main role' (*poshlovatyi, tupovatyi, myl'nyi serialets s figuristoi madam v glavnoi roli*). Another writes, 'After watching *Niania* I get the feeling that I've become ten times thicker [*potupel v 10 raz*]. It's like watching stupid Beavis and Butthead cartoons. No, I'd rather read.' However, they receive sharp ripostes: 'Some have written about the uncultured nature of the serial. But ... I would like to express the point of view that the fans are better educated and more cultured than the anti-fans'; 'You've laid it on thick [*pereborshchili*] with all your depth and fine breeding ... Miss Zavorotniuk is after all playing a nanny, not Anna Karenina' (www.ruskino.ru/movie/forum; accessed 17 April 2006).

12 For a discussion of *Generation 'P'* in these terms, see Hutchings 2004: 174–87.

13 Thus, a female correspondent suggests that the programme

> is leading a propaganda campaign for theatres and other [cultural] spectacles since Maksim Viktorovich is a cultured person [*litso kul'turnoe*], and, more precisely, a producer, not a banker as they had originally wanted to make him, and Konstantin is propaganda for a civilised upbringing [*propaganda vospitannosti*].

Another praises the sitcom for its 'plot lines, humour, sense of intrigue and the fine skills of its actors' (*khoroshaia akterskaia igra*), to which she receives a sarcastic response: 'I'd be interested to know where in this "masterpiece" anyone could find humour and intrigue ... in my view it is just vaudeville' (www.ruskino.ru/movie/forum; accessed 17 April 2006). A third goes as far as praising *My Fair Nanny* for its 'originality and psychologism' (http://serialmag.ru/forum/archive/index.php/t-66.html; accessed 18 April 2006).

14 A male correspondent rages:

> Surely you can't want to laugh at the exploits of this dumb Ukrainian bumpkin [*tupoi derevenskoi khokhlushki*]? But if you watch this serial you could be forgiven for thinking that there are such people. You people really think that we've all sunk to the level of your heroes ... I'm really sorry for you if you do ... It's complete nonsense [*bred*] and it is terrible that our people continue to make such rubbish and that there are those who continue to swallow with a squeal everything that is shoved in front of them.
>
> (www.ruskino.ru/movie/forum; accessed 17 April 2006)

15 A correspondent from Donestsk asserts of *My Fair Nanny* that it is 'One of the few serials which you can relax normally with and in which there is no pink snot [*rozovykh soplei*]. I'm really pleased by the lack of high pretensions ... If you want something for the soul, then you can always watch Tarkovskii' www.ruskino.ru/movie/forum; accessed 17 April 2006).

16 Rebutting the views of those who object to the distasteful materialism of Zhanna Arkad'evna, a Krasnoiarsk viewer makes a rather improbable comparison with the satire of Gogol:

> Zhanna Arkad'evna attracts opprobrium [*vyzyvaet nepriazn'*]. But she is teaching children that, if they drink, they will become like her, and grown-up women that one shouldn't become hooked on one man, but instead continue to look for others, like Vika. This serial is more complex than *Dead Souls* [*zakruchenei 'Mertvykh dush'*] it is so instructive [*pouchitelen*].
>
> (www.ruskino.ru/movie/forum; accessed 17 March 2006)

17 A Zaporozh'e viewer rejects an accusation that her remarks contain all the hallmarks of illiteracy with the following sarcastic rejoinder:

What a pity that you haven't found work as a copy editor [*korrektor*] on this site. Why do you think newspapers have copy editors? It's not because the journalists are illiterate. ... You'd do better to pay attention to the way of thinking [in the serial].

(www.ruskino.ru/movie/forum; accessed 17 April 2006)

18 A Moscow viewer characterises *My Fair Nanny* as 'the only serial in which there are no corpses, porno [*pornukhi*], fighting or any of the other shit [*govna*] which accompanies our television'. A second adds that 'in this serial there is none of the vulgarity [*poshlosti*], violence, or murder you find in American cinema'. Another even sees fit to compare *My Fair Nanny* with *The Nanny* and claim of the latter that 'it is much more vulgar than our version', suggesting 'Look at Fran and look at Anastasia. Vika is our own girl [*nasha, rodnaia*]. She has that inner quality [*tsenz*] of which there is no hint in Fran' (www.ruskino.ru/movie/forum; accessed 18 April 2006).

19 A Crimean viewer puts it bluntly:

> Maybe it is a copy from America [*amerikanskaia kopiia*], but they are at least our jokes [*prikoly*], our actors and, in general, our life and there is no need to refer to plagiarism here. We have learned to do what they do and we even do it better than them.

(www.ruskino.ru/movie/forum; accessed 17 April 2006)

20 According to a Moscow viewer:

> The actors are good but the serial itself is idiocy in its pure, unadulterated form [*idiotism v chistom, nezamutnennom vide*]. Vulgar [*poshlye*] texts and vulgar performances [*vul'garnye vykhodki*] by the actors. It's just offensive that they are trying to feed us with this rancid American slop [*protukhshim Amerikanskim varevom*]

And in an indignant response to attempts to compare the programme with Push-kin and Charlie Chaplin, another correspondent objects 'It's a sin to even mention [*i zaikat'sia grekh*] Aleksandr Sergeevich in this context ... And you shouldn't touch the masters of Soviet comedy either' (www.ruskino.ru/movie/forum; accessed 17 April 2006).

21 A Khar'kov viewer mounts a particularly acerbic assault on the would-be (male) defenders of Russian cultural purity against the illiteracy of *My Fair Nanny*'s young (female) fans:

> Who is it that writes the one-line commentaries like 'Nastia is Super!'? It's mainly children, teenagers, for the most part young girls. And suddenly a man, say, 5 years older, appears, who has read, say, 5 more books, has learned to write 200–300 Russian words without a mistake and got the hang of [*osilil*] the 'Idiot' serial. And here he adopts the pose of an intellectual, a defender of Russian culture. That'll do, gentlemen. That's enough of 25-year old uncles asserting themselves over teenage girls ... In another 5 years you'll marry and watch the very same serial with your own family.

(www.ruskino.ru/movie/forum; accessed 17 April 2006)

22 Some put the linguistic objection in particularly uncompromising terms: 'This lady [*osoba*] with her exaggerated [*gipertrofirovannym*] accent and complete lack of taste just drives me mad [*besit*]. It's a curse [*chuma*] – all these rip-offs [*kal'ki*]

from American serials' (http://serialmag.ru/forum/archive/index.php/t-66.html; accessed 18 April 2006). Others are especially irritated by Vika's 'put on guttural sounds' (*narochitoe gakan'e*), seen as 'unnatural' and 'stuffed full of vulgarity' (*zabito poshliatinoi*) (www.ruskino.ru/movie/forum; accessed 17 April 2006).

23 A Kiev viewer is fulsome in her praise: 'A cool [*prikol'nyi*] serial. She's a far out chick [*uletnaia chuvikha*], this Nanny. It's immediately obvious that she's our *khokhlushka!*' (www.ruskino.ru/movie/forum; accessed 17 April 2006).

24 Some see Vika as 'propaganda for the idea of the unity of all Slavic peoples (most of all, Russia and Ukraine)'. For others, the programme's unifying aspect is a positive feature: 'I was also born in the Soviet Union and now I don't distinguish Russia from Ukraine; it's bad when people try to do this on our behalves'. Yet others, whilst arguing from the same political position (that of the value of re-aligning the countries of the former Soviet Union), see *My Fair Nanny* as an example of anti-Ukrainian xenophobia: 'The authors of serials as popular as MFN should respect viewers from all regions, beliefs and nationalities ... The image of Vika represents an anti-Ukrainian advert [*antikhokhliatskaia reklama*]' (www.ruskino.ru/movie/forum; accessed 17 April 2006).

25 A Vladivostok viewer expresses her approval of *My Fair Nanny* with a knowing nod to the hallmark speech traits of her heroine: 'Oh,my God! (*Mama dorogaia!*) What a serial. Insaaaaane! [*Aaaaachumet'!*]' (www.ruskino.ru/movie/forum; accessed 17 April 2006).

26 A female correspondent comments, 'Do you know how many times a day I hear "Insaane!" [*Ochumet'!*] And it's not me saying it, but those around me.' (www. ruskino.ru/movie/forum; accessed 17 April 2006).

27 In Lotman's semiotic theory of culture, it is the gap and the movement between periphery and centre which guarantees 'semiotic dynamism' in a system (Lotman 1990: 134).

7 (Mis)appropriating the western game show

1 This is the outcome of the focus group interviews. Among Moscow participants, there was a lady whose daughter studies at a theatre institute. She related how her daughter and other students of the institute had been auditioned for several parts on *Okna*. During our interviews in Moscow in 2006, we also met a female journalist who writes scripts for *Court Hour* (*Chas suda*).

2 Vladislav List'ev (10 May 1956 – 1 March 1995) was a Russian journalist and head of the ORT TV Channel (now Channel 1 in Russia).

3 All the *Field* programmes quoted in this article were recorded on Channel 1 *Vsemirnaia set'* as broadcast in the UK. The dates are noted in brackets in the text.

4 The definition of ritual phase is based on the definition of 'ritual' as given in *Collins* dictionary.

5 For comparison, we reproduce Skovmand's quantitative analysis of *Wheels* in USA, Scandinavia, Northern Europe and Denmark (1997–8).

Wheel of Fortune (USA)

			Minus Ad Blocks
Game	13 mins 38 secs	48.20%	65.23%
Talk	5 mins 24 secs	19.09%	25.84%
Shopping	1 min 52 secs	6.60%	8.93%
Ad Blocks	7 mins 23 secs	26.10%	
Total	28 mins 17 secs		

Lyckohjulet (TV3, Scandinavia)

			Minus Ads
Game	15 mins 27 secs	49.41%	56.11%
Talk	6 mins 47 secs	21.70%	24.64%
Shopping	5 mins 18 secs	16.95%	19.25%
Ads	4 mins 44 secs	15.14%	
Total	32 mins 16 secs		

Glücksrad (Sat1, Northern Europe)

			Minus Ads
Game	9 mins 43 secs	31.67%	45.33%
Talk	5 mins 18 secs	17.27%	24.73%
Shopping	6 mins 25 secs	29.91%	29.94%
Ads	9 mins 15 secs	30.15%	
Total	30 mins 41 secs		

Lykkehjulet (TV2, Denmark)

Game	14 mins 15 secs	57%
Talk	5 mins 15 secs	21%
Shopping	5 mins 30 secs	29.94%
Total	25 mins	

6 International Women's Day has lost its original Soviet meaning as the day of solidarity of women all over the world. For decades it has been a holiday to celebrate femininity and confirm gender stereotypes. In translation into western idiom, it has become a strange mix of Mother's Day and Valentine's Day.

7 To openly advertise commercial products is accepted practice on Russian TV. For a discussion of Russian advertising and commercials, see a forum on television advertising in *Iskusstvo kino*, 7, (2004): 5–37.

8 *Blue Light* is a post-Soviet variety show originating in the Soviet period and consisting of music, humour and light entertainment. It has usually been broadcast on New Year's Eve.

8 Russian regional television

1 These statistics are from one of many statistical surveys carried out by Russia's Public Opinion Foundation (*Fond Obshchestvennogo Mneniia*) and published on its website at http://bd.fond.ru/cat/societas/mass_media (accessed 31 August 2007).

2 See Constitution of Russia, Part One, Chapter 3, Article 65, 'The Russian Federation', available at www.kremlin.ru/articles/ConstChapter3.shtml (accessed 26 June 2007).

3 See Chapter 9 for full details of the fieldwork we carried out.

4 The mysterious deaths of the journalist Anna Politkovskaia in 2005, and of the former FSB agent, Aleksandr Litvinenko, in 2006, are cases in point.

5 Among other characteristics of the neo-Soviet model of the media listed, Oates refers to a 'rejection of balance or objectivity', 'self-censorship' and 'government interference'.

6 Details of the history of Perm television are based on the account given in *Govorit i pokazyvaet Perm* (Perm: FGUP Permskaia GTRK "T7" and OOO Raritet Perm, 2002).

7 Quoted from an interview conducted in June 2006.

8 Quoted in a report on the Russian media issued by the 'Internews' media monitoring organisation in 2004. See http://internews.ru/internews/publications/tvproducer.html; accessed 27 July 2004.

9 We owe this observation to our colleague, Dr Galina Miazhevich, a specialist in Belarusian national identity.

10 These insights were developed in discussions with Dr Miazhevich, to whom we are very grateful.

9 Television through the lens of the post-Soviet viewer

1 The Educated Media Foundation (EMF, formerly known as Internews Russia) suspended its work following a search in its Moscow headquarters on 18 April 2007. For more details, see www.internews.org/prs/2007/20070503_russia.shtm (last accessed, 23 May 2008).

2 For a discussion of *stiob* in military dramas, see Chapter 5. For a treatment of *stiob* in post-Soviet military parades see Hutchings and Rulyova 2009.

Bibliography

Aldridge, M. (2007) *Understanding the Local Media*, Milton Keynes, Open University Press.

Allan, R.C. (ed.) (1992) *Channels of Discourse Reassembled*, London, Routledge.

Altman, R. (1999) *Film/Genre*, London, BFI Publishing.

Anderson, B. (1991) *Imagined Communities: Reflections on the Origin and Spread of Nationalism*, London, Verso.

Ang, I. (1985) *Watching Dallas: Soap Opera and the Melodramatic Imagination*, London, Methuen.

——(1995) *Living Room Wars: Rethinking Media Audiences for a Postmodern World*, London, Routledge.

Bakhtin, M. (1981) *The Dialogic Imagination*, ed. M. Holquist, trans. C. Emerson, Austin, University of Texas Press.

——(1984) *Rabelais and His World*, Bloomington, Indiana University Press.

——(1986a) *Speech Genres and Other Late Essays*, Austin, University of Texas Press.

——(1986b) *Estetika slovesnogo tovorchestva*, Moscow, Iskusstvo.

Barker, A. (ed.) (1999) *Consuming Russia: Popular Culture, Sex and Society Since Gorbachev*, Durham (NC), Duke University Press.

Barthes, R. (1972) *Mythologies*, trans. A. Lavers, New York, Noonday Press.

Bausinger, H. (1990) *Folk Culture in a World of Technology*, trans. E. Dettmar, Bloomington, Indiana University Press.

Bennett, W.L. and R. Entman (2001) *Mediated Politics: Communication in the Future of Democracy*, Cambridge, CUP.

Benveniste, E. (1966) *Problemes de linguistique generale*, Paris, Gallimard.

Beumers, B. (2002) Review of *Russian Ark* (*Russkii kovcheg*, 2002), online at www.kinokultura.com/reviews/Rark.html.

Beumers, B., S. Hutchings and N. Rulyova (2009) *The Post-Soviet Russian Media: Power, Change and Conflicting Messages*, London, Routledge.

Bonnell, V. and G. Freidin (1995) 'Televorot: The role of television coverage in Russia's August 1991 coup', in N. Condee (ed.), *Soviet Hieroglyphics: Visual Culture in Late Twentieth Century Russia*, Bloomington, Indiana UP, pp. 55–121.

Bonner, F. (2003) *Ordinary Television: Analyzing Popular TV*, London, Sage.

Borenstein, E. (1999) 'Public Offerings: MMM and the Marketing of Melodrama', in A. Barker (ed.), *Consuming Russia*, Durham NC, Duke University Press, pp. 49–75.

——(2000) '"About That": Deploying and deploring sex in post-Soviet Russia', *Russian Culture of the 1990s. Studies in Twentieth Century Literature*, 24 (1), pp. 51–83.

Borenstein, E., Lipovetskii, M. and Baraban, E. (2004) 'Forum: Innovation through iteration: Russian popular culture today', *Slavic and East European Journal*, 48.

Bourdieu, P. (1992) *Language and Symbolic Power*, Cambridge, Polity Press.

Boyd-Barrett, O. and T. Rantanen (2004) 'The international news agenda', in A. Sreberny and C. Paterson (eds), *International Flow of News*, Luton, University of Luton Press, pp. 31–46.

Boym, S. (2001) *The Future of Nostalgia*, New York, Basic Books.

Cannadine, D. (1983) 'The context, performance and meaning of ritual: The British monarchy and the "invention of tradition", c.1820–1977', in E. Hobsbaum and T. Ranger (eds), *The Invention of Tradition*, Cambridge, CUP, pp. 101–65.

Castells, M. (1996) *The Rise of the Network Society*, Oxford, Blackwell.

Chivers, C.J. (2006) 'The school', *Esquire*, June 2006, pp. 143–60.

Clark, K. (2000) 'Stalinskii mif o "velikoi sem'e"', in E. Dobrenko and H. Gunther (eds), *Sotsrealisticheskii kanon*, St Petersburg, Akademicheski proekt, pp. 784–96.

Collins, J. (1992) 'Postmodernism and television', in R.C. Allan (ed.), *Channels of Discourse Reassembled*, London, Routledge, pp. 327–54.

Condee, N. (2009) 'Vicarious catastrophe: The third empire watches *Gibel' imperii*', in B. Beumers, S. Hutchings and N. Rulyova (eds), *The Post-Soviet Russian Media: Power, Change and Conflicting Messages*, London, Routledge, pp. 178–185.

Curran, J. (2002) *Media and Power: Communication and Society*, London, Routledge.

Davydova, M. (2005) 'Ne zabud'te vykliuchit' televizor', *Iskusstvo kino*, 1, pp. 91–94.

Dayan, D. and E. Katz (1985) 'Electronic ceremonies: Television performs a Royal Wedding', in M. Blonsky (ed.), *On Signs: A Semiotic Reader*, Oxford, Blackwell.

——(1992) *Media Events: The Live Broadcasting of History*, Cambridge, Massachusetts, Harvard UP.

Deleuze, G. and F. Guattarri (1987) *A Thousand Plateaus: Capitalism and Schizophrenia*, Minneapolis, University of Minnesota Press.

Dies, N. (1997) *Russian Talk: Culture and Conversation During Perestroika*, Ithaca, Cornell UP.

Doane, M.A. (1990) 'Information, crisis, catastrophe', in P. Mellencamp (ed.), *Logics of Television: Essays in Cultural Criticism*, Bloomington, University of Indiana Press, pp. 222–40.

Dunn, J. (2004) 'Humour and satire in post-Soviet Russian television', in L. Milne (ed.), *Reflective Laughter: Aspects of Humour in Russian Culture*, London, Anthem Press.

Dyer, R. (1979) *Stars*, London, BFI.

Ellis, F. (1999) *From Glasnost to the Internet: Russia's New Infosphere*, Basingstoke, Macmillan.

Ellis, J. (1992) *Visible Fictions: Cinema, Video, Television*, London, Routledge.

——(1999) 'Television as working-through', in J. Gripsrud (ed.), *Television and Common Knowledge*, London and New York, Routledge, pp. 55–71.

——(2001) *Seeing Things: Television in the Age of Uncertainty*, London, I.B. Tauris, pp. 1–38.

Fairclough, N. (1995) *Media Discourse*, London, Edward Arnold.

Feuer, J. (1992) 'Genre study and television', in R.C. Allan (ed.), *Channels of Discourse Reassembled*, London, Routledge, pp. 138–61.

Fiske, J. (1987) *Television Culture*, London, Methuen.

——(1986) 'Television: Polysemy and popularity', *Critical Studies in Mass Communication*, 3 (4), pp. 391–408.

——(1989) *Reading the Popular*, London, Routledge.

——(2006) *Understanding Popular Culture*, London, Routledge.

Foucault, M. (1978) *The History of Sexuality: An Introduction*, New York, Random House.

Geertz, C. (1973) 'Thick description: Toward an interpretive theory of culture', in *The Interpretation of Cultures: Selected Essays*, New York, Basic Books, pp. 3–30.

Gitlin, T. (1980) *The Whole World is Watching: Mass Media in the Making and Unmaking of the New Left*, Berkeley, CA, University of California Press.

Glynn, K. (2000) *Tabloid Culture: Trash Taste, Popular Power and the Transformation of American Television*, Durham NC, Duke UP.

Goffman, E. (1981) 'Footing', in E Goffman, *Forms of Talk,* Philadelphia, University of Pennsylvania Press, pp. 197–259.

Golub, M. (2001) Interview. Host Ksenia Larina. Ekho Moskvy. 25 February; last accessed 19 July 2007 at http://echo.msk.ru/interview/13759/index.phtml.

Gripsrud, J. (1999) 'Scholars, journalism, television: notes on some conditions for mediation and intervention', in J. Gripsrud (ed.), *Television and Common Knowledge*, London, Routledge, pp. 34–53.

Grymov, I. and Lysenkov, A. (2000) Interview. Host Sergei Korzun. Ekho Moskvy. 20 April; last accessed 19 July 2006 at http://echo.msk.ru/interview/10394/index.phtml.

Gunther, H. and E. Dobrenko (eds) (2000) *Sotsrealisticheskii kanon*, St Petersburg, 'Akademicheskii proekt'.

Hafez, K. (2007) *The Myth of Media Globalization*, London, Polity Press.

Hall, S. (1980) 'Encoding/decoding', in S. Hall, D. Hobson, A. Love and P. Willis (eds), *Culture, Media, Language: Working Papers in Cultural Studies, 1972–79*, Boston, Unwin Hyman, pp. 128–138, 294–295.

——(1994) 'Reflections upon the encoding/decoding model', in J. Cruz and J. Lewis (eds), *Viewing, Reading, Listening: Audiences and Critical Reception*, Boulder, Westview, pp. 253–74.

Handler, R. and J. Linnekin (1989) 'Tradition, genuine or spurious', in E. Oring (ed.), *Folk Groups and Folklore Genres*, Logan, Utah State University Press.

Hannerz, U. (1991) 'Scenarios for peripheral cultures', in A. King (ed.), *Culture, Globalisation and the World System*, London, Macmillan, pp. 107–28.

Hartley, J. (2003) 'Democratainment and DIY citizenship', in R.C. Allen and A. Hill (eds), *The Television Studies Reader*, London, Routledge, pp. 524–34.

——(2004) 'Television, nation and indigenous media', *Television and New Media*, 5 (1), pp. 7–25.

Hartley, J. and Alan McKee (2000) *The Indigenous Public Sphere*, Oxford, OUP.

Heller, D. (2003), 'Russian "sitkom" adaptation: the Pushkin principle', *Journal of Popular Film and Television*, pp. 1–10.

Hobsbaum, E. and T. Ranger (eds) (1983) *The Invention of Tradition*, Cambridge, CUP.

Holmes, S. and D. Jermyn (2003) *Understanding Reality Television*, London, Routledge.

Hopkins, M. (1970) *Mass Media in the Soviet Union*, New York, Pegasus.

Hosking, G. (2004) 'Forms of social solidarity in Russia and the Soviet Union', in I. Markova (ed.), *Trust and Democratic Transition in Post-Communist Europe*, Proceedings of the British Academy, 123, 2004, pp. 47–62.

Hunter, S. (2004) *Islam in Russia: The Politics of Identity and Security*, London, M.E. Sharpe.

Huntington, S. (1996) *The Clash of Civilizations and the Remaking of World Order*, New York, Simon and Schuster.

Hutchings, S. (2004) *Russian Literary Culture in the Camera Age: The Word as Image*, London, RoutledgeCurzon.

Hutchings, S. and N. Rulyova (2008) 'Commemorating the past/performing the present: television coverage of World War 2 victory celebrations and the (de)construction of Russian nationhood', in B. Beumers, S. Hutchings and N. Rulyova (eds), *The Post-Soviet Russian Media Power, Change and Conflicting Messages*, London, Routledge, pp. 135–157.

Hutchings, S., G. Miazhevich, C. Flood and H. Nickels (2007) 'The impact of "Islamic extremism" on television news representations of multiculturalism: A comparative analysis', *Russian Communication Studies*, 1, pp. 43–70.

Iakubovich, L. (2002) News. Ekho Moskvy. 23 January; last accessed 19 July 2006 at http://echo.msk.ru/news/76468.phtml.

——(2004a) Chelovek iz televizora. Host Matvei Ganapol'ski. EkhoMoskvy. 24 July; last accessed 19 July 2006 at http://echo.msk.ru/programs/persontv/26432/index.phtml.

——(2004b) Telekhranitel. Host Elena Afanas'eva. Ekho Moskvy. 21 November; last accessed 19 July 2006 at http://echo.msk.ru/programs/tv/33090/index.phtml.

Inkeles, A. (1950) *Public Opinion in Soviet Russia: A Study in Mass Persuasion*, Cambridge, MA, Harvard UP.

Jakobson, R. and Iu. Tynianov (1978). 'Problems in the study of literature and language', in L.Matejka and K.Pomorska (eds), *Readings in Russian Poetics – Formalist and Structuralist Views*, Ann Arbor, Michigan UP.

Kachkaeva, A. (2004) 'Smotrim televizor: Osveshchenie rossiiskim televideniem torzhestv v Sankt Peterburge', online at www.svoboda.org/programs/tv/2003/tv:060203.asp.

Katz, E. and Liebes, T. (1990) *The Export of Meaning: Cross-Cultural Meanings of Dallas*, Oxford and New York, Oxford University Press.

Katzman, K. (2005) 'CRS Report for Congress' www.law.umaryland.edu/marshall/crsreports/crsdocuments/RS220492102005.pdf; last accessed 27 December 2005.

Khakhordin, O. (1999) *The Collective and the Individual in Russia: A Study of Practices*, Berkeley, University of California Press.

Klioutchkine, K. (2005) 'Fedor Mikhailovich lucked out with Vladimir Vladimirovich: The "Idiot" series in the context of Putin's culture', *KinoKultura*, 9 (July 2005); www.kinokultura.com/articles/jul05-klioutchkine.html; last accessed 12 April 2006.

Koltsova, O. (2005) *News Media and Power in Russia*, London, Routledge.

Kress, G. (2001) *Multimodal Discourse*, London, Edward Arnold.

Kristeva, J. (1982) *Powers of Horror: An Essay on Abjection*, New York, Columbia UP.

Kuhn, R. and E. Neveu (eds) (2002) *Political Journalism: New Challenges, New Practices*, London, Routledge.

Lacan, J. (1977) *Écrits*, trans. R. Sheridan, New York, W.W. Norton.

Lembo, Ron. (2001) *Thinking through Television*. Cambridge, Cambridge University Press.

Liebes, T. (1990) *The Export of Meaning: Cross-Cultural Readings of 'Dallas'*, New York, OUP.

Litosseliti, Lia. (2003) *Using Focus Groups in Research*, London and New York, Continuum.

Livingstone, S. (1990) *Making Sense of Television: the Psychology of Audience Interpretation*, Oxford, Pergamon.

Livingstone, S. and P. Lunt (1994) *Talk on Television*, London, Routledge.

Lotman, Iu. (1990) *Universe of the Mind: A Semiotic Theory of Culture*, Indianapolis, Indiana UP.

——(1992) 'Tekst v tekste', in Iu. Lotman, *Izbrannye stat'i v trekh tomakh*, vol. 1, Tallinn, Aleksandra, pp. 148–61.

McCabe, C. (1999) *The Eloquence of the Vulgar: Language, Cinema and the Politics of Culture*, London, BFI Publishing.

MacFadyen, D. (2007) *Russian Television Today: Primetime Drama and Comedy*, London, Routledge.

McLuhan, M. (1964) *Understanding Media: The Extensions of Man*, London, The New English Library.

McNair, B. (1991) *Glasnost, Perestroika and the Soviet Media*, London, Routledge.

——(2000) *Journalism and Democracy*, London, Routledge.

——(2003) *An Introduction to Political Communication*, 3rd edition, London, Routledge.

Marshall, P.D. (1997) *Celebrity and Power: Fame in Contemporary Culture*, Minneapolis, University of Minnesota Press.

Martin Barbero, J. (1993) *Communication, Culture and Hegemony: From the Media to Mediations*, trans. E. Fox and R.White, London, Sage.

Mauss, M. (1954) *The Gift: Forms and Functions of Exchange in Archaic Societies*, trans. from the French by I. Cunnison, London, Cohen & West.

Mellencamp, P. (1990) 'TV time and catastrophe, or beyond the pleasure principle of television', in P. Mellencamp (ed.), *Logics of Television: Essays in Culural Criticism*, Bloomington, University of Indiana Press, pp. 240–67.

Mickiewicz, E. (1988) *Split Signals: Soviet Television in the Age of Glasnost*, New York and Oxford, OUP.

——(1997) *Changing Channels: Television and the Struggle for Power in Russia* London and New York OUP.

——(2008) *Television, Power, and the Public in Russia*, Cambridge, Cambridge University Press.

Miller, J. (2005) 'Another Beslan?', www.channel4.com/news/2005/02/week__basayev. html; accessed 2 December 2005.

Mitchell, W.J.T. (1994) *Picture Theory: Essays on Verbal and Visual Representation*, Chicago and London: Chicago UP.

Mittell, J. (2001) 'A cultural approach to television genre theory', *Cinema Journal*, 40 (3), pp. 3–24.

Moran, A. (1998) *Copycat TV: Globalisation, Program Formats and Cultural Identity*, Luton, University of Luton Press.

Moran, A. and J. Malbon (2006) *Understanding the Global TV Format*, Bristol, Intellect.

Morley, D. (1980) *The Nationwide Audience: Structure and Decoding*, London, British Film Institute.

——(1992) *Television, Audiences and Cultural Studies*, London, Routledge.

——(1999) 'Finding out about the world from television news: Some difficulties', in J. Gripsrud (ed.), *Television and Common Knowledge*, London, Routledge, pp. 136–59.

——(2006) 'Globalisation and cultural imperialism reconsidered: Old questions in new guises', in J. Curran and D. Morley (eds), *Media and Cultural Theory*, London and New York, Routledge, pp. 30–43.

Morson, G.S. (1996) 'The reader as voyeur: Tolstoi and the poetics of didactic fiction', in M. Katz (ed.), *Tolstoy's Short Fiction*, New York, Norton, pp. 379–94.

Munson, W. (1993) *All Talk: The Talk Show in Media Culture*, Philadelphia, Temple University Press.

Neale, S. and F. Krutnik (1990) *Popular Film and TV Comedy*, London, Routledge.

Norris, P., M. Kern and M. Just (2003) *Framing Terrorism: The News Media, the Government and the* Public, London, Routledge.

Oates, S. (2007) 'The neo-Soviet model of the media', *Europe-Asia Studies*, 59 (8), 1279–1297.

——(2006) *Television, Democracy and Elections in Russia*, London, Routledge Curzon.

Olson, S.R. (2004) 'Hollywood planet: Global media and the competitive advantage of narrative transparency', in R. Allen and A. Hill (eds), *The Television Studies Reader*, London, Routledge, pp. 111–130.

Oslon, A. (2003) 'V tiskakh reitinga', *Iskusstvo kino*, 5, pp. 9–14.

Perrie, M. (1998), '"Narodnost": Notions of national identity', in C. Kelly and D. Shepherd (eds), *Constructing Russian Culture in the Age of Revolution: 1881–1940*, Oxford, Oxford UP, pp. 28–36.

Petrovskaia, I. (2002) Interview. Host Matvei Ganapolsky. Ekho Moskvy. 1 July; last accessed 19 July 2006 at http://echo.msk.ru/interview/18948/index.phtml.

Petrovskaia, N. (2004) 'Molchanie gosudarstvennikov', *Ivestiia*, 4/9/04, p. 7.

Pietiläinen, J. (2003) 'Media audiences in a Russian province', *Nordicom-Review*, 1, pp. 79–88.

Pilkington, H. and E. Omel'chenko (2002) *Looking West? Cultural Globalization and Russian Youth Culture*, University Park, PA: Pennsylvania State UP.

Pole chudes (2007) www.1tv.ru/owa/win/ort5peredach.peredach?; last accessed 19 June 2007.

Poluekhtova, Irina (2003) 'Telemeniu i telepotreblenie', in *Otechestvennye zapiski*, Konets SMI, 3, pp. 371–83.

Potter, C. J. (2000) 'Payment, gift or bribe? Exploring the boundaries in pre-Petrine Russia', in S. Lovell, A. Rogachevskii and A. Ledeneva (eds), *Bribery and 'Blat' in Russia: Negotiating Reciprocity from the Middle Ages to the 1990s*, Basingstoke, Palgrave, pp. 20–34.

Rantanen, T. (2002) *The Global and the National: Media and Communications in Post-Communist Russia*, New York and Oxford, Rowman & Littlefield Publishers.

Ries, N. (1997) *Russian Talk: Culture and Conversation During Perestroika*, Ithaca and London, Cornell University Press.

Robertson, R. (1997) 'Comments on the "global triad" and "glocalisation"', in N. Inoue (ed). *Globalisation and Indigenous Culture*, Kokugakuin University, Japan, Institute for Japanese Cultural Classics.

Rulyova, N. (2005) 'Piracy and narrative games: Dmitry Puchkov's translations of "The Lord of the Rings"', *Slavic and East European Journal*, 49 (4), pp. 625–38.

Russell, J. (2005) 'Terrorists, bandits, spooks and thieves: Russian demonisation of the Chechens before and since 9/11', *Third World Quarterly*, 26 (1), pp. 101–16.

Ryazanova Clarke, L. (2000) 'The dichotomy of totalitarian and post-totalitarian in the language of Russian public discourse (1990s)', *Essays in Poetics*, 25 (Autumn), pp. 169–86.

——(2005) 'Criminal rhetoric in Russian political discourse', *Language Design*, 6, pp. 141–60.

Sennett, R. (2002) *The Fall of Public Man*, London, Penguin.

Silverstone, R. (1994) *Television and Everyday Life*, London, Routledge.

Skomvand, M. (1992) 'Barbarous TV international: Syndicated Wheel of Fortune', in M. Skomvand and K. Schrøder (eds), *Media Cultures: Reappraising Transnational Media*, London and New York, Routledge, pp. 84–103.

Smith, A. (1991) *National Identity*, London, Penguin.

Stanley, A. (1997) 'On Russian TV: Sincerest form of frivolity', *New York Times*, January 12.

Thompson, J. (1995) *The Media and Modernity: A Social Theory of the Media*, Stanford, Stanford University Press.

Timbey, B. (2002) *Television Talk: A History of the Television Talk Show*, Austin, Texas, Texas UP.

Tolstoi, A. (1936) *Zolotoi kliuchik ili priklucheniia Buratino*, Leningrad, Detskaia literatura.

Turner, G. (2001) 'Genre, hybridity and mutations', in G. Creeber (ed.), *The Television Genre Book*, London, BFI.

Turovskaia, M. (2003) *Binokl': Zametki o Rossii dlia nemetskogo chitatelia. Zametki o Berline dlia rossiiskogo chitatelia*, Moscow, Novoe literaturnoe obozrenie.

Uspensky, B. (1976) *The Semiotics of the Russian Icon*, Lisse, Peter de Ridder Press.

Van Dijk, T. (1991) *Racism and the Press*, London, Routledge.

——(1998) *Ideology: A Multidisciplinary Approach*, London, Sage.

Varese, F. (2001) *The Russian Mafia: Private Protection in a New Market Economy*, Oxford, OUP.

Vertov, D. (1984) *Kino-Eye: The Writings of Dziga Vertov*, ed. A. Michelson, trans. K. O'Brien, Berkeley and Los Angeles, University of California Press.

Williams, R. (1974) *Television: Technology and Cultural Form*, London, Collins.

Wilson, A. (2005) *Virtual Politics: Faking Democracy in the Post-Soviet World*, New Haven CT, Yale UP.

Wilson, T. (1993): *Watching Television: Hermeneutics, Reception and Popular Culture*, Cambridge, Polity Press.

Wood, H. (2006) 'The mediated conversational floor: An interactive approach to audience reception analysis', *Media, Culture and Society*, 29 (1), pp. 75–103.

Youngblood, D. (2001) 'A war remembered: Soviet films of the great patriotic war', *The American Historical Review*, 106 (3), pp. 839–52.

Yurchak, A. (2006) *Everything was Forever, Until it was No More: The Last Soviet Generation*, Princeton, Princeton UP.

Zassoursky, I. (2004) *Media and Power in Post-Soviet Russia*, Armonk, NY, M.E. Sharpe.

Zizek, S. (2000) *The Fragile Absolute: Or, Why is the Christian Legacy Worth Fighting For?* London, Verso.

——(2001) *Did Somebody Say Totalitarianism? Five Interventions in the (Mis)use of a Notion*, London and New York, Verso.

——(2002) *Welcome to the Desert of the Real: Five Essays on September 11 and Related Dates*, London and New York, Verso.

——(2004) *Iraq: The Borrowed Kettle*, London, Verso.

——(2006a) *The Parallax View*, Cambridge MA, The MIT Press.

——(2006b) 'The thing from inner space', www.ivorytowermedia.com/; last accessed 17 November 2006.

Zvereva, V. (2004) 'Telereklama: prostranstvo virtual'nogo shopinga', *Iskusstvo kino* 7, pp. 5–13.

Index

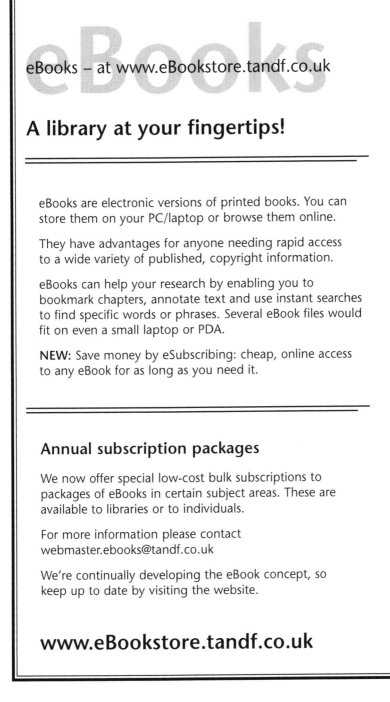